India and Iran

An Assessment of Contemporary Relations

India and Iran

An Assessment of Contemporary Relations

Edited by
Anwar Alam
Professor and Director,
Centre for West Asian Studies,
Jamia Millia Islamia, New Delhi.

New Century Publications
New Delhi, India

NEW CENTURY PUBLICATIONS
4800/24, Bharat Ram Road,
Ansari Road, Daryaganj,
New Delhi – 110 002 (India)

Tel.: 011-2324 7798, 4358 7398, 6539 6605
Fax: 011-4101 7798
E-mail: indiatax@vsnl.com • info@newcenturypublications.com
www.newcenturypublications.com

Editorial office:
LG–7, Aakarshan Bhawan,
4754-57/23, Ansari Road, Daryaganj,
New Delhi – 110 002

Tel.: 011-4356 0919

First Published: **July 2011**

ISBN: **978-81-7708-276-0**

Published by New Century Publications and printed at Salasar Imaging Systems, New Delhi.

Designs: Patch Creative Unit, New Delhi.

PRINTED IN INDIA

About the Book

Indo-Iran relations have been the subject of intense debates and discussions in recent years, particularly post-9/11 period. The growing Indo-US relations are considered to have cast a shadow on Indo-Iran ties. Given the anti-Iranian thrust in US foreign policy, particularly on nuclear issue, the Indian foreign policy faces a daunting task of maintaining a balanced outlook towards Iran. It is in this background that this book discusses the whole gamut of issues in Indo-Iran relations including energy security, military and defence co-operation, Iranian nuclear programme, terrorism, commerce, and political, economic and cultural ties. These dimensions of Indo-Iran relations are examined with reference to the influencing factor of US, China, Pakistan, Israel, Afghanistan, and Central Asia. The 19 research articles in this volume, authored by scholars in the field, provide deep insights into the complexities of Indo-Iran relations in contemporary times in terms of their continuity, limitations, strengths and weaknesses.

Editor's Profile

Anwar Alam is Professor and Director, Centre for West Asian Studies, Jamia Millia Islamia, New Delhi. He has served as a Lecturer in the Department of Political Science, Aligarh Muslim University (AMU), and Assistant and Associate Professor at the Centre for West Asian and African Studies, School of International Studies, Jawaharlal Nehru University (JNU), New Delhi. He was awarded the ICSSR Doctoral Fellowship (1991), International Visitor Programme (Islamic) Scholarship, USA, (2002), Indo-French Social Scientist Exchange Programme Fellowship (2003) and Alexandor Von Humboldt Post Doctoral Fellowship (2004-06).

He was Visiting Fellow at Maison des Sciences de l'Homme (MSH), Paris, France, (March-April 2005), Centre for Citizenship and Ethnicity, Department of Sociology, University of Bristol, Bristol, UK, (May-June 2005) and International Institute for the Study of Islam in the Modern World (ISIM), Leiden, Netherlands, (July-August 2005). Currently, he is a Visiting Professor at Fatih University, Istanbul, Turkey.

He has authored/edited 5 books: *Religion and State: A Comparative Study of Contemporary Egypt, Iran and Saudi Arabia* (1998); *India and West Asia in the Era of Globalisation* (2008); *Iran and Post-9/11 World Order* (2009); *Contemporary West Asia* (2010) and *India, Global Powers and West Asia* (2011). Besides, he has contributed several articles in national and international referred journals and chapters in edited books. His areas of research interest include international politics, political theory, religion and politics, political Islam, globalization and Muslim society.

Contents

INDIA AND IRAN: CULTURAL DIMENSIONS

Preface

India and Iran are two great historical civilizations. Centuries of interactions has deeply affected each other's life and mode of thinking. However, as these two cultural civilizations move into the direction of becoming modern nation states, it has brought a different set of problems and challenges of mutual adjustment. In other words, the transformation of these two cultural entities from civilization into a nation state was/is accompanied by *fissures, temporary breakdown* and at times *rupture* in the amicable relationship between the two. In recent times, both India and Iran, given their different location in the trajectory of global power politics, are finding it difficult to accommodate concerns of each other. If one set of national interest brings them closer, another set of national interest moves them apart. The shared history, culture and memory appear to be not much helpful in fostering close political relationship between the two. In short, a simultaneous *push and pull* factors characterize the relationship between the two in the present time.

This book aims at providing an understanding of various dimensions of Indo-Iran relations in recent times. The various chapters in the book seek to assess the changing contours of the relationship between the two nations. It investigates almost all important factors and issues that influence the relations between these two civilizations. This ranges from history, culture, military, defence, nuclear, political-bilateral, energy, economy, trade, and terrorism and includes such countries and regions as US, China, Pakistan, Afghanistan, Israel, Central Asia and West Asia that have bearings upon the relationship between these two nations.

The volume is a product of the deliberation of an international conference on 'India-Iran Relations in Contemporary Times (1979-2009)' that took place at Jamia Millia Islamia, New Delhi. Though there were many papers presented during the course of three day long conference, all of them could not find a place in this volume. The articles included in this volume were selected keeping into consideration the nature, thrust and scope of this book.

Many efforts have gone in making this book a reality. First of all, I am thankful to all participants and contributors to this volume for taking out time not only to participate in the conference but also for submitting their manuscripts well within time. I deeply acknowledge the financial support granted by my own university, Jamia Millia Islamia, New Delhi and Indian Council of Social Science Research, New Delhi that helped me in efficiently organising this conference. I also sincerely thank the students of Centre for West Asian Studies, Jamia Millia Islamia, New Delhi, for their tireless efforts to make the conference a success. I owe special thanks to Pervez Nayarrie, without whose support and efforts this conference would not have been possible.

I do not have words to express my gratitude and feeling for my wife Zubia and daughter Sanober whose love, comfort and cooperation provided me strength, both mental and emotional, to execute this project right from organising the conference to its publication in the form of the present book.

Last but not the least, I am thankful to Mr. Sandeep Sury, CEO of New Century Publications, New Delhi for placing this book in the public domain.

New Delhi **Anwar Alam**
May, 2011

Contributors

Amir H. Zekrgoo is currently Professor at Islamic and Oriental Arts International Institute of Islamic Thought and Civilization (ISTAC) International Islamic University Malaysia. He is an artist, art historian, indologist and a scholar of comparative religious art. In 1995, he was awarded the prestigious Hirayama Fellowship by UNESCO to carry out a research on "The Evolution of Islamic Calligraphy and the Evolution of Buddhist Iconography along the Silk Roads". In 1997, he was made a Member of UNESCO's First International Team of Buddhist Studies.

Professor Zekrgoo is a member of the Iranian Academy of Arts and the Iranian Academy of Sciences; Founding Member of Islamic Manuscript Association (TIMA) and honorary member of All India Arts and Crafts Society (IFACS). He has been engaged in teaching art, history of art, philosophy of Islamic and Oriental Arts, and comparative studies in religious and sacred arts since 1982.

He is an established painter, calligrapher and a photographer. His art works have been displayed in many national and international, solo and collective exhibitions in America, China, Czechoslovakia, India, Iran, Malaysia, Pakistan, Switzerland and UAE since 1977.

He has to his credit eight books and over a hundred articles on subjects such as Islamic art and Manuscript Studies, Indian philosophy and mythology, oriental art and iconography, Islamic literature and mysticism.

Ashok K. Behuria is a Research Fellow at the Institute for Defence Studies and Analysis (IDSA), New Delhi, India.

Atul Aneja is the West Asia Correspondent with The Hindu newspaper, based in Dubai. He has an M.Phil. degree in international relations from Jawaharlal Nehru University, New Delhi. After a brief tenure at the Institute of Defence Studies and Analysis (IDSA), New Delhi, Atul joined "The Hindu" Newspaper in 1991 as its defence and foreign affairs correspondent. Out of Delhi, he covered the Kargil War and then from Kabul and Dushanbe, the Afghan conflict after 2001. As a West Asia correspondent, first based in Bahrain and then Dubai, he covered from Beirut, the Lebanon War in 2006. He has been a regular visitor to Tehran, covering two major presidential elections, first in 2005 and then in June 2009. He was assigned in January 2011, to cover from Cairo, the pro-democracy movement in Egypt. Atul has a special interest in West and Central Asia, where he has been following pro-democracy movements, human rights issues as well as the shifting terrain of geopolitics.

Chintamani Mahapatra is currently Professor of American Studies at Jawaharlal Nehru University, New Delhi. He has been awarded several international fellowships and scholarships, such as, Fulbright Fellow, Salzburg Seminar Fellow, Visiting Fellow at Australian Defence Studies Centre, Foreign Policy Fellow, University of Maryland, Commonwealth Scholar at School of Oriental and African Studies, University of London.

Professor Mahapatra regularly lectures at various Indian military training colleges and Foreign Service Institute of the Ministry of External Affairs, Government of India. He has authored/edited five books and several articles in reputed national and international journals. His latest book is, *US Approach to the Islamic World in Post-9/11 Era*. Moreover, he is a consistent contributor of articles in national and local dailies. He has given interviews to BBC, CBS, CNBC, CNN/IBN, DD News and several other audio-visual media.

Elaheh Koolaee has obtained her Ph.D. in international relations and became a faculty member of Faculty of Law and Political Science in University of Tehran. She has written many books and articles about Russia, Central Asia, Caucasus,

Iran's foreign policy and women issues. She was elected for Iran's Parliament (*Majlis*) in 2000-2004, and was a member and Speaker of the National Security and Foreign Policy Commission. She was an active member of the Women Faction of the Reformist Parliament (6th Parliament). She is currently a full-professor of Regional Studies in University of Tehran.

Faisal Ahmed is Assistant Professor of International Business and Strategy; Program Director of International Business Program; and Joint Co-ordinator of International Academic Exchange Programs at Asia-Pacific Institute of Management, New Delhi. He has been teaching at MBA and executive levels. He is also a trade and geopolitical analyst on India's engagements with WANA, CIS and Latin America. He holds Master of International Business Management (MIBM) degree from Aligarh and Ph.D. in Economics (in the area of international trade) from Udaipur. Dr. Ahmed has published more than twenty five research papers in refereed national and international journals and conference proceedings. He is also a Member of the Academy of International Business (USA)-India Chapter; Committee Member (Reviewer), ACI, England; and, a Member of the Indian History Congress. Dr. Ahmed is invited by premier universities, think tanks, chambers of commerce, and other professional bodies as a speaker and expert panelist and has also been quoted in international newspapers. His teaching areas are international business, foreign trade, WTO and strategic management; while his research interests include regional integration, trade policy and geopolitics. His consulting interests lies in trade facilitations (country-level) and public diplomacy.

Hamid Ahmadi is a Professor of Political Science, at the Faculty of Law and Political Science, University of Tehran. He secured his Master in Political Science from the University of Tehran and obtained his Ph.D. in Political Science from

Carleton University in Ottawa, Canada. He was a visiting professor of international relations in METU (Middle East Technical University) in Ankara, Turkey in 2004. He teaches Iranian and Middle Eastern politics. Some of his works include: 'The Dilemma of National Interests in the Islamic Republic of Iran', in, Homa Katouzian and Hossein Shahidi, (eds), Iran in the 21st Century, Politics, Economy and Conflict, (London: Routledge, 2007); 'Islam and the West in the Wake of September 11 Attacks', Discourse: an Iranian Journal, Vol. 4. No 2 (Fall 2002); Bonyaad haaaye Hoviate melli Irani (the foundations of Iranian national identity), Tehran, 2009; and Ravaabete farhangi Iran va Turkey (Iran-Turkey Cultural Relations), Tehran, 2010.

Jajati K. Pattnaik is Associate Professor at the Department of Political Science, Indira Gandhi Government College, Tezu, Arunachal Pradesh. He received M.Phil. and Ph.D. degrees from the West Asian Studies Division, School of International Studies, Jawaharlal Nehru University, New Delhi. He also served as a visiting scholar at the Gulf Studies Programme, School of International Studies, Jawaharlal Nehru University, New Delhi. He has published works in edited volumes, journals, periodicals and national dailies. He has presented papers in national as well as international seminars. He specializes in comparative politics and his areas of interest are international politics and foreign policy with special focus on West Asia.

Javed Ahmad Khan is an Associate Professor at the Centre for West Asian Studies, Jamia Millia Islamia, New Delhi. He holds a Ph.D. in Economics from Aligarh Muslim University, India. His publications include: *Iraq Reconstruction–The Arabs Response to an Imperial Design* (2008); *India's Energy Security and the Arabian Gulf: Oil and Gas Market in Decontrolled Regime* (2005); *Islamic Banking in India - Scopes and Challenges* (ed., 2003); *India and West Asia:*

Emerging Markets in the Liberalization Era (1999) and *Islamic Economics and Finance: A Bibliography* (1995).

Kaveh L. Afrasiabi is an expert on Iran's foreign and nuclear policies. He has also authored such woks as *Iran's Nuclear Program: Debating Facts versus Fictions*; *Readings in Iran's Foreign Policy after September* (co-authored with Abbas Maleki). He was also formerly advisor to Iran's nuclear negotiation team (2004-2005).

Mandana Barkeshli is a conservation scientist and currently an Associate Professor and Head of Department of Applied Arts and Design in Faculty of Architecture and Environmental Design, International Islamic University, Malaysia (IIUM). From 2006 till present she has been one of the Committee Board Members and Head of Conservation Sub-Committee of The Islamic Manuscript Association (TIMA), University of Cambridge, UK. She has been appointed as Editorial Board Member of the Restaurator Journal, a prestigious International Journal for the Preservation of Library and Archival Material in Munich, Germany from March 2008. From October 1999 to November 2003, she has been the Head Curator at the Islamic Arts Museum Malaysia, where she has been instrumental in the establishment of the Curatorial Department and assisted the establishment of Conservation Centre for the Museum. She has co-authored the book, *Conservation and Restoration of Paper Documents* in 1997 published by Indian Council of Conservation Institute (INTACH) which was subsequently translated to Hindi in 2001. She has made numerous contributions to journals and publications, and participated in international conferences, lectures and workshops on art and conservation. Dr. Barkeshli is internationally recognized in conservation scientist community for her scientific researches on materials technology of historical Persian and Indian Manuscript and miniature paintings.

Masoud Imani Kalesar obtained his Ph.D. from the School of International Studies, Jawaharlal Nehru University, New Delhi. His main areas of study and interest are geopolitics and energy security in and around the Caspian Sea, Caucasus and Central Asia.

Masoud has been active at the academic level by publishing articles and participating in conferences. He is fluent in several Central Asian languages and a regular contributor to the Central Eurasia Program of the Tehran University.

He worked as a Radio and TV announcer in Iran for several years. Afterwards, he studied and lived in India for a decade. In 2010, he joined European Union Institute for Security Studies in Paris as a visiting Fellow and currently, he works as a journalist for Euronews, based in Lyon, France.

M.H. Ilias is Associate Professor at India-Arab Cultural Centre, Jamia Millia Islamia, New Delhi, India. Ilias completed his doctoral research in International Relations form the Centre for West Asian Studies, Jawaharlal Nehru University (JNU), New Delhi. His current research addresses a range of issues relating to society and culture in the Gulf countries. His areas of interest also include film and popular culture in West Asia, Hadrami migration on the Malabar Coast, Islam and International Relations, Muslims and New Media etc. His published books include: *India-West Asia Relations: Understanding Cultural Interplays* (co-edited); *Space, Memory and Jewish National Identity; Society and Change in the Cotemporary Gulf* (co-edited); *Arabs in India: Society, History and Culture* (co-edited). Ilias has been the recipient of Ford Foundation Fellowship for Post-doctoral Research (2007) at Oxford University and Post-doctoral Visiting Research Fellowship (2008) at the Centre for Modern Orient, Berlin. His articles and chapters have appeared in many collections as well as in internationally reputed journals.

Mohammad A. Mousavi did his Ph.D. from the University of Durham (England) in Political Economy in 1994. He received his B.A. from University of Tehran (Iran) and his M.A. from Manchester University (England), both in economics. He has been a career diplomat, before joining the academic life at the University of Tehran in 2005. His last position was as Ambassador of Iran to Canada. He is currently a Professor of North American Studies at the Faculty of World Studies, Tehran University, Tehran. He is also the Vice-President of the University of Tehran in International Affairs. He has taught various courses including Iranian economy, political economy of oil, US Constitution and Government, US foreign policy in Middle East, Iran and the process of globalization, and political economy of globalization.

Some of his recent publications include: *US Public Diplomacy on Iran: Evaluating Voice of America; Iran-US Nuclear Standoff: A Game Theory Approach; Indo-Iran Strategic Relations under the US Shadow; Globalization and Regionalism: Juxtaposition of Conflict?; Some Notes on the Caspian Energy and Ethnic Conflicts in the Caucasus; Revolutionaries Get in Concert: Iran's Relationship with the New Left in Latin America*. His areas of interest are the US foreign policy and government, globalization, energy and political economy of oil, and the political economy of Iran.

Monika Chansoria is presently a Senior Fellow at the Centre for Land Warfare Studies, New Delhi. She has done post-doctorate in International Relations as a Hermès Post-Doctoral Fellow at the Centre for International Studies and Research, Paris (France), during the academic year 2007-08. She also holds a Ph.D. degree in international relations from the American Studies Division of the School of International Studies, Jawaharlal Nehru University, New Delhi. Dr. Chansoria was awarded the 2010 French Senior Fellowship by the Foundation Maison des Sciences de l'Homme, Paris, as a Visiting Professor and Associate Director of Studies (Directeur d' études associé). Her areas of research interests include American security policy and strategy in Asia with special reference to China and proliferation of WMD.

Chansoria is the author of books including, *China: Military Modernisation and Strategy* (2011) and *Chinese WMD Proliferation in Asia: U.S. Response* (2009) and co-author of *Afghanistan: India's Strategic Stakes* (2010); and *Iran Analysis: A Net Assessment* (forthcoming). Besides, she has contributed numerous research papers and articles in various edited books, academic journals and national and international dailies.

Shebonti Ray Dadwal is a Research Fellow with the Institute for Defence Studies and Analyses, (IDSA), specialising on energy security and climate change-related issues. She has worked as Senior Editor in The Financial Express and also served as Deputy Secretary at the National Security Council Secretariat. She has presented several papers in national and international conferences and has written several peer-reviewed articles and papers on her area of work. She is also a member of the IDSA Editorial Board for its flagship journal 'Strategic Analysis'.

Ms. Dadwal was awarded the Foreign and Commonwealth Office (FCO) Chevening Fellowship on The Economics of Energy in April 2009. She has been on the Steering Committee of the CII which was formed to conduct a study on "Energy Assets Acquisition: A Comparative Analysis of India and China Policy", which was published in December 2010, as well as a member of the IDSA Task force on Climate Change. The report titled, "Security Implications of Climate Change for India", was published in 2009.

Srikanth Kondapalli is Professor in Chinese Studies at Jawaharlal Nehru University, New Delhi. He is also an Honorary Fellow at Institute of Chinese Studies, Delhi and Research Associate at Centre for Chinese Studies, University of Stellenbosch, South Africa. He served at Institute for Defence Studies & Analyses, New Delhi for nearly 12 years. He is educated in Chinese studies in India and China with a specialisation in Modern Chinese History in Master of Arts at Osmania University, Hyderabad; Master of Philosophy and Doctor of Philosophy in 1989 and 1995 respectively in Chinese Studies Division of School of International Studies, Jawaharlal Nehru University, New Delhi. He learnt Chinese language at Beijing Language and Culture University and was a post-doctoral Visiting Fellow at People's University, Beijing from 1996-98. He was a Visiting Professor at National Chengchi University, Taipei in 2004, a Visiting Fellow at China Institute of Contemporary International Relations, Beijing in May 2007 and an Honorary Professor at Shandong University, Jinan. He also received the *K. Subramanyam Award for Excellence in Research in Strategic and Security Studies*. He has published two books, two monographs, co-edited two volumes and several articles in edited books and in national and international journals and newspapers.

Sujata Ashwarya Cheema, is Assistant Professor at the Centre for West Asian Studies, Jamia Millia Islamia, New Delhi. She was awarded the Government of Israel Graduate Fellowship (2002-03) to conduct research at Hebrew University of Jerusalem and Hermes Post-Doctoral Fellowship (2007) at Maison des Sciences de l'Homme (MSH), Paris. She was also awarded a Visiting Fellowship (2009) at the MSH under the Indo-French Cultural Exchange Programme. Her research specializations include Israeli politics and foreign policy, Arab-Israeli conflict, and politics in West Asia. Her publications include *Structures of Political Violence in Palestinian-Israeli Conflict* (New Delhi, 2005 and *West Asia: Civil Society, Democracy and State* (New Delhi, 2010).

Vishal Chandra is an Associate Fellow at the Institute for Defence Studies & Analyses (IDSA), New Delhi. His area of research is politics of Afghan conflict. Apart from publications in IDSA's refereed journal 'Strategic Analysis', he has many other articles and book chapters to his credit. He regularly delivers lecture on Afghan affairs at several Indian institutions. He has also been to Afghanistan for his research.

Among his select publications are: *India in the Afghan Maze: Search for Options, Debate*, (Strategic Analysis, January 2011); *Idea and Politics of 'Reconciliation' with the Taliban in Afghanistan*, in Reconstructing Afghanistan: Prospects and Limitations, Delhi, 2011; *Will NATO Stay On in Afghanistan*?, (Strategic Analysis, September 2009); *The National Front in Afghan Politics: An Exploratory Study* (Strategic Analysis, July 2009); *Making of the New Afghan National Army: Challenges and Prospects* (Strategic Analysis, January 2009); *The Taliban Resurrection and the Changing Course of Afghan Civil War in Afghanistan: The Challenge*, New Delhi, 2007; *Warlords, Drugs and the War on Terror in Afghanistan: The Paradoxes*" (Strategic Analysis, January 2006).

He has also co-edited a book on *India's Neighbourhood: Challenges Ahead*.

1

Introduction: Travelling through Indo-Iran Relations in Contemporary Times

Anwar Alam

INSTRUMENTAL RATIONALITY characterizes 'modern' nation or state or nation-state. Relations between two nations are normally context specific guided by each other's application of instrumental rationality. In other words, relations between the two are conditioned by each other's understanding of political, economic and strategic considerations, domestic factors and international context as well as ideological matrix of political leadership at a given time and space. Political leadership on behalf of '*imagined*' nation and its *undefined, unspecified* mascot 'national interest' ruthlessly harnesses all resources at its disposal–people, culture, civilization, history, soft and hard power–to legitimize the making or unmaking of relations with each other. The shared culture and civilizational affinities between the two nations does not automatically translate itself into establishing strong political relationship between the two.

Power or what is called 'sovereignty' is another characteristic feature of modern nation state. Being habitués in seeing the history of world through the prism of power, nation state conducts its diplomacy principally to augment and project its power which is contextually dependent. This, notwithstanding the fact that such diplomacy is normally conducted in discourse of promoting 'Peace', 'Friendship', 'Stability' and 'Growth'. The *fluctuations* in the relationship between the two nations emanates from *unstable* structure of nation state and its instrumental rationality.

The Indo-Iran relation is not an exception to the above framework of inter-state relationship. This partly explains why despite the exchange of several high profile visits including head of governments (see Appendix) made during last two decades, relationship between India and Iran did not move beyond the normal working diplomatic and political gamesmanship required for conducting inter-state relationship. In other words, centuries of shared cultural and civilizational affinities, which is normally invoked in the meetings of government delegations between the two, did not prove to be of much help in building mutual trust and establishing durable political and strategic relationship despite a mutual desirability on each other's part to achieve the same.

A simultaneous 'convergence and drift' approach characterizes the relationship between the two in recent times. If both nations converge on such issues as tackling the challenges of terrorism in general and of Taliban in particular, stability of Afghanistan, idea of a gas pipe line running from Iran to India, the issue of energy security and security of sea routes, diversification of commercial activities from oil based trade to non- oil areas, the strategic importance of construction of Chahbahar and Bandar Abbas port and sharing of multi-polar world order, they differ widely on the role of United States in West Asia, Central Asia and Afghanistan, Pakistan's role in Afghanistan and its linkage with terrorism, Iran's nuclear issue and viability of constructing Iran-Pakistan-India (IPI) gas pipe line. Such convergences and divergences on the range of issues like above partly emerges from power trajectory of each-other; self belief and imagination that historically they constitute a regional power and are in the process of becoming a supra regional and global power. This then entails the prioritization of issues, selection of strategies and building of political alliance that supplement and help in consolidating the long cherished goal of becoming a 'global power'.

The market driven economic nationalism and sustained economic development at the growth rate of 7-8 percent over the past two decades has fuelled the long suppressed political ambition of India's political leadership and its middle class to acquire the status of global power. [1] The massive modernization of Indian army that began in 1990s is intended to achieve this status. [2] Given this matrix, the preferred policy of Indian political leadership at this stage is to forge a closer relationship with United States to achieve the following 'national' objectives: to ensure latter's support for its economic development and recognition of its 'global status', to end its nuclear isolation imposed by the international community since its first nuclear test in 1974 and Indo-US Civil Nuclear Deal (2009) was visualized as first step to achieve this goal, to secure India's claim to permanent seat in the Security Council of the revamped UN structure in future, to check the 'rogue behaviour' of China and Pakistan towards India and to ensure political stability in West Asia, particularly in the Persian Gulf, and Central Asia which is vital for India's energy security and rapid economic development.

From this perspective India does not see US' physical presence in the Persian Gulf and in Central Asian republics as *necessarily* a destabilizing force, but one that is crucial for the stability of region, dealing with challenges of militant radical Islamic groups, continuous movement of oil and gas products and other trade commodities through the protection of sea lanes in Persian Gulf and Arabian Ocean and flow of remittances of Indian migrants. [3] However, notwithstanding the high priority that the US has come to enjoy in the Indian political vision at this stage of history due to variety of reasons including the ones that are listed above, India will not go as far as becoming a 'strategic partner' of United States, like Israel, in order to preserve its interest and hence prefers to retain its strategic autonomy.

On the other hand while Iran has emerged stronger at the cost of US's military intervention in Afghanistan (2001) and Iraq (2003) that resulted in the elimination of two of Iran's political adversary (Saddam's Iraq and Taliban's Afghanistan at its western and eastern frontier respectively) and emergence of *Shiism* as a political force in large part of West Asia. It sees the presence of US as *destabilizing force* in the region and a *principal* obstacle in its emergence as supra regional power. Given the US's belligerent approach towards 'Islamic' Iran since 1979 revolution as manifested in its unilateral imposition of economic sanction for last three decades, its doctrine of regime change and demonization of Iran as a part of 'axis of evil', mobilization of UN and other European nations to pressurize Iran to thwart its nuclear ambition and holding the card of use of force alive if diplomacy failed to deliver the desired result, Iran *naturally* feels threatened in the midst of being encircled by US forces all around its territory. This in part has necessitated the Iranian speed to acquire the nuclear technology, which it claims to be meant for civilian and peaceful purposes while the West suspects its intention to acquire nuclear technology for making a bomb.

The issue of nuclear technology in today's Iranian context has become a question of its national identity and pride and therefore no Iranian government in the present or in the near future can think of initiating measures that hamper the realization of this long cherished goal. Regionalism is a deeply embedded feature of Iran's foreign policy [4] and given its threat perception vis-à-vis United States, it is not difficult to understand why Iran *unequivocally* demands the withdrawal of US forces from the region including Afghanistan (where it shares with US a similar objective in eliminating the threat of Sunni Pashtun based Afghan Taliban) as a *primary condition* for the return of peace and stability in the region. Iran therefore advocates the regional security structure against the US led security structure in the region in order to manage regional conflicts. India needs to be sensitive about the threat perception of Iran at this juncture in order to send a message across the political leadership of Iran that its growing ties with the United States and Israel will not be at the cost Iran's security.

The divergent perception of Iran and India with regard to the role of United States will continue to influence the relations between the two in the foreseeable future or till the time when Iran and US patch up their differences which is unlikely in the near future. Several contributors in this volume have highlighted the various dimensions of US factor that have constrained the Indo- Iran relations from reaching its optimal level. One significant fallout of divergent perception of Iran and India vis-à-vis the role of the US is that in recent years Iran has emerged as *a test case for measuring* the strategic autonomy of Indian foreign policy. In this context the growing Indo- US-Israeli tie is considered to be premised on an idea of circumventing Iran as well as to fight 'Islamic' terrorism at global level.

In addition to Iranian political leadership, a section of intelligentsia in both countries carries a strong point of view that Indo-Iran relation is increasingly becoming a hostage to Indo-US ties. In other words, India is increasingly coming under US pressure while conducting its diplomatic relationship with Iran. In this regard, the three consecutive Indian votes against Iran on the nuclear issue in the International Atomic Energy Association (IAEA-September 2005, February 2006, November 2009) along with India's reluctant and slow response to implement IPI (Iran-Pakistan-India) gas pipe line project, its adherence to US and UN economic sanctions against Iran and more recently (in December 2010) the Reserve Bank of India's decision to scrap the Asian Clearing Union (ACU)-an institutional mechanism that helped to bypass the US sanctions for facilitating financial transaction between the two countries-are cited as concrete examples of India's growing complicity to US pressure and interest in the region.

Mohammad A. Mousavi and Kaveh L. Afrasiabi have inquired along this axes concerning Indo-Iran relationship in the present time. Mousavi in his paper on *Indo-Iran Relations since New Delhi Declarations* provides a comprehensive account of emerging orientation and position of Indian and Iranian state on a host of issues that concern them. These issues range from strategic and security matters including the security of sea lanes, military and defence cooperation, Iranian nuclear issue, energy security, LNG and IPI gas pipe line, trade, terrorism and bi-lateral relationship in the context of Afghanistan, Pakistan, Central Asia and Israel. He sees 'US shadow' on Indo-Iran engagements on all these issues. In the course of his analysis he demonstrates that how due to 'US factor' a political demarcation between the 'area of cooperation' and 'area of constraint' has come to stay between India and Iran. It is an account of 'US factor' and Indian understanding of the need of United States in particular that is hampering the realization of full cooperation between the two nations. The author concludes that though Iran remains a significant factor in India's strategic calculation for a variety of reasons including the fact that nuclear energy does not supplement the demand of hydrocarbon energy, India, given its understanding of US' role in its developmental trajectory, is unlikely to assert its independent position and pursue the diplomatic lines of Turkey and Brazil viz.-a viz. Iran.

Kaveh analyzes the US factor in Indo-Iran relations, particularly in the context of Iranian nuclear issue. In his paper on *Nuclear Equation in Iran-India Strategic Relations,* Kaveh first highlights the juxtaposition in India's position on nuclear non-proliferation as evident in the declaration of Non-Aligned Movement Conferences and its negative approach towards Iranian nuclear issue and accuses the Indian government of going too far in preventing the nuclear trade between India and Iran in order to appease the US government and its non-proliferation lobby which is otherwise not required as per the provision of IAEA and UN sanctions. He cautioned the Indian government of losing a lucrative nuclear market in Iran to other powers like Russia, France and even United States due to its 'bifurcated' stance on Iranian nuclear issue and strongly recommends a possibility of 'controlled nuclear cooperation' between India and Iran within the framework of IAEA and UN Sanctions.

On the other hand, Ashok K. Behuria and Chintamani

Mahapatra do acknowledge the US' role in Indo-Iran relationship but do not see Indian foreign policy towards Iran as solely dictated by US consideration. Behuria in his paper on *India and Iran: In Search of a New Rhythm* also provides a comprehensive account of all those issues that have been raised by Mousavi in the context of Indo-Iran relations. In particular he examines the graphic movement of Indo-Iran relationship that began in the early 1990s and reached new heights in the form of Delhi Declaration (2003) but exhausted itself by the end of 2010. He identifies India's negative vote against Iran at IAEA, stalemate over IPI gas pipeline as arising out of differences over pricing of gas, transit fee and security of supply of gas, Ahmadinijad's rhetorical anti-West and anti-Israel politics and US' latent pressure over India as crucial factors in bringing the relationship between the two to such a pass. However notwithstanding the relative decline in terms of political relationship between the two, the economic engagements between the two countries continue to grow despite the UN and US economic sanctions against Iran. The mutual imperative, according to him, requires what he calls a 'new rhythm' or a new perspective to sustain and consolidate their relationship.

Chintamani in his paper on *India, Iran and the United States: Nuclear Diplomacy* looks at the complexity of political diplomacy by nations around the issue of non- nuclear proliferation and argues that nuclear diplomacy cannot be understood as isolated from other political, economic and strategic factors that influence foreign policy behaviour of a state. While he acknowledges US as factor in shaping the response of Indian policy makers towards Iranian nuclear issue, he dismisses the argument that Indo- Iran relations has become a hostage to India-US ties; that India has lost its independent foreign policy and is toying the US line on variety of international and regional issues including Iran's nuclear and IPI gas pipeline. He notes that though the balancing act of Indian diplomacy between United States and Iran has so far not paid off as neither the Indo-US nuclear cooperation has taken off nor the Iran-Pakistan-India gas pipeline; the reason for this does not lie in the complicated diplomacy of Indo-Iran-US relations but in the complications of operationalization of each project which is independent of 'US' or 'Iran' factor.

In addition to the United States and Pakistan, there are two other important nations that have attracted the attention of a segment of intelligentsia and policy makers in India and in Iran. This attention has been in terms of their policies having important bearings on contours of Indo- West Asia relations in general and Indo-Iran relations in particular. These two countries are People's Republic of China and Jewish State of Israel. China with its nuclear status, having second largest economy in the world, a strong military power and its growing influence in global affairs including parts of West, Central and South Asia and given its troubled political history and relationship with India is bound to have an impact on the direction of Indo- Iran relations.

China along with India has emerged as the largest consumer of hydrocarbon products in the world. Both India and China are today engaged with similar issues in the Gulf: energy security, the security of the Persian Gulf, the security of Sea Lanes of Communication (SLOC), military cooperation, arms sales, oil and gas pipelines and flow of Arab investments in their respective domestic markets. In particular, China is vigorously pursuing its policy of energy security with a particular focus on capping the oil and gas resources of Persian Gulf and Central Asia. This has led to huge Chinese investment in the sector of oil and gas both in Persian Gulf and Central Asia. From this perspective, Iran is a very important nation that fulfills partly the requirements of Chinese energy consumption.

Srikanth Kondapalli examines *China Factor in Indo-Iranian Relations* and provides a detailed account of growing political, economic, strategic and military relationship between China and Iran. China values its growing ties with Iran in managing its restless segment of Muslim population in Xinjiang Uighur region as well as in procuring oil and gas resources. He examines the China-India-Iran relationship in the context of energy factor, Iranian nuclear issue and Afghanistan crisis and demonstrates the issue-specific position of China on all these issues. Thus while China converges with India on the necessity of stability of region from the point of view of uninterrupted supply of oil and gas products, it changed its initial opposition to US led punitive action against Iran and supported the UN sanctions against Iran on its nuclear issue but at the same time also supports Pakistan and Taliban in Afghanistan. He concludes that while at present stage China lacks the capacity, something that US has, to influence the Indo- Iran relations, however its potential to become *the* major player in the region and its adverse repercussion on Indo- Iran relations cannot be ruled out in the near future.

On the other hand, given the negative Muslim proclivity and sensitivity towards Israel in the light of occupation of Palestine and particularly of 'Islamic' Iran's ideological hostility to Israel, it was expected that growing ties between India and Israel will hamper or adversely affect the Indo-Iran relationship. Sujata Ashwarya Cheema's *Indo-Iranian Ties: Is there an Israel Factor?* examines the issue of Israeli factor in influencing Indo- Iran relations and found out that Indo-Iran relations is not a hostage to Indo- Israeli ties and vice versa. According to her, while Iran has been generally indifferent towards India's proximity to Israel, the latter has expressed concerns over many issues in New Delhi-Tehran relations. However, Israel's concern particularly in the field of transfer of Israeli defence technology to Tehran has not affected the deepening ties between India and Iran. She highlights the 'strategic autonomy' of India's foreign policy and contends that within the structure of its strategic autonomy, India has been successful in balancing its diplomacy between Israel and Iran.

Diplomacy is not *a zero sum game* and as India struggles to become a responsible global power it faces enormous challenges in terms of harmonizing its relationship with multiple competing global and regional power structures including Iran. In fact the balancing act of diplomacy which India is currently pursuing in international affairs is not only a calculated political strategy but is also a product of far reaching changes in the international structure that took place in early 1990s. A host of factors including the disintegration of erstwhile Soviet Union, the end of the ideological Cold War, the gradual de-ideologisation of India's foreign policy, the decreasing moral and ethical underpinnings of its world view that once characterize India's foreign policy, its gradual acceptance of power centric view of world order in post cold war period [5] and economic competitions and complementarities that replaced the political-ideological competition in the fast emerging globalised world –has freed India to pursue a simultaneous improvement in its relations with all the major powers including the United States, Europe, Japan, China and Russia and to play an active role in the formation of G-20, BRIC (Brazil, Russia, India and China) and IBSA (India, Brazil and South Africa).

The same process and opportunities has also guided the Indian policy makers to intensify simultaneously its relationship with Iran, Saudi Arabia and Israel-the three states around which Indian foreign policy in the region revolves today. It is interesting to note that India has been able to maintain its growing ties with all three states despite the mutually antagonistic relations that exist among them and the prevailing negative attitude of US and Israel towards Iran. More or less, the same factors and processes are also at work in the context of Islamic Republic of Iran that allows it to follow a more *pragmatist and flexible* foreign policy during President Rafsanjani and Khatami's era in the mid 90s and early period of first decade of twenty first century till the coming of Ahamedinejad as President of Iran in 2004 that brought back the centrality of ideology in its conduct of foreign affairs, although not in the similar fashion that was witnessed during the period of Ayatollah Khomeini (1979-1989). Khatami's bold formulation of 'Dialogue of Civilizations', which was later adopted by the UN General Assembly facilitated a room for dialogue between Iran and the West, particularly United States, that did take place between the two concerning issues related to stabilization of Afghanistan and Iraq. However, the subsequent hardening of position by both the US and Iran hardly leaves any room for further progressive dialogue between the two.

This period also witnessed the consolidation of bilateral ties between India and Iran as evident from the frequent exchange of high level governmental delegations (see Appendix to this chapter) that resulted in Tehran (1997) and Delhi (2003) Declarations which established the framework of joint cooperation in many fields. The factors that contributed (and continue to work) to the consolidation of ties between the two in the changed international context of 1990s were/are: the need of Iran for more partners to ends its 'international isolation', the mutual recognition of the need for hydrocarbon trading. Iran desperately need an outlet to sell its Oil and Gas resources to augment its cash stripped economy and India emerges as one of biggest consumer of oil and gas products in the world and saw Iran as one of important sources to supplement its energy needs. Iran also found India attractive to secure its service and technological cooperation in many other fields, specifically in defence, modernization of Iranian Army, nuclear cooperation, medicine, information technology, and above all in the sharing of threat perception on the issue of terrorism in general and Afghan Taliban in particular. The mutual complementarities of each other was well recognized in Tehran (1997) and Delhi (2003) Declarations.

This slow but steady growth in bilateral relations between the two has been highlighted by various contributors in the volume. However, it was the defence and military cooperation that first brought the two nations together in early 1990s. In the post Soviet period, Iran sought India's help in modernizing its Russian made conventional arsenals including tanks, combat aircraft, submarines and ships as India had considerable know-how and experience in dealing with Russian made military equipments. In particular, Iran sought Indian help in developing batteries for the three Kilo-class submarines. The Submarine batteries that Russia had provided were not appropriate for the warm waters of the Persian Gulf, and India had substantial experience in operating Kilos in warm water. Monika Chansoria's *Indo-Iranian Relations and Defence Cooperation* provides a detailed account of nature of defence and military cooperation between the two. She considers the defence cooperation between the two as crucial for India in order to protect its significant geopolitical and energy security stakes that lies in West and Central Asia. She cautions the Indian government of the need to maintain a very fine diplomatic balance between Iran and United States while strategizing its defence policy and concludes how defence cooperation between the two nations would serve as an essential tool of foreign policy thereby strengthening mutual trust and enhancing security and stability in the region.

Jajati K. Pattnaik's paper on *India-Iran Bilateral Relations in the Contemporary Period* provides a theoretical understanding of the bilateral relations between India and Iran which is based upon the simultaneous interplay of the principles of idealism, realism, pragmatism and multilateralism between the two. According to him, India and Iran are strategically located in the Asian continent and are inevitable to each other. India is the bridge to Iran's Look East policy and the reverse is the example for India's access towards West Asia, Central Asia and Caspian Sea region. He concludes by projecting a better prospect for the future relationship between the two as the relationship is based more on the elements of convergence than divergence.

Hamid Ahmadi's paper on *Iranian Foreign Policy towards India* makes an interesting observation how the nature of state does not determine its foreign policy and affects the bilateral relations between the two nations. He examines this in the context of Iran and finds out that the secular Phalavi regime of Iran was more friendly disposed towards 'Islamic' Pakistan than a 'Secular' India, wherein the 'Islamic' Republic of Iran developed more cordial ties with Secular India than Islamic Pakistan. The author analyzes the events and contexts and the role of civil society in shaping Iranian foreign policy toward India. In this regard he makes an insightful observation that while cold war structure brought Pakistan and Iran closer under US tutelage, it was particularly the role of Islamic groups and individuals in Iran (though not sufficiently elaborated) that influenced and tilted the orientation of post revolutionary Islamic government in Iran in favour of Pakistan which was otherwise favourably disposed towards India in the initial years of its existence.

The fact that state remains the basic unit of understanding in the field of international relations or conducting inter-state diplomacy, the role of civil society in influencing the inter- state relations has not received the adequate attention in the academic scholarship except in case of the United States of America where 'politics of lobbying' is a legitimate means of influencing government's decision making process. This despite the fact almost all states retain the linkage with civil society for a variety of purposes including matter concerning foreign policy. In this regard, it will be worthwhile to mention here that Pakistani government has successfully used Islam and Islamic groups throughout the Muslim world to mobilize the 'Muslim public opinion' either through the instrument of OIC (Organisation of Islamic Conference) or other civil society channels in order to draw favourable and sympathetic attention towards her as 'feeble Muslim state' against the 'hegemonic Hindu State of India'. In other words Pakistan, like Israel, has been successful in projecting its 'victimhood' in the Muslim world in order to gain Muslim sympathy.

The popular perception about the 'Partition of Indian Sub Continent' that exists in the Muslim world (including the segments of its intelligentsia) is that almost all Muslims from India have migrated to Pakistan and the same has been skilfully reinforced by the Pakistani diplomacy over the years, thereby monopolizing the 'Islamic space' in South Asia despite the fact that India is a home of third largest Muslim Population after Indonesia and Pakistan and second largest Shii Muslim population after Iran in the world. [6] The Indian governments will continue to face the challenges of 'Islamic card' of Pakistani diplomacy in the Muslim world. Given this imperative and the nature of discourse of secularism in India that recognizes the role of religious identity in public sphere, it will not be improper nor will it dilute the 'secular democratic image' of the

Indian state if it were to utilize the soft power of Islam as 'cultural capital', if not 'political-ideological tool', as used by the Pakistani state, to overcome its 'Islamic deficiency' in the Muslim world. Such an exercise would rather help the Indian government in consolidating its ties with the Muslim world including Iran.

In addition to defence and maritime cooperation, energy cooperation between Iran and India has been the major incentive for these two nations to come closer. The component of energy factor received the central focus in both Tehran (1997) and Delhi (2003) Declarations. The Teheran Declaration stated "the geographical situation of Iran and its abundant energy resources along with the rapidly expanding Indian economy and energy market on the other, create a unique complementarity which the sides agree to harness for mutual benefit". [7] According to the New Delhi Declaration (January 2003), "India and Iran have a complementarity of interests in the energy sector as a strategic area of their future relationship. Iran with its abundant energy resources and India with its growing energy needs are natural partners". [8] India, in recent years, has emerged as one of world's largest consumers and importers of petroleum products. It has experienced a growing energy supply-demand gap as its domestic production of oil and gas has failed to keep pace with rising consumption needs. It is estimated that India's gas import dependency is expected to jump to 91 percent by 2025, while the oil import dependency is expected to reach 78 percent in the same period. For India, energy relations are even more vital as energy security is seen as an absolute necessity, if India is to achieve great power status—hence, India's quest to diversify its external sources of supply.

Iran, on the other hand, is endowed with enormous energy resources, and is therefore keenly interested in exporting its surplus oil and natural gas to India. In fact, it has the second largest natural gas reserves in the world after Russia, estimated at 23 trillion cubic meters. Therefore, Iran has figured prominently in India's strategy to establish and expand its energy relationship with the Gulf countries. For the same reason India is still exploring the viability of IPI gas pipeline. The Indian Government has approved the IPI Gas pipeline Project in 2005. Currently India imports 17 percent of oil products from Iran while Iran imports 40 percent gasoline or refined oil from India. Thus the energy cooperation promises to serve both countries' immediate and long-term needs.

In this context Elaheh Koolaee and Masoud Imani Kalesar's *India's Energy Security and Caspian Sea Region* provides a very comprehensive and critical analysis of India's energy security policy in the Caspian Sea Region (CSR). It not only highlights the significance of Iran for India in securing latter's energy security and providing a gateway to facilitate the trade and commerce for India in Central Asia but goes into a detailed evaluation of various options of pipeline projects that exist for India to secure energy security. The authors conclude that while India has recognized the importance of access to energy resources in CSR but there exists a wide *gap* between India's declaratory intent, conceptualization of various schemes and its implementation. The authors further contend that since nuclear energy is not an alternative to hydrocarbon energy in terms of volume and magnitude of energy consumption required in India, it should explore all possibilities first to secure hydrocarbon based energy security rather than running around securing nuclear energy.

Shebonti Ray Dadwal's *Indo-Iran Cooperation in Energy and Energy Security* also looks at the state of Iran-India energy relations, and proposes that despite the fact that relations, including ties in the energy sector, between these two important Asian countries have undergone some problems and have dipped from the high point of 2003-2005, the scope for strengthening and broadening ties in the energy sector are there. Having examined the feasibility of various pipe line projects between India and Iran, she recommends the adoption of policies that are not only in their national interest but is also reflective of their status as rising powers, both at the regional and global level.

Though oil and gas related products constitute the bulk of economic transaction between India and Iran, there is a growing realization on part of both the countries to diversify their trade and commercial relations in non-oil sector. Javed Ahmad Khan's *Indo-Iran Economic Relations since 1990s* and Faisal Ahmed's *Indo-Iran Engagements: A Geo-Economic Analysis* explore the pattern of growing trade and economic relations between the two countries since early 1990s.

Along with energy sand defence cooperation it was primarily the context of threat of Taliban in Afghanistan that brought India and Iran closer. Incidentally, during the 1990s, Pak-Iran relations started deteriorating, due to their perceived varying interests in Afghanistan, conflicting attitudes towards the Taliban, economic rivalry over opportunities in Central Asia and the rise of sectarian terrorism in Pakistan. This helped India in cementing its ties with Iran and they continue to cooperate in Afghanistan vis-à-vis Taliban. In this context the cooperation between the two ranges from supporting Northern Alliance against the Taliban, sharing of intelligence, undertaking infrastructural projects and working on strategies that deny any effective role to Taliban in the post (western) withdrawal phase of Afghanistan.

However, how strong is this cooperation? Is this cooperation strategic or tactical in nature? Vishal Chandra has raised these questions in his paper titled *Growing Afghan Maze: An Opportunity for Indo-Iranian Re-engagement.* He explores the international and regional dimensions of Afghanistan in order to partly answer these questions and partly to reflect upon the future political scenario in the event of withdrawal of Western forces from Afghanistan. He finds that Indo- Iranian relationship vis-à-vis Afghanistan is conditioned by other factors as Iran-US relations, Pakistan-Iran relations, US-Pakistan relations and Indo-US relations and in conjunction with their wide differences particularly over the role of Pakistan vis-à-vis terrorism and the role of United States in Afghanistan and region, concludes that the relationship between the two in the context of Afghanistan is likely to remain at best *fragile, unstable* and *tactical.*

Pakistan mediated cross border terrorism in Iranian territory that became evident from the series of suicide bombing in its Seistant and Bluchistan region [9] and the growing sectarian *Shia-Sunni* conflict within the territory of Pakistan, compelled Iranian political leadership to re-evaluate its relations with the Pakistan. For the first time the Iranian government has called upon the Government of Pakistan to rein in Pakistan based *Sunni* Islamic fundamentalist organizations such as Jund Allah and the Pakistan Taliban who are targeting the *Shii* population across the Iranian border in Siastan and Bluchistan. Such toughening of Iranian postures vis-à-vis Pakistan on the issue of terrorism might be welcomed from the Indian point of view but will not be adequate enough to strongly cement the ties between the two unless Iranian government shares the Indian perception about the role of Pakistani establishment, directly or indirectly, in abetting terror across the region. In this context it is sad to note that much of the Muslim world including Iran saw the terrorist attack on Mumbai on 26 November 2008 as the handiwork of Christian- Jew conspiracy (rather US-Israel/CIA-MOSSAD) in order to draw India into 'US-Israeli conception of security' to fight the international menace of 'Islamic Terrorism' and did not out rightly condemn the role of Pakistani establishment in abetting this heinous crime. [10]

In response to Mumbai terror attack Iranian President Ahmadinezad said in a statement that 'the ugly phenomenon of terrorism has its root in an unfair international order and occupationist and disuniting policies'. [11] The former Iranian foreign minister Manuchehr Mottaki echoed the same position and said on December 31, 2008 that "certain extra-regional powers are carrying out activities that cause instability in South Asia. They have organized plans that lead to extremism". [12] On November 29 2008, the Iranian newspaper Al-Wifaq, prompted that, 'Israel has shown terrorism in Middle East and the entire world. It added that the attacks in India had a Zionist background with goals of interfering in regional matters. According to the article, ten years ago, the U.S. and the Zionists started spreading to India to encourage a civil war within India and strife between India and its neighbours. Their intention was to impose their hegemony in the region. Thus, it is not enough to put an end to the military attack, the true American string pulling behind the terrorist attack must also be exposed". [13]

Similarly the Iranian government did not condemn the ISI-mediated Taliban suicide bombing of Indian Embassy in Kabul in October 2009 that killed 41 persons including four Indian officers posted in the Embassy. Such an attitude will not be helpful for building trust among the Indian political leadership particularly in a context when all investigations into a majority of terrorist related incidents within and outside India points out its connection with Pakistan. The Indian insistence on the recognition of Pakistan's role (direct or indirect) in abetting terrorist activities within and outside region is not intended to isolate Pakistan internationally or to destabilize her internally, but to make a point that Pakistan's policy of using terrorism as an instrument of state policy or its role in politicization of Islamic ideology has inherent tendency not only to destabilize herself, as the current spate of terrorist bombings inside Pakistan does indicate, but will have repercussion on the stability of world order. It is therefore imperative to build strong international consensus so as to put pressure upon Pakistan to dismantle its infrastructure of terror and desist from using terrorism as a tool of foreign policy. India is extremely concerned with the internal developments of Pakistan as it strongly believes that a destabilized Pakistan is not in the interest of India. India needs a stable Pakistan and stability in the region for its continuous growth. [14]

It is not only energy driven needs or historical civilizational ties or geo-strategic location of Iran (Iran controls Strait of Harmuz from where the bulk of oil tankers and other shipments passes and is the gateway of India for access to Central Asia in the present context) that propels India to maintain close ties with Iran but also a political recognition of growing influence of Iran in West and Central Asia. By all accounts Iran has emerged as one of the strongest power in the region of West and Central Asia following the US's invasion of Afghanistan and Iraq in 2001 and 2003 respectively. Its prestige, influence and domination have tremendously increased in the several quarters of the Arab World and Central Asian countries. In today's context its role is crucial in securing the political stability in the region, particularly in the Persian Gulf countries where India has vital economic stake.

Atul Aneja in his significant piece on *Iran, Turkey and the Reshaping of West Asia in the Post-9/11 Scenario: Implications for India* highlights this assertive and growing role of Iran in post-9/11 regional scenario in West Asia and demonstrates how the major stakeholder in the region—Iran, Turkey, Syria and Saudi Arabia—are coordinating their activities in order to maintain the regional stability (which also includes the stability of existing regimes) in region against the US-Israeli design of creating a 'Greater Middle East' that is, according to him, bound to destabilize the entire region. He concludes by making an insightful observation: while the US invasion of Iraq and Afghanistan intended to establish absolute US-Israeli hegemony in the region, the course of events and development of political forces following 9/11 as well as the actions of these stakeholders in the region indicates a loosening of Western hegemonic influence and the emergence of greater autonomous space for regional forces and influences to work that will shape West Asia's destiny in the future. The current ongoing popular democratic upsurge that started from Tunisia and Egypt and has now spread to almost all Muslim countries of West Asia and North Africa (WANA) is bound to strengthen further this emerging regional autonomy of the region.

Given this emerging political scenario in West Asia how will

Indian foreign policy respond? In other words what are the implications for Indian foreign policy in the region? Atul partly reflects on this question and draws attention of the Government of India to the need of establishing close ties with Iran in particular and other powers of the region in order to protect its interest in the region. Given this regional scenario, he argues that India does not have any alternative but to cement ties with Iran by either finalizing the IPI gas pipe line project or alternatively deep sea pipeline, if IPI is not possible in view of Pakistan factor, or SAGE (South Asia Gas Enterprise) involving Qatar, Iran, Iraq and Oman.

The American failure in Afghanistan and Iraq has led to a rethinking within a section of American establishment to seek the support of Iran in stabilizing Iraq and Afghanistan. The Indian government cannot be oblivious of this emerging political reality and therefore Iran will continue to occupy strategic position in India's foreign policy. For this reason and in accordance with its world view India has never shared the US and Israeli's projection of 'Islamic' Iran as 'rogue state' and a threat to peace and stability of region; neither endorse the Western position that suspects Iranian intention to misuse nuclear technology for making nuclear bomb, nor buys the US's classification of 'good and bad Taliban' as political strategy to fight the menace of terrorism (read Islamic terrorism). Further, India has entered into defence security related agreements with many of Persian Gulf countries including Saudi Arabia, Oman, Qatar and Bahrian. It also conducted joint naval war fare with Iran in 2003 and 2006. India is keen to project its military power projection in the region so as to be part of emerging alternative security arrangement vis-à-vis US in the Persian Gulf and Central Asia. India has already commissioned two air military bases in Central Asia. The underlying idea of enhanced defence and military cooperation with Iran and other littoral states of Persian Gulf is that India with the cooperation of Persian Gulf countries should be ready in shouldering the responsibility of providing regional security structure in the Persian Gulf as and when the situation warrants.

On the nuclear issue the successive governments of India has consistently maintained that within the structure of rights and obligations of NPT Iran has legitimate right to use nuclear technology for peaceful civilian purposes. Its three consecutive votes against Iran in the Board Meeting of IAEA was guided by the following pragmatic national considerations:-First, it was intended to convey a message to the West, particularly United States, that India can be a reliable partner and its position is in congruence with the leading power of the world; second, to secure and operationalize the Indo-US Civil Nuclear Deal in order to end the 'nuclear isolation of India' that was imposed on it since Pokhran nuclear Test in 1974 and to partly fulfill its energy requirements; third, to manage the anti-nuclear proliferation lobby in the United States; fourth, to share the concern of Arab Gulf countries who have strong misgivings about Iranian nuclear programme [15] and finally, India is wary of having another nuclear power state in its neighbourhood.

The crux of the matter is that not only Indian economy is strongly linked with the economy of Western nations and Persian Gulf countries but its future growth as global power is contingent upon the support, goodwill and recognition of these two regions, particularly the West. Further, the 'Chinese factor' binds US-India relations in future. Despite the fact that China is the largest trading partner of India, she along with Pakistan continue to be considered as a *'hostile nation'* in the public perception of India and therefore India needs the support of United States to deal with the Chinese threat in future. On the other hand, by all accounts, the current policy of US government in South Asia aims to augment Indian powers to contain the increasing influence of China at global level. It was these set of considerations that forced Indian government to vote against Iran in the IAEA's Board Meetings.

However, these negative votes were, unlike the West, not intended to punish Iran for its 'wrong doing'. This partly also explains why India displayed its reservation to the recent UN economic sanctions (2010) against Iran and decided to work out 'creative ways' [16] that mitigates the impact of sanctions on Indian economy and insulates the Indian companies from the same. These included joining a consortium with companies from Russia, China, and/or Kuwait, making it difficult to single out single countries or firms, and creating new corporate entities with no financial ties to the US or EU, to insulate them from any retaliation from the West.

Other 'creative mechanism' recommended by Ministry of External Affairs in this regard are:

- A Rupee-Rial arrangement for settling bilateral trade to avoid a ban on Indian banks from accessing the US or EU financial system.
- An arrangement to open letters of credit in Rial, as suggested by

the Iranians at the 16th session of the India-Iran Joint Commission.

- Investment by Indian firms through joint ventures in mining, fertilizer, food processing, pharmaceuticals and automobile projects that are not currently sanctioned.
- Opening of warehouses for fast-moving Indian products in Iranian Free Trade Zone with a mechanism to provide insurance cover for political and economic risks.

In a speech on July 5, 2010 at an India-Iran strategic dialogue in New Delhi, the Indian Foreign Secretary Nirupama Rao said, "we are justifiably concerned that the extra-territorial nature of certain unilateral sanctions recently imposed by individual countries, with their restrictions on investment by third countries in Iran's energy sector, can have a direct and adverse impact on Indian companies and more importantly, on our energy security and our attempts to meet the development needs of our people". [17]

Similarly, the perception that India is unwilling to formalize the IPI pipeline gas project due to US pressure is also not correct. One cannot rule out the implications of US role that might have affected the finalization of deal but for Indian governments the issue of pricing of gas, the transit fees, the security of uninterrupted supply of gas, the security of pipelines and the cost of distributive pipelines that will run throughout the territory of India are crucial for finalizing this deal. Given the history of *bad faith* between India and Pakistan and in the present context of spectrum of terrorism in Pakistan that is posing a serious threat to Pakistani state, it is near impossible for any Indian government to mortgage a vital part of its security in the hand of Pakistan by signing this agreement.

The Iranian government is fully aware of these concerns and apprehensions of Indian government and therefore remains open for negotiations without ever blaming the Indian government for not formalizing the deal. Further, Iran knows well that given its international isolation, cordial relationship with India at this juncture provides legitimacy to Iranian government, a booming market for Iranian hydrocarbon products, its requirements of refined oil that it imports (almost 40 percent) from India, access to relatively cheap and high quality educational opportunities in India for Iranian middle class who can no more afford the cost of education in the West due to its failing economy. Moreover, a nation which is close to western power structure at present conjecture can be useful for mediation between Iran and the West in the possible future.

Thus, in the light of above and from the point of view of balancing act of Indian diplomacy between Iran and West, particularly the United States, Indian response to Iranian nuclear issue appears to be a *measured one.* On the other hand the Iranian political response that see India's negative vote against Iran at IAEA as nothing but *a case of betrayal* and *national hurt* and link it with 'American pressure at work' reflects a case of *misplaced expectation* on the part of Iranian political leadership. The fact remains that the two do not constitute a *'strategic partner'* as nurtured through long history of friendship and trust and political agreements; hence there does not arise a question a *feeling of betrayal and hurt* on any part. After all Iran supported Pakistan in its war against India (1965, 1971) and routinely supports Pakistan sponsored resolution against India in Organisation of Islamic Conference (OIC). Further, Iran has not been sensitive to India's concern on the issue of Kashmir and role of Pakistan in fomenting terrorism inside India. It is as recently as on 16th November 2010 the Iranian Supreme Leader, Ayatollah Khamaenie, on the occasion of *Eid* appealed to the Muslim *Umma* to help 'struggling' Muslim nations including Kashmir. Such reference to Kashmir from the highest leader of Iran is certainly not helpful in building cordial relationship, trust and confidence between the two nations. [18]

It is also amusing to find a 'near silent' Iranian response to the Chinese and Russian vote against Iran in the IAEA deliberations on its nuclear issue or in favour of imposing sanctions against Iran in UN Security Council. This dualism on the part of Iran begs a question: does the Iranian political response betray its cultural conception about India? How does India figure in the collective national imagination of Islamic Republic of Iran? What is the strategic importance of India for Iran? Where does India figure in the Iranian regional security structure? Or, whether India figures at all? This question has rightly been raised by Vishal Chandra in his piece on Afghanistan. While significance of Iran for India is fairly established discourse among the intelligentsia both within India and outside including Iran, there is little that one knows about the significance of India for Iran except the two dimensions: market for the consumption of Iranian oil and gas and influence of Persian culture and literature on Indian society.

It is important to note here that the relationship between the two that was forged in the mid 90s continue to work despite the political hiccup and murmur one hears from thc Iranian side on the Indian behaviour on Iranian nuclear issue or IPI gas pipeline or what Iran calls 'Peace Pipe Line'. Prior to this all previous engagements between the two beginning with 1950 Peace and Friendship Treaty has for one or other reason floundered and did not materialize beyond a point. The institutional mechanism of Indo- Iran Joint Commission Meeting (JCM) that was established in 1998 in the backdrop of Tehran Declaration (1997) is very much in operation and its 15th Meeting took place in October 2008.

The JCM covers range of issues including cooperation in the field of energy, science and technology and transportation and transit. Despite several constraining factors in Indo-Iran Relations the bilateral trade between the two today has reached from US$ 2 billion in 2001-02 to US$ 13.4 billion in 2009-10 and US$ 30 billion dollar if one includes the trade routed through third country. The purpose of strengthening bilateral relations between the two can be better served if both countries demonstrate ample flexibility and pragmatism in dealing with each other. This calls on the part of Iranian political leadership not to see every Indian response and action towards her through the prism of United States and accommodate the Indian sensitivity on Kashmir. On its part, the Indian government urgently needs to undertake some measures to implement some provisions of Tehran and Delhi Declarations in order to restore confidence among the Iranian political leadership as well as be sensitive to the threat perception of Iran at a political juncture where Iran is facing international isolation.

This volume would have remained incomplete without a discussion on the cultural dimension of Indo- Iran relations. While politics divides, culture unites people and civilizations. Centuries of cultural interactions and movement of ideas between Hindustan and Faras (a civilizational space), not India and Iran (a modern political entity) deeply affected each other's mode of thought, ways of interactions, culture of hospitality, sense of dressing and cuisine. In particular, Faras deeply impacted Hindustan in terms of art, architecture, administration, cuisine, culture of greetings and Persian language that was gradually absorbed into, indigenized and enriched the cultural diversity of Hindustan so much so that this cultural interaction gave a birth to a new Indian language called Urdu which unfortunately, owing to various modern political factors, has now been reduced as the language of 'Muslim community of India'. The reverence and warmth of each-other as shaped through the history of cultural interactions can still be felt in each-other's bylanes, streets, *mohallas* (neighbourhood) and *gallis*. However as Hindustan and Faras became embedded in the project of modernity and consequently became 'India' and 'Iran' (The Islamic Republic of Iran further enhance the project of modernity) respectively, they erected a 'political-national barrier' that not only hampered cross cultural interaction but also deflected and distorted the form of this rich interaction.

The dilemma of preservation of culture and heritage and unfettered continuity of cultural interaction between 'two peoples' and among cultures and civilizations within the 'structure of nation-state' haunts many critical scholars today. Mandana Barkeshli's *Preservation of Cultural Heritage between Iran and India* and Amir H. Zekrgoo's *Reflections on Indo-Iranian Relations* deals with this dimension of cultural relations between India and Iran. Mandana first reflects upon the rich cultural heritage that both India and Iran share and underlines that the very notion of preservation of cultural and heritage is modern one. She subsequently goes on to describe the various attempts and contributions of various individual scholars including her own that have been made to institutionalize the preservation of culture and heritage. The 1979 Islamic revolution helped in focusing upon the culture of Eastern Civilization including India that resulted in the exchange of cultural products between the two countries and also initiated the joint cooperation and collaborations between concerned institutions in India and Iran in order to preserve the cultural heritage of both countries.

Amir H. Zekrgoo in his paper provides a powerful critique of modern notion of human life—which is narrow, structured, contaminated through modern entities called nation and its interest based politics that establishes a fragile, limited, contemporary relationship based on interest and intends to recapture or restore the *'original self'* of mankind which is eternal and establish human relationship across cultural societies without the barrier of political territories. He argues in favour of re-establishment of notion of cultural territory against the notion of political territory that facilitates the inter-cultural dialogue and communication and helps in preserving cultural diversity without political borders. He highlights the significance of cultural products like Silk Route—a symbol of globalization that connects and enriches many human civilizations through mutual cultural interactions. He reflects on how the two civilizations–Persian and Indian- communicated and enriched each other in the writings of many *Sufis*, saints, *Sadhus*, *Rishis* and Great Souls, in paintings, and in other art products and thereby constructing a common, *timeless spiritual self* in both civilizations. He then describes his efforts in creating a piece of Art that symbolizes constant communication, harmony and living together between the two civilizations, which he successfully managed to complete. One can find his piece of Art hanging in the main hall of Iranian Embassy at New Delhi. Zekrgoo's understanding of common cultural heritage is very much evident from the amount of good will that exist for Iran in the Indian society and vice versa. This partly explains why India's adverse actions on Iranian nuclear issue struck an emotional code in the bylanes of Lucknow, Delhi and other places and gets translated into a political mobilization at the call of political parties to protest against the action of government of India.

M.H. Ilias's paper on *Iranians and Bollywood Cinema* seeks to make an enquiry into how Bollywood cinema as a 'translocal cultural entity' is being perceived by the Iranians within the boundaries of their imagination and aesthetic sensibilities. He highlights such dimensions of Indian Cinema as freedom, love, sacrifice, sanctity of family, nationalism, victory of good over evil etc and how these become important in the contemporary condition of Iranian political and national life. Given the authoritarian nature of Iranian polity and 'strangulated freedom', these symbolisms of Bollywood resonates with the cultural sensibilities of Iranian population and help in imagining their dream of freedom from day-to-day struggle for a dignified life in a dignified free nation.

The sub text of three these three papers is the recognition of the role of civil society in building a human relationship—which is not a promotion of politically mediated notion of peace and friendship as practiced in modern world- but something genuine, spiritual, cultural, aesthetic which is based upon mutual recognition of each other difference but with equal respect and dignity and inter-cultural understanding of each other life. In this context it is worthwhile to point out here that the permission of Islamic Government in Iran to open Indian Cultural Centre in Tehran, something along the line of Iranian Cultural Centre in Delhi, will go a long way to bring these two civilizations closer to each other.

A reading of this volume throws other interesting questions, in addition to those that have been raised in the above text, that are important from the point of view of understanding the contour of Indo- Iran relationship at the present conjecture. Some of these questions are: does the convergence of interest and increasing cooperation between the United States and India on a set of issues that range from inflow of FDI, terrorism, civil nuclear cooperation, defence cooperation and stability in the region of West and Central Asia amounts to a capitulation of India's foreign policy? Does the enhanced cooperation between India and United States should necessarily be seen as premised on anti-Iranian agenda as is normally considered in the Iranian political circle? Should Iran normalize its relations with the US in near future, will then Iranian political leadership continue to see Indo- US ties as premise of containing Iran or for that matter China?

Similarly, does Indo-Israeli growing ties, particularly in the field of defence and military, has anti- Iranian component? What has been reaction of Iran to the growing Indo-US and Indo-Israeli ties? Should India perceive closer Iran-Pakistan ties as a sign of anti-India axis? Why Iran continues to maintain its steady relations with Pakistan despite latter being a satellite of United States and posing a direct threat to Iranian interest in Afghanistan and in Central Asia by first helping Taliban to capture Afghanistan and latter though officially participating in American led war against Taliban but retaining enough manoeuvring capacity to keep Taliban alive as a Sunni Islamic militant movement? What is the impact of phenomenon of cross border terrorism on Indo-Iran relationship? What is the role of civil society in building good will and trust between the two nations?

Given these set of debates, perceptions and questions surrounding India's policy towards Iran and vice versa, what are the future prospects of the relationship between the two? Will the relationship between the two grow or relapse given the present conjecture of global politics that demands the cooperation of international community in preventing and isolating Iran from pursuing its ambition of becoming a nuclear power? The collection of articles in this volume has attempted to deal with these and other questions that have been raised in the context of Indo-Iran relations. Some are answered but some remain unanswered. In sum and taken together, the articles in the volume provide a broad parameter and perspective to understand the complexities of Indo-Iran relationship:

its continuity, limitations, strength and weakness.

Appendix: India-Iran Diplomatic Visits Since 1993

S.N	Visits	Date
VVIP Visits (From India)		
1	Shri Narasimha Rao, Prime Minister	September 1993
2	Shri K.R. Narayanan, Vice-President	October 1996
3	Atal Bihari Vajpayee, Prime Minister	April 2001
VVIP Visits (From Iran)		
4	Akbar Hashemi Rafsanjani, President	April 1995
5	Mohammad Khatami, President	January 2003
6	Mahmoud Ahmadinejad	April 29, 2008
Other High Profile Visits (From India)		
7	P R Dasmunshi, Minister of Water Resources	February 26-27, 2005
8	Rajiv Sikri, Secretary (East), Ministry of External Affairs	April 30-May 2, 2005
9	Mani Shankar Aiyar, Minister of Petroleum, Natural Gas and Panchayati Raj	June 10-14, 2005
10	K. Natwar Singh, Minister of External Affairs	September 3-5, 2005
11	E Ahamad, Minister of State for External Affairs	February 20-22, 2007
12	Saifuddin Soz, Minister for Water Resources	May 12-14 , 2006
13	Pranab Mukherjee, Minister of External Affairs	February 6-7, 2007
14	E Ahamad, Minister of State for External Affairs	March 6-8, 2007
15	Murli Deora, Minister for Petroleum and Natural Gas	April 25-26, 2007
16	E Ahamad, Minister of State for External Affairs	September 3-4, 2007
17	T C A Raghavan, Joint Secretary (PAI)	November 11-13, 2007

18	Prof. Saifuddin Soz, Minister for Water Resources	November 23-25, 2007
19	Shivshankar Menon, Foreign Secretary	December 16-17, 2007
20	Kumari Selja, MOS for Housing and Urban Poverty Alleviation	February 2-5, 2008
21	R Swaminathan, Joint Secretary (CPV)	February 18-20, 2008
22	K C Jena, Chairman, Railway Board	April 11-15, 2008
23	E Ahamad, Minister of State for External Affairs	May 4-5, 2008
24	Kumari Selja, MOS for Housing and Urban Poverty Alleviation	May 1-14, 2008
25	T C A Raghavan, Joint Secretary (PAI)	May 10-12,2008
26	P M Meena, Joint Secretary (Consular)	June 28-30, 2008
27	Pranab Mukherjee, Minister of External Affairs	July 28-30, 2008
28	Pranab Mukherjee, Minister of External Affairs	November 2, 2008
29	Smt. Nirupama Rao, Foreign Secretary of India	February 2-3, 2010
30	Shri S. M. Krishna, External Affairs Minister	May 15-18, 2010
Other High Profile Visits (From Iran)		
31	Bijan Namdar Zangeneh, Oil Minister	January 6-7, 2005
32	Kamla Kharrazi, Foreign Minister	February 21-22, 2005
33	Gholam Ali Haddad Adel, Majlis Speaker	February 27- March 3, 2005
34	Ali Larijani, Secretary Supreme National Security council	August 30-31, 2005
35	Mehdi Safari, Deputy Foreign Minister for Asia, Oceania and CIS Countries	February 23-24, 2006
36	Esfandyar Rahim Moshaee, Vice President and President of Iran's Cultural Heritage and Tourism	March 25-29, 2006

	Organisation	
37	Mehdi Safari, Deputy Foreign Minister for Asia, Oceania and CIS Countries	August 3-4 , 2006
38	Manouchehr Mottaki, Foreign Minister	November 16-17, 2006
39	Mohammad Abbasi, Minister for Cooperatives	January 23-23, 2007
40	Parviz Fattah, Energy Minister	February 25-27, 2007
41	Mehdi Safari, Deputy Foreign Minister for Asia, Oceania and CIS Countries	September 5-7, 2007
42	Mostafa Pour Mohammadi, Minister of Interior	November 7-8, 2007
43	Ayatollah Ahmad Jannati, Secretary, Guardian Council	November 24-December 1, 2007
44	Davoud Danesh Jafari, Minister of Economic Affairs	January 14-19, 2008
45	Sayyed Mohammad Hosseni, MFA Spokesman	February 9-17, 2008
46	Esfandiar Rahim Mashaie, Vice president of Culture	April 29- May 4, 2008
47	Manouchehr Mottaki, Foreign Minister	November 16-17, 2009
48	Dr. Mohammad Ali Fathollahi, Deputy Foreign Minister for Asia and Oceania	August 5-8, 2010

End Notes

1. According to the World Bank's World Development Report 1999-2000, India's economy is gigantic in terms of overall gross national product (GNP). It ranks eleventh in the world, with a total figure of US$ 421 billion, compared with China's US$ 929 billion, and Japan's US$ 4,090 billion. When measured by purchasing power parity (PPP) taking into account local rates of exchange, India scores higher with US$ 1,661 billion, the fourth largest in the world. As international politics recognizes states as the main actors, these figures should rank India among the leading 'powers' of the world. *Subrat K. Mitra,* 'Engaging the

World: the Ambiguity of India's Power' in Subrat K. Mitra and Bernard Rill, ed; *India's New Dynamics in Foreign Policy*, 2006, Haans Seidel Stiftung V, Munich, p. 9.

2. The budget allocation for Defence expenditure in 2005-06 was ₹ 80548.98 crore; in 2006-07 ₹ 85494.64 crore; in 2007-08 ₹ 92500.00 crore and in 2008-09 ₹ 1,56,000.00 crore. India's defence expenditure is 2.5 percent of its GDP. For details see, 2009-10 Report, Ministry of Defence, Government of India. http://mod.nic.in/reports/welcome.html retrieved on February 10, 2011.
3. In 1990-91 remittances from overseas Indians were a modest US$ 2.1 billion. The Reserve Bank of India has reported that Indians living abroad transferred US$24.6 billion in the fiscal year 2005-06 making it the leading recipient of remittances in the world. Source: http://www.rbi.org.in/scripts/Publications. In the year 2003, the total volume of remittances received by India rose to US$ 17.4 billion compared to US$ 11.1 billion in the year 2001 showing an increase of US$ 6.3 billion. About 50-60 percent of total remittance received by India has come from Middle East countries. Nayyar D. (1994). *Migration, Remittances and Capital Flows: The Indian Experience.* New Delhi: Oxford University Press, p. 27.
4. Abbas Maleki, 'Iran', New Silk Road, 168-72 http://www.silkroadstudies.org/new/docs/publications/GCA/GCAPUB-06.pdf.
5. One indication of India's gradual acceptance of power centric world view is its diplomatic sensitivity about acquiring the permanent seat in the Security Council of revamp United Nations in future. India was offered permanent seat in the Security Council of the United Nations at the time of its formation. However India preferred to decline the same owing to its moralist conception of world politics and order. Today India is at the forefront of mobilizing international public opinion in favour of its claim to permanent seat in the Security Council of revamp United Nations as and when it gets materialized. Earlier the 1962 Chinese aggression against India and 1965 Indo-Pakistan war along with global responses to these events jolted the Gandhian-Nehruvian moralistic conception of world order and politics. This led India to first to participate in the liberation war of Bangladesh (1971), brought her in the sphere of Soviet

orbit through Peace and Friendship Treaty (1972) and conducted its first nuclear device in 1974. The 'realist' impulse continue to guide Indian political establishment that reflected in its assertion as pre-eminent power in South Asia, deployment of IPKF (Indian Peace Keeping Force) in Sri Lanka in mid 1980s, explosion of second nuclear device (1999) and its growing proximity with United States and Israel.

6. This observation is based on my interaction with academia and common people in Iran and in Turkey during the course of my several visits.
7. For Text of Tehran Declaration see, http://pib.nic.in/archive/pmvisit/pmvisit_iran/pm_iranre14.html.
8. For the text of the New Delhi Declaration see, http://meaindia.nic.in/event/ 2003/01/25events01.htm.
9. Since 2007 the Pakistan based Sunni Islamic Fundamentalist organization, Jundallah, has carried out a series of suicide attack in this border region of Iran. The most recent such attack took place on December 14, 2010 in which two suicide bombers targeted a group of Shiite worshippers at a mourning ceremony a day before Ashoura near a mosque killing at least 39 people.
10. Atul Aneja, "How West Asia Views Mumbai Attacks" (op-ed), *Hindu* (Chennai), December 17, 2008.
11. 'Arab and Muslim Reactions to Mumbai Attacks', available at http://news.zionism-israel.com/2008/12/arab-and-muslim-reactions-to-mumbai.html.
12. Iran says ready to broker India-Pakistan talks" Iranian news channel Press TV website on 31 December 2008 at BBC.
13. Ibid.
14. See Anwar Alam, 'External Policy Implications of Islamic Militancy in India' in Dr. Rajiv Kumar and Ambassador Santosh Kumar, *The National Interest Project: Papers on Security Issues, Companion Volume 1 to the Main NIP Report*, Submitted to Ministry of External Affairs, Government of India, May 2010. pp. 162-217.
15. The apprehension of Arab States, particularly Persian Gulf Arab countries, have been confirmed by Cable release of WIkileaks, see http://chhpak.com/wikileaks-documents-expose-arab-states-anxiety-over-iran-1610.html, retrieved on February 9, 2011.
16. http://www.indianexpress.com/news/to-engage-iran-india-looks-to-beat-us-un-sanctions-by-being-creative/655365/2 accessed on

August 17, 2010.

17. 'India 'concerned' over sanctions on Iran', http://www.presstv.ir/detail/133540.html, retrieved February 9, 2010.
18. 'Khamenei urges Muslims to 'help' Kashmir', http://timesofindia.indiatimes.com/world/middle-east/Khamenei-urges-Muslims-to-help-Kashmir/articleshow/6935375.cms accessed on 16th November 2010).

2

Indo-Iran Relations since New Delhi Declarations

Mohammad A. Mousavi

Historical Background

India has enjoyed close relations with Iran ever since Iran was Persia and India was ruled by the Mughal dynasty. This historical relation is rich in terms of cultural, economical and political relations. What is noticeable is the result of the over a millennium amicable relation which is the presence of Iranian culture in India today and manifest itself in architecture, art, colloquial and official language and culture.

In the post- World War II period, such relation entered a new phase. On March 15, 1950, New Delhi and Tehran signed a friendship treaty which called for 'perpetual peace and friendship' between the two, committing the two states to amicable relations. Through Iran's participation in the Baghdad Pact (CENTO) in 1960s and 1970s, the Shah had close ties to the United States and Pakistan. During the 1965 and 1971 wars between India and Pakistan, Iran provided military assistance to Pakistan, its 'strategic depth'. Such alliance was always rejected by Indian policy makers: "a wrong approach, a dangerous approach, and a harmful approach". [1] While India championed the Non-Aligned Movement and forged close ties with the former Soviet Union, US were the primary defence supplier of Iran and Soviet for India.

Victory of the Islamic Revolution in Iran led to the exit of Iran from the sphere of the Western capitalism and the centre-periphery circular. Iran closeness to Non-Aligned Movement (NAM) in which India was a leading power, led to closing of the two states. India largely welcomed Iran's 1979 Revolution and this was a notable period of positive engagement, which the two sides sustained economic ties, particularly on energy issues. Iran too was generally well disposed towards India. Iran was more critical of the Soviet invasion of Afghanistan than was India. [2] During the Iraqi imposed war (1981-88), India tried to simultaneously protect its oil interests in both states.

The end of the Cold War witnessed the significant improvements in bilateral relations. Although the late Indian Prime Minister Mr. Narshima Rao's state visit to Iran in 1993 was a 'turning point' in bilateral relations, the visit by then Iranian President Rafsanjani in 1995 led to solidify mutual economic interests. Following the Tehran Declaration signed in 2001 by the then India's Prime Minister Vajpayee in his visit to Tehran and laid the foundation of strategic relations between the two countries; The Delhi Declaration (2003) galvanized the military relations in the following areas:

- Sea-lane control and security.
- Indo-Iran joint naval exercises.
- Upgrading Iran's Russian made defence systems.
- Joint working team on counter-terrorism and counter-narcotics.

The timing of the Delhi Agreement was concurrent with the U.S. military build up in the Persian Gulf in order to invade Iraq as well as with extensive expansion in US-Indian military ties. Other than robust defence cooperation between the two, the key areas include concrete steps on oil and gas projects, the commitment to expand non-hydrocarbon trade and joint effort to further develop the Chahbahar port complex, the Chahbahar-Fahranj-Bam railway link and the Marine Oil Tanking Terminal. The document committed both sides to Indo-Iran Strategic Dialogue and institutional interaction on national security concerns.

Delhi Declaration announces "The Republic of India and the Islamic Republic of Iran are resolved to exploit the full potential of the bilateral relationship in the interest of the people of the two countries and of regional peace and stability...with a vision of a strategic partnership for a more stable, secure and prosperous region and for enhanced regional and global cooperation...explore opportunities for cooperation in defence in agreed areas, including training and exchange of visits" (New Delhi Declaration, January 25, 2003, Foreign Ministry of India). The declaration called upon the two states to broaden their strategic collaboration in third countries, which include Afghanistan.

Declaration and the Security Concern of Indian Ocean Basin

Some analyst emphasizes the Indian Ocean basin as the

extended strategic neighbourhood [3] for India. India likes to be recognized as the pre-eminent power and further to be-and to be seen as--a global power in due course [4] and "a truly multi-polar world, with India as one of the poles. [5]

A 'Look to East' policy of India has maintained a very sophisticated greater Middle East policy that includes Israel, Iran, and several Central Asian and Arab states. Of particular importance for this relationship is India's continuous effort to consolidate its strategic footing in Afghanistan and other parts of Central Asia, including two airbases in Tajikistan. Iran is critical to these efforts in many ways, because it provides India much-needed geographical access to these theatres.

India wants to be a supra-regional power, in Central Asia, which includes Afghanistan along with Iran. Only some of India's interests in Central Asia are Pakistan-focused. India's approach to this region is not only guided by a security measure but also to secure access a reliable source of energy, it also sees Central Asia and Iran as enormous potential consumer markets for Indian products and its manpower.

While India enjoys strong relations with Israel, military cooperation in particular, for Tehran such state is for the world's final apartheid benefiting from America's blind support. On Afghanistan both countries share similar concerns. The majority of Afghans share strong religious and cultural links with Iran and Iran has invested heavily in the relatively more stable north, particularly in infrastructure. Trade has risen sharply with Afghanistan and "moderate Sunni and Shiite who were supported by Iran when the United States effectively allowed the then-Saudi-and UAE-funded Taliban to overrun the country, look increasingly to Iran for support". [6] The recent leaked documents on Wikileaks shows that Saudi Arabia is still the largest financial supporter of the Taliban. This is true for almost all of the undemocratic Arab regimes in the Persian Gulf region who are still funding the Taliban and hardliner Salafi groups. "This has always been an open secret in this part of the world. Indeed, not only are these states funding the Taliban, they are effectively funding the Taliban ideology, which has strong similarities to that of Al-Qaeda, throughout the world. Closing eyes to Saudi support for worldwide, are making things more difficult for the region stability". [7]

Why Iran is Important for India: As understood from the

Delhi Declaration, energy and security are the two important reasons that propel India to have close relations with Iran. In recent years, India has been working to deepen its ties to Tehran for two reasons. First, India's economic boom—growth that it is counting on to lift hundreds of millions of its people out of poverty—requires energy. Indo-Iranian cooperation had "acquired a strategic dimension flourishing in the fields of energy, trade and commerce, information technology and transit". [8]

Both states seek to undermine uni-polarity, uncomfortable with the role that the United States have played and will likely continue to play in the Middle East. India needs Iran to achieve its varied objectives in Central Asia. Both states share concerns about the Sunni ultra-fundamentalist as a source of domestic security concern in the region. India further focuses on security threats that Pakistan poses to the region and beyond.

Close ties with Iran and other Muslim countries help to diminish some Muslims' fears at home and abroad that in India Islamophobia persist, particularly under the shadow of India's efforts to promote a tripartite relationship with the United States and Israel, the rise of Hindu nationalism, and the growing anti-Muslim violence. National Security Advisor to the Prime Minister Vajpayee and Israeli Deputy Prime Minister Lapid has called for explicit US-India-Israel axes to counter Islamist terrorism. [9] For India, such ties also help circumvent Pakistan's efforts in multilateral forum (such as the Organization of Islamic Countries) to raise the issue of Kashmir. India was always wary of Kashmiri self-determination. [10]

Why India matters for Iran: As in the Delhi Declaration which emphasize on the military/defence relations and promotes trade and economic cooperation, the two elements in which Iran is very much interested. Iran is looking for a market to export. A large but financially growing Indian market is an extremely good destination. For India, Iranian commodity market is a good and strong consumption market. Iranian tourists have become one of the top nationalities in number to arrive in India in 2010. This is growing trend which will have not only financial gain for India but also it will lead to a better understanding of one another culture, a human face to face contacts.

Closer ties between New Delhi and Tehran especially in the realm of defence cooperation shall be of critical significance to both nations even as it might impact upon the West Asian politico-strategic dynamic. Indian and Iranian defence cooperation could well prove to be an essential tool of foreign policy thereby strengthening mutual trust and enhancing security and stability in the region that may radically alter the geopolitics of the region.

Indian officials consistently explained their actions at the IAEA to domestic and Iranian audiences alike that India went to great lengths to *help* Iran during the various IAEA standoffs. Indian officials dilated upon the fact that India worked assiduously to ensure that the United States, France, Germany, and Britain did not "ride roughshod over Iranian interests" and lobbied the Europeans to amend their 2005 resolution, which called for an immediate referral to the UN Security Council. Following the February 2006 vote to refer Iran to the UNSC, Indian Prime Minister Manmohan Singh explained this decision in terms of helping to provide diplomatic solutions to the impasse and encouraging all parties to eschew confrontation and inflexibility. Such kind of explanation was not acceptable for Iranians. Nonetheless, they would clearly know that the Indian government is under tremendous pressure from the United State and this was to some extent understandable for them.

Bilateral Energy Interests

India's energy, economic, and other strategic interests have important overlaps with those of Iran. Among these issues for India, energy is the primary one. As reflected in the 2001 Tehran Declaration and the 2003 New Delhi Declaration, India and Iran want to move ahead on commercial and energy issues. Iran after Saudi Arabia has been the second producer of India's energy need.

India's Energy Need: With plenty of domestic coal reserves but modest oil and gas reserves, India's policymakers are systematically looking for the widest possible set of alternatives to meet their growing energy needs. India is currently the world's sixth largest energy consumer, with more than half of its electricity production based upon coal. [11] In India, coal accounts for 55 percent of current power generation. In total, thermal sources (coal, gas, diesel) accounts for 66 percent of India's production. In 2003, India produced 33 million tons of crude oil and imported 90 million tons or 73 percent of its total requirement of 123 million tons. [12]

Some analysts believe that by 2020, India may become the fourth largest consumer, following only the United States, China, and Japan. [13] Its energy consumption will rise to 27.1 quadrillion

BTUs by 2025, up from 12.7 in 2000—the largest expected increase in energy use after China. Nuclear power at this point accounts for some 2.6 percent of India's electricity; the most ambitious plans now under discussion would increase this share to some 12 percent by 2020. Much of the estimated 8 percent annual increase in demand will therefore have to come from oil and gas, with gas demand growing more rapidly than any other part of India's energy market. This growing appetite for new energy sources and reliance on foreign sources to fulfil that demand make Iran an attractive partner. This is where Iran (by having the third largest reserve of oil, with proven reserves of over 132 billion barrels and the second largest proven reserve of gas with 1000 trillion cubic feet) fits in as the OPEC's second-largest oil producer and sits on 10 percent of the world's proven oil reserves and the world's second-largest natural gas reserves. [14] Such energy needs seems to be a source of competition between the two Asian giants, China and India.

Indian crude oil imports from Iran range about 14 percent of India's total crude oil imports, a figure set to grow markedly in the next ten to fifteen years as India pushes ahead for a steady and fast economic growth, and with plans to substantially boost its refinery capacity for Middle East crude. [15] India also wants to purchase Iranian natural gas and has invested heavily to help Iran develop its gas fields. Based on a US$ 22 billion deal between India's GAIL and Iran's NIGEC, a subsidiary of the National Iranian Oil Company, LNG will be supplied over a 25-year period, commencing from 2009. To this end GAIL has committed to help construct an LNG plant in Iran. As American components are generally necessary for such plants, it will be a difficult task to succeed. India intends to invest heavily in Iranian **Farzad and South Pars gas** fields as it strategically pursues controlling the global oil and gas resources. To this end, Indian companies expanded the investment in Iran's oil and gas sector. In 2009, Indian oil companies committed to invest around 6.5 billion US dollar in Iran's gas sector. Furthermore, ONGC was after a share of 20 percent in one of the phases of the South Pars project.

One of the symbols of strengthening energy cooperation between the two countries has been the 'Peace Pipeline'. A pipeline, while resolving the energy needs of India and Pakistan, provides prosperity and development and ultimately leads to peace between India and Pakistan.

The Peace Pipeline is turning out more as a dream for the time being. In the post-Mumbai terrorist attack, India has had the fear from Pakistan's hostage policy on the safe passage of gas from Iran to India. Hence, it has dragged the negotiation to a stall point. Although in 2007-08, with Pakistan supporting the possible extension of IPI to China, India backed Gazprom to finance the pipe line to enlarge the stake holders for what it considers an unhindered supply line into India. Not having India a partner, and not attracting needed 'techno-investment', hence, there is no clear future for the pipeline, although Iran and Pakistan decided to go forward on the Iran-Pakistan part of the Pipeline.

Bilateral Trade: Overall, the bilateral trade picture appears to be promising. The total value of trade for the fiscal year ending March 2010, exceeded 14 billion US dollar, from 13 billion in 2007. Statistics provided by the clearing Union's Website shows that Iran's trade through the clearinghouse rose to US$ 12.2 billion in the first 11 months of 2010, from 7.8 billion in the same period in 2009 (wall Street 2010). This was mainly the advice of Iran's government to the local and Indian companies to use Asian Clearing Union (ACU) as a way of avoiding international sanctions.

Nonetheless, the US put pressure on Indian government to close this already established method by the United Nations in 1974 (to help facilitate trade in South Asia and headquartered in Tehran), which had been a way of trade between 9 countries of the region. This is while if one adds the indirect trade (re-export from other countries) between the two countries, the bilateral trade reaches over 30 billion US dollar.

However, the unilateral sanctions by the United States and her continuous pressure on other states to abide with, led to a financial decision by India's Central Bank. On December 27, 2010, the Reserve Bank of India (RBI) announced that: "In view of the difficulties being experienced by importers and exporters in payments to and receipts from Iran, the extant provisions have been reviewed and it has been decided that all eligible current account transactions including trade transactions with Iran should be settled in any permitted currency outside the ACU mechanism until further notice". [16] On January 7, 2011, the State Bank of India (SBI) refused to issue fresh Letters of Credit (LCs) to public and private sector refineries. This move had the potential to 'halt' oil import from Iran altogether. This stance by the RBI has led Reliance

Industries to abandon its plans to invest in an oil refinery in Iran.

One of the means that boost the trade between the two is the **North-South Corridor**. India and Iran continue to make progress on their commitment to build such corridor with Russia. Iran, India and Russia signed the inter-governmental agreement on International North-South Transport Corridor in September 2000 in St. Petersburg. Since this corridor is a part of an Indo-Iranian initiative to facilitate the movement of goods across Central Asia as well as Russia, both India and Iran entered into an earlier trilateral agreement with Turkmenistan in 1997. According to early reports in 2002, officials expected the corridor to handle 15 to 20 million tons of freight at US$ 10 billion per year. However, due to both political cloud and economic downturn the project is far from its objectives.

Defence and Military Ties

One of the chief issues of Delhi Declaration was the establishment of Strategic defence partnership. In 2001, Indian Defence Secretary Narain met with his Iranian counterpart Shamkhani to explore arm sales to Iran. According to the Indian press, India has trained Iranian naval engineers in Mumbai and at Visakhapatnam. Reportedly, Iran was also seeking combat training for missile boat crews. Iran also anticipated that India can provide midlife service and upgrades for its MiG-29 fighters and retrofit its warships and submarines in Indian dockyards. India helped Iran develop batteries for its submarines, refit and maintain Iran's T-27 tanks and selling Iran the Konkurs anti-tank missile. [17] India and Iran conducted their second naval exercise on March 3-8, 2006, overlapping with President Bush's trip to Afghanistan, India, and Pakistan. A spokesman for the Indian Navy's Southern Command reportedly explained that Indian naval instructors briefed nearly 220 sailors. "India and Iran have enjoyed good maritime relations that include high-level political and military visits, joint-naval exercises, naval technology cooperation, and maritime infrastructure developments symbolized by port development in Chahbahar. Naval cooperation between the two sides dates back to the mid-1990s when the Indian Navy helped the Iranian Navy to adapt four Russian-built Kilo-class submarines for warm water conditions in the Persian Gulf".

In November 2009, India started Iranian military training program, provided satellite services, and joint naval manoeuvre in

Persian Gulf, first of such manoeuvre done in March 2003. [18] "The complexities of Indo-Iranian ties could be attributed to the 'American angle' that looms large over this equation as New Delhi walks a tightrope whilst its ties with the United States (US) burgeon" (ibid). Hence, while these two states have been talking about "strategic relations" for some time with few concrete results, they have instituted a strategic dialogue that has met four times between October 2001 and early 2007. This dialogue is the forum designed to explore opportunities for cooperation in defence in agreed areas, including training and exchange visits based on the 2003 New Delhi Declaration. [19] Some analyst used the timing and symbolic importance of such an exercise, to argue that India's foreign policies would not be dictated by Washington. [20]

The other example of such autonomous symbolism in India's foreign policy came in March 2007 when Washington conducted its war games in the Persian Gulf-its largest show of force in the region since the 2003 invasion of Iraq involving USS Eisenhower and USS Stennis. This coincided with the visit of the Iranian Naval Chief to India-a reflection of the importance that Iran attached to its growing defence ties with India. Additionally, a naval cadet training ship visited India, and in 2007, the Indian government allowed a limited number of Iranian officers to participate in joint training courses with officers from several other countries.

On the other hand, some Indian strategic analyst argue that the presence of Indian engineers at Chahbahar and of Indian military advisors and intelligence officials in Iran confers to India a significant access to Iran. This access has tremendous import for India's ability to project power vis-à-vis Pakistan and Central Asia. It clearly provides India an enhanced ability to monitor Pakistan and even launch sub-conventional operations against Pakistan from Iran. As Chansoria [21] argues, commencing a defence dialogue could be envisaged, which could be progressed based on international and regional developments, providing opportunities for greater cooperation with Iran.

Military Cooperation: The band of opportunities is not necessarily sequential or time constrained and could be envisaged in the following fields:

- Assistance in modernisation of defence forces.
- R&D assistance in defence research.
- Strategic defence dialogue.

- Defence infrastructure development.
- Training and exercises.
- Maintenance assistance, supply of spares and ancillaries.
- IT application at the armed forces.

As far as Army-to-Army cooperation is concerned, it could entail the following:

- Course at the National Defence College (NDC) and Defence Services Staff College (DSSC).
- Training of UN peacekeeping operations.
- Joint anti-terrorist exercises.
- Offer assistance in training as well as maintenance and repair of key Russian equipment like Kilo submarines and MIG-29 fighters.
- Maintenance and training support for Iranian T-72 Tanks, BMPI and II infantry carrier vehicles.
- Selling Advanced Light Helicopters (ALH) and jet trainer aircraft.

According to reports appearing in September 2007, [22] Iran has been negotiating with India to purchase advanced radar systems designed for fire control and surveillance of anti-aircraft batteries. Iran is seeking an unspecified number of Indian radar systems called Upgraded Support Fledermaus from the Indian state-owned Bharat Electronics Ltd (BHEL). However, New Delhi faces intense pressure from Washington to not to sell the radars to Iran, as it is convinced that the request is part of Iran's military effort to protect its nuclear weapons facilities in question. The upgraded Super Fledermaus is mono-pulse radar used in 35-mm air defence batteries and designed to detect low-flying objects, such as unmanned air vehicles (UAVs). The digital system contains a built-in simulator as well as a signal jammer. Crucially, BHEL has gone on record and confirmed Iran's request for these upgraded radars. Executives at the plant stated that Iran sought the same fire control and surveillance radar that the company upgraded for the Indian Army way back in 2001.

Political Significances and Constraints in Bilateral Relations

The end of the Cold War and the weakened independent blocks in the international arena, led to the world leaning more toward the United States of America. Influential and independent countries tried to take positions in world politics (even toward Western capitalism) based on their national interest.

Part of India's direction toward US is due to its security concerns. This includes:

- Kashmir.
- Afghanistan.
- Pakistan.
- Al Qaeda and fundamentalist ideology in India's surrounding.
- Central Asia as a source of stability and security.
- Security of Indian Ocean as the see trade and security of energy.

No doubt, the border and internal security is the prime objective of India's foreign policy. Stable and moderate government of Karzai in Afghanistan on the one hand and having stability in Central Asia on the other is a source of security in India. The following discusses some of these significances and constraints in Indo-Iran bilateral relations.

US Constraint: While Iran is important to India, there are constraints that restrict India's reach into Iran. The United States and Israel consulted and pressed India to minimize defence, energy, and strategic relations with Iran. Despite the Bush Administration's explicit forbearance on the Iran factor, Indian strategists and policymakers ultimately understand that US patronage is likely necessary for it to achieve all that it aspires. In the past, India reasonably had few hopes to believe that the United States could or would support India's bid for great power aspirations and to assume its rightful global role.

Some Congresspersons were disconcerted by the second Indian-Iranian naval exercise that took place in March 2006. This was coincident with President Bush's visit to South Asia. On December 18, 2006, President Bush signed the US-Indian civilian nuclear deal into law. At the time US Senate and the House tried, but failed, to forge a precondition for nuclear cooperation with India which was to end its military engagement with Iran. [23] US officials' argument was that the civilian nuclear engagement would diminish India's reliance upon Iran, or at least provide the opportunity for the United States to shape India's relationship with Iran. One of the reasons put forward by Condoleezza Rice, the then Secretary of State, was that the deal will help India "meet its rising energy needs without increasing its reliance on unstable foreign sources of oil and gas, such as nearby Iran" (Rice, 2006). Furthermore, Congressional Research Service in its report examining the extent of the relationship, acknowledged some differences in preferred policy towards Iran between the two countries, but concluded that "India's motivations to pursue relations with Iran were primarily rooted in India's growing energy needs and therefore are relatively benign to U.S. interests". [24]

Following Mukherjee's, the then Indian Foreign Minister, February 2007 visit to Tehran, the new chairman of the House Foreign Affairs Committee, Tom Lantos, publicly opined that India was not keeping its commitments regarding the nuclear deal. He said "...in order to become a strategic ally of the United States... India must recognise some basic facts, specifically some facts with respect to Iran: It is a terrorist state whose current regime strives to develop nuclear weapons. At this committee's first hearing on the proposed nuclear deal, I and others on this committee made it clear that a 'business as usual' relationship with the current terrorist regime in Tehran is unacceptable behaviour by any country seeking to be our strategic partner". [25] In 2005, officials from the Bush Administration expressed confidence that the relationship does not adversely affect major U.S. interests. [26]

Hence, one may argue that part of the justifications for India's votes and recent distance from Iran may be analyzed under the pretext of Washington's consternation. Three years ago, senior members of the U.S. Congress sent a toughly-worded letter to Prime Minister Singh, linking final approval of the nuclear cooperation agreement to New Delhi's stance on Iran's nuclear program. One should bear in mind that, nevertheless, India has seemed critical of US further deep penalization of Iran. Following Obama's tough new unilateral sanctions law against Iran later quarter of 2010, India became critical of this policy: this is "a direct and adverse impact on Indian companies and, more importantly, on our energy security and our attempts to meet the development needs of our people". [27]

From Iran's stance, the votes against Iran in the International Atomic Energy Agency, created furies among Iranians. From 2003, India has twice voted against Iran in IAEA, the latter of which recommended referring Iran to UN Security Council for violating international obligations. Due to India's complex interests in Iran, its shift in policy toward Iran created a furore in the Communist Party and other leftist parties on whose votes Prime Minister Singh's Congress Party–led coalition relies for a parliamentary majority. They argued that the government was abandoning its foreign policy autonomy and becoming subservient to Washington. Upon such pressures, Prime Minister Manmohan Singh took the unusual step of explaining India's vote in a formal statement to parliament. [28] In January 2006 when US Ambassador to India, publicly connected India's vote against Iran to the US nuclear deal with India, the furies of opposition parties in Delhi augmented.

In 2010, President Obama signed into law a set of tough new unilateral penalties against companies helping the Iranian petroleum sector, a move that affects a number of Indian enterprises that want to develop oil and natural gas fields there. Such pressure is not only on the Indian government, but also on the Indian companies which face the UN Security Council and US unilateral Sanctions' consequences as well. Though there is no direct evidence that American pressure is operating on Indian companies, however, there are indications that it is quite likely that firms like Reliance were coerced to withdraw from Iran if they wanted to keep their prospects alive in the Shale Gas sector in USA. To partially corroborate this hypothesis, according to WikiLeaks, the officials of the US government had warned executives of France's Total and Italy's Eni SPA that investments in Iran "could possibly impact their Shale gas investments in the US." Moreover, the Wall Street Journal recently reported that US officials had issued a similar warning to the Indian companies.

Hence, what is currently noticeable is that India has started a more diplomatic position toward Iran, consistently urging the international community to handle their nuclear concerns about Iran through diplomacy rather than confrontation. India tried to use the trip of President Ahmadinejad to Delhi as a means of convincing him that India's position was not an anti-Iran move. "Ahamdinjead's visit is an opportunity for India at course correction and put its relations with Iran back on solid footing after vote against Iran at the IAEA". [29] India tried to walk a fine line when making decisions regarding Iran, to use diplomatic skills to reconcile strategic considerations with domestic political compulsions. Though, such moves are slow and limited. Even in the Brazil-Turkey proposal of resolving the standstill swap of enrich Uranium which led to 2010 Tehran declaration, India was totally absent.

Israeli Element: On the hand, Israel serves as an important impediment to India's efforts to engage Iran. As India's largest arms supplier, Sharon (the then-Prime Minister) expressed apprehension about India's ties with Iran during his 2003 visit to India, and again during the Indo-Israeli Joint Working Group on Counterterrorism in November 2004. Israel has helped India with avionics upgrades with its MiG jetfighters, and in turn, India hopes to provide similar services to countries throughout the region (as both India and Israel enjoy having expertise in providing maintenance and upgrades for Russian weapons platforms) (Pant 2004). As India is not insensitive to Israelis discomfiture, Israel "remain a part of New Delhi's decision calculus *vis-à-vis* Iran for the policy-relevant future" (Fair 2007). Israel has always raised concerns vis-à-vis New Delhi's ties with Iran resting upon apprehension that India could divert Israeli military technology to Iran. However, Israel, for Iran, is a state sponsoring terrorism, the country which has denied forcefully and illegally the right to livelihood of Palestinians and continues to do so by depriving them from their natural right of choice and live. Hence, being the last apartheid state on the earth, a warm Indo-Israel relations has been a source of discomfort for Iran as well.

Afghanistan: India and Iran relationship harps on shared geopolitical interests and the security issues that are cantered on the conflict in Afghanistan. Iran has been a great supporter of Northern Alliance alongside with India in Afghanistan. It seems that Iranians have started looking ahead beyond the post US- exit scenario (2014) and hence alliance with regional countries to smoothen out its influence in Afghanistan. India also perceives that post US withdrawal from Afghanistan (2014) remain secured for India with the crucial help of Iran. New Delhi wants to prevent Afghanistan from becoming a Pakistani proxy state (Kahn 2010). During Afghanistan's civil war, Tehran supported the ethnic Hazaras—who are Shiite Muslims—against the Pashtun Taliban, Sunnis backed by Pakistan. India, meanwhile, funded ethnic Uzbek and Tajik warlords. New Delhi may seek to create an alliance of these non-Pashtun groups in Afghanistan to thwart Islamabad's designs on Kabul. What's more, India needs to maintain good relations with Tehran so that it can continue to send equipment and supplies for its aid mission in Afghanistan through Iran, since Pakistan will not permit Indian aid to pass through the country. [30]

Central Asia: Central Asia has been of great importance for Iran as it holds the national security of Iran. For India, influence over Central Asia is part of its extended security appraisal. It will control Pakistan security backyard and further provides stability and moderation in Afghanistan. Indo-Iran cooperation in construction of railway linking network to that of Central Asia (considerably reduces Pakistan's strategic leverage over these landlocked states thus providing them alternative corridors to the sea) and development of the Iranian port of Chahbahar (for India this is development of 'alternative access routes'-bypassing Pakistan- for reconstruction of Afghanistan). [31] Moreover, India's construction of 218 kilometres long Zaranj-Delaram highway links Afghanistan to the Iranian port of Chahbahar as part of the Afghan circular road that connects Herat and Kabul via Mazar-e-Sharif in the north and Kandahar in the south- thereby providing easier access to Afghanistan and possibly even further, to Central Asia via Iran. This may presumably facilitate trade and is part of a larger Indian Ocean to North Sea initiative involving Russia and others, and mainly cantered on the Iranian port of Bandar Abbas.

Pakistan & Kashmir Issue: No doubt, Iran is bound with its neighbour Pakistan. The Eastern border of Iran has always endangered by the terrorist and narcotic activities rooted in Pakistan and Afghanistan. Hence for Iran, control of such security concerns through partial political relations with the neighbouring countries has been a priority. For Iran having good relation with Pakistan as its neighbour with major security concern of Al-Qaida-Taliban infiltration, has led to security cooperation between the two countries wherein the institutional linkages between the two intelligence and security institutions are sequentially developing. The dramatic arrest of Abdolmalek Rigi, head of Jundallah group may be a result of such cooperation. Rigi, a fundamentalist terrorist Sunni, who was responsible for multiple terrorist attacks in South-eastern province of Sistan and Baluchistan of Iran against innocent people and some military personnel, was linked to US and to the network of Islamist extremist organisations based in neighbouring countries, particularly in Pakistan.

In the current ambiguous and normal-problematic relations between India and Iran, Pakistan is trying to use of this situation to increase the existing bond between herself and Iran.

Iran in its bid for re-alignment of the forces in the post US withdrawal and the growing ideological approach of the government of President Ahmadinejad has shown some renewed interest in expanding its ties with Pakistan; regular meetings between the high ups of both governments are examples. The regular interaction has gone to increase the mutual understanding of each other's strategic interests and developed more space to accommodate each other. The generous help provided by the Iranian government and its people to Pakistan's flood affected people is a way of reflection of existing bonds between the two countries. Critical and cautious of US-Pakistan rapprochement, India refutes to view international relations as a zero-sum game: "The United States has its relationship with Pakistan, which is separate from our own relationship with them... Our relationship with Iran is peaceful and largely economic. We do not expect it to affect our continuing good relations with the United States". [32] Dr Pasha, an Indian scholar, argues: "Friendly ties with Iran are important for India. Given incestuous alliances between militants the world over, any instability in the region can spill over into Indian territories like Kashmir,". [33]

Furthermore, the Kashmiri issue is an open wound in the Muslim world. The Kashmir issue has upgraded from an Indian national to a regional (Muslim World) level, hence a regional security concern for the Indian government. The statement of Iranian spiritual leader Ayatollah Khamenei supporting to listen to the people of Indian held Kashmir who are struggling for their rights was misread in India. Actually, India, while trying to keep the status quo over Kashmir, cannot tolerate any statement on Kashmir. One can argue that one of the objectives of the Indian government's request from the United States for a permanent membership seat in UN Security Council is to resolve the Kashmir issue which is still pending on the 1948 Resolution of the Security Council.

Conclusion

No doubt that Iran holds particular importance for India as it provides unique access to Afghanistan and Central Asia, two theatres in which India seeks to project greater influence. As New Delhi promulgates a 'look to the east policy' to develop and sustain a multifaceted presence in the greater Middle East, Iran unquestionably is an instrumental player in this set up. [34] Furthermore, Iran lies at the core of the world's energy heartland formed by the Middle East and Central Asia. As such, enlightened self-interest demands that India should engage Iran in a constructive manner to safeguard its significant geopolitical and energy security stakes. Because of Iran's strategic importance and its own goal of ensuring a stable energy, it is difficult for New Delhi to abandon its relationship with Tehran. Iran takes the direction of its foreign policy from the West to East, as

India is giving more importance to 'look the East' policy as well. Furthermore, Iran gives a great deal of importance to regional integration. For both India and Iran, the Persian Gulf has an important position in the country's foreign policy.

However, United State of America has become the central point in India's new direction in foreign Policy. India has few objectives from this new relation with US:

- Seeking its place in world polity as a major player.
- Reconstructing its military/naval forces.
- Wishing to secure a permanent seat in United Nations Security Council.
- Resolving the Kashmir issue.
- Acquiring US nuclear technology to secure the supply of over 12 percent of its needed energy from nuclear one.
- Controlling its security concerns through information sharing and institutional intelligence collaboration with US.

Hence, India follows the US sensitivity on Iran's Nuclear Program. In Indo-Iran bilateral relations, it has distinguished between Iran's nuclear position and other areas of cooperation. While India continues its selective cooperation with Iran in pursuit of its own national interests, New Delhi has supported US anti-Iran efforts over its nuclear program. Given that Indian government is unlikely to totally sacrifice its energy and strategic interests with Tehran for its relationship with Washington, the United States has increased its pressure on India over its defence relations with Iran on the one hand, and demands categorical Indian support of US efforts on Iran's Nuclear Profile on the other. India's votes at the International Atomic Energy Agency (IAEA) 'against Iran' in September 2005 and February 2006 were important tests for Washington policymakers who were uncertain about India's intentions.

India's leaders are likely to continue opposing an Iranian nuclear weapons program to appease USA, though this will be uncomfortable for them and will generate political heat. They are also likely to continue pursuing a vigorous energy relationship as well as enough of a security connection to give them access to Pakistan's Central Asia backyard. Their hope is that their emerging partnership with Washington will be strong and sophisticated enough to go along with this two-pronged approach to Iran. From Washington's point of view, the most important question is how vigorously India is willing to join in international efforts to prevent

Iran's emergence as a nuclear power, though Iran continuously have announced its peaceful intention for nuclear activities and showed readiness for whatever inspection within the framework of NPT.

Earlier in 2010, Brazil and Turkey infuriated the Obama administration when they announced just ahead of a critical United Nations vote on sanctions against Iran that they had brokered a deal to reprocess Iran's low-enriched uranium. To Washington, it looked like a throwback to the bad old days of the non-aligned movement: two big developing nations trying to resolve an international issue without the big powers involved. One would wonder if India, one of the old leaders of NAM will be the next to break ranks on Iran. Though, India could mount legal challenges to the West's new unilateral sanctions, however if pressed by the United States and Europe, New Delhi will likely acquiesce. It is unlikely that India will follow the lead of Brazil and Turkey and cast a "no" against Western anti-Iran policy. Why? If India undermines U.S and EU policy on Iran, not only the current development process of India will perish but the dream of a permanent seat on the U.N. Security Council may go array.

End Notes

1. Naaz, Farah, 'Indo-Iranian Relations 1947-2000', *Strategic Analysis*, Vol. 25, No. 10 (May 2001).
2. India, under Prime Minister Indira Gandhi, avoided public condemnation even though privately she was deeply vexed that Moscow brought superpower confrontation into India's extended strategic environment.
3. It includes Strait of Hormuz and the Persian Gulf as westernmost frontier of this strategic area stretches; the Strait of Malacca as the eastern point; and Central Asia to the north; and extends to Antarctica to the south (Fair 2007).
4. Perkovich, George "Is India a Major Power," The Washington Quarterly, Vol. 27, No. 1, winter 2003-04, pp. 129-44, also, Fair, Christine, 'India and Iran: New Delhi's Balancing Act', *The Washington Quarterly*, vol. 30, no. 3, Summer 2007b, at http://muse.jhu.edu/login?uri=/journals/washington_quarterly/v030/30.3fair.pdf.
5. Government of India, *Ministry of Defence Annual Report 2005-2006,* p. 78.
6. Marandi, Seyed Mohammad, 'Iran, US and the balance of power

in Middle East', *Conflict Forum*, January 14, 2011.
7. Ibid.
8. Government of India, *Ministry of Defence Annual Report 2005-2006,* p. 76.
9. Fair, Christine, 'Indo-Iranian Ties: Thicker than Oil', *The Middle East Review of International Affairs*, Vol. 11 No. 1, March 2007, pp. 41-58.
10. Fair, Christine, 'Indo-Iranian Relations: Prospects for Bilateral Cooperation in post-9-11', in Robert Hathaway (ed.), *The Strategic Partnership Between India and Iran,* Asia Program Special Report, No. 120, April 2004, p. 120.
11. Government of India, Ministry of Power website, http://powermin.nic.in/.
12. IEA Energy Statistics, *Oil in India*, IEA: Washington, 2003, at http://www.iea.org/textbase/nppdf/free/2003/key2003.pdf.
13. Neogi, Saikat "Oil Diplomacy Beyond Tehran," *The Hindustan Times*, February 5, 2006.
14. Mousavi, Mohammad A., 'Some Notes on the Caspian Energy and Ethnic Conflicts in the Caucasus', *Iran and the Caucasus*, Vol. 14, No. 1, 2010, pp. 159-168.
15. Kahn, Jeremy, 'India's Nuclear Diplomacy: Why New Delhi Is Courting Tehran', July 22, 2010.
16. Quoted in Mukherjee, Uddipan, 'The Oil Payments: New Twist in India-Iran Relations', at http://www.eurasiareview.com/analysis/the-oil-payments-new-twist-in-india-iran-relations-13012011/, January 13, 2011 retrieved 14/1/ 2011.
17. Chansoria, Monika, 'India-Iran Defence Cooperation', *Indian Defence Review*; Vol. 25:1, 2010.
18. Ibid.
19. Maitra, Ramtanu, 'Why courting Russia and Iran makes sense', *Asia Times Online*, October 2, 2003.
20. Fair, Christine, 'India and Iran: New Delhi's Balancing Act', *The Washington Quarterly*, vol.30, no. 3, Summer 2007, at http://muse.jhu.edu/login?uri=/journals/washington_quarterly/v030/30.3fair.pdf.
21. Chansoria, Monika, 'India-Iran Defence Cooperation'.
22. Ibid.
23. Fair, Christine, 'Indo-Iranian Ties: Thicker than Oil'.
24. Kronstadt, Alan, Katzman, Kenneth, 'India-Iran Relations and

U.S. Interests', *CRS Report For Congress*, Washington: Thomson Gale, 2006.

25. http://in.rediff.com/news/2006/apr/06ndeal1.htm retrieved.
26. See Nicholas Burns, Under Secretary of State for Political Affairs, US on 'The U.S. India Civilian Nuclear Deal' May 16, 2006, http://www.google.com/#sclient=psy&hl=en&q.
27. Quoting Indian Foreign Secretary, Nirupama Rao, Kahn, Jeremy, 'India's Nuclear Diplomacy: Why New Delhi Is Courting Tehran p.122.
28. Other than US pressure, he also noted concerns about a thinly veiled reference to Pakistan, in India-Iran Relations: Changing the Tone? CSIS, March 8, 2006, at http://csis.org/files/media/csis/pubs/sam92.pdf.
29. Qamar Agha, in INAS 2008, at http://www.thaindian.com/newsportal/uncategorized/ahmadinejads-visit-to-halt-drift-in-india-iran-ties_10042594.html.
30. Bassam, Javed, 'Indo-Iran Relation; Who's Hostage?' January 10, 2011, at http://www.thenews.com.pk/TodaysPrintDetail.aspx?ID=24905&Cat=2&dt=1/9/2011 retrieved on Jan 11, 2011.
31. Indian Ministry of External Affairs, Annual Report 2004-2005, New Delhi, at http://meaindia.nic.in/meaxpsite/annualreport/30ar01.pdf.
32. India's Ministry of External Affairs stated in January 2005, in Chansoria 2010.
33. IANS 2008, at http://www.thaindian.com/newsportal/uncategorized/ahmadinejads-visit-to-halt-drift-in-india-iran-ties_10042594.html.
34. Kahn, Jeremy, 'India's Nuclear Diplomacy: Why New Delhi Is Courting Tehran'.

3

India and Iran: In Search of a New Rhythm

Ashok K. Behuria

Background

India and Iran share deep historical, cultural and civilizational linkages. The contacts between the people and civilizations of these two regions 'go back to the dawn of history'. [1] Streams of culture have flown in either direction since remote past and ensured a natural bonding which has weathered phases of relative lassitude in relationship at the official level. The first prime minister of India, Jawaharlal Nehru, during his trip to Iran in September 1959, referred even to 'common stock from which the two peoples and languages of Iran and India arose' and emphasised the point that there were no two countries 'in the world which had such close and long historical contact as Iran and India'. [2] During the medieval and colonial period Iran was an important neighbour with which India shared a border till 1947.

During the post-colonial period, after independence, India established diplomatic links with Iran on March 15, 1950. India-Iran bilateral relations continued on an even keel boosted by high level visits till the Islamic revolution in 1979. The Shah of Iran visited India in February/March 1956 and Nehru paid a return visit in September 1959. Indira Gandhi visited Iran in April 1974 and Morarji Desai visited in June 1977. The Shah, in turn, visited India in February 1978. It is true that the Shah's close relationship with the US was viewed with suspicion in India, a close friend of the former USSR, during the cold war years. The US supported the earlier Shah regime and opposed the Islamist government of Ayatollah Khomeini, whereas India maintained a cautious and friendly relationship with Iran.

Post Revolution Iran

The Islamic Revolution of 1979 which led to a change of regime was followed by a short period of lull in the bilateral relationship. The new regime was busy consolidating its position in Iran. It revised Iran's foreign policy vis-à-vis the US, because the US had supported the earlier Shah regime and opposed the Islamist movement of Ayatollah Khomeini. Despite the Islamic government's sympathy for jihad in Afghanistan, Iran kept a studied distance from it because it was sponsored by the US. The Cold War was at its peak by mid 1980s and eventual withdrawal of Soviet forces in 1989 brought about a change in the regional strategic environment. It must be noted here that in 1983, the two countries established the India-Iran joint Commission which sought to strengthen defence and security ties between them. With the rise of Taliban, an intensely sectarian group, wedded to the idea of turning Afghanistan into a Sunni Islamic state, there was some convergence of interest between India and Iran in Afghanistan in the early 1990s. Moreover, the economic liberalisation in the 1990s which led to unprecedented growth in Indian economy, made it necessary on the part of India to look for energy resources around the world. It was natural that Iran with its vast hydrocarbon resources would attract India's attention. The bilateral relationship began to prosper since the 1990s.

New Phase in Relations (1993-2005): Too Short-lived?

A new phase of engagement began with exchange of high level visits of Indian Prime Minister Narasimha Rao in September 1993, Iranian President Akbar Hashemi Rafsanjani in April 1995 and Indian Vice President K.R. Narayanan in October 1996. In 1993, Iran requested for Indian help to develop three Kilo class submarines Iran had acquired from Russia. Iran held that the Indian experience of operating in warm water would be of great help for its navy. India, as a major recipient of Soviet weapons for almost two decades by then, was also approached to provide spare-parts as well to upgrade Russian defence hardware which ranged from tanks, warships and submarines to MIG-29 fighters.

This trend was consolidated and enhanced at the turn of the millennium by the initiatives of the National Democratic Alliance (NDA) government which was in power during this phase when India embarked upon an ambitious multilateral foreign policy of establishing ties with countries as far apart as Iran and the US. Interestingly, the NDA government led by right-of-the centre Bharatiya Janata Party (BJP) also made efforts to mend India's relationship with Pakistan at the same time. Moreover, President Khatami of Iran, who was known for his liberal views, also evinced lot of interest in his country's relationship with India. Against this backdrop, Indian Prime Minister Atal Behari Vajpayee made a visit to Iran in 2001. The 'Teheran declaration' was signed on April 10, 2001 and it was followed by six MOUs.

On the eve of President Mohammad Khatami's visit to India in January 2003, when he was also the Chief Guest at the Republic Day function, the two countries signed a defence cooperation agreement in Teheran (on January 19, 2010) which was hailed by the Iranian defence attaché in India as 'a milestone' agreement. This agreement envisaged Indian help in the construction of warship repair facilities at the Iranian port of Chabahar, stationing of Indian aeronautical engineers at Iranian military bases to maintain and provide mid-life upgrades for Iran's MIG-29 fighters, and sending Indian engineers to Iran to refit and maintain T-72 tanks.

During Khatami's visit the leaders of the two countries signed the "New Delhi Declaration" on January 25, 2003, and pledged to start a "strategic partnership". India and Iran also signed seven substantive agreements. Indian oil companies had started investing in prospecting of oil and gas in Iran since 2001, however, following 2003 agreement, there was even more interest in this field. According to the landmark declaration, the two countries resolved "to exploit the full potential of bilateral relationship" in the interest of the people of both the countries outlined among other things greater Iranian access to Indian military technology and "explore opportunities for cooperation in defence in agreed areas, including training and exchange of visits".

In the post-Taliban Afghan scenario, the two countries also agreed to give a further push to "the trilateral agreement between the Governments of India, Iran and Afghanistan to develop the Chahbahar route through Melak, Zaranj and Delaram", which, they held, "would facilitate regional trade and transit, including to Afghanistan and Central Asia, contributing thus to enhanced regional economic prosperity". India and Iran held joint naval exercises in March 2003. The emerging India-Iran relationship was seen with concern both in US and Pakistan. Some Pakistani analysts held that New Delhi had "finally found a viable defence partner in the Middle East for which it [had] been searching for quite some time" and argued that "any Indian presence on Iranian military bases...even if it is solely for the purpose of training the Iranians, would allow India a more subtle operational use of early warning, intelligence gathering, and other facilities against Pakistan". [3] Others hoped that the relationship would face difficulties in future, because New Delhi was expected to factor in US concerns regarding Iran for "the benefits that India can expect from its close relations with Israel and the US, far outweigh those it can get from its friendship with Iran". [4]

In US also India's relationship with Iran, a country designated as a member of then President George Bush's 'axis of evil', was viewed with concern and anxiety. A leading think-tank in te4h US, the Woodrow Wilson Centre, came out with a special report in April 2004, titled "The "Strategic Partnership" between India and Iran", [5] where some analysts noted that Indian cooperation with Iran in certain areas, like Space and Nuclear, were of particular concern. The October 2003 media report that former chairman and managing director of the Nuclear Power Corporation, Dr. Y.S.R. Prasad, took a job in Iran after his retirement in July 2000 [6] was particularly flagged to indicate that the relationship was indeed strategic and had made "substantive advances in relatively little time". It was also concluded that "both states needed each other politically now more than ever" and it was unlikely that India would roll back its relationship with Iran. Some analysts in the report also suggested that India would jeopardize its relationship with Israel and the US by deepening ties with Tehran.

US Factor and its Impact on the Ties

Around this time in June 2004, there was a change of government in New Delhi. The new United Progressive Alliance (UPA) government led by the centrist Congress Party mostly retained the foreign policy orientation of its predecessor. In January 2005, India signed an agreement with Iran to import 7.5 million tonnes per annum of liquefied natural gas (LNG), starting 2009, over a period of 25 years. The deal was later clinched in June 2005 and was reported to bc worth US$ 21 billion. [7] However, during 2005-2006, the relationship between India and Iran showed increasing signs of strain as India's relationship with the US prospered immensely. It must also be mentioned here that exactly around the time India and the US signed the framework agreement for Civilian nuclear Cooperation (July 2005), Iran witnessed a change in leadership in August 2005 and Mahmoud Ahmedinejad, known for his conservative views, came to power. He reversed the reformist measures adopted by Khatami and adopted a hawkish stance vis-à-vis. the US, the United Kingdom and Israel. Ahmedinejad rejected the incentives, financial and otherwise, offered by France, Germany and the UK and restarted uranium conversion, which sparked further international suspicions about Iranian nuclear programme. At this juncture, the Indian Prime Minister— immediately after signing the Indo-US nuclear deal in his interview with *Washington Post*—was seen to be advocating a constructive solution to the Iranian issue by working with other likeminded countries and even offered India 'as a bridge', even as he indicated, in an oblique reference to Iran, that "countries which take solemn international obligations, that they must honour those obligations". [8]

It is debatable whether it was the un-accommodative posture of the Bush administration or a revival of Islamist politics in Iran, which brought about a shift from the reformist politics followed by Khatami during his tenure. However, Ahmedinejad's aggressive posture on issues like Palestine and clandestine nuclear efforts was partly responsible for Iran's growing isolation at the international level which might have played a role in gradual reduction in Indian emphasis on its 'strategic partnership' with Iran. There is hardly any doubt, at the same time, that there was latent pressure on India from the US to deemphasise its relationship with Iran. [9] As discussions on Indo-US civilian nuclear cooperation gathered momentum (during 2005-2008), and the relationship acquired some critical potential, there was a subtle shift in India's international position on Iran.

Indian Votes in IAEA

On September 24, 2005, soon after the signing of the Indo-US framework agreement and Ahmedinejad's assumption of office (August 3, 2005), India voted with the US in the IAEA for the implementation of the non-proliferation safeguards agreement in Iran. In this particular voting at the IAEA meeting of the Board of the Governors, Russia and China abstained while India chose to vote along with US and the West. The US termed this support 'significant'. [10] India said that its vote was meant to avoid a major confrontation between Iran and the international community. India urged that Iran must fulfil its obligations as a signatory to the Nuclear Non-proliferation Treaty (NPT) and held that the passage of the resolution could not be the basis of a "renewed punitive approach or new sanctions" against Iran. [11]

Indian stance was regarded by Iran as a turn-around in its approach towards Iran. Iran's reaction was swift and it threatened immediately to cancel the LNG deal struck between the two countries in June 2005. The media reports said that soon after the Indian vote, the Iranian Ambassador in Vienna came up to Indian representative Dr. Sharma and conveyed the message from Iran's top nuclear negotiator, Ali Larijani, that Iran was no longer willing to go ahead with the US$ 21-billion LNG deal. [12] India voted again against Iran in February 2006 following which Iran made its displeasure even more apparent. In fact, Iran even went to the extent of refusing permission to India fighter jets to fly over its territory to take part in Red Flat air-combat exercise in the US in September 2008. [13]

From 2005 onwards, Iran would quote a higher price for the LNG and make the process of negotiations over the issue difficult for the Indian side to accept. Finally in November 2008, an Iranian government official was quoted as stating in the media that the deal was "dead because the whole arrangement was based on the clause that unless the National Iranian Oil Co's (NIOC) board of directors approve the deal, it will not be approved. The board of directors did not approve it."

Pipeline or Pipedream?

The Iran-Pakistan-India pipeline has been a victim of deteriorating relations with Iran on the one hand and adverse relations with Pakistan on the other. Conceived as a pipeline with great potential for the three countries, India signed a MOU with Iran on the pipeline in 1993. India had its concerns about the pipeline's route through Pakistan right since the beginning of the project. The 2775-km land pipeline was supposed to start from Assaluyeh fields in Iran, pass through Balochistan in Pakistan and end at the Indian border at Barmer, Rajasthan. The Initial cost was estimated at US$4 billion, which was later increased to US$ 7.6 billion. According to the feasibility study by BHP Billiton in 2003, the project fundamentals were strong and it could provide long-term affordable energy supply. The Indian cabinet approved of the IPI project in 2005. There were seven tripartite meetings and India participated in six of them till 2007. The sticking points for India were pricing, transit fee for Pakistan and Pakistani assurance of security of supply.

Iranian proposal was to supply gas at US$ 4.93 per mbtu (million British thermal unit) at oil price US$ 60 per barrel and to remain the basis of pricing of gas for the entire 25-years of contract. However, later it sought modification of this proposal and asked for revision of the pricing every three years. India also had the problem of fixing the transport and transit fee with Pakistan. India stopped participating in the discussions since September 2007 and said that it had its concerns regarding safe and secure transit through Pakistan. India wanted Iran to be responsible for safe passage of gas through 1,035 km. pipeline in Pakistan and would pay for the fuel only when it is delivered at Indian border, however, it was not acceptable to Iran. Pakistan and Iran finally signed the Heads of Agreement (HOA) and Operational Agreement that would pave way for construction of a gas pipeline on March 16, 2010 in Istanbul, and the sovereign guarantee agreement on May 28, 2010, in Islamabad. [14] During the negotiation stage in 2008, with India reluctant to join without its concerns being addressed, Iran and Pakistan had also toyed with the idea of inviting China into the project. [15] However, after initial reactions that it was studying the project, China has largely maintained silence over the project. [16] Media reports in December 2010 suggested that India was still interested in joining the pipeline project if the gas pricing issue was resolved. [17]

Economic Engagements: Will they Stand?

Economic and commercial ties between the two countries have largely prospered because of continued Indian import of Iranian crude oil over the years. India provides Iran with the third largest market for Iranian crude. India exports petroleum products, rice, machinery and instruments, manufactures of metals, primary and semi-finished iron and steel, drugs/pharmaceuticals and fine chemicals, processed minerals, manmade yarn and fabrics, tea, organic/inorganic/agro chemicals, rubber manufactured products, etc.

Even if the trust gap is widening between the two countries at the moment, it is interesting to note that the talks between India and Iran are going on over projects like the IPI gas pipeline, supply of LNG, development of the Farsi oil and gas blocks, South Pars gas field and LNG project, Chabahar container terminal project and Chabahar-Faraj-Bam railway project, etc. Several joint ventures such as the Irano-Hind Shipping Company, the Madras Fertilizer Company and the Chennai Refinery have managed to sustain the relationship even if it is at a low keel. Indian companies such as TATA, and ESSAR do have a presence in Iran. India is also a member of the International North-South Corridor project. The two countries are in the process of finalizing a Bilateral Investment Promotion & Protection Agreement (BIPPA) and a Double Taxation Avoidance Agreement (DTAA). In fact, the 35-year-old Indo-Iranian shipping joint venture, Iran-o-Hind, was placed under sanctions as per the UN Security Council Resolution 1929 on Iran. Given India's stance that it would not violate UN resolutions on Iran it is expected to find alternate ways of transporting crude from Iran. Sensing Indian sensitivity to the sanctions and apprehending further Indian disengagement, Iran has sought to tie India down with other projects which were lying in cold storage for some time. For example, at the 16th joint commission meeting in New Delhi, Iranian delegation renewed the offer to India to build the strategic Chabahar port which would provide an alternate route to central Asia via Afghanistan through the Zaranj-Delaram road which has been built in Afghanistan with Indian assistance.

While Iranian nuclear programme has led to the county's increasing isolation and impacted his economy in adverse ways, Iran's economic relationship with India has, in a way, been of critical significance for Iran. On the other hand growing energy needs has compelled India to engage Iran to its own advantage, despite pressures from the West to get out of the Iranian embrace. Table 3.1 shows the trade relations between the two countries.

Table 3.1: Bilateral Trade Balance and Growth Rate*
(US$ Million)

Year	Exports from India	Imports by India	Trade Balance	Total Bilateral Trade	Growth Rate (%)
2005-2006	1188.35	702.46	485.89	1890.81	43.70
2006-2007	1446.48	7818.55	6372.07	9065.03	379.43
2007-2008	1943.92	10943.61	-8999.69	12887.53	42.17
2008-2009	2534.01	12376.77	-9842.76	14910.78	15.70
2009-2010	1853.17	11540.85	-9687.68	13394.02	-10.17

*Data taken from MEA Website, Government of India, 2011.

Bilateral Interaction: Recent Phase

The Iranian President Dr. Mahmoud Ahmadinejad visited India

on April 29, 2008. The two countries have several bilateral consultative mechanisms at various levels whose meetings take place regularly. India and Iran hold regular bilateral talks on economic and trade issues at the Indo-Iran Joint Commission Meeting (JCM). The 15th JCM was held in Tehran on October 31-November 2, 2008 and the 16th JCM was held in New Delhi on July 8-9, 2010. During the JCM, 6 MoUs/agreements were signed. India and Iran also hold Joint Business Council meetings regularly. The 10th meeting of the JBC was organized by the Federation of Indian Chambers of Commerce & Industry (FICCI) in New Delhi on November 13, 2009. Consultations/Strategic Dialogues at the level of foreign ministries of the two countries are also going on since 2003. The seventh round of meeting was held in Teheran and the Indian foreign secretary, Nirupama Rao, visited Iran at the invitation of her counterpart, Dr. Mohammad Ali Fathollahi, Deputy Foreign Minister for Asia and Oceania, on February 2-3, 2010 for the consultations. Dr. Fathollahi, visited New Delhi on August 5-8, 2010 for the 8th round of Foreign Office Consultations. There were extensive discussions on bilateral relations during this visit and views were exchanged on Afghanistan, cross-border terrorism and other matters of regional and global relevance.

The Indian External Affairs Minister, S.M. Krishna, visited Iran during May 15-18, 2010 to attend the 14th G-15 Summit. In his address on May 17, Krishna emphasised on creation of an "effective platform not only for South-South cooperation but also for policy articulation in the global discourse in the areas of trade, money and finance, equitable development, food & energy security, climate change, etc.

In addition, at the semi-official level, the Institute of Defence Studies and Analyses (IDSA) of India, a think tank entirely funded by the Ministry of Defence, Government of India, and the Institute of Political and International Studies (IPIS) of Iran, run by the Ministry of Foreign Affairs, Iran, have a bilateral arrangement whereby they hold regular meetings to exchange views and ideas on bilateral and multilateral issues. At the official level, ministerial level visits are taking place regularly. The Iranian Foreign Minister Manouchehr Mottaki led a high-level delegation to India on November 16-17, 2009. During this visit the agenda for bilateral relations to be pursued by the two governments for the medium term was laid out. During the visit, Mottaki met the Vice-President and the Prime Minister of

India and met the External Affairs Minister, Shri S.M. Krishna and held discussions on a whole range of bilateral issues including economic cooperation, energy security, expansion of bilateral trade, surface transport, and regional issues and common concerns about terrorism.

Indian Presence in Oil and Gas Sector also Affected

Indian oil-major Oil and Natural Gas Corporation (ONGC) was involved in the exploration of the Farsi Block in the South Pars field since 2002. A consortium of Indian companies (ONGC-Videsh Limited with 40 percent, IOC with percent and OIL with 20 percent of the equity value) [18] signed a contract to carry out exploration in the Farsi Block. [19] The contract was worth US$ 27 million in exploration. In October 2004, the ONGC along with the Chinese SINOPEC negotiated a long-term deal with the National Iranian Oil Company (NIOC) for the development of Yadavaran, Iran's biggest onshore oil field with a stake of 29 percent (while SINOPEC had a 51 percent stake). There was another related deal to allow ONGC to develop part of the South Pars natural gas field. These deals were worth over US$ 100 billion. In January 2005, the LNG deal between India and Iran also offered further opportunity for Indian companies. It was reported that OVL would get a 20 percent share in the development of Iran's biggest onshore oil field, Yadavaran, and 100 percent in 30,000 barrels per day from the Jufeyr field.

The 20 percent in Yadavaran would translate into 60,000 barrels per day of crude oil for India. In November 2006, it was reported the consortium struck oil at three offshore exploration wells in the Farsi block. Iran is also seen as a gateway to the resource rich Central Asian republics, which energy-starved India is keen to gain access to. By November 2008, the consortium had struck crude oil in three wells in the Farsi block, 90 km off Bushehr port and it was reported that the consortium (OVL:IOC:OIL = 40:40:20) had the service contract for the in the 3,500 sq km Farsi offshore block where they would be reimbursed 35 percent plus US$90 million investment they made during the exploration phase. If the consortia would get the developmental rights, they would be paid a 15 percent rate of return over and above the investments they make.

The commercial viability report prepared by OVL—the operator of the field—said in 2006 that the least gas volume was 9.48 Tcf and the high-case estimate was 21.68 Tcf after independent studies by

Fugro Robertson Ltd of the UK and ONGC's Institute of Reservoir Studies. Further, the commerciality report established that in the worst-case scenario of 9.48 Tcf where National Iranian Oil Company, Iran (NIOC) would earn a net cash of US$ 71.792 trillion by producing 83 million barrels of condensate and 7.354 trillion cubic feet of gas over 30 years. In May 2009, it was reported that the Indian consortium were likely to invest about US$4 billion to start production from this gas field in the next 3-4 years. The investments for development of the this field would be in the range of US$4 billion and the Indian firms wanted to liquefy the gas and ship it to India in the form of liquefied natural gas (LNG), it was reported.

Indian companies have found it difficult to operate in Iran because of the sanctions imposed by UN, the US and the EU on Iran since 2006. These sanctions bar nuclear, missile and many military exports to Iran and target external investments in oil, gas and petrochemicals, exports of refined petroleum products, as well as the Iranian Republican Guard Corps (IRGC), banks, insurance, financial transactions and shipping. The UN Security Council imposed fresh sanctions on Iran over its nuclear programme vide resolution 1929 adopted on 9 June 2010. The resolution covers nuclear and ballistic missile activities, conventional arms transfers to and from Iran, Iran's shipping and banking sectors and entities related to Iranian Revolutionary Guards Corps (IRGC). The UN Security Council resolutions [20] on Iran have been adopted under Chapter VII of the UN Charter, and it is mandatory for all UN members to comply with their provisions.

Latest RBI Directive and the ACL Controversy

Iran is India's biggest oil supplier after Saudi Arabia and India imports about 21 million tons of crude from Iran annually. [21] Indian companies Mangalore Refineries and Petrochemicals Limited (MRPL), a subsidiary of ONGC, Hindustan Petroleum Corporation Limited (HPCL), Indian Oil Corporation (IOC) and Essar Oil import about 400,000 bpd Iranian crude. [22] The Reserve Bank of India (RBI) issued a directive on December 27, 2010 that "all eligible current account transactions including trade transactions with Iran should be settled in any permitted currency outside the ACU mechanism until further notice". [23] This step taken by the RBI drew positive reaction from the US. White House spokesman Tommy Vietor said in an email that "the Reserve Bank of India has made the right decision to carefully scrutinize and reduce its financial dealings with the Central Bank of Iran", and this "latcst action adds to the growing list of companies, financial institutions and governments that are increasingly concerned about Iran's misuse of trade and financial relationships to support illicit activity, including its nuclear program." [24]

Mehdi Fakheri, vice president of international affairs at the Iran Chamber of Commerce, Industries and Mines, said in an interview in Mumbai on January 28, 2011, that Iran might halt crude shipments to India in two weeks if a gridlock over payments that threatened US$ 9.5 billion of oil trade between the nations would not be resolved. Indian refiners owed Iran about US$ 900 million for crude oil after payments stopped in December 2010. Kakheri also indicated that if there was no payment solution, Iran would sell its oil to other countries and the Iran-India trade exchanges would drop to almost 20 percent of the current level. [25] So far, the payments to Iran were being settled through Asian Clearing Union (ACU), a longstanding clearinghouse system run by the Asian central banks since 1974. The ACU, based in Teheran, settles trade transactions among nine countries, viz. Bangladesh, Bhutan, India, Iran, Nepal, Pakistan, Maldives, Myanmar and Sri Lanka. These transactions are settled by the central banks of these countries, which makes it difficult to identify the individual companies involved in the transaction. There is pressure on India from the US to stop transacting with Iran through ACU, because it allows Iran to bypass financial restrictions imposed on it by the US. In 2010, Iran routed US$ 13.19 billion through ACU whereas cumulatively there was a transaction worth US$ 41.27 among the nine countries. [26] India and Iran together accounted for nearly 76 percent of the total transactions. Following the RBI decision the oil companies importing oil Iranian crude have taken some reverses in the stock market. The shares of MRPL fell as much as 4.4 percent to ₹ 65.65 on January 28, 2011 and closed at ₹ 68.40. Essar Oil dropped 4 percent to ₹ 120.25 and group company Essar Energy Ltd. declined 2.6 percent to 529 pence at 10:55 a.m. in London. [27]

Iranian proposal to use the European-Iranian Trade Bank (EIH), based in Germany for payment transactions was not acceptable to Indian companies. Under this arrangement, the Indian companies would have had to open individual accounts with the State Bank of India (SBI) which in turn would have opened an account with EIH to make payments to Iran. SBI did not want to take any risk since EIH was blacklisted by the U.S. Treasury Department in September 2010, and the US had announced then that any bank that would do business with EIH would risk US sanctions. [28] Iranian officials also suggested the names of two other banks based in the UAE, which refused to oblige. Iran has been under pressure to find a bank which is not under US sanctions and is ready to handle these transactions. Be that as it may, this row seems to make it difficult for Iran to sell its oil, and force Indian refiners to find replacements for Iranian crude.

Assessment

As it stands at the beginning of 2011, the relationship between India and Iran seems to have turned full circle, i.e., from height of enthusiasm in 2003 to the bottom of exasperation in 2010. The twists and turns in the relationship since 1990s in a way shows the extremely unpredictable nature of realist politics based on changing nature of national interest geopolitical realities. India and Iran rediscovered each other as countries with deep linguistic, cultural and civilizational contacts in the 1990s and realised that their relationship was guided by their common interests in regional politics (Afghanistan), economic compulsions (energy trade) as well as security imperatives (Indian need to have a friend in the Islamic world and Iranian need to break out of international isolation through strategic partnership with India). However, before the relationship could gather momentum, the two countries were sucked into the orbit of global power politics. Iran, dubbed as a member of 'axis of evil' by the then American president in 2002, did little to convince the international community of its intentions and chose to take measures which pushed it deeper into isolation, making it increasingly difficult for India to sustain the relationship.

With the busting of the nuclear black market by A.Q. Khan of Pakistan in 2004, the Pakistan-Iran nuclear nexus came to the fore and the US tried to ensure that Iran would not go nuclear in future. This was the time when India's emerging ties with Iran came under closer American scrutiny. Although India had an unenviable record as a non-NPT and *de facto* nuclear state, its economic and security engagements with Iran was viewed as enablers for Iranian nuclear venture. It is interesting to note that analysts in the US read more into India-Iran relations than what was actually there and went to the extent of arguing that India will try its best to balance its separate strategic partnerships with Iran and the US, and it might not side with the US even on principled issues.

Even if India has voted with the US thrice at IAEA (September 24, 2005, February 4, 2006 and November 27, 2009), there are suspicions that India may not be fully backing the American line on Iran. Even after first two crucial votes at IAEA by India, the long scheduled joint naval exercises between India and Iran (that, of course, coincided with Bush's visit to India in March 2006), were taken as an instance of Indian efforts to toe an independent line on Iran. [29] US officials have admitted to the fact that the Indian votes on Iran were to some extent coerced. [30] From then on, the US left no stone unturned to build pressure on Iran contrary to the Indian position that "Governments [ought to] exercise restraint and choose the peaceful path of persuasion and negotiations". India has also time and again reiterated its stand that Iran has the right to develop peaceful use of nuclear energy while fulfilling all its international commitments and obligations. It has also expressed its concerns about use of military force against Iran and held that any "military strike on Iran would have disastrous consequences for the entire region, affecting the lives and livelihood of five million Indians resident in the Gulf, and the world economy". Indian maintained in May 2008:

Iran must be engaged purposefully and candidly - not by demonising its social and cultural mores but by recognizing their internal dynamic even while we may not accept them for ourselves. For those of us who inhabit the same region as Iran and are aware of the richness of its history and culture, and the pride they take in their civilization, it is axiomatic that threats against or denigration of the country will not work. Iran has to be mindful of its international obligations, but progress on the issues that concern us will not be possible by the use or the threat of use of force or sanctions. It is only engagement which will enable us to see that Iran views following its international obligations as being in its pragmatic self interest. It is a country of tremendous natural and human resources and the development of these resources will make Iran a factor for regional security. The threat or the implied threat of use of military or economic force will not.

Simultaneously, India has urged Iran to fulfil its obligations as a NPT signatory. Undoubtedly, the IAEA findings on Iran have left room for suspicion about Iranian intentions. As the newly appointed Director General of IAEA, Yukiya Amano, stated in January 2011, Iran hid information about its nuclear facility at Qom until IAEA discovered in 2009. Similarly, Iran did not discuss the construction of other nuclear plants with IAEA ahead of time and announced their establishment suddenly. It has not yet furnished IAEA with comprehensive information regarding these facilities. There are many 'unanswered questions', as Amano would put it, like what purpose do components for a highly explosive ignition system serve and what are neutron triggers needed for? [31] It is true that Iran does have a sovereign right to produce nuclear energy, but since it has chosen to be part of the non-proliferation treaty it has to come clean on its nuclear efforts. Rather than seeking to misguide and hoodwink international community, it must cooperate with the IAEA and share all relevant information related to its nuclear programme.

There is a view that Iran operates in a highly insecure neighbourhood—as a Shia majority country it is surrounded by Sunni states and it also has an aggressive Israel to contend with—to keep the bogey of nuclear capability afloat to ward off any possible aggression. However, the current strategy adopted by Iran of either defying or duping international community will force its friends and well-wishers to desert him and it will find itself increasingly cornered at the global stage. Moreover, it has been particularly suspicious of India and deemphasised on its relationship with India in contrast to its position vis-à-vis China and Russia, who abstained the first vote but have consistently voted with the US on the Iranian question ever since. India has consistently opposed moves against Iran over the issue of human rights. Even in response to the recent Iranian position on the Kashmir issue, India abstained the motion against Iran on human rights at the UN, while Russia and China voted against Iran.

India may be seeking to strengthen its relationship with the US and decelerating the pace of its engagement with Iran, but this is real-politik and states do have to take such decisions in their self-interest. India, which is pursuing a neo-liberal agenda in its foreign and economic policy, seeks to strike a fine balance and thus it walks a tightrope between US and Iran as some observers would argue. [32] The leadership of India at the moment is making Machiavellian calculations of benefiting immensely from its relationship with the US because, it thinks there is s synergy of views between the two democracies and their interests are also coinciding to certain extent. This is however not a monochromatic view of a nation of more than one billion people. There is substantial opposition to the position taken by the UPA government in power today. There are countervailing forces in the polity too who would argue that India could have chosen to abstain rather than join the bandwagon and played a crucial role in persuading Iran to implement the NPT safeguards agreement on its own.

Iranian leadership must understand that the nuclear option that they are seeking for themselves stands in clear violation of their commitment as a NPT member. Iran can secure its interests by projecting its interests and security concerns in a non-offensive manner. As a relatively more open society in the region, with a rich civilization and cultural heritage, Iran and Iranians must leave the path of confrontation and chose a path of open dialogue with the West. While a war or short and swift attack on Iranian facilities may not take place at all, Iran must take measures which will preclude such a possibility. India on its part, even if its foreign office is understaffed and its leadership lacks the Nehruvian confidence, should try to facilitate dialogue between the US and the Iran in the coming days. That may lend a different dynamic and a new rhythm to India-Iran relations.

End Notes

1. Jawaharlal Nehru, *India's Foreign Policy, Selected Speeches, September 1946-September 1961*, The Publications Division, Ministry of Information and Broadcasting, Government of India, Delhi, 1961, p. 249.
2. Ibid., p. 413.
3. Rizwan Zeb, The Emerging Indo-Iranian Strategic Alliance and Pakistan", February 12, 2003 issue of the *CACI Analyst* online, at http://www.cacianalyst.org/?q=node/902.
4. Kashif Mumtaz, "Changing Patterns Of Iran-India Relations", *Strategic Studies*, Vol. XXVI, Number 2, Summer 2006, at http://www.issi.org.pk/ss_Detail.php?dataId=388.
5. "The "Strategic Partnership" Between India and Iran", Asia Program Report, No 120, April 2004, See the full report at http://www.iranwatch.org/privateviews/WWICS/perspex-wwics-stategicpartnership-0404.pdf.
6. C. Christine Fair, "Indo-Iranian Ties: Thicker Than Oil", *Middle*

East Review of International Affairs, Volume 11, No. 1, March 2007,
http://meria.idc.ac.il/journal/2007/issue1/jv11no1a9.html#_edn4.

7. The deal was signed between National Iranian Gas Export Co. (NIGEC), and Indian companies GAIL (India) Ltd, Indian Oil Corp. Ltd and Bharat Petroleum Corp. Ltd. It was reported that the LNG imported would be marketed by Gail, IOC, ONGC and OIL in the proportion of 40:25:25:10. Reported *Indian Express*, January 8, 2005, at
http://www.indianexpress.com/storyOld.php?storyId=62321.
8. In his breakfast meeting with editors and writers of Washington Post, Prime Minister Manmohan Singh said, "We have strong civilisational links with Iran. Also I would say Iran is the largest Shia Muslim country in the world. We have the second largest Shia Muslim population in our country and I do believe that thanks to our unique history we can be a bridge." Quoted in *Indian Express*, July 25, 2005.
9. See for details K. Alan Kronstadt and Kenneth Katzman, "India-Iran Relations and U.S. Interests", CRS Report for Congress, August 2, 2006, at
http://fpc.state.gov/documents/organization/70294.pdf.
10. The US Under Secretary of State Nicholas Burns said, "It's very significant to the US that India voted with the majority. That is a blow to Iran's attempt to turn this debate into a developed world versus a developing world debate.... So we're very grateful for India's support and it's significant that India is now working very closely with the United States and Europe to prevent Iran from becoming a nuclear power ".
11. India also went with the IAEA's findings and said that "Iran's failure to notify the Agency of the existence of this facility until September 2009...was inconsistent with its obligations under the Subsidiary Arrangements to its Safeguards Agreement and ....Iran´s late declaration of the new facility reduces confidence in the absence of other nuclear facilities under construction in Iran which have not been declared to the Agency. Rediff.com, "Why India voted against Iran in IAEA", November 27, 2009 at
http://news.rediff.com/report/2009/nov/27/why-india-voted-against-iran-in-iaea.htm
12. Reported Amit Baruah, "LNG deal is off: Iran ", *The Hindu*, September 28, 2005, at

http://www.hindu.com/2005/09/28/stories/2005092818651500.htm.

13. As reported in the *Times of India*, September 19, 2008.
14. Under the gas sale purchase agreement signed between the Iranian National Oil Company and Interstate Gas System of Pakistan, Iran will provide 750 million cubic feet of gas per day to Pakistan for the next 25 years.
15. "Ahmadinejad Would Welcome Chinese Role in Gas Pipeline", Xinhua News Agency April 28, 2008.
16. Analysts believed that the "massive investment required to link China to the pipeline would be susceptible to many risks since it falls along a major fault line of instability....Beijing might just be feigning interest in the IPI pipeline to get a better deal in negotiations with Russia on relatively safer Siberia-China gas pipelines. Stephen Blank, "Will China Join the Iran-Pakistan-India Pipeline?", China Brief, Volume: 10 Issue: 5, March 5, 2010, Jamestown Foundation, at http://www.jamestown.org/programs/chinabrief/single/?tx_ttnews[tt_news]=36122&tx_ttnews[backPid]=25&cHash=0e88d5e465.
17. "India reiterates interest in IPI", *Teheran Times*, December 30, 2010 at http://www.tehrantimes.com/index_View.asp?code=233186.
18. *The Telegraph* (Calcutta) December 27, 2002.
19. See the report titled "OVL, IOC, OIL to invest US$ 4 bn in Iran gas field", in *Economic Times* (Delhi), May 01, 2009, available at http://economictimes.indiatimes.com/news/news-by-industry/energy/oil--gas/ovl-ioc-oil-to-invest-4-bn-in-iran-gas-field/articleshow/4472044.cms, Also see detailed report at rediff.com, at http://www.rediff.com/money/2009/may/01iran-oil-majors-to-invest-4-bn-dollars.htm.
20. The sanctions imposed by the United Nations Security Council resolution so far are (i) Resolution 1737 passed on December 23, 2006, (ii) Resolution 1747 passed on March 24, 2007, (iii) Resolution 1803-passed on March 3, 2008, and (iv) Resolution 1929 passed on June 9, 2010.
21. Iran is the second largest crude oil supplier after Saudi Arabia to India. For the April-September 2010-11 period, of the total 75,575 TMT (75.575 million tonne) crude oil imported, 8,839

TMT (8.839 million tonne) came from Iran. "Iran payments: MRPL petitions RBI for status quo for 3 months", Business Line, January 09, 2011, at http://www.thehindubusinessline.in/2011/01/09/stories/2011010950950100.htm.

22. MRPL has a capacity to process 11.8 million tonne per annum (mtpa) of crude oil. In India, MRPL is the biggest importer of Iranian crude oil, sourcing about 7.1 mtpa. MRPL buys about 7-8 cargoes a month from Iran. HPCL imports a little over 3 mtpa and Indian Oil Corporation, about 3 mtpa. Private refiner Essar Oil imports about 2-3 mtpa. In India, MRPL is the biggest importer of Iranian crude oil, sourcing about 7.1 mtpa. MRPL buys about 7-8 cargoes a month from Iran.
23. See the full circular at http://www.rbi.org.in/SCRIPTs/NotificationUser.aspx?Id=6172&Mode=0.
24. See the report by Reuters at http://in.reuters.com/article/2010/12/30/idINIndia-53840020101230.
25. Report titled "Mangalore Refinery, Essar Fall on Iran Supply Concerns", in *Bloomberg Business week*, January 28, 2011, at http://www.businessweek.com/news/2011-01-28/mangalore-refinery-essar-fall-on-iran-supply-concerns.html. Also see "Oil Flow to India Continues, *Iran Daily*, at http://www.iran-daily.com/1389/11/9/MainPaper/3882/Page/4/Index.htm.
26. *Asian Clearing Union Newsletter*, Volume 29, No.12, December, 2010m available at http://www.asianclearingunion.org/Publications/MonthlyNewsletter.aspx.
27. "Mangalore Refinery, Essar Fall on Iran Supply Concerns", *Bloomberg Business week*, January 28, 2011 at http://www.businessweek.com/news/2011-01-28/mangalore-refinery-essar-fall-on-iran-supply-concerns.html.
28. In June 2010, the United Nations stepped up punitive measures against Iran over its nuclear ambitions, applying a fourth round of sanctions. The U.S. and European Union later imposed additional restrictions. Iran says it's enriching uranium for power generation.
29. See for example the analysis by C. Christine Fair, "India and Iran: New Delhi's Balancing Act", *The Washington Quarterly*,

Volume 30, Number 3, Summer 2007, pp. 145-159.

30. Stephen G. Rademakcr—who quit his job as Assistant Secretary for Non-proliferation and International Security at the U.S. State Department in December 2006, said during a talk at the New Delhi based think tank Institute for Defence Studies and Analyses (IDSA) on February 17, 2007, that the votes were coerced. See report in *The Hindu*, February 18, 2007. The US Ambassador denied any such pressure later, however, the general impression that the US exerted lot of pressure on India on the issue has caught on.
31. See Amano's interview with German news paper Der Speigel on January 11, 2011. Available at http://www.iaea.org/newscenter/transcripts/2011/derspiegel110111.html.
32. Harsh Pant, A Fine Balance: India Walks a Tightrope between Iran and the United States, *Orbis,* Summer 2007, pp. 495-509.

4

Iranian Foreign Policy towards India

Hamid Ahmadi

Iran and India during the Pahlavi Era (1947-1979)

Iran and India had many commonalities during the Pahlavi era, which could have logically brought the two states closer, if not together, at least in the realm of foreign policy and establishing good relations. These commonalities included:

1. Both were secular states having developmental and modernizing policies in order to raise their domestic and international place of their countries in post colonial era.
2. Iran and India had a rich civilizational background and shared common ethnic and cultural ties which had their roots in the ancient Aryan traditions and later Vedic and Zoroastrian religious traditions.
3. Common cultural ties, especially in linguistic realms with respect to the influence and popularity of the Persian language during Islamic sultanate dynasties in India.
4. The popularity of the contemporary Indian art, music and cinema in Iran.

However, despite the early good relations between the two countries, and the fact that they had reached agreements such as Air Transport in November 1948 [1] and signed the Treaty of Peace and Friendship in March 1950 [2], bilateral relations did not flourish well due to several reasons including the spread of the cold war to the Third World countries.

In the beginning, the Shah of Iran tried to prevent the deterioration of the relations by paying his first visit to India in February 1956; right after Iran became a member of Baghdad Pact, and assured the Indian leadership that Iran's close relations with Pakistan were not directed against India. [3] Though India too welcomed him and Jawaharlal Nehru, the then Prime Minister of India, had his formal visit to Tehran in 1959, the two countries were following opposite lines in their coalition and alliance formation in international system.

Iran's support to India in Indo-China war of 1962 and the positive visit of Dr. Radhakrishnan, the then Indian President, to Tehran in May 1963 on the one hand, and the beginning of the Washington and Moscow détente policy in the early 1960s on the other, paved the way for improving the cold war torn Tehran-Delhi relations. However, Indo-Pakistan war of 1965 and continuation of the conflict after that prevented closer relations between Iran and India.

Despite the importance of Iran's alliance with the West and the Shah's resentment of Indo-Soviet warm relations, the swift strategic developments in the Persian Gulf region following the British withdrawal in the late 1960s and the early 1970s, made him to have a more independent foreign policy. Believing on the necessity of making the regional states neutral in the future Iran–Arab conflict over the Persian Gulf issues (Iran's claim over Bahrain and the three Islands of the Lesser and Greater tombs and Abu Musa), Shah decided to prevent any further alienation of India from Iran. Having this consideration in his Persian Gulf strategy, he took initiative in melting the ices in Indo-Iranian relations. Shah's 12 days visit to India in January 1969 was a clear sign of his new policy. It was in the same visit that he declared Iran's policy of non-intervention if the people of Bahrain decide to have an independent state.

Once again the Pakistani factor, i.e., the new Indo-Pakistan conflict of the early 1970s, put its mark on Indo-Iranian relations and halted the improvement of their bilateral relations. Being aware of the importance of such relations, India for its turn took the initiative for warming up the Indo-Iranian ties during the visit of Swaran Singh, the then Indian foreign minister to Tehran in July 1973. [4] The continuous efforts of India under the leadership of Mrs. Indira Gandhi for bringing Iran, the superpower of the Persian Gulf region, to India's friends circle, had important effects on Iran and paved the way for further friendly relations. This happened during Mrs Gandhi's visit to Tehran in May 1974 that resulted in a series of agreements signed between the two countries. The most important aspect of these multilateral agreements was their cooperation in the realm of nuclear energy. The next year witnessed the most important result of this cooperation when the two sides agreed on nuclear cooperation in February 1975. This was the beginning of a new era in bilateral relations between India and Iran.

The widening disagreement between Iran and the United State of America over OPEC's oil policy for increasing the oil prices convinced the Shah of Iran for having more close relations with powerful states such as India. Iran's policy of bringing peace and stability to the Persian Gulf region and supporting India's policy for Indian Ocean, required more cooperation with India. That was the reason behind the Shah's visit to India in October of 1974. [5] It seemed that the rise of the military government of Zia al Haq in Pakistan in the late 1970s and his *Shari's* policy led to the Shah's resentment and his willingness toward reinforcing political and economic relations with India. His trip of February 1978 to Delhi indicated this willingness. However, the Shah's wishes of having more friendly and strategic relations with India did not fulfil because of the political turmoil which led to his fall in the next year.

Secular Iran and the Islamic Pakistan: Surprising Relations

Despite the strength of Indo-Iranian cultural and civilizational ties and the mutual tendency of their elites toward each other, it was surprising that Iran was the first state which recognized Pakistan as an independent state. The Shah of Iran, too, was the first head of state who visited Pakistan in May 1950. [6] Of course, Pakistani leaders were very active in getting as much support as they could from the international community, especially the Islamic world. By naming Pakistan an 'Islamic Republic', they put much emphasis on gaining the sympathy of the Muslim countries.

The Iran-Pakistani relations got a new momentum due to the spread of the Cold War into the Middle East in the mid 1950s. As the important members of the Baghdad pact, both countries started warm relations, and by the rise of the Non-Align Movement in 1955, Iran-Pakistan bilateral relations improved at the expense of the Indo-Iranian relations. Tehran-Islamabad axis got a new impetus when the Central Treaty organization (CENTO) replaced the Baghdad pact after the Iraqi military coup d'etate of 1958 which toppled the second Arab monarchy following the Free Officer military coup of June 1952 in Egypt. [7] While Washington did not have a membership position in Baghdad Pact, except in its military committee, it became the main source behind the creation of CENTO. Facing the Soviet threat, Iran had more impetus to join the new organization.

The Iranian-Pakistani friendship proved its fruitfulness when the Shah of Iran backed Islamabad in Indo-Pakistani war of 1965. One reason, probably, for Iran's support was the bitter fact, as the Shah believed it, that Washington did not gave military support to its ally in the war and pursued a policy of neutrality. The same fact, according to some analysts [8], led to the resentment of the CENTO members and encouraged them for more regional cooperation. One result of this tendency was the formation of Regional Cooperation Development (RCD) between Turkey, Iran and Pakistan in 1964. [9]

Iranian support to Pakistan was not limited only to Indo-Pakistani conflict, but also included other important aspects. Iran was the main factor behind the failure of Afghanistan's irredentist pan-Pashtun trends which tended to instigate Pashtun ethnic turmoil in Pakistan. The Shah of Iran always warned Afghanis, especially during the 1970s, that any move in that direction would face the Iranian resistance and Tehran-Islamabad alliance. [10] Iran also was the main provider of the financial and military support for Pakistan in its fight against the Baluchi ethnic insurgency during the 1960s and 1970s. [11] Fear of a similar phenomenon on the Iranian Baluchistan, which somehow became a reality due to the support of Iraq, the arch enemy of Iran in the Middle East in the late 1960s and early 1970s [12], encouraged Iran's support to the central government in Pakistan. Another important dimension of Iran's support to Pakistan involved economic and financial issues. In addition to financial helps, Iran used to give cheap oil to Pakistan. Though Butho's government worried about the Shah's reluctance to continue this in the aftermath of the oil price increases after 1974, this did not happened. According to Asadullah Alam, the Iranian Minister of the Court, Iran accepted Butho's demand for the supply of the cheap oil to Pakistan as did it before. [13]

To sum up, the foreign policy of Iran toward Indian subcontinent during the Pahlavi era had more Pakistani orientation at the expense of India. This was an irony which contradicted the common logic of foreign policy of the states. Both Indian and Iranian states had much more in common in terms of the nature of the political system, rich background of friendship and cultural-civilizational commonalities.

Iranian Foreign Policy towards India in the Islamic Era (1979-2009)

The foreign policy of the Islamic Republic of Iran toward India can be divided into almost three periods, each having a different orientation toward India. The first period included the dominance of the liberal government of Mehdi Bazargan (1979-1980), the leader of the Liberation Movement of Iran who somehow pursued a realist foreign policy and could provide a basis of good relations with India. After withdrawing Iran from CENTO and joining Non-Aligned Movement (NAM), Bazargan followed the classic pattern of Negative Balance (*Mowaazeneye Manfi*) foreign policy of Muhammad Mussadiq, the nationalist Iranian Prime Minister of early 1950s, whose government was toppled as a consequence of the British-American military coup of 1953. [14] By stressing close similarities between Negative Balance policy of Mussadiq and the principles of the Non-Alignment policy, the followers of Mussadiq insisted on Iran's membership in Non-Aligned movement since the late 1950s. [15] Bazargan's foreign policy toward India was based on good and cooperative relation as he considered Mussadiq and Nehru the leading heroes of the Non Aligned movement. Thus, Iran and India could lead a constructive foreign policy of the Third World countries in the beginning of the second cold war following the Soviet invasion of Afghanistan.

Bazargan's fall following the US hostage crisis by the radical Islamic students in October 1980, marked the beginning of the second period of Iran's foreign policy toward India. Though Iran still continued to be a member of Non-Aligned Movement, two factors led to the deterioration of Tehran-Delhi relations. First, the thrust of revolutionary foreign policy of the new government was export of the revolution and support of the Islamic movements around the world. Because of the Kashmir problem and the conditions of the Indian Muslims, the Indo-Iranian ties became strained. [16] The second factor was different positions of Iran and India toward the question of the Soviet invasion of Afghanistan. [17]. The fact is that in spite Iran's revolutionary policy on the Islamic issues, and its strained relations with most Arab countries of the Middle East over this, Indo-Iranian relations was not based on Iran's Islamic principles of foreign policy. Though Kashmir has been one of the basic issues of the Islamic world for many Islamic fundamentalist groups, the Islamic Republic of Iran had tried to have a somewhat neutral stand on it.

However, other issues such as the Iran-Iraq war and the Indian policy of having balance between the two oil exporting countries, prevented further warmer relations between Iran and India. [18] Despite this, normal ties between the two countries continued and according to some Indian analysts, mutual cooperation in economic terms was growing during the 1980s. This included the possible nuclear cooperation when Iran asked India's help for completing the Bushehr nuclear reactor project in 1980 after West German halted work on it. [19]

The third period of Iran's foreign policy toward India was in fact the turning point for Indo-Iranian relations in contemporary times. This period started by the rise of Taliban in Afghanistan in the early 1990s when this fundamentalist group began its gradual dominance in Afghani politics. The common challenge of Islamic fundamentalism in Afghanistan and Pakistan brought India and Iran together and convinced them on improving mutual relations. This common challenge led to a series of formal high level state visits between the two countries. Ali Akbar Velayati, the then foreign minister of Iran paid a visit to New Delhi in November 1992, which led to the visit of Prime Minister Narasimha Rao in September 1993. Hashemi Rafsanjani, who started a new era of détente in Iranian foreign policy in the late 1980s, visited India in April 1995. That marked the highest level of Indo-Iranian relations and the beginning of an era which other Iranian statesmen continued to follow.

The era of Muhammad Khatami (1996-2004), the Iranian reformist President, witnessed the remarkable improvement in Indo-Iranian relations. Khatami's personality and thought which brought about positive prestige for the Islamic republic after two decades of international isolation, was an opportunity for a new breakthrough in Indo-Iranian ties. Indian political elites proved that they were rational enough for using such opportunity for their own national interests. The high profile four-day visit of Atal Behari Vajpayee, the then Indian Prime Minister in April 2001, was warmly welcomed by the Iranian president, who described it as "a new chapter in the field of human and international relations". [20] The result of this visit was the signing of Tehran declaration in which both sides agreed to launch a new phase of constructive and mutually beneficial cooperation, covering in particular, the areas of energy, transit and transport, industry, agriculture and service sector. The sides reaffirmed their commitment to strengthen transport and transit cooperation. They also agreed to actively promote scientific and technological cooperation, including among others, joint research projects, short and long-tern training courses and exchange of related information on regular bases. [21]

Tehran declaration was, in fact, an introduction for further cooperation during Khatami's reciprocal visit to India in January 2003. India considered Khatami's visit very important and welcomed him as the Chief Guest at India's Republic Day's parade. [22] It was during this visit that the famous "New Delhi Declaration" and "the Road Map to Strategic Cooperation" were signed by both leaders. Beside these two important documents, seven other agreements were signed in the realm of economic exchanges, science and technology, information technology, educational training, reconstruction of Afghanistan and anti-terrorism. Defence cooperation and training and exchange of visits were other parts of mutual cooperative agreements. [23]

One aspect of the Delhi Declaration of 2003, with 16 articles, was mutual willingness of both countries for energy cooperation. According to article seven of the Delhi Declaration:

India and Iran have a complementarily of interests in the energy sector which should develop as a strategic area of their future relationship. Iran with its abundant energy resources and India with its growing energy needs as a rapidly developing economy are natural partners. The areas of cooperation in this sector include investment in upstream and downstream activities in the oil sector, LNG/natural gas tie-ups and secure modes of transport. [24]

Bilateral cooperation in energy arena reached its peak when India and Iran signed a multi-billion dollar deal in June 2005 under which Iran will supply India with 7.5 million tons of liquefied natural gas annually for 25 years beginning 2009. The deal also envisaged Indian participation in the development of the Yadavaran and Jufeyr oilfields in Iran. [25] It is noteworthy that Indian exporters provide about 40 percent of gasoline that keeps Iran moving. [26]

Beside energy, Indo-Iranian trade has had remarkable increase after the Delhi Declaration. According to the Indian Embassy in Tehran, India "exports goods worth US$ 1.937 billion to Iran and imports goods worth US$ 11.049 billion from Iran. India's imports from Iran include crude oil and petroleum products worth US$ 10.06 billion and India's exports include petroleum products worth US$ 850 million. Thus trade volume between Iran and India has reached almost US$ 13 billion in 2007 after business between the two countries grew by 80 percent". [27]

One important aspects of mutual cooperation includes the question of defence and military. This dimension of Indo-Iranian relationship goes well back to the early 1990s and even beyond that time to the early 1980s. In fact, after forming an Indo-Iranian Joint Commission in 1983, India and Iran established steady but relatively low-level defence and military relations. In 1988 Iran began rebuilding its conventional arsenal with purchases of tanks, combat aircraft, and ships from Russia and China. In 1993 Iran turned to India for help in developing batteries for the three Kilo-class submarines that the Islamic Republic had bought from Russia. Submarine batteries that Russia had provided were not appropriate for the warm waters of the Persian Gulf, and India had substantial experience operating Kilos in warm water. [28] India reportedly hoped that the 2003 New Delhi Declaration would pave the way for sales to Iran of upgrades of Iran's Russian-made conventional weapons system. While Indo-Iranian deals along these lines have not yet materialized, Iran has sought Indian advice in operating missile boats, refitting T-72 tanks and armoured personnel carriers, and upgrades for MiG-29 fighters. [29]

Iran-Pakistan Relations after the Revolution: Non-Relevance of the Islamic Factor

Comparing to the Pahlavi era, Iran and Pakistan bilateral relations have not been as good as it presumed to be according to the conventional wisdom. Though both the post-revolutionary Iran and Pakistan are Islamic states and lay their legitimacy on the basis of the Islamic *Shari'a*, their relations have had many ups and downs after 1979. Considering Zia al Haq policy of *Shari'* a, and with respect to the existence of the important Islamic movements such as Jama'at Islami and Islamic thinkers such as Mawdudi, the theoretician of the Islamic State [30], it seemed that the Islamic republic of Iran would follow the Pakistani path of Islamic politics. However, the Shiite nature of the Iranian Islamic republic and the independent nature of the Shiite jurisprudence did not allowed such things to happen.

The Shiite revival in Pakistan and the traditional links between Iran and the religious Shiite circles (Hawza Ilmiya) in Pakistan instigated the sensitivity of the anti-Shiite extremist Deobandi and other *Sunni* Wahhabi fundamentalist groups. The formation of Sipaahi Sahaabe in 1983 and its confessional anti-Shiite terrorist attacks against the Pakistani Shiite places and leaders, led to a vicious circle of violent activities which not only took the lives of many Pakistanis, but also brought about the resentment of the Islamic

Republic of Iran regarding the silence of the Pakistani government toward such subversive confessional activities. This problem reached its peak when a group of Iranian military personnel in the diplomatic mission were assassinated by the anti-Shiite extremist groups in Pakistan in 1985. Thus, Islam and the Islamic cause strained the formal relations of the two Islamic states rather than bringing them together.

Though Iran and Pakistan could keep their bilateral relations at the conventional level, especially on economic cooperation, the course of the events did not help to prevent the deterioration of their relations. The rise of the Taliban in Afghanistan and Pakistan's policy of supporting this radical Islamic fundamentalist group made Iran more skeptics toward Islamabad's policy toward Afghanistan. Taliban's moves against Iran in 1997, during which groups of Iranian diplomats were killed in Mazari Sharif, had more negative effects on Pakistani-Iranian relations. As mentioned earlier, these events were turning points for Iran's foreign policy toward India and Pakistan. India and Iran had a common strategy in supporting the Northern Alliance, led by Ahmad Shah Masud, against Taliban.

Following the US invasion of Afghanistan (2001), Parviz Musharraf, the former military ruler of Pakistan, launched the anti Taliban policy and also initiated tough measures against the extremist confessional anti-Shiite groups in Pakistan and brought to the justice of the killers of the Iranian diplomats. However these political gestures of Pakistan government did not help much in improving its ties with Islamic Republic of Iran. The Iran-Pakistan relations remained at a lower level comparing to Indo-Iranian relations during the late 1990s and the first decade of the twenty first century. Moreover, the rise of the Pakistani based extremist anti-Shiite groups in Iranian Baluchistan, particularly Jund Allah of Abdul Malik Rigi, who has launched several violent anti-Shiite operations inside Iran during 2006-2009, has strained Tehran and Islamabad relations.

Irony of Iranian Foreign Policy towards India

To explain the surprising nature of Iranian foreign policy toward India during the Pahlavi state, it is necessary to present multifaceted explanation rather than one single factor. For most part, the structure of the international system and the opposite place of Iran and India in it, was the cause of an irony, in which two secular state with many historical and cultural commonalities reflected different stances on the regional and international issues. However, this factor should not make us to neglect other important factors such as the personal role of the Shah as the main foreign policy decision maker in Iran. Though Iran and India were members of the two opposite Cold War political organization (Baghdad Pact-CENTO vis-à-vis. Non-Align Movement), and this made them to have different foreign policy orientations on regional and international issues, the personal rivalry or better to say animosity between Jamal Abdul Nasser, the leader of Egypt and the Shah of Iran played an important role in alienating Iran from the Non-Align Movement. Nasser's position toward Iran, Iranian interests and sovereignty in the Persian Gulf had made the Shah sensitive toward NAM. In fact, if Egypt was not a member of the NAM, it was easier for Shah to accept Iran's membership in NAM.

Iran's cordial relations toward Pakistan in the beginning, i.e., the late 1940s and the early 1950s, were basically a result of the influence of the forces of civil society than higher political elites such as the Shah. During the 1940s strong religious groupings and figures, such as Fadaeeyane Islam (Islam's Devotees) and Ayatollah Kashaani had strong presence in Iranian politics. They used to play the role of Islamic lobbies and tried influence Iranian foreign policy in favour of the Islamic causes such as Palestine and Pakistan. The Shah of Iran at that time was too young to have big influence on Iran's foreign policy. He was basically more involved in military affairs and the Iranian army than politics. It was after 1953 coup d'etate that he could have more control of foreign policy. Nevertheless, his independent personality as a decision maker had not yet gets the proper shape in order to impose his ideas on foreign policy.

Moreover, his fear of communism and the Soviet penetration in Iran made him to rely on American support. However, he gradually began to play independent roles in domestic and foreign policy on the basis of his own reasoning and ideas rather than the dictates of his foreign allies. This was the case particularly during the late 1960s and the early 1970s when he started to challenge Oil Consortium, made up of a group of western oil companies who controlled Iranian Oil industry, and even US energy politics. It was during this period that he started better relations with India. His support of Pakistan during the Indo-Pakistani conflicts was basically under the influence of the cold war mechanisms. His financial and military support of Pakistani government *vis-à-vis.* the domestic and foreign challenges, such as the question of Baluchi insurgency and Greater Pashtunistan, was based on his policy of maintaining regional peace and stability in south west Asia.

Bilateral relations between Iran and Pakistan during the last three decades (1979-2009) had taken a form similar to that of Iran and India during the Pahlavis. The common logic tended to foresee cordial and warm relationships between the states that had based their legitimacy on Islamic rules and principles. However, the factional differences within Islam did not let this to happen. From the early 1980s, by the rise and spread of Shiia-Sunni violent conflicts within Pakistan, it was clear that the interests of the two states would not coincide in a foreseeable future. That happened due to the rise of Taliban in Afghanistan and the strategic support which Pakistan used to give to it in order to insure its benefits in Afghanistan and also in Central Asia. The complexity of the domestic politics and power structure in Pakistan in which the strong fundamentalist extremist Islamic groups have been able to exert their influence in domestic and foreign policy of the state has prevented the expansion of cordial relations between Iran and Pakistan. Though Taliban has been ousted of power, yet other factors such as the rise of the Pakistani-based extremist anti-Shiite groups, has increased the level of deterioration between Iran and Pakistan.

Future Challenges of Indo-Iranian Relations

While the relations between Iran and India in its different aspects and dimensions have improved remarkably during the first decade of the twenty first century, multifaceted domestic, regional and international factors facing the two countries may challenge their relations in future. These challenges can stem from both countries. On the Iranian side, the continuation of the neutral policy toward Kashmir problem which has been the traditional policy of the Islamic Republic should continue, otherwise any Islamist oriented position in this regard can resent India and distort friendly bilateral relations. Rather than emphasizing on the question of Kashmir as an Islamic problem, Iran can play more useful and acceptable role as the mediator in Indo-Pakistani conflict. Both Iran and India are vulnerable toward the radical extremist Islamic terrorism which has targeted both countries during the last years. The Taliban-Al-Qaida linked extremist groups who have resorted to confessional violence against India and Iran do not like to see any improvement in Indo-Iranian relations. As before, Iran should distinguish between the moderate and extremist Islamism and condemn any anti-Indian Islamist activity by radical extremist groups. On the international level, it is up to Iran not to confuse Indo-American or Indo-Israeli ties, as long as they do not harm Iranian national interests, with Indo-Iranian relations.

For India, the challenges come from the international pressure, such as those of the US, for subverting or at least reversing the healthy course of Indo-Iranian relations. Considering the fact that powerful states such as the United States or regional powers such as Israel have their own problems with Iran, they may use their ties with India as an instrument of pressure to affect Indo-Iranian relations. India's last two experience of voting against Iran with the United States on September 24, 2005 on an IAEA resolution finding Iran in non-compliance with its international obligations and again on February 4, 2006 for referring Iranian nuclear case to the security council [31], were clear signs of the international pressure for taking anti-Iranian stances. Though it was clear for Iran and many Indian and western analysts [32] that India had voted under the US pressure, but any kind of further similar moves may have negative effects on bilateral relations. It is up to India to convince its friends in the west or in the region that they must distinguish between Iran's nuclear crisis and its relations with India.

End Notes

1. A.H.H Abidi. 1996. 'Relations between India and Iran, 1947-1979,' *The Iranian Journal of International Affairs,* Vol. vii, No. 4, p. 881.
2. John Calabrese. 2002. 'Indo-Iranian relations in Transition,' *Journal of South Asian and Middle Eastern studies,* Vol. xxv, No. 5, pp. 61-62.
3. Kashif Mumtaz. 2006. "Changing patterns of Iran-India relations," http://www.issi.org.pk/journal/2006_files/no_2/article/al.htm accessed Nov, 11, 2009.
4. Abidi. op.cit, p. 894.
5. Mumtaz, op. cit.
6. Abidi. op.cit. p. 881.

7. Shahram Chubin. 1997. "Iran," in Yzid Sayigh and Fred Halliday, eds. *The Cold War and the Middle East.* New York: Oxford University Press, p. 248.
8. Hushang mahdavi. 1994. *Siyasate Khareji Iran dar Asre Pahlavi.* Tehran: Alborz, p. 335.
9. Chubin. Op.cit. p. 228.
10. Amir Asadullah Alam. 1993. *Alam's Notes*. Tehran: Maziyar, p. 152.
11. Harrison; Shah gave 6 modern helicopters to Pakistan at the midst of Baluchi insurgency, see Alam, op.cit., p. 125.
12. Harrison, op.cit. pp. 148-152.Baluchi Iran.
13. Alam. op.cit.
14. Mark J. Gasiorowski. 1987. 'The Coup d'etate in Iran,' *International Journal of the Middle East Studies.* Vol. 19. No. 3.
15. Mahdavi, op.cit.
16. Farah Naaz. 2005. *The West Asia and India: Changing Perspectives*. Shipra Publications, New Delhi.
17. Mumtaz, op.cit. quoting Calabrese, op.cit. p. 63.
18. Ibid.
19. Mumtaz, op.cit. quoting http://www.nti.org/e_research/profiles/1825_1826.htm
20. Afzal Mahmood. 2001. 'Iran's strategic handshake', *Dawn* (April 23).
21. "Foreign Secretary's Remarks at Discussion Session, 2001. 'India-Iran: From Dialogue to a Convergence of Views' at the India Economic Summit (New Delhi, December 4, 2001)", *Strategic Digest,* Vol. XXXI, No. 12, p. 1624.
22. Mumtaz, op.cit. p. 3.
23. Maghsud ul Hasan Nuri. 2003. "India and Iran: Emerging Strategic cooperation?" in *IPRI JOURNAL,* Vol. III, No. 2, p. 49. Quoted by Mumtaz, op.cit.
24. http://www.meaindia.nic.in/declarestatement/2003/01/25jdl.htm accessed 2009/11/11.
25. Mumtaz. Op.cit. quoting Sudha Ramachandran, "The glue that binds India, Iran, " http://www.atimes.com.pk
26. Howard LaFanchi. 2009. 'Does US road to better relations with Iran pass through India'? http://www.csmonitor.com/2009/0718/p25s05-usfp.htm accessed 2009/11/11.
27. Press TV, 2008. "US$ 13 bn: New Record in Iran-India Trade,"

http://www.presstv.ir/ accessed 2009/11/11.

28. Backgrounders. 2007. "Iranian FM Visit: Backgrounder Indo-Iranian Ties, "http://www.realite-eu.org/site/apps/nlnet/content3.aspx accessed 2009/11/11 quoting Fair, C. Christine, "Indo-Iranian ties: Thicker than oil," *Middle East Review of International Affairs*, June 14, 2007.
29. Ibid. quoting The State Department was seen as complacent, saying New Delhi had reassured Washington that the agreement "doesn't involve military and technical assistance," ("Iran-India pact not a security concern,' State Department official says," *Inside the Pentagon*, February 13, 2003; "India-Iran military ties growing," *Strategic Affairs*, June 16, 2001.
30. Charles J. Adams. 1983. "Mawdudi and the Islamic State", in John L. Esposito, ed., *Voices of Resurgent Islam*. New York: Oxford University Press, pp. 99-134.
31. Weisman, Steven. 2005. "India balks at confronting Iran, straining its friendship with US," *New York Times*, September 15; Misra, Neelesh. 2006. "India says vote against Iran at nuclear agency not under US pressure," Associated Press, September 24.
32. IRNA. 2007. "India's anti-Iran votes were coerced, says former US official," http://www.payvand.com/07/feb/1214.htm accessed 2009/11/11.

5

Nuclear Equation in Iran-India Strategic Relations

Kaveh L. Afrasiabi

This paper deals with what is undoubtedly an important dimension of relations between the Government of India (GOI) and the Islamic Republic of Iran (IRI) today, that is, the nuclear dimension. As "near neighbours" with strong historical and cultural ties, Iran and India share a great deal in the international arena as well as regionally, with the potential to further their mutual interests by expanding cooperation on a range of economic, trade, regional and global issues pertaining to peace and stability, anti-terrorism, counter-narcotics, etc.

The nuclear dimension constitutes a select aspect of these relations that is of special concern to not only Iran and India but also the external powers and which has, historically, acted as both an opportunity as well as a break, indeed a *paradoxical state of affairs* that will likely remain for the foreseeable future and experience the tumults of varying ups and downs depending on the contingent circumstances and changing (geo) strategic atmospherics dominating the overall context of relations between Tehran and New Delhi. The paper is divided into three parts: defining the issue, exploring the areas of feasible nuclear cooperation, and, finally, policy recommendations.

Part One: Defining the Issue

At the outset, a pertinent question: Is there a "nuclear dimension" to Iran-India relations? The answer is, no, yes, and may be. To some extent, this is a dimension on future credit rather than existing arrangements, and above all, it is both a positive and a negative relations that denotes normative as well as policy ambiguity rather than transparency, thus making it difficult to decipher and prognosticate.

On India's part-whose nuclear relations with Iran have been

mortgaged to its new strategic relations with the United States per (if not the explicit terms) the overall understanding of the India-US nuclear cooperation agreement and the relevant US legislations, such as the Hyde Act that explicitly mandates annual review of India's performance on issues of proliferation concern such as Iran–one can nonetheless detect the uncomfortable traces of a built-in bifurcation.

A clue to this bifurcation can be seen in India's endorsement of the September 2006 Havana Declaration on the Non-Aligned Movement on Iran's nuclear right–that "reaffirmed that states choices and decisions in the field of nuclear technology and its fuel cycle policies must be respected." [1] This clearly runs contrary to India's explicit bandwagoning with the US against Iran, twice at the IAEA in September 2006 and February 2006, as well as through repeated official statements, dating back to July 2005, conveying an Indian 'falling into line' while, simultaneously, basking in the rewards of its exemplary "proliferation mainstream." In retrospect, the US-India deal appears increasingly in the light of a pre-emptive agreement, inked by the US to ensure the viability of India's "model" behaviour. [2]

While it remains to be seen how the Obama administration will implement or operationalize the nuclear deal-and there are unmistakable signs of India having "lost ground to China in the new administration's Asia policy" [3] and whether or not New Delhi will leverage its proliferation potential to bring the Obama administration into line on the historic deal that benefits the development of India's civilian nuclear program while at the same time retaining aspects of the 34 year-old sanctions regime on enrichment, reprocessing, dual-use technologies, etc. nonetheless it is abundantly clear that India's incongruent or rather bifurcated stance on Iran will continue to bedevil its foreign policymakers, [4] reflecting an ideological cleavage touching on India's external identity, with several intended and unintended consequences. One such consequence is the *attrition* of India's *prestige* (as an independent actor), ironically just as its nuclear *status* is being elevated due to the so-called "123 agreement." Needless to say, this is an unpleasant trade-off and much depends on the Indian government's diplomatic savvy, and the state's choices and decisions in the months and years to come, to protect all aspects of its national interests in tandem, given the Iran litmus test. However, to do justice to the above-stated question on the nuclear dimension, one must explore both the civilian and (proto) military aspects and do so by making the necessary distinctions between perceptions and misperceptions, facts and fictions.

From Iran's point of view, India's nuclear proliferation is not necessarily a curse and, in fact, contains certain dividends for Iran's national security interests that, in turn, dampen any proliferation tendency in Iran, primarily by virtue of locking the Sunni-led nuclear-armed Pakistan perpetually away from Iran. But, the growing nuclear asymmetry favouring India, that is today bolstering its second strike capability via its nuclear submarines, is a disquieting factor that raises Tehran's concerns about nuclear imbalance in the region, [5] irrespective of New Delhi's presentation of its rapid nuclear superiority in defensive language. This, together with India's concert with the US, represent "game-changing" templates that inevitably affect the calculations of all neighbouring states including Iran.

This aside, both Tehran and New Delhi are today grappling with similar problems–both are facing serious external limitations on their indigenous nuclear fuel cycle, both are pressured on the adoption of the voluntary Additional Protocol, and are commonly concerned about guaranteed nuclear fuel supply, notwithstanding their similar experiences with reneged foreign contracts and frustrated expectations, e.g., the Australian government has reversed its earlier decision to sell Uranium to India once the US-India pact was signed, "on the basis that safeguards fell short of the NPT requirements." [6] Of course, Tehran has fresh memory of how in 1991 India signed an agreement to provide Iran with a 10-megawatt research reactor but cancelled under pressure from the US.

In addition to turning superfluous its own NAM pronouncements on Iran's nuclear program, the fallout on India's energy security as a result of India's "Faustian bargain" with the US is also a matter of interest when probing the nuclear dimension in Iran-India relations. India's ability to leverage the power of NAM for furthering its own goals has now been hampered partly as a result of its new "great power" obsessions that have supplanted the previous globalist preoccupations with a "just world order." A gradual, albeit structural, transformation of India's foreign policy, gleaned from the official discourses surrounding the nuclear deal with the US, raises the spectre of India increasingly acting like the US and its *machtpower* projections.

For sure, the pundits' idea of a "paradigm shift" in India's foreign policy may turn out to be exaggerated and the continuity of a prudent, cautious, and part-idealistic Indian power may well turn out to be the hallmark of its future external behaviour. This is certainly a distinct possibility, yet who can with certainty discount alternative scenarios whereby India's regional pre-eminence and nuclear prowess would fuel interventionism and 'above the horizon' power projections? Such anxieties about India's "ambitions" and, perhaps, even a "grand strategy," abound in West Asia nowadays and need to be put to rest by serious efforts on the part of New Delhi to build confidence in the region and beyond that India does not thread the path of (neo) imperialism, but rather regional cooperation, interdependence and reciprocity. In the absence of such efforts, the close nuclear rapport between US and India will most likely have the unintended consequence of augmenting the proliferation pressures in the continent.

Part Two: Exploring India-Iran Nuclear Cooperation

As is well-known, the government of India has taken several concrete steps in tandem with the implicit linkage of its US agreement with the "non-proliferation" issues in general and Iran in particular: it has passed the WMD Act (in 2005) in conformity with UN Resolution 1540, it has issued directives banning the trade of nuclear material to Iran, it has upgraded its export control regime in coherence with the Nuclear Suppliers Group (NSG), [7] and has put inordinate emphasis on "extreme vigilance" in licensing issues involving Iran, in light of a few past examples of Indian companies found in breach of prohibited trade with Iran. [8]

On the surface, India's behaviour appears to be in conformity with the UN sanctions resolutions on Iran, that are Chapter VII resolutions invoked in the language of world peace and security, yet on closer examination it is clear that India has deliberately omitted a nuanced understanding of those resolutions and, in fact, has *overcommitted* itself to the US's chariot of Iran policy that is also unmindful of those resolutions' own nuances.

Lest we forget, contrary to popular perception, seemingly so widespread in India as well, the UN resolutions do not block the transfer of dual-use technology to Iran. Rather, they call on states to make a determination of whether or not an item sought by Iran would be directly useful in specific programs–enrichment, heavy water, or missiles–and to deny exports based on that determination. Case in point, Paragraph 3 of UN Security Council Resolution 1737, prohibits trade with Iran of "good and technology which could contribute to Iran's enrichment-related, reprocessing or heavy-water related activities, or to the development of nuclear weapon delivery systems."

What is more, these UN resolutions provide for exceptions, i.e., the light-water reactor in Bushehr is exempted from the sanctions' purview and Russia is not barred from supplying nuclear fuel to Iran. Nor is there any bar on IAEA's technical assistance to Iran, in light of some 55 Iran nuclear projects assisted by the agency (curtailed by 40 percent as of 2007); at least one Indian scientist, Dr. Y.S.R. Prasad, has been involved with the IAEA's Iran assistance programs in the past.

This means that there is no legal bar, either by the UN Security Council or the IAEA, against expanding Iran-India nuclear cooperation on a whole range of civilian nuclear activities pertaining to medical, industrial, agricultural, or environmental purposes. Yet, the application of unilaterally enforced, generalized prohibitions on nuclear cooperation with Iran by the Indian government is in contravention of the limits and scopes of the UN resolutions and have, as a result, frozen the possibility of a civilian nuclear agreement between the two countries within the parameters of NPT and IAEA. For India, which has so far signed seven such agreements, such as with Mongolia, Kazakhstan, and more recently with Argentina, the "Iran proliferation concerns" remain the dominant reason why it does not even contemplate a similar agreement with Iran.

In his recent meeting with Iran's president Mahmoud Ahmadinejad, Brazil's president, Lula de Silva, has stated, "We recognize Iran's right to develop a peaceful nuclear program in compliance with international accords." [9] Certainly, various top Indian officials including Prime Minister Dr. Manmohan Singh have repeatedly echoed a similar sentiment, and Dr. Singh has even told the Indian Parliament (in February 2006) that India is opposed to "Iran being declared in non-compliance with its safeguard agreements." Since then, several developments favouring Iran have made it more incumbent, logically speaking, for India to come down on Iran's side more forcefully irrespective of how it may raise some eye brows in the west. Briefly:

1. The 2007 UN National Intelligence Estimate has concluded that

Iran's nuclear program has been peaceful since 2003.

2. The IAEA has repeatedly confirmed the absence of any evidence of military diversion from Iran's peaceful nuclear program, this after extensive inspections that have found "consistency" in Iran's nuclear declarations. [10]
3. All the six "outstanding issues" that were the primary reasons for referring Iran to the IAEA have been resolved in Iran's favour as a result of an IAEA-Iran Work plan, as per the February 2008 report of the IAEA; according to the concluding paragraph of this work plan, Iran's nuclear dossier would be treated as "normal" after the completion of the Work plan.
4. Iran has initiated the idea of a "fuel-for-fuel" swap and has agreed in principle to the framework of an IAEA proposal regarding the exchange of Iran's low-enriched uranium (LEU) for high-enriched fuel required by the small medical reactor in Tehran, and as of this writing the negotiations regarding this matter are on-going.

Considering the latter, it is noteworthy that the US and other "P5 + 1" nations engaged in nuclear talks with Iran (i.e., Russia, China, France, England and Germany) have explicitly consented to the above-said transaction involving Iran's LEU that, from the prism of UN resolutions, has been procured rather illegally, that is, in defiance of the UN Security Council order to suspend Iran's enrichment program. Thus, the mere fact that Iran's 'contraband' LEU has been subjected to a new discourse of implicit if not explicit approval, simply means that the world community has treated the contested Iran nuclear standoff *flexibly* and with *pragmatism*, irrespective of whether or not this deal would eventually go through or, inversely, collapse for one reason or another. In a word, this shifting discourse has the side-effect of introducing a minor tremor in the hitherto robust Indian policy of no nuclear cooperation with Iran. Ironically, at the same time, some of these nations, above all US, have cornered India to a much higher standard, by insisting on a highly restrictive, and extra-legal (from the prism of international law) non-cooperative mode on India's part with respect to Iran's civil nuclear program, pursuant to Iran's NPT "inalienable right" to acquire nuclear equipment and technology for peaceful purposes.

As a result, nuclear cooperation between Iran and India has stalled, despite the fact that countries such as France and even the US may now enter the Iran 'nuclear market" via the IAEA-proposed nuclear fuel deal mentioned above. The US has reportedly considered the option of assisting Iran with "modern instruments" for the safety of Tehran reactor, while France has been named as a candidate for the delivery of fuel rods to Iran. The west's insistence on the outward shipment of a bulk of Iran's LEU, on the ground that it depletes Iran's resources for nuclear weapons, is itself a confirmation of the US's intelligence finding that Iran is not marching toward nuclear weapons, for if there were more than a "proliferation concern" and serious evidence of "weaponization" on Iran's part, then this whole insistence would have been superfluous.

As regards the future prospect of Iran-India nuclear cooperation, it is bound to be impacted by the developments above-mentioned, the net result of which is, theoretically speaking, to open the door a jar on this cooperation, without necessarily overhauling the present export control regime by the Indian government, only altering it by introducing timely adjustments that address the problems of *unbounded prohibitions* incongruent with the UN resolutions mentioned earlier on the one hand and, on the other, the importance of bringing India's Iran policy closer in line with the letters and spirits of NPT standards and IAEA norms, not to mention India's NAM commitments.

Part Three: Recommendations

In order to make possible a revised script for the hitherto absent Iran-India nuclear cooperation, one that would be cognizant of the potential backlashes against India in US Congress, etc., any progress in this area is contingent on its legalism, that is, conformity with the present international sanctions regime on Iran and the set limits and scopes mentioned above. Specifically, this calls for the following recommendations:

1. A joint Iran-India-IAEA review committee to explore the areas of bilateral and trilateral cooperation (with the IAEA) that falls outside the purview of UN sanctions;
2. A review of India's export control policy and the upgrading and fine-tuning of the licensing and end-user certificates of non-diversion and peaceful use, in order to facilitate the areas of further nuclear cooperation between the civilian atomic organizations of Iran and India;
3. A feasibility study, commissioned by the governments of India and Iran, respecting other areas of cooperation, such as

combating nuclear terrorism and cooperation on a region-wide export control and nuclear accountancy, in light of Iran's recent proposed package for constructive negotiations that promises Iran's cooperation in "an effort to encourage other states to control the export of nuclear material and equipment."

In conclusion, the nuclear dimension in Iran-India relations need not be either stationary or mainly negative, projecting the image of a "zero-sum" relations when, in fact, this can be a "win-win" situation, whereby India's willingness to enter a new chapter of *controlled nuclear relations* with Iran for purely civilian purposes, under stringent IAEA safety and safeguard regulations, would carry important dividends for the country's regional and international prestige as an independent actor on the world stage, while simultaneously introducing a qualitative improvement in bilateral relations between the two countries. A final word and that is, the nuclear equation is and, for the foreseeable future, will be a work-in-progress shaped and reshaped by world politics, and to a lesser extent regional realities, and never simply a technical issue.

End Notes

1. India's "schizophrenic" positions cited in this paper may be rooted in the country's changing global status and the absence of a "grand strategy" as lamented by various Indian pundits such as Pratap Bhanu Mehta. See "Still under Nehru's Shadow? The Absence of Foreign Policy Framework," *Centre For Policy Research* (September 2009).
2. The Hyde Act, Section 104g(2)E(1), calls for annual report to the US Congress by the president on India's foreign policy, to ensure its being "congruent to that of the US" and specifically to ascertain that India follows the US's effort to isolate and put sanctions against Iran.
3. Quoted in Ishaan Tharoor, "Making the Case For India," *Time Magazine* (November 24, 2009).
4. In the past, India appears to have made use of subtle use of threat of assisting Iran in order to curry favours with the west. This might explain Foreign Minister Singh's statement to the Parliament in December 2003 that "India has and would continue to help Iran in its controversial bid to generate nuclear energy."
5. See Pat M. Holt, "US Shift on India Nuclear Policy Tilts

Regional Balance," Christian Science Monitor (August 4, 2005); also, Glen Hallick, "Nuclear Balance in Asia Shifts," *The Valley Leader* (Nov. 2009). India already has plans to have three more nuclear submarines in addition to the one, Arihant, that it commissioned in late 2009. A point missed by many western pundits is that the US's selling the nuclear agreement in terms of bolstering India as a "counterweight" to China belies the US's insistence that the agreement is a step forward for the non-proliferation regime. On the latter, see Nicholas Burns, "America's Strategic Opportunity with India," *Foreign Affairs* (Nov/Dec 2007).

6. "India Seeks US Support of Nuclear Pact," *The Age,* November 24, 2009.
7. See Sema Galhault, "India Export Control Policy," www.NPSGlobal.com.
8. For more on this see Sharon Squassoni, "India and Iran: WMD Proliferation Activities," CRS Report for Congress (November 2006).
9. Associated Press, November 24, 2009.
10. For more on this see Afrasiabi, Iran's Nuclear Program: Debating Facts Versus Fictions (Booksurge, 2007). Also, Afrasiabi, "Keeping Iran's Nuclear Potential Latent," Harvard International Review (Winter 2005).

6

India, Iran and the United States: Nuclear Diplomacy

Chintamani Mahapatra

India, Iran and the United States all in principle support the idea of nuclear non-proliferation. The United States, the first state to achieve nuclear weapon status, is the leading nation in promoting non-proliferation. While Washington always desired to maintain its nuclear monopoly by championing the cause of no further proliferation, some of its rivals, adversaries, allies and friends tried and acquired nuclear weapon capability of their own over the decades since the nuclear bombs devastated two Japanese cities during Second World War.

The USSR, the erstwhile superpower rival of the US, was the first to break the US nuclear monopoly. Then the British and the French joined the nuclear club. When China detonated the nuclear explosive in 1964, the nuclear weapon states at the time happened to be the permanent members of the UN Security Council. Although the PRC (People's Republic of China) did not occupy the seat in the UN Security Council, none had any doubt that it would do so soon and the day came after a few years when the PRC was admitted and Taiwan was removed from the UN in 1971.

The US then decided to stop any further proliferation and expansion of the nuclear club and took initiatives with the USSR and its European allies to attain that goal. Neither China nor France acceded to the Nuclear Non-Proliferation Treaty (NPT), but ultimately changed course and joined the NPT. India has refused to sign the NPT until date, but Iran became a member of the NPT. While staying outside the NPT, New Delhi adhered to all the norms of non-proliferation. But India tested a nuclear device of its own in 1974—just four years after the NPT came legally into force. India, by doing so, did not violate any international treaty or law. Moreover, it continued to profess non-proliferation and did not go overtly nuclear. It then changed track after about twenty-four years, conducted a series of nuclear tests in 1998 and declared itself as a nuclear weapon power state! India once again did not violate any international treaty or law, but its decision to do so in the post-Cold war era shocked many in the international community, particularly because the prevailing mood was supportive of additional non-proliferation efforts, as reflected in the negotiations leading to signing of the Comprehensive Nuclear Test Ban Treaty (CTBT). India soon faced a barrage of criticism and a range of international sanctions, particularly imposed by the United States. But in a couple of years, the US approach towards India turned positive with President Bill Clinton's path-breaking trip to India in March 2000. During eight years of administration by President George W Bush US-India relations further improved to an extent that resulted in the signing of a civil nuclear cooperation agreement between the two countries. One of the reasons why the Bush Administration desired to end India's isolation in civilian nuclear market was New Delhi's track record in abiding by the principle of supporting non-proliferation and even championing the cause of establishing a nuclear weapon free world.

Iran's nuclear programme has been in sharp contrast to that of India and the US attitude towards Iranian nuclear programme too has been markedly different from that towards India's. Iran has been a member of the NPT. This membership itself symbolizes Iran's commitment to non-proliferation. It has had a civilian nuclear programme that has got "good behaviour" certificate from the UN watchdog—International Atomic Energy Agency (IAEA) for several years. But the American, Israeli and possibly European intelligence reports have raised doubts about the peaceful nature of Iran's nuclear programme. It is suspected that Iran has nuclear weapon ambitions and that if Iran manages to achieve that status, it would have wide ranging negative repercussions in the security scenario of oil-rich and volatile region of the Persian Gulf. This in turn could affect the economic and security milieu around the globe.

India has been caught in the complex nuclear diplomacy related to Iranian nuclear programme. This paper seeks to address this complexity involving India, Iran and the United States. Nuclear diplomacy cannot be understood in isolation of other political, economic and strategic factors that influence foreign policy behaviour of a state. Hence, it is imperative to outline the broad parameters of US-India, US-Iran and Indo-Iranian relationship before explaining the Iranian nuclear programme.

US-India Strategic Partnership

The emerging strategic partnership between India and the United States indubitably influences the perception and policy of India regarding Iranian nuclear question.

For long, during decades of the Cold War, India and the United States remained estranged democracies, sometimes cooperating, sometimes quarrelling and at other times at logger heads on international issues. There were perennial differences over Kashmir issue, arms transfer to Pakistan and nuclear issues between the United States and India. But the relationship changed direction once the Soviet Union disintegrated and the Cold War terminated.

India and the United States were good trading and investment partners even during the Cold War, but what revolutionized the relationship in the aftermath of the Cold War was steady improvement in defence and security ties between the two. India was opposed to the presence of Great Power navies in the Indian Ocean during the Cold War, but began to do naval exercises with the American navy after the Cold War. Maritime cooperation in dealing with piracy, securing the sea lanes and interdicting drugs peddlers and terrorists on the high seas became the hallmark of Indo-US naval cooperation. The high point in this relationship was cooperation in disaster management during the Tsunami in the Indian Ocean region.

The military exercises between the two countries have not been confined to navy alone and rather encompasses the entire sectors of the military establishment, including army, air force and even counter-insurgency forces. In addition, security cooperation also has been expanded to areas, such as arms trade, intelligence sharing, counter-terrorism cooperation and high level military exchanges to conduct policy dialogues.

US-Iran Confrontation

In sharp variation to Indo-US relations, the United States has followed a policy of containing, confronting and isolating Iran, especially since the 1979 Islamic Revolution in Iran. When India and the US were unable to coordinate their national security policies during the early decades of the Cold War due to alliance formation strategy of the US and non-aligned foreign policy approach of India, Iran had opted for a strategic alliance with the US. It had joined the

US sponsored regional security groupings, such as CENTO or Central Treaty Organization. While CENTO itself was not a very effective anti-Soviet bloc, Iran was not hesitant to join the American-led anti-Soviet bloc politics. This organization was disbanded in 1979, the very year Iran witnessed a successful Islamic Revolution, but during the 1970s when India forged closer security understanding with the Soviet Union, Iran was still with the US on policy issues.

After the revolution, Iran did not switch sides and rather walked a lonely path. The Soviet invasion of Afghanistan could have restored the intimate ties between Iran and the US, but it did not materialize. Iraq, allegedly inspired by Washington, waged war with Iran that continued for about eight years. The Reagan Administration clandestinely sold weapons to Tehran and perhaps desired to restore relationship with Tehran as part of a strategy to counter Soviet military presence in Afghanistan. But the outcome was rather politically disastrous for President Reagan who was hunted by the Iran-Contra scandal and finally Colonel Oliver North became the sacrificial goat. The war with Iraq, dwindling oil revenue, and confrontational policy towards the US contributed towards isolation of Iran.

The end of the Cold War did not alter the situation much. President Bill Clinton's administration decided to adopt a "dual containment" strategy that would simultaneously seek to contain Iraq and Iran. By taking unilateral measures against Iran and enacting even extra-territorial legislation in the form of Iran-Libya sanctions Act, Washington continued its containment policy vis-à-vis Iran.

There have been many attempts since the 9/11 terrorist attacks to establish reasonably good contacts or at least to limit damages in the bilateral relationship. But paradoxical developments have only added to the confusion. For instance, Iran was quite helpful in the US efforts to invade Afghanistan in the aftermath of 9/11, but this turned out to be a temporary phase when the Bush Administration declared Iran to be part of an axis-of-evil. The US complaints have been revolving around the allegation that Iran has been anti-Israel and a sponsor of anti-US and anti-Israel terrorism.

Nuclear Bug

Washington recognizes Iran's constructive position on Iraq and Afghanistan affairs, there have been occasional dialogues between American and Iranian officials on the sidelines of conferences, but the real bug since 2006 has been Iran's nuclear programme.

In 2007, a US National Intelligence Estimate pointed out that Iran ceased to have any nuclear weapon related efforts since 2003. While Iran had already been branded as part of an axis-of-evil in 2002 and this official policy position remained intact, why did the NIE report was made public in 2007? In any case, the Israeli and some European intelligence agencies did not endorse the NIE conclusions and suspected continued Iranian efforts to acquire bomb making capability.

In the backdrop of several IAEA reports absolving Iran of any wrong doing related to nuclear weapon build-up, Iran could claim that no agency had conclusive prove that Iranian government was seeking a nuclear weapon status. The allegations were in the realm of speculations and intelligence analysis. The United States, on the other hand, kept challenging Iran's less than transparent activities and unconvincing answers to revelations of hitherto clandestine effort to enrich uranium.

International doubts over Iran's real ambitions compounded due to Iran's behaviour. First of all, Iran came up with periodic revelations about its enrichment facilities—Qom to Fodar—only after western media reports of such facilities citing intelligence sources. Secondly, Iran adopted a dialoguing and stalling tactics giving rise to suspicion that it was only buying time. Thirdly, Iran took considerable time in responding to international proposals to resolve the issue and then responded only with its own set of counter-proposals. Fourthly, Iran not only refrained from signing the Additional Protocol of the IAEA, but also occasionally threatened to walk out of the NPT. Last but not least, Iran disregarded the UN Security Council Resolutions calling for halting of its uranium enrichment activities.

The US was initially reluctant to negotiate directly with Iran to resolve the nuclear question and outsourced the diplomatic efforts to European troika, consisting of Germany, France and Britain. When the European efforts did not bear fruit, next step was US participation in multilateral effort to negotiate with Iranian leadership. This was known as the P5+1 process consisting of Russia, China, Britain, France and Germany and the US representatives.

While George Bush Administration adopted a dual track policy of engagement and intimidating offering carrots during negotiations and keeping the military options open in response to Iranian defiance, the Obama Administration at first stood up for dialogue and diplomacy. Obama's approach towards Iran has actually not been drastically different from that of his predecessor. While voicing the need for giving diplomacy enough chance and avoiding the language of gun-boat diplomacy, President Obama has not excluded the use of force as an option.

In the American debate among the strategic analysts, one finds the hawks advocating military strike, the doves championing diplomacy and the owls calling for "smart sanctions" to prevent Iran from acquiring nuclear weapon capability. There are also others who desire a regime change. Both the pros and the cons of all these options have been contemplated and valid questions have been raised. To give a few examples, the regime change option is doubted in view of the fact that a new regime may not abandon the nuclear path or that call for regime change may actually strengthen the current Iranian regime and bolster patriotism among the masses.

Secondly, those who oppose Iran as a nuclear weapon state argue that this capability may embolden Tehran to support terrorism, threaten closure of the Strait of Hormuz and spark a war between Israel and Iran. In response, others point out that Iran already promotes terrorism, provokes Israel through outrageous remarks and may not close the Strait of Hormuz because it would affect its own economy and enrage its allies/supporters as well. In response to the military option, it has been contended that Iran has greater strategic depth than Iraq; that the lessons from US military interventions in Iraq and Afghanistan are not positive and that in any case military strike may not be able to eliminate hidden bombs, if any. Even sanctions have well known limitations. After all, Iran has been under some kind of sanctions or other for above three decades and it still retains the capacity to maintain its strategic autonomy and defy the international community and US Security Council Resolutions!

There are some in the United States who appear to have concluded that Iran is not far from being a nuclear weapon capable country, although it may not make an actual weapon. Tehran is in possession of thousands of centrifuges and indulged in enriching uranium. It has certainly the ability to enrich uranium by 4 percent; it claims a capacity to enrich up to 20 percent and thus is not far from being able to enrich it to above 90 percent to acquire fissile material. Recently, when Secretary of State Hillary Clinton spoke of a defence umbrella over the Middle East to meet any Iranian nuclear threat, some interpreted it as if the US Government has already reconciled to the existence of a nuclear Iran.

In replying to the advocates of military strike, who consider Iran's air defence as rudimentary and propose use of stealth aircraft by electronically shutting down Iran's radars and surface-to-air missiles, Defence Secretary Robert Gates pointed out that a military strike could only delay the construction of nuclear bombs in Iran. This is also interpreted as an indication of Washington's reconciliation to the reality of living with an Iranian nuclear weapon capability sooner or later.

In any case, a perception is slowly emerging in the United States that Iran may not actually go for the nuclear bomb, but move towards the nuclear threshold to reap all the benefits of being regarded as nuclear weapon capable state with little cost to bear that would have been the case if weapons were made. But the US policy makers consider even this scenario as substantially threatening to American interests. As a result efforts are on to prevent Iran from moving towards the threshold. The latest success of the Obama Administration in getting a UN Security Resolution passed for the fourth time imposing sanctions on Iran is reflective of this. The US Congress in addition has passed legislation imposing stricter sanctions on Iran, particularly elements of the Iranian Revolutionary Guards who are directly or indirectly responsible for the country's nuclear programme.

Complicating Factors

The main reasons of US failure to induce Iran to relinquish its nuclear programme are many. First of all, Iran has been a member of the NPT and has all the legitimacy to set up a civilian nuclear programme for peaceful purposes. Secondly, it is well established that nuclear energy is safe and clean and fossil fuels are non-renewable sources of energy and Iran easily justifies its civilian nuclear programme on these grounds. After all, increasing number of countries have now been seeking nuclear energy as either alternative or additional sources of energy and that includes the US, China, Russia, India, UAE, Ecuador, Poland and many others. Thirdly, there is no unanimity of assessments among intelligence agencies on the status of Iran's nuclear design. While the NIE of the US claimed that Tehran stopped its quest for the nuclear bomb in 2003, Israel's

Mossad believes Iranian government is incessantly pursuing a nuclear weapon capability. Fourthly, IAEA faces serious problems in the absence of unanimity of views on Iran's nuclear status, since it is empowered to deal with nuclear materials and has no power to make intelligence and document analysis.

Fifthly, when western and Israeli intelligence inputs accuse Iran of acts of commission and commission, Iran challenges those assessments. But the US and Israel maintain that they cannot possibly reveal all their sources to prove their points, because of security reasons and fear of exposing their sources. Sixthly, Russia, China, India, some European countries have extensive trade and business investments and reluctant to punish Iran for unproved nuclear ambitions to an extent that would affect their respective economic interests. Significantly, American big businesses do not have very high stakes in Iran and thus it is relatively easy for US administrations to seek imposition of stricter sanctions on Iran. Finally, North Korea has overtly gone nuclear and more difficulties the US faces in tackling the nuclear tangle more inspired Iran becomes. Tehran watches with certain amount of amusement inability of the US and its allies to speak of military action against North Korea even after its dispute with South Korea over sinking of a submarine with death of more than 40 South Korean sailors. Tehran in a way claims moral high ground by repeatedly mentioning its nuclear programme as the one meant for peaceful uses only.

Notwithstanding these complicating aspects of Iran's nuclear programme, the Obama Administration, like his predecessor, seems to be determined to constrain and contain Iran's alleged nuclear ambition. Here comes the dilemma and difficulties for India.

India's Tightrope Walks

As has been explained earlier, India has had a vibrant relationship with the United States culminating in a strategic partnership between the two countries. But India has also been trying to give a proper shape to its strategic partnership with Iran at least since January 2003. This date is important, since it came after the US declaration of Iran as part of an axis-of-evil. India and Iran share common strategic goals in stabilizing Afghanistan, preventing the return of the Taliban to rule from Kabul, checking spread of extremism and radicalism in the region, promoting peace and stability in Central Asia and cooperating with each other to maintain energy security.

As part of an exercise to maintain a viable strategic partnership, Tehran and New Delhi have also conducted naval exercises, allowed to port calls to each other's naval ships, shared intelligence information, and explored ways of enhancing mutual military training and realizing the potential of arms trade.

India's most ambitious initiative to forge long-term partnership with Iran was through establishment of a gas pipeline between the two countries through Pakistan for supply of Iranian gas to energy hunger India.

India has actually been trying to maintain a de-hyphenated relationship between the United States and Iran. Two countries and two different trajectories of relationship were Indian foreign policy establishment's ambitious goals. But this effort came in for enormous challenge when India sought civilian nuclear cooperation with the US and gas supply arrangement with Iran at the same time. India succeeded in signing a civilian nuclear cooperation agreement with after years of negotiations and hard bargaining. But in the process, its gas deal with Iran did not move smoothly, partly because of the US factor, partly due to Iran's nuclear policy and also because of difficulties of laying the pipeline through Pakistan.

When the United States exerted diplomatic pressure on India to abandon the gas pipeline proposal, India refused to do so. Washington did not want India to reward Iran financially at a time it was seeking to isolate Iran on the ground of its nuclear ambition, but India refused to sacrifice its energy requirements in the midst of its high economic growth and rising demands for energy. But when the Iranian nuclear issue came for discussion in the IAEA and a US-sponsored resolution was introduced to refer the case to the UN Security Council, India voted in favour it. Subsequently India voted twice in the IAEA on the nuclear issue that went against the Iranian interest. Iran was no doubt outraged. The gas pipeline proposal also went into doldrums. Currently, neither the Indo-US nuclear cooperation has taken off nor the Iran-Pakistan-India gas pipeline.

It is in India's interest to successfully achieve both. What India needs to do is to explain its position to both the capitals through diplomatic channels. It would certainly require a diplomatic tight-rope walking. India needs to harp on its position in Tehran that it is not opposed to its civilian nuclear programme. Its vote in IAEA was, among other things, the result of timing. The US Congress was in the process of debating the civilian cooperation agreement and some of the US legislators made their support to the bill conditional upon Indian votes in the IAEA against Iran. India could not have done otherwise when the gas pipeline proposal was going nowhere and the nuclear cooperation agreement with the US was in its supreme national interest to do so. Moreover, India voted along with the majority views, including that of Russia and China, and its vote thus should not be seen in isolation as an anti-Iranian move.

Tehran needs to understand too that India has always opposed any military action against Iran on the ground of its suspected nuclear programme. India has always supported a negotiated settlement of the nuclear issue. India also is not opposed to the civilian use of nuclear energy by Iran.

Likewise, India requires a serious dialogue with the US policy makers on its Iran policy. India has to convince Washington that its strategic partnership with the US could not flourish at the cost of India's vital national interests and that cordial and cooperative ties with Iran are in the critical national interest of the country. India has to ask the US why it has permitted Pakistan to go ahead with the gas deal with Iran, while expecting India to walk out of it. India has to reiterate its position in Washington that it does not support the emergence of a nuclear Iran. So its strategic partnership with Iran should not construe as either anti-American or pro-proliferation.

Conclusion

There is little doubt that the nuclear issue in the Persian Gulf has affected India's ties with the United States as well as Iran. But Indian foreign policy behaviour cannot just be explained by drawing wrong conclusions from rising Indo-US strategic cooperation. There are many Indian scholars and possibly some Iranian scholars who strongly believe that India's vote against Iran in the IAEA was the product of American pressure. By this logic, India has ceased to have an independent foreign policy and that closer defence and security relations with the US has increased American leverage on India to an extent where India is constrained from taking independent position on international issues, such as Iranian nuclear question.

Is it really credible reasoning to maintain this position? First of all, India is not an alliance partner of the United States like that of, for example, Pakistan or Britain or Israel. Secondly, strategic partnership between India and the United states is still under construction and it will take a long while before it becomes a finished product. Thirdly, the United States is not the only country with which India has been trying to forge strategic partnership. Fourthly, India does not go the whole hog with the US to address issues and problems in its neighbourhood. New Delhi and Washington have divergent policies and perceptions of developments in Pakistan and Afghanistan. India refused to contribute military troops to stabilize Iraq, despite serious requests from the Bush Administration. Last but not the least, India and the US are not in the same wave length when it comes to dealing with strategic issues of Asia.

In other words, India continues to maintain an autonomous position on world affairs. Its foreign policy decisions and approaches are dictated by national interest considerations and that its position on the Iranian nuclear issue also can better be explained in terms of national interests as understood and defined by the government in power.

It is also a discernible event that US-Iran confrontation is a signature development in world politics. It has made foreign policy choice difficult for many countries, including India. The future of the Iranian nuclear programme is still uncertain. There are many scenarios. One is that a regime change may lead to a negotiated settlement of the issue. Secondly, Iran may actually go nuclear and the rest of the world has to willy-nilly accept it. Thirdly, there may be surprise military strike by Israel and its consequences are difficult to imagine. Fourthly, the current rounds of tough sanctions may ultimately persuade Tehran to adopt means that would not affect its nuclear energy requirements but would not enable it to achieve weapon capability. Tough days are ahead!

7

India-Iran Bilateral Relations in the Contemporary Period

Jajati K. Pattnaik

The study of India-Iran bilateral relations in the backdrop of foreign policy making offers immense scope for an in-depth and analytical inquiry of the subject from theoretical as well as empirical perspectives. The contours of India-Iran bilateralism are based on the twin philosophies of realism and idealism to cherish their foreign policy objectives in the contemporary international relations based on trust and interdependence. The age-old ties and the strategic considerations signify the importance of prioritizing the objectives of national interest and drawing the future course of bilateral relations in mutually beneficial modes. Peeping into the theoretical formulations and the historicity of bilateral relations, this paper endeavours to map the convergences and divergences in diverse spectrums.

A closer scrutiny of the subject indicates that foreign policy construct is an act of preference of ends over means exhibited by the sovereign states in the international system. The broad objectives defined by the states prioritize the long term goals in terms of national interest. The avowed realists describe national interest in the idiom of power, perceived from the angle of material or military capability. On the contrary, the idealists interpret national interest in the language of universal moral principles for attaining world peace at the cost of military capability of a nation. The moderate realists or idealists draw a line between the two extremes and synthesize the national interest with the universal moral principles. India made a balanced approach and fused the doctrinal foundations of realism and idealism into a coherent whole for pursuing India's national interest in the international sphere. [1] The policy expressed in the cold war era was based on the principles of non-alignment; peaceful co-existence; promotion of world peace: decolonization; elimination of racialism; economic development through international co-operation and democratization of international systems. [2]

The Iranian revolution of 1979 that dethroned Shah's regime brought a new political set-up wherein the system laid emphasis on its Islamic moorings. The foreign policy of Iran also underwent transformation which called for rejection of external supremacy over Iran; preservation of the policy of non-alignment with the dominant powers and independence of Iran in all respects; consolidation of relations with the states searching for peace; repudiation of Iranian ascendancy over others; preservation of solidarity with the Islamic world called 'Islamic-Worldism' and the Third world called 'Third Worldism. [3] No doubt, the principle of non-alignment and opposition to domination or ascendancy paved the way for symmetry in bilateralism, albeit the differences between India and Iran during this stage.

With the demise of Soviet Union in 1989, the cold war politics came to an end. The neo-liberal philosophy order was advanced in the last decade of the twentieth century envisaging free movement of trade, capital, knowledge technology and people across the globe. India ushered economic reforms in the nineties to deal with the emerging trends of globalization. The sustained growth rate during this period brought India's global economic influence and this success led to projections that that India would succeed many European countries as well as Japan by 2020 and United States by 2050. [4]

The economic breakthrough redeemed India's position as a major political player in the global politics. [5] The think-tank of Indian foreign policy interprets the developments in the realm of three concentric circles. The first circle reflects India's emergent relations with the major powers. The second circle connects India to the 'extended neighbourhood' in the region of Indian Ocean comprising of Africa, Central Asia, East Asia, Middle East and Persian Gulf. The third circle incorporates India's linkage immediate neighbourhood nations in South Asia. [6] These concentric circles reflect India's engagement with the global community.

Correspondingly, pragmatism surfaced in the political establishment of Iran after the demise of Ayatollah Khomeini in June 1989.The reformists launched the so-called "Reform Movement" which became a significant political force and popular demands played a greater role in the process of interest articulation. [7] Ali Akbar Hashemi Rafsanjani after assuming the office of the President in the post Khomeini era sought to bring reforms inducting liberal forces called 'pragmatists' a conglomerate of neo-capitalists, entrepreneurs, profit-making farmers, professionals, bureaucrats and technocrats in the decision-making system. [8] He introduced reforms based on his 'LPG' thesis (Liberalization, Privatization and Globalization) to revamp the war-torn economy of Iran and scuttle its isolation through increasing interaction at the regional and global level. [9]

During this period, Rafsanjani struck a balance between the liberal-humanitarian philosophy of the emerging civil society and the revolutionary ethos of institutional mechanism to steer the trajectory of development in Iran. After assuming the office of the Presidency in 1997, Khatami carried on internal and external reforms upholding Islamic ethos and Iranian supremacy across the region and the globe. [10] He mooted the idea of détente to resolve the disputes with the other nations. The strategy of 'Neither East nor West' was gradually replaced by the 'North and South' approach in bilateral relations. [11] Iran's diplomatic support to the US war efforts to contain the Taliban in 2001, silent approval of US attempts to dislodge Saddam Hussein in 2003 and endeavour for diplomatic engagement with the US illustrates 'eclectic pragmatism' of its foreign policy behaviour. [12]

After Mahmoud Ahmadinejad assumed power in 2005, foreign policy of Iran cantered on 'Look to the East', 'Third Worldism' and 'nuclear question'. He followed a 'confrontationist—assertive and accommodationist—active' strategy to define the foreign policy of Iran. The accommodationist policy was applied towards the non-western countries while the assertive policy was meant towards the western countries. However, Iranian Scholars analyze the foreign policy of Ahmadinejad with optimism and define it in the background of 'defensive realism' rather 'hegemonism within the framework of offensive realism'. [13] Notwithstanding the confrontationist or assertive nature of the foreign policy of Iran, certainly, the accommodationist part influenced by the neo-liberal principles would drive her towards forging ties with the nations around the world, and in this perspective its relations with India would be highly significant.

Bilateral Relations

India-Iran bilateral relations have come a long way in recorded history. In the aftermath of Indian independence, it was formalized with a friendship treaty on March 15, 1950 which stated that "there shall be perpetual peace and friendship between the Governments of the two countries and that their differences shall be settled through ordinary diplomatic channel, by arbitration and by such peaceful means as deemed suitable by them." [14]

Much to the chagrin of many, 'Treaty of Friendship' was marred by distrust and animosity. Iran's unswerving support to Pakistan became a major barrier for steady bilateral relations. Further, the military and diplomatic support accorded by Iran to Pakistan during the two Indo-Pak wars also impinged the relations. [15] The bilateralism that was marked by suspicion during the Khomeini era received an impetus after a long time with the coming to power of President Rafsanjani in 1989. The quest for friendship and co-operation on both sides sought to clear the mutual distrust between India and Iran. The visit of Indian Prime Minister P.V. Narasimha Rao to Tehran in 1993 was particularly important since Iran rallied round India's stand of non-interference and called upon all the states to desist from terrorism and subversion in the region. [16] President Rafsanjani even called for cooperation between India, Iran and China and viewed that the three major Asian Powers should take initiative to crystallize it in a proper form to have significant role in global politics. Rafsanjani stated: "If the Asian cooperation is going to be achieved India will be one of the most important axis of such an inter-Asian co-operation." [17] He reiterated that this cooperation existed in other continents in multiple ways but had proved futile in the Asian subcontinent. As he remarked: "Very important countries are in Asia as far as population, industry and markets are concerned. If we cooperate, we, in Asia will be able to have a say in international affairs." [18]

The growing affinity in bilateral relations was observed with the visit of President Rafsanjani to New Delhi in April 1995. [19] During the exchange of views at the highest level, Rafsanjani underlined the significance of the need for increasing strategic cooperation between Tehran and New Delhi to remove external intervention and hegemony in the Asian region. He said "co-operation among Iran, Pakistan, India and China will give no pretext for foreign forces to interfere in the region." [20] On the bilateral economic matters, a good deal of success marked the discussions between the two countries. Both Tehran and New Delhi agreed to expedite the process of laying a gas pipeline from Iran to India. [21] The most successful achievement was the signing of a Memorandum of Understanding (MOU) in April 1995 between Iran, India and Turkmenistan on direct transit facilities for Indian goods into Central Asia through Iran.

The Memorandum also contained cooperation in other fields, i.e., "tourism, telecommunication, postal services, prevention of narcotic drugs and psychotropic substances" among the respective governments. [22] It was anticipated that these agreements would form the core of the efforts for regional economic cooperation with the Central Asian Republics. Iran comprehended the geo-political importance of India as its 'strategic neighbourhood' spread over to the Persian Gulf in the west and the South China Sea in the East. [23] So, the Iranian policy makers coined' Look East policy' in 1997 to improve relations with India, China and Central Asian states to secure access to the Central Asia for natural resource; facilitate the entry of India and the Persian Gulf states to the Central Asian states and serve as a transit point between Central Asia and the Indian Ocean to reap economic dividends for the country. [24] India also offered positive response to the Iranian overture.

Indian Prime Minister Atal Behari Vajpayee paid a visit to Iran in April 2001 and the Tehran declaration was signed on 10 April 2001 to achieve a new breakthrough in their bilateral ties. Both India and Iran realized their historical linkages and desired to materialize this opportunity in political, strategic, technical and cultural fields for regional peace and stability. The two sides also avowed to respect the principles of sovereignty, territorial integrity, equality and non-interference and espouse the thesis of 'Dialogue among civilization' for pluralism, diversity and tolerance in the conduct of international relations. They denounced terrorism in all respects and appealed the Comity of the Nations for initiating strong measures to counter international terrorism. They raised concern over the developments in Afghanistan and resolved to assist in the formation of a broad based government for ensuring peace and stability in the country. [25] The mounting spirit of Indo-Iranian relationship was noticed when President Mohammad Khatami came to India as the Chief Guest in the Republic Day of 2003 and the Delhi Declaration was signed along with the " Road Map to Strategic Co-operation" for a stable ,safe and flourishing region. [26]

However, India's vote for a resolution sponsored by EU-3

(France, Germany and Unite Kingdom) on the nuclear issue of Iran at the International Atomic Energy Agency (IAEA) Board Meeting in September 2005 raised apprehensions among the foreign policy watchers to persist stable and secured bilateral ties. New Delhi clarified those doubts by saying that India did not want any crisis out of the prevailing situation. The spokesperson of the Indian Ministry of External Affairs said "In our explanation of [the] vote, we have clearly expressed our opposition to Iran being declared as non-compliant with its safeguards agreements. Nor do we agree that the current situation could constitute a threat to international peace and security. [27] He further said "Nevertheless, the resolution does not refer the matter to the Security Council and has agreed that outstanding issues be dealt with under the aegis of the IAEA itself. This is in line with our position and therefore, we have extended our support to it." [28] Equally, it was perceived that India sought a negotiated settlement based on conciliation. Justifying this Spokesperson also said: "It should also be borne in mind that India has all along been supportive of the EU-3 initiative to negotiate a fair and reasonable understanding with Iran on this issue. Our support to the resolution should also be seen against this background. We have been in close touch with the EU-3, and External Affairs Minister has himself been meeting with and talking to his French, German, and British counterparts regularly in the past couple of weeks, to try and encourage a conciliation approach." [29] Besides, India also showed concern over this subject and counselled Iran to adopt flexibility. [30]

Indo-Iranian relations were hampered when India voted along with the twenty seven nations at the IAEA Board Meeting to refer the Iran issue to the United Security Council in 2006. Clarifying India's stand on voting against Iran, the Spokesperson of the Ministry of Affairs said it "should not be interpreted as in any way detracting from the traditionally close and friendly relations we enjoy with [that country]". "It is our conviction that our active role, along with other friendly countries, enabled the tabling of a resolution that recognizes the right of Iran to peaceful uses of nuclear energy for its development, consistent with its international commitments and obligations, while keeping the door open for further dialogue aimed at resolving the outstanding issues within the purview of the IAEA". [31]

Subsequently, Minister of External Affairs Pranab Mukherjee

paid a visit to Tehran in February 2007 to give a fresh impetus to Indo-Iranian relations. He said that India and Iran have historical bonds and their strength lies over centuries of cooperation. He anticipated that India and Iran can explore the opportunities in various spheres for cementing their ties. [32] Later, President Mahmoud Ahmadinejad visited India in April 2008 and expressed satisfaction over India's "good and appropriate response" to the US diplomacy for raising the nuclear enrichment issue during his trip to New Delhi. [33] He said that "Each vote has its own impact" and Indo-Iranian bilateral relation is "deeper than a vote". "It is related to the past and we are looking forward." [34] He expressed that India and Iran are ready to strengthen wide-ranging aspects to give a new direction to Indo-Iranian relations. [35]

Again the growing spirit of friendship was marked with the visit of Iranian Foreign Minister Manouchehr Mottaki to New Delhi on November 16-17, 2009. During his sojourn, he discussed matters on energy security, economic cooperation, and regional as well as common threats on terrorism with the Indian counterparts. [36] India yet again voted along with twenty five nations in November 2009 in favour of a resolution at the IAEA to send the nuclear issue of Iran to the UN Security Council while indicating in the explanation vote that it "cannot be the basis of a renewed punitive approach or new sanctions." [37] New Delhi also reiterated its stand to resolve this matter through dialogue at the IAEA Meet. [38] There was no marked departure in Indo-Iranian relations during this period. Likewise, the Indian External Affairs Minister, S.M. Krishna also showed positive response to Iranian approach during his recent visit to Tehran on May 15-18, 2010 on the occasion of G-15 summit and shared his views on bilateral, regional and international developments with the Iranian establishment. [39] The developments as well as the recent overtures in bilateral relations signify India and Iran are again poised to promote friendship and co-operation to reap the dividends in an era of interdependent world for mutual benefits irrespective of their reservations.

Mapping the Convergences and Divergences

The theoretical underpinnings as well as various developments in bilateral relations provide us key inputs for mapping the convergences and divergences between India and Iran. Objective interpretation of the subject would divulge its veracity and offer new parameters to steer the course of Indo-Iranian bilateral relations in future.

Civilizational as well as historical ties between India and Iran pave the way for convergence in bilateral relations. There is an effort to champion the thesis on Dialogue among Civilizations to ensure peace, security and development in international relations. Dialogue among civilizations can be achieved through "actual instances of interaction and penetration of cultures with each other resulting from a variety of factors, present one mode in which this dialogue takes place." [40] This mode is natural determined by geographical position, historical incidence and social occurrence. [41] It also indicates a "deliberate dialogue among representative members of various civilizations such as scholars, artists and philosophers from disparate civilizational domains". [42]

The question raised here is: Has the Thesis on "Dialogue among Civilizations" become a universal paradigm to ensure peace in the contemporary world? Of course, answer is not derived in absolute terms. The experts on international politics opine that the thesis has not yet provided "a paradigm in the Thomas Kuhnian meaning of a conceptual resource applied to make sense of the world," rather "it is at best a problematisation in the Foucauldian sense that serves to debunk the clash of civilisations counter-theory, and to create concepts that are pivotal for the maintenance of a just and peaceful world order." [43] The dialogue as a discourse creates an atmosphere for 'collective legitimization' and the derivatives are drawn at the bilateral as well as multilateral levels through pluralistic approach rather than any monolithic or hegemonic one. [44] As a synthesis of differing values, the thesis can be interpreted through the world view of 'utopian realism'. [45] Contemplating the utopian considerations of the thesis, Khatami had stated: "From an ethical perspective, the paradigm of dialogue among civilizations requires that we give up the will for power and instead appeal to the will for empathy and compassion. Without the will for empathy, compassion and understanding there would be no hope for the prevalence of order in our world." [46]

What is noticed here is that the ideological schism between the oriental and occidental perspectives would lead to nowhere. Rather, a symbiotic approach imbued with the Eastern and the western values or fusion among them would facilitate in building up a universal paradigm as well as materializing a truly global society. In this context, India and Iran sharing the ethos of their great civilizations in history, culture, art, architecture, science and medicine can substantially contribute to the development of present day world afflicted with challenges on many fronts.

India and Iran are strategically located in the Asian continent and are mutually inevitable to each other. India is the bridge to Iran's Look East policy and reverse is the example for India's access towards West Asia, Central Asia and Caspian Sea region. India's strategic setting is perceived in the broader canvass of Indian Ocean and its strategic depth in the west spreads up to the Eastern Coast of Africa through the Strait of Hormuj, and in the East it extends up to the South China Sea including the Strait of Mallaca, and in the South it expands up to Antarctic. [47] India has a significant role in the region looking from its policy of 'Extended Strategic Neighbourhood.' The Ministry of Defence, Government of India, in the Annual Report (2005-2006) mentions "slow but steady" development in attaining "a truly multi- polar world, with India as one of the poles." [48] Depending upon its economic and political influence, it seeks to play a positive role and deter any threat to maintain peace and stability in the region.

Iran being strategically located in the Persian Gulf region would add to India's advantages to secure its national interest, and Indo-Iranian co-operation in this sphere would accord primacy to India in materializing its objectives in its extended strategic paradigm. Moreover, twenty first century is dubbed as an Asian century. India and Iran being the significant Asian neighbours with immense potentialities can really shape the destiny of Asia roping in other neighbours for common Asian Union with common currency plus visa regime. This project would dissipate the differences and realize the strategic think-tanks' vision of turning 21st century into an Asian Century in near future.

India and Iran being the members of Non-Aligned Movement share common perceptions in their bilateral relations and have affirmed in the times of yore to champion the principles of sovereignty, territorial integrity, non-interference and equity for peace and security at the regional and global level. The question raised here is how far the Non-Aligned movement is relevant in the present day world order? The answer is that the NAM is not be mirrored in a myopic vision of cold war politics of the twentieth century, rather it is to be revitalized in the context of changing contours of contemporary international relations. The neo-liberal paradigm that guides the foreign policies in the present day world order aims at securing growth and development through an interdependent and harmonious world. However, the gap between the developed and developing countries increased in spite of the benefits of global capitalism. It augmented global inequity and created 'a world of winners and losers'-a few blooming with prosperity and many sunk in a life of distress. [49] Thus, India and Iran along with the other members are to rejuvenate the NAM to bridge the economic divide between the developed and the developing nations and halt the discriminatory policies of the neo-liberal regime. Moreover, they should address the challenges confronted by the world community on international terrorism, global warming, climate change and ecological hazards to pave the way for peace and sustainable development in the contemporary international relations.

The formation of Asian Union as a corollary to the European Union would promote neo-liberal mode of development linking East with the West or orient with the occident. North-South Corridor project in terms of time and space affords better opportunities for both India and Iran to have access with Europe and Russia. The Corridor links India and Iran with Europe and Russia involving four fold transportation processes. These are:

1. Firstly, there would be transhipment of goods from the ports in India to the ports of Bandarabbas and Chabahar in Iran.
2. Secondly, there would be transit of goods by the Iranian railways to the ports of Bandar Anjali and Bandar Amirabad of Caspian Sea.
3. Thirdly, there would be passage of goods through the Caspian Sea to the Port of Astrakhan in Russia.
4. Fourthly, there would be transit of goods through road and railways in Russia across Eastern Europe to Central and Western Europe. [50]

An optimistic introspection of the project indicates that it would fetch gains for the parties engaged in it. One major advantage of North-South Corridor is that it covers 6,245 kilometres, whereas the present maritime transport route across the Mediterranean Sea and the Red sea is 16,129 kilometres. [51] Undoubtedly, the North-South Corridor would reduce the cost of transportation by thirty percent and transit period by forty percent. [52] Further, if this is connected with the ongoing South-East Asian transport corridor, it would provide outlet to both India and Iran for better economic integration with other regional economic groupings such as European Union (EU) and Association of South East Asian Nations (ASEAN). However, the realization of the project hinges upon the political will as well as interest of the international investors and transport bidders to undertake such mega project.

Afghanistan is the conduit between Central, South and West Asia and could be a major transit point for trade and energy between India and Iran. The 217 kilometer Zaranj-Delaram highway built up by India is linked with the 'garland highway' of Afghanistan connecting Zaranaj with Kabul, Kandahar, Herat, Mazar-e-sharif and kunduz. Indian and Iranian goods from the chabahar port across the land corridor of Iran would traverse Zaranj and other cities of Afghanistan through these highways. [53] Similarly, goods from Afghanistan would disembark at the Chabahar port through the land route of Iran. Further, India and Iran using the transit corridor of Afghanistan can transport the goods to the central Asian countries. [54] The region can emerge as a potential centre for multilateral trade if peace and stability is upheld in Afghanistan. The multilateral diplomacy to resolve the Afghan crisis at London called for security, reintegration, and governance, regional and international co-operation. A sustained political system free from inherent domestic conflict can only generate peace and stability in the region and fetch gains for India and Iran. No doubt, India relies upon an indigenous integration model comprising of groups that could renounce terror and violence, and adhere to the Afghan constitution based on the principles of democracy, pluralism and human rights. [55] Thus, India and Iran sharing values of political assimilation can reinforce the institution building process and restore peace and stability of Afghanistan.

The Iran-Pakistan-India (IPI) gas pipeline is a potential trilateral project being accorded priority for economic and strategic considerations. Iran thinks through this trilateral venture it can reap economic dividends as well as extend its relations with both India and Pakistan. Of course, the Idea of gas pipeline termed as the 'peace pipeline' was mooted in 1993. It was projected that the India-Iran-Pakistan (IPI) Gas pipeline covering around 2,275 kilometres would start from South Pars Gas field of Iran in the Persian Gulf and after passing through Khuzdar city of Pakistan, one of the branches would reach Karachi and the other India by Multan. [56]

President Mohmoud Ahamadinejad during his visit in July 2008 reassured Iran's full co-operation for the success of IPI trilateral project and envisaged for quadrilateral agreement including China in this arrangement. Indian political establishment expressed keen interest for carrying out the IPI pipeline to meet the growing demand for energy. However, New Delhi put forth suggestions to Iran regarding the source, security of the gas pipeline in Pakistan and prospective participation of Indian companies in Pakistan in this joint endeavour. [57]

Besides this, there are major problems crop up before India for laying IPI gas pipeline project. These are:

1. Pakistan might provide lukewarm response towards participation of Indian companies in Pakistan.
2. It might disrupt the gas pipeline route to due to any incompatible interest with India.
3. It might not provide adequate security to the gas pipeline given the nature of recent spate of terrorism.
4. The military establishment might not allow going ahead with such grand project which in latter's perception might be more beneficial for India political regime of Pakistan might go ahead with the proposal.

In the event of these uncertainties, the off-shore gas pipeline is being considered as an alternative and being studied by South Asia Gas Enterprises private Limited (SAGE). It is being viewed that the under water gas pipeline ,if starts from the Chabahar port in Iran would cover around 684 miles across the bed of Arabian Sea to deliver gas at the Gujarat coast in India. [58] The gas pipeline would be financed by the international investors and possibly the Italian enterprises would undertake this project. "The carrying capacity of the gas pipeline's first leg will be a total of 31billion cu.m. annually, with the cost of construction estimated at US$ 4 billion," observed T.H.P. Pao, Head of the Supervisory Board of South Asia Gas Enterprise Private Ltd. (SAGE). [59] A through study of the above projects indicates that the success of onshore project is for the benefit of India, Iran and Pakistan. There is need for political will as well as pragmatic diplomacy on the part of all the stakeholders for the early finalization of IPI. The realistic scenario demands India, Pakistan and Iran being the immediate neighbours should sort out their differences over IPI through trilateral negotiations reckoning the benefits accrued from this, and pave the way for IPI project to ensure growth and development of the region.

India has become a strategic partner of the United States in the changing global environment. Iranian foreign policy establishment does not approve of such tie-up owing to her estranged relations with the US. But Indo-US partnership is a natural corollary of India's policy of global engagement in the neo-liberal age of integration. Equally, it is also felt that a secluded Iran is not in the interest of India as it would have adverse impact upon the peace and stability of the South west Asia. [60] So, Confrontation between Iran and US would not pay benefit to either in the long run perspective; rather it would create tension or conflict in the region. An attitude of co-operation and collaboration would fetch gains for both Iran and US paving the way for common collaboration. Furthermore, in the event of melt down of ice between Iran and US, it would transform the regional equation in favour of India compared to other Asian neighbours because of India's age-old proximity with Iran. In this context, India as an important power can be the negotiator and can bring Iran and US to the negotiating table through diplomacy and global leadership.

India's voting over the Iranian nuclear issue in the IAEA Board of Governors Meet in the past created eyebrows in the political establishment of Iran. However, India has clarified that it sought peaceful resolution of the nuclear issue through dialogue and conciliation. It supports Iran's right for peaceful use of nuclear technology. It does not approve of force or sanctions to solve the problem. While dealing with the EU-3 earlier, it signalled for fair and reasonable approach on Iran through mutual understanding. India envisages that its policy of engagement would facilitate Iran for negotiated settlement.

The UN Security Council enforced fourth round of sanctions against Iran in June 2010 suspecting development of nuclear weapons which Tehran claims solely for peaceful purposes. Iran described the resolution "illegal" and pronounced 'it will take retaliatory measures if Iran's legitimate interests are jeopardized'. [61] Recently, India is elected as a non-permanent member to the UN Security Council and given its principled stand for peaceful resolution of conflict at the international fora; it would act considerably to the resolve the nuclear question of Iran through pacific means. Obviously, External Affairs Minister of India, S. M. Krishna, in a press conference said "On sanctions India's position is fairly well known. On Iran we have had occasions to exercise our vote on one or other occasion. So, India will certainly take a constructive view. We believe that all questions between nations will have to be resolved by mutual discussions. And India will continue to work in that direction." [62] Positively analyzed, this would be steppingstone towards the resolution of Iranian nuclear issue with a fresh perspective.

Likewise, India's response to the American unilateral sanctions against Iran is quite reasonable. It is to be noted that the US has imposed fresh sanctions on Iran in July 2010 for alleged infringement of nuclear norms containing the third countries to clinch any deal or contract with the energy firms in Iran. No doubt, the imposition of unilateral sanctions on Iranian Firms would mar the economic interest of India in the energy sector. It is also apparent that India holds up the rights of all states for peaceful use of nuclear energy in consonance with the international norms and seeks to resolve the matter through dialogue evading confrontation. [63] India views that the International Atomic Energy Agency (IAEA) 'continues to provide the best framework for addressing technical issues related to the Iranian nuclear programme'. [64]

The Foreign Secretary of India Nirupama Rao said in this context: "We are justifiably concerned that the extra-territorial nature of certain unilateral sanctions recently imposed by individual countries, with their restrictions on investment by third countries in Iran's energy sector, can have a direct and adverse impact on Indian companies and more importantly, on our energy security and our attempts to meet the development needs of our people." [65] Thus, the need of the hour is to facilitate sustained dialogue between Iran and US to bridge the trust deficit and subsequently pave the way for mutual rapprochement in the long term interest of India, Iran and US.

To revisit India-Iran relations in the context of changing international relations, one would really come across a great deal of convergence in the nature of bilateralism. The perception of Tehran over growing Indo-US co operation as well as India's role in the past at the IAEA over the Iranian nuclear issue remains the major divergences, albeit New Delhi has clarified its stand to Iran on several occasions. Never the politics of distrust, but the politics of partnership can transform the nature of bilateralism or multilateralism. Thus, India and Iran should carry forward their ties based on pragmatism as well as idealism to overshadow the divergences and cherish their mutual objectives in an enduring partnership.

End Notes

1. J. Bandyopadhyaya, *The Making of India's Foreign Policy*, (New Delhi: Allied Publishers Private Limited, 1987), pp. 4-5.
2. M.S. Rajan, *Recent Essays on India's Foreign Policy*, (Delhi: Kalinga Publications, 1997) pp. 22-23.
3. Amir M. Haji-Yousefi, *Iran's Foreign Policy During Ahmadinejad: Confrontation to Accommodation,* Paper Presented to the Annual Conference of the Canadian Political Science Association, June 2-3, 2010, Concordia University,Montreal,Canada,www.cpsa-acsp.ca/papers-2010/Haji-Yousefi1.pdf Accessed on 22 August 2010.
4. C. Raja Mohan, "Indian Foreign Policy", *World Focus,* vol.xxviii,No.11&12, November-December 2007, p. 392.
5. Ibid, pp. 392-393.
6. Ibid.
7. Mehran Kamran and Manochehr Dorajji, *Iran Today, An Encyclopaedia of Life in the Islamic Republic,* (London: Greenwood Press, 2008), pp. 423-426.
8. A. H. H .Abidi, " Iran: Resilience at Home ,Problems Abroad" in Girijesh Pant, P. C. Jain and A. K. Pasha (eds.),Gulf Studies Programme, School of International studies, Jawaharlal Nehru University, New Delhi, *Contemporary Iran and Emerging Indo-Iranian Relations,* (New Delhi: Neelkanth Publishers,1996), p. 18.
9. Ibid.
10. Arshin Adib-Maghaddam, *Iran in World Politics: The Question of Islamic Republic,* (London: Hurst and company, 2007), p. 74.
11. Yousefi, n. 3.
12. Adib-Maghaddam, n. 10, p. 74.
13. Yousefi, n. 3.
14. A.H .H. Abidi, "Relations between India and Iran :1947-1979", *Working Paper,* Gulf Studies Programme, Centre for west Asian Studies, School of International studies, Jawaharlal Nehru University, New Delhi,1994,p. 6.
15. Jajati K. Pattnaik, "Prospects for Indo -Iranian Relations", *The Pioneer,* 12 October 1994.
16. Iran Endorses India's Stand on Interference, *The Times of India,*

21 September 1993.

17. India, Iran, China Cooperation, *The Hindustan Times*, 19 September 1993.
18. Ibid.
19. Iran Moots Strategic Regional Cooperation, *The Hindu,* April 20, 1995.
20. Ibid.
21. India, Iran, Turkmenistan Sign MOU on Transit Facilities, *The Times of India,* April 19, 1995.
22. MOU Signed on Trade with Iran, Turkmenistan, *The Hindu*, April 19, 1995.
23. C. Christine Fair, "Indo- Iranian Relations: Prospects for Bilateral Co- operation Post 9-11" *Asia program Special Report*, No. 120, April 2004, http://www.iranwatch.org/privateviews/ww/cs/perpex-wwwics-strategic partnership-0404.pdf Accessed on 23 November 2009.
24. J. Roshandel, "The overdue Strategic Partnership between Iran and India," *Asia Program Special Report*, No.120, 2004, http://www.iranwatch.org/privateviews/ww/cs/perpex-wwwics-strategic partnership-0404.pdf Accessed on November 23 2009.
25. Tehran Declaration, Ministry of External Affairs, Government of India, New Delhi. http://www.mea.nic.in/events/2001/04/10event01.htm Accessed on November 23, 2009.
26. John Cherian, "An Entente with Iran", *Frontline*, Vol. 20, No. 3, 1-14. February 2003.
27. Amit Baruah, India's IAEA Vote was Decided in Advance, Accessed on 1 December 2009, www.hindu.com/2005/09/26/.../2005092606971100.htm Accessed on December 1, 2009.
28. Ibid.
29. Ibid.
30. Ibid.
31. MEA Official Spokesperson Response to Questions on India's Vote on Iran nuclear Issue at the IAEA Board Meeting in Vienna, February 4, 2006 http://svaradarajan.blogspot.com/2006/02/iaea-votes-to-refer-iran.html Accessed 21 October 2006.
32. Visit of Hon'ble Minister for External Affairs, H.E. Mr. Pranab Mukherjee to Tehran, Embassy of India, Tehran,

www.indianembassy-tehran.ir/press_release.php?id=16 Accessed on November 28, 2009.

33. IPI Gas Pipeline Deal Soon, Says Iran President, http://www.hindustantimes.com/IPI-gas-pipeline-deal-soon-says-Iran-President/Article1-307828.aspx Accessed on December 1, 2009.
34. Ibid.
35. Culled from an Interview with the Foreign Minister of Iran, Manouchehr Mottaki by Siddharth Vardarajan, "Iran hopes President Obama can deliver on his Promises", *The Hindu*, November 17, 2009.
36. "India-Iran bilateral relations", Embassy of India Tehran,http://www.indianembassy-tehran.ir/india-iran_relations.php Accessed on October 22, 2010
37. Pranab Dhal Samant, "Again, India Votes against Iran's nuclear Programme", http://www.expressindia.com/latest-news/Again-India-votes-against-Irans-nuclear-programme/547319 Accessed on 21 October 2010. See "India Vote against Iran at IAEA", http://timesofindia.indiatimes.com/india/India-votes-against-Iran-at-IAEA/articleshow/5276462.cms Accessed on October 24, 2010.
38. Ibid.
39. http://www.indianembassy-tehran.ir/india-iran_relations.php Accessed on October 20. 2010.
40. "Round Table: Dialogue among Civilizations," New York: United Nations, September 5, 2000, *Provisional Verbatim Transcription Address* by H. E. Mr. Mohammad Khatami, President of the Islamic Republic of Iran, www.unesco.org/dialogue /en/khatami.htm Accessed on May 11, 2010.
41. Ibid.
42. Ibid.
43. The "United Nations and the Idea of Dialogue among Civilsations", Kaveh L. Afrasiabi, *Global Dialogue*, Vol. 3, No. 1, Winter 2001, http://worlddialogue.org/content.php?id=135 Accessed on May 11, 2010.
44. Ibid.
45. Ibid.
46. Khatami, n. 40.
47. C Christine Fair, "Indo-Iranian Ties Thicker than Oil, *The*

Middle East Review of International Affairs, Vol. II, No. I, March 2007, http://meria.idc.ac.il/journal/2007/issue1/jv11noa9.html Accessed on 19 October 2010.

48. Cited in Ibid.
49. Anthony Giddens, *Runway World: How Globalization is Reshaping Our Lives*, (London: Profile Books, 2004), p. 15. Jajati K Pattnaik, "A Critique of Neo-Liberal Development," *Mainstream*, Vol. XLVI, No. 26 p. 15.
50. Sudha Rmachandran, "India, Iran Russia Map out Trade Route", www.atimes.com/ind-pak/DF29f02.html Accessed on August 15. 2010.
51. Ibid.
52. North-South Corridor, A Special Opportunity for Iran's Activation in International Trade, *Iran International Magazine*, No. 26, November 2003, http://www.iraninternationalmagazine.com/issue_26/text/north-south.htm Accessed on May 15, 2010.
53. Sudha Ramachandran, "India Takes a Slow Road", 27 January 2007, http://www.atimes.com/atimes/South_Asia/1A27D04.html Accessed on August 15, 2010.
54. Ibid.
55. Statement by External Affairs Minister S. M. Krishna at Kabul Conference, July 2010, http://www.indianembassy.org/prdetail1559/statement-by-external-affairs-minister-mr.-s.m.-krishna-at-kabul-conference Accessed on October 22, 2010.
56. Ariel Cohen, Lisa Curtis and Owen Graham, "The Proposed Iran-Pakistan- India Gas Pipeline: An Unacceptable Risk to Regional Security," *The Heritage Foundation*, May 30 2008,http://www.heritage.org/research/reports/2008/05/the-proposed-iran-pakistan-india-gas-pipeline-an-unacceptable-risk-to-regional-security Accessed on September 1, 2010.
57. Excerpts from an Interview with S. Rahim Mashaee by Atul Aneja "Iran has Addressed India's Concern on Gas Pipeline Project", *The Hindu*, August 6, 2008.
58. "Under water Gas pipeline with India on Track" http://www.zawya.com/story.cfm/sidZAWYA20100526043759/Underwater percent20Gas percent20Pipeline percent20With percent20India percent20on percent20Track Accessed on

October 19, 2010.

59. Ibid.
60. Girijesh Pant, "India, Iran and US in Post-9/11 Period" in Anwar Alam (ed.), *Iran and Post-9/11 World Order*, (New Delhi: New Century Publications, 2009), pp. 105-106.
61. "Iran Vows Firm Response to Illegal Resolution 1929" http://www.tehrantimes.com/index_View.asp?code=221577 Accessed October 23, 2010.
62. Press Conference by EAM on India's Election to UNSC, http://meaindia.nic.in/mystart.php?id=190016563 Accessed October 15, 2010.
63. http://www.thehindu.com/news/national/article501500.ece Accessed on September 17, 2010.
64. Ibid.
65. Ibid.

8

Indo-Iranian Relations and Defence Cooperation

Monika Chansoria

Introduction

As nations in Asia compete to project a greater role for themselves, the tool of defence cooperation could well complement diplomatic enterprise towards issues that prove to be of common interest. This phenomenon has progressively been accredited the world over. Sprouting geo-strategic realities call for engagement with significant players in the Asian region and the case of India and Iran is best applicable to this veracity. Of all the controversies that have surrounded Iran of late, India has made lucid efforts to project the Iranian case as symbolic of the sovereignty of its foreign policy orientations. The complexities of the Indo-Iranian ties could be attributed to the 'American angle' attached to this equation as New Delhi walks a tightrope whilst its ties with the United States (US) burgeon. In addition, fostering a close relationship with Israel also proves to be a litmus test for New Delhi vis-à-vis Tehran.

Since the end of the Cold War, New Delhi has been slowly but surely forging a comprehensive relationship with Tehran based on energy and commercial cooperation, infrastructure development in Iran and beyond, and purported military and intelligence ties. [1] Iran holds particular importance for India as it provides unique access to Afghanistan and Central Asia, two theatres in which India seeks to project greater influence. [2] As New Delhi promulgates a "look-east" policy to develop and sustain a multifaceted presence in the greater Middle East, Iran unquestionably is an instrumental player in this set up. [3]

The two nations display a range of converging interests encompassing regional and international issues that include countering terrorism, the fluid security situation in Afghanistan and energy security—acknowledged by India's Ministry of External Affairs on March 28, 2009 when it released a statement stating the same. During discussions between National Security Advisor MK Narayanan and Iran's Secretary of the Supreme National Security Council Saeed Jalili, while he was on a visit to India, cooperation in combating terrorism flowing from the region assumed prime importance. Recently, Indian External Affairs Minister, SM Krishna, condemned the terrorist attack in Iran's south-eastern province of Sistan-Baluchestan terming it as 'savage.' As many as 41 people including top commanders of the Islamic Revolution Guards Corps (IRGC) were killed in this attack for which, Pakistan-based Jundallah terrorist group claimed responsibility. [4]

Defence and Military-to-Military Collaboration: A Proclivity

India and Iran's strategic partnership has significantly put in place military and energy deals valued at over US$ 25 billion. The broad range of cooperation involving all three military services is quite a turnaround in the strategic situation in Southern Asia in the last two decades. In fact, in its 2005-06 Annual Report, Ministry of External Affairs in New Delhi claimed that Indo-Iranian cooperation had "acquired a strategic dimension flourishing in the fields of energy, trade and commerce, information technology and transit." [5]

The establishment of the Indo-Iran Joint Commission in 1983 was instrumental in so far as forging New Delhi's defence and military ties with Tehran were concerned. As the Iran-Iraq war drew to a close in 1988, Iran felt the need to rebuild its conventional arsenal and initiated the process with purchases of tanks, combat aircrafts and ships from Russia and China. Further, Iran reportedly asked for Indian assistance in 1993 to help develop new batteries for three Kilo-class submarines it had purchased from Russia. The submarine batteries provided by the Russians were ill suited to the warm waters of the Persian Gulf, and India possessed substantial experience operating Kilos in warm water. [6] In addition, Iran is also inclined for acquiring Indian assistance with other upgrades to Russian-supplied military hardware, crucially including MiG-29 fighters, warships, subs, and tanks.

Defence ties between India and Iran further evolved post signing a Memorandum of Understanding (MoU) on defence cooperation in 2001. It was in the same year that India's Defence Secretary, Yogendra Narain, met his Iranian counterpart, Ali Shamkani, and supposedly discussed arms sales to Iran including Indian Konkurs anti-tank guided weapons and spare parts. [7] India and Iran are hopeful that New Delhi will become a source of conventional military equipment and spare parts for Iran, provide expertise in electronics and telecommunications, train Iran's armed forces, and grant assistance with upgrades for many of Iran's Russian weapons systems. Iran also wants India to provide combat training for missile boat crews as well as simulators for ships and submarines and purportedly anticipates that India can provide midlife service and upgrades for fighters, warship, and subs in Indian dockyards. [8]

Bilateral defence and security ties received a boost as Iranian President Hojjatoleslam Seyyed Mohammad Khatami paid a state visit to India in January 2003 where he was the guest of honour at India's Republic Day. In a landmark accord, the two nations agreed upon future Iranian access to Indian military technology. According to the declaration:

The Republic of India and the Islamic Republic of Iran are resolved to exploit the full potential of the bilateral relationship in the interest of the people of the two countries and of regional peace and stability with a vision of a strategic partnership for a more stable, secure and prosperous region and for enhanced regional and global cooperation... Explore opportunities for cooperation in defence in agreed areas, including training and exchange of visits. [9]

The New Delhi Declaration called upon the two states to broaden their strategic collaboration in third countries—a clear reference to Afghanistan. Significantly, the New Delhi Declaration sought to upgrade defence cooperation between India and Iran specifically in the following areas:

1. Sea-lane control and security.
2. Discomfort with mounting US military presence in Persian Gulf.
3. Indo-Iran joint naval exercises.
4. Indian assistance to Tehran in upgrading its Russian made defence systems—something that has not yet come to fruition.
5. Establishment of working groups on terrorism and counter-narcotics.

According to reports, India would purportedly be given access to Iranian military bases in the event of a war with Pakistan. [10] India reportedly hoped that the 2003 New Delhi Declaration would pave the way for sales to Iran of upgrades of Iran's Russian-made conventional weapon systems. While Indo-Iranian deals along these lines have not yet materialized, Iran has sought Indian advice in operating missile boats, refitting Iran's T-72 tanks and armoured personnel carriers, and upgrades for MiG-29 fighters. [11] Although there was a clear mention of military ties expanding further, the US State Department expressed contention and dismissed any anxiety over the developments stating that New Delhi had reassured Washington that the agreement "doesn't involve military and technical assistance." [12]

Two months after President Khatami's visit to India, in March 2003, Tehran and New Delhi conducted their first joint naval manoeuvres in the Arabian Sea. Sea-lane control and security, as well as discomfort with the emerging US presence in the Persian Gulf, were partially responsible for this exercise and another one held in March 2006. Defence cooperation beyond this, however, has been sporadic and low-level. [13] The timing of the second naval exercise in March 2006 was crucial as it overlapped with President George W. Bush's trip to Afghanistan, India and Pakistan. Given its timing, the conduct of the exercise signalled to Tehran and Washington alike that Washington will not dictate India's foreign policies. [14] As a matter of fact the joint naval drill in 2006 prompted US Congressional criticism, but both the Bush Administration and Indian officials insisted the exchange emphasised mutual sport activities rather than military techniques. [15]

According to reports appearing in September 2007, Iran negotiated with India to buy advanced radar systems designed for fire control and surveillance of anti-aircraft batteries. Iran is seeking an unspecified number of Upgraded Support Fledermaus radar systems from the Indian state-owned Bharat Electronics Ltd (BHEL). The deal could reach US$ 70 million and mark the first major defence agreement between New Delhi and Tehran. However, New Delhi faces intense pressure from Washington not to sell the radars to Iran, as it is determined that the request is part of Iran's military effort to protect its nuclear weapons facilities. The Upgraded Super Fledermaus is a monopulse radar used in 35-mm air defence batteries and designed to detect low-flying objects, such as unmanned air vehicles (UAVs). The digital system contains a but-in simulator as well as a signal jammer. Crucially, BHEL has gone on record and confirmed Iran's request for these upgraded radars. Executives at the plant stated that Iran sought the same fire control and surveillance radar that the company upgraded for the Indian Army way back in 2001.

Adding on to the nascent military ties, India has also developed intelligence outposts in Iran, including the Indian consulate in Zahedan and a relatively new consulate in Bandar Abbas, which will permit India to monitor ship movements in the Persian Gulf and the Strait of Hormuz. [16] Undertaking the task of cooperation in the area of space research, India and Iran claim collaboration as well. [17] Moreover, India can also offer medium-technology weapons such as medium-range howitzers, and more prominently, jointly train with the Iranian forces.

Developing Port Facilities and Road Links

India has vital geopolitical and energy security stakes in the Gulf region in general and Iran in particular. Iran provides strategic land corridors/access to the sea to the landlocked states of Central Asia and Afghanistan. As India assists Iran to construct railway spurs linking its rail network to that of Central Asia, the process considerably reduces Pakistan's strategic leverage over these landlocked states thus providing them alternative corridors to the sea.

New Delhi has undertaken vital development of Iranian port facilities along with the construction of road and rail links. Indian engineers have contributed immensely towards the up gradation and development of the Iranian port of Chahbahar. In fact, in its annual report, India's Ministry of External Affairs claimed, "New Delhi and Tehran have agreed to "join hands" in the reconstruction of Afghanistan and to support the development of "alternative access routes" to that country (bypassing Pakistan) via Iran's Chahbahar port." [18]

This shall presumably facilitate trade and is part of a larger Indian Ocean to North Sea initiative involving Russia and others, and mainly cantered on the Iranian port of Bandar Abbas. Goods move through Iran via rail to the Caspian Sea and onward to northern Europe and Russia. [19] As a part of this corridor, India is developing Chahbahar and is laying railway tracks to connect it to Zaranj in Afghanistan, proclaiming that this would be a commercial port. Additionally, India has constructed the 218 kms long Zaranj-Delaram highway that now links Afghanistan to the Iranian port of Chahbahar as part of the Afghan circular road that connects Herat and Kabul via Mazar-e-Sharif in the north and Kandahar in the south—thereby providing easier access to Afghanistan and possibly even further, to Central Asia via Iran. [20]

Tool of Defence Cooperation to Achieve Strategic Congruence

Towards this end, defence cooperation proves critical in facilitating regional security and further cementing alliances with nations in the extended neighbourhood. Defence cooperation with Iran would go far so as to project India's role in the regional security structural design.

Assessing the opportunities available for military cooperation with Iran, it is evident that Tehran is searching for sustained support in modernisation of its armed forces which have been suffering from lack of access to advanced technology, maintenance and spares support. Developing early stakes in the process would be a major advantage for India. For this purpose, commencing a defence dialogue could be envisaged which could be progressed based on international and regional developments providing opportunities for greater cooperation with Iran without necessarily impinging upon India's relations with other states in the region or with the United States. [21] The band of opportunities is not necessarily sequential or time constrained and could be envisaged in the following fields:

1. Assistance in modernisation of defence forces to include supply of arms and equipment as per India's national policy from time to time.
2. Defence research and development (R&D) assistance.
3. Strategic defence dialogue.
4. Training and exercises.
5. Courses.
6. Defence infrastructure development.
7. IT*isation* of the armed forces.
8. Maintenance assistance, supply of spares and ancillaries. [22]

It would also be evident that there are very limited reverse spin offs that would be accrued to the Indian military. However, defence cooperation would very effectively serve the larger aim of building a strategic relationship with Tehran as and when such an opportunity becomes visible or is envisaged. Being situated on Pakistan's western borders, Iran provides significant politico-strategic advantage for India. This provides a strong congruence of Indo-Iranian interests in ensuring a moderate regime in Kabul that is not a client of Pakistan. Afghanistan is critical to India's security and Iran can provide a major stabilising influence there. Accordingly, India must clearly distinguish between Iran's nuclear position and other areas of cooperation—which by itself should not come in the way of

Indian energy and economic relations with Iran. Engagement of Iran implies an engagement with its Armed Forces and the need for fostering military-to-military relations. This could translate into sharing of intelligence regarding terrorist groups operating out of Afghanistan and curbing the activities of narcotics smugglers and drug traffickers. India and Iran have a major stake in keeping the Gulf waterways open for trade and energy flows. Towards this end India and Iran had envisaged naval cooperation for sea-lane control and security. Indo-Iranian naval exercises such as the ones held in March 2003 and 2006 need to be resumed. Furthermore, bilateral naval exercises could also encompass anti-piracy operations and cooperation. [23] As far as Army-to-Army cooperation is concerned, it could entail the following:

1. Joint anti-terrorist exercises.
2. Provision of course vacancies for Iranian officers at the National Defence College (NDC) and Defence Services Staff College (DSSC).
3. Provision of training for UN peacekeeping operations.
4. Training in English language and IT skills for Iranian armed forces personnel.
5. Offer assistance in training as well as maintenance and repair of key Russian equipment like Kilo submarines and MiG-29 fighters.
6. Maintenance and repair and training support for Iranian T-72 Tanks, BMP infantry fighting vehicles [BMP1 and BMP2 ICVs] and Russian origin artillery equipment (105 mm, 130 mm and 122mm towed artillery Field Guns).
7. Provision of spares would be a major component of military ties.
8. India could consider selling Advanced Light Helicopters (ALH) and jet trainer aircrafts.

However, assistance in these areas would be contingent upon a scaling down of Iran's hostility levels with the US and Israel. India receives major quantities of cutting edge equipment from Israel and as such cannot be seen as undermining its security by upgrading the perceived threat from Iran.

US and Israeli Factor: A Paradox

Despite these many forms of collaboration, more than a few constraints are likely to curtail the extent to which India might reach out to Iran in defence association. The field of defence cooperation is subjected to close scrutiny and sensitivity as it comes under the scanner of the US and Israel. Refuting to view international relations as a zero-sum game, India's Ministry of External Affairs stated in January 2005:

The United States has its relationship with Pakistan, which is separate from our own relationship with them...Our relationship with Iran is peaceful and largely economic. We do not expect it to affect our continuing good relations with the United States.

Nonetheless, the impact of Tehran's nuclear programme did cause considerable strain in Indo-Iranian ties when New Delhi cast its vote at the IAEA Board of Governors in 2005 in favour of a resolution finding Iran in "non-compliance with its safeguards obligations under the NPT" and expressing "the absence of confidence that Iran's nuclear programme is entirely for peaceful purposes," and then voted to refer Iran to the UN Security Council in February 2006. New Delhi's ultimate decision to vote for the resolution came in as a surprise to many, underlining thereby, the growing influence of budding Indo-US ties, especially since signing of the civilian nuclear agreement. Moreover, tensions over Washington's pressure on New Delhi rose when former US Ambassador to India, David Mulford, cautioned India regarding the future of the landmark nuclear cooperation pact in case it voted against sending the Iranian issue to the Security Council. Subsequently, Tehran was incensed by India's vote against it at the IAEA and outlined that American pressure on New Delhi against Iran had indeed played a decisive role. [24]

During an April 2006 hearing of the Senate Foreign Relations Committee to discuss proposed US-India civil nuclear cooperation, Secretary of State Condoleezza Rice was inquired about New Delhi's relationship with Tehran. Of immediate interest to some Senators was an American press report on Iranian naval ships visiting India's Kochi port for "training." Indian officials downplayed the significance of the port visit, and Secretary Rice challenged the report's authenticity. [25] Secretary Rice did however, sent a message across when she stated, "The US has made very clear to India that we have concerns about their relationship with Iran." [26]

Iranian President Mahmoud Ahmadinejad's first official visit to India in April 2008 came at an opportune time with an aim to iron out diplomatic differences between India and Iran. Ahmadinejad's visit was viewed through the prism of intensifying ties between the two countries by means of deliberations in numerous key sectors ranging from energy, the Iran-Pakistan-India gas pipeline project, talks on the two multi-billion dollar energy deals and bilateral investments. However, the visit was shrouded in controversy, with Washington, apparently uneasy about the India-Iran ties, kept a close tab on the Iranian President's movement in South Asia. [27] The sentiment was deftly reflected in the statement made by US State Department Deputy Spokesman Tom Casey where he also pointed at Tehran's support for promoting terrorism in Iraq:

New Delhi should urge Iran to curtail its nuclear programme and to cease enriching uranium. India should also put pressure on Iran to become a more responsible actor on the world stage and ask Iran to end its rather unhelpful activities with respect to Iraq.

The US statement received flak by the Ministry of Foreign Affairs in New Delhi further indicating that President Ahmadinejad's trip had flashed diplomatic barbs between New Delhi and Washington. The MEA released a statement strongly rebuking Washington that stated:

India and Iran are ancient civilisations whose relations span centuries. Both nations are perfectly capable of managing all aspects of their relationship with the appropriate degree of care and attention and neither country needs any guidance on the future conduct of bilateral relations. [28]

India's camaraderie with Iran especially in the field of defence collaboration incessantly carries a potential risk of putting it at odds with simultaneous improvement in ties with Israel and the US. Israel is concerned about India's defence ties with Iran resting upon apprehension that India could divert Israeli military technology to Iran—a nation it describes as the "epicentre of terrorism." During Israeli Prime Minister Ariel Sharon's visit to India in September 2003, Sharon was reported to have demanded explicit guarantees from India that it would not transfer any technology acquired from Israel to any third country, especially Iran. [29]

It should be highlighted that the cornerstone of the Indo-Israeli strategic partnership is military and defence cooperation. New Delhi's decision to launch the Israeli Tescar spy satellite in January 2008 signifies New Delhi's potential willingness to enhance Israel's security vis-à-vis Iran, especially with regard to Iran's nuclear programme. [30] Therefore, as Iran seeks Indian facilitation in refitting and maintaining tanks, infantry fighting vehicles, and artillery guns, the collaboration has episodically disconcerted Israel, which provides spare parts and technology upgrades to India. [31] Yet another episode that established India's autonomous foreign policy approach came in March 2007 when Washington conducted its war games in the Persian Gulf—its largest show of force in the region since the 2003 intervention in Iraq involving USS *Eisenhower* and USS *Stennis.* This coincided with the visit of the Iranian Naval Chief to India—a reflection of the importance that Iran attached to its growing defence ties with India. [32] Additionally, a naval cadet training ship visited India, and in 2007, the Indian government allowed a limited number of Iranian officers to participate in joint training courses with officers from several other countries. [33]

In April 2007 it was widely reported that eight leading US senators led by Jon Kyl, (Republican from Arizona) and Barbara Boxer, (Democrat from California) further including Senators Trent Lott, Robert P. Casey Jr., Richard Durban, David Vitter, Gordon Smith and Bill Nelson urged India to suspend its 'military cooperation' with Iran until it completely ceased its pursuit of nuclear weapons, so as to remove a 'potentially serious barrier' to future cooperation between New Delhi and Washington. In a letter to Prime Minister Manmohan Singh, the Senators stressed:

We were disturbed to read recent reports that Iran and India have agreed to form a joint defence-working group. This agreement, which is purported to build off the India-Iran strategic partnership accord of 2003, will serve to undermine the efforts of the international community to isolate the regime in Tehran. Such an announcement would serve the long-term security interests of both India and the United States and remove a potentially serious barrier to future cooperation between our two nations. [34]

Thus on the one hand there is an assumption that Iranian-Indian ties are benign to US interests even if they imply future policy disagreements between New Delhi and Washington. On the other hand Chairman of Business Executives for National Security, Stanley Weiss, points out, "India's new ties with Iran make it more, not less, valuable to Washington…it should recognise that India and Iran are the key to regional stability and join New Delhi and Tehran in an axis of friendship." [35]

Conclusion

It needs to be absorbed that the lynch pin of Indo–Iran strategic cooperation hinges upon coordinating their actions in Afghanistan and Central Asia. The very fact that Iran shares 936 kms. of border with Afghanistan and a 909 kms. border with Pakistan, imbibes it with tremendous strategic significance for India. As New Delhi strives to consolidate its strategic presence in Central Asia, including setting up air bases in Tajikistan and further expanding its footprint in Afghanistan, Tehran offers India geographical proximity and access to these regions so as to flex its power projection capabilities. Tajikistan allows Indian combat aircrafts to use its Farkhor air base coupled with use of Tajikistan's Aini air base, as reported. [36]

India will have to compete for influence in Iran and military to military ties would go a long way to cement relations with Iran. Iran lies at the core of the world's energy heartland formed by the Middle East and Central Asia. As such, enlightened self-interest demands that India should engage Iran in a constructive manner to safeguard its significant geopolitical and energy security stakes.

As of now, the cooperation appears sporadic and slowly shaping up to becoming robust. Clearly, in its dealings with Tehran, India is bound to walk a tightrope as it tackles the conflicting imperatives of domestic politics and strategic interests while making efforts towards skilfully matching them. Closer ties between India and Iran especially in the realm of defence cooperation shall be of critical significance to both nations even if it might impact upon the West Asian politico-strategic dynamic. In its quest for better relations with the US, India will have to guard against being painted into a corner in Asia by an adverse grouping of major states that could include Russia, China and Iran. Despite the fact that resisting unvarying US pressure towards keeping its diplomatic and political channels open vis-à-vis Tehran, New Delhi should maintain an independent line while strategizing its foreign policy sans any threads binding the same. At the same time, India could volunteer to act as a mediator between Washington and Tehran so as to resolve what rapidly appears to be becoming a ceaseless impasse.

Thus, in a move that could radically alter the geopolitics of the region, Indian and Iranian defence cooperation shall prove to be a significant pointer towards emerging strategic calculations in the Persian Gulf and the Arabian Sea. Defence cooperation between the two nations would serve as an essential tool of foreign policy thereby strengthening mutual trust and enhancing security and stability in the region.

End Notes

1. C. Christine Fair, "Indo-Iranian Ties: Thicker Than Oil," *The Middle East Review of International Affairs*, Vol. 24, No. 1, March 2007.
2. For more on this subject see, Stephen Blank, "Central Asia's Deepening East Asian Relations," *Analysis Biweekly Briefing*, November 8, 2000.
3. Subhash Kapila, "India-Saudi Arabia: The Strategic Significance of the New Delhi Declaration," *South Asia Analysis Group*, Paper No. 1734, January 2006.
4. SM Krishna condemned the attack by means of a letter to his Iranian counterpart, Manouchehr Mottaki, as reported by Iranian *Islamic Republic News Agency* (IRNA) on October 26, 2009.
5. Ministry of External Affairs, *Annual Report* 2005-06, New Delhi.
6. Cited in K. Alan Kronstadt and Kenneth Katzman, "India-Iran Relations and US Interests," Congressional Research Service (CRS) Report for Congress, August 2006, p. 4; also see, Fair, n. 1.
7. Calabrese, "Indian-Iranian Relations in Transition"; "India-Iran Military Ties Growing," *Strategic Affairs*, June 16, 2001.
8. For more details see, Stephen Blank, "India's Rising Profile in Central Asia," *Comparative Strategy*, Vol. 22, No. 2, April-June 2003, pp. 139-157.
9. For more details see Joint Statement by the Republic of India and the Islamic Republic of Iran, "The New Delhi Declaration," January 25, 2003, Ministry of External Affairs, New Delhi.
10. Donald L. Berlin, "India-Iran Relations: A Deepening Entente," *Asia-Pacific Centre for Security Studies Special Assessment*, Honolulu, October 2004, p. 1.
11. "Iran-India pact not a security concern-State Department official says," *Inside the Pentagon*, February 13, 2003; also see, "India-Iran Military Ties Growing," *Strategic Affairs*, June 16, 2001.
12. Ibid.
13. Ronak D. Desai & Xenia Dormandy, "India-Iran Relations: Key Security Implications," Report by the Robert and Renée Belfer Centre for Science and International Affairs, Harvard Kennedy School, April 2008.
14. C. Christine Fair, "India and Iran: New Delhi's Balancing Act," *The Washington Quarterly*, Vol. 30, No. 3, Summer 2007,

p. 151; also see, House Committee on International Relations, The US-India Global Partnership, 109th Congress, Second Session, 2006.
15. CRS Report, n. 6, p. 5.
16. Berlin, n. 10.
17. "India, Iran Cooperating on Space Research," *The Times of India*, February 1, 2003; also see, Yiftah S. Shapir, "Iran's Efforts to Conquer Space," *Strategic Assessments*, Vol. 8, No. 3, November 2005.
18. Indian Ministry of External Affairs, *Annual Report* 2004-2005, New Delhi; also see, "Iran Sees Good Ties With India Despite India-US Nuclear Deal," *Agence France Presse*, March 30, 2006.
19. Regine A. Spector, "The North-South Corridor," *Central Asia-Caucasus Institute Analyst*, July 3, 2002.
20. Rizvan Zeb, "Gwadar and Chabahar: Competition or Complimentarity," *Central Asia-Caucasus Institute Analyst*, October 22, 2003.
21. Monika Chansoria, GD Bakshi and Rahul Bhonsle, "Iran Analysis: A Net Assessment," Project Study for the Centre for Land Warfare Studies, New Delhi, February 2009.
22. Ibid.
23. Ibid.
24. For more details see, Monika Chansoria, "Iran's Nuclear Quagmire: Trends and Challenges," Manekshaw Paper No. 7, (New Delhi: KW Publishers Pvt Ltd. and Centre for Land Warfare Studies), December 2008.
25. Vivek Raghuvanshi and Gopal Ratnam, "Indian Navy Trains Iranian Sailors," *Defence News*, March 27, 2006.
26. Transcript, "Senate Foreign Relations Committee Holds Hearing on US-India Atomic Energy Cooperation," April 5, 2006.
27. Chansoria, n. 24.
28. Statement released by the Indian Ministry of External Affairs, New Delhi, April 24, 2008.
29. "Tel Aviv worried about New Delhi's Ties with Iran," *The Times of India*, September 11, 2003.
30. Desai, et al., n. 13.
31. Fair, n. 14, p. 150.
32. Harsh V. Pant, "A Fine Balance: India Walks a Tightrope between Iran and the United States," *Orbis*, Vol. 51, No. 3,

Summer 2007, pp. 498-99.

33. As cited in Teresita C. Schaffer and Suzanne Fawzi, "India and Iran: Limited Partnership, High Stakes," *South Asia Monitor*, Centre for Strategic and International Studies, no. 114, December 2007, pp. 2-3.
34. "India Should End Military Ties with Iran: US Senators," *NNN-PTI News*, April 22, 2007.
35. Stanley A. Weiss, "India + Iran = Foundation for Stability," *International Herald Tribune*, February 6, 2003.
36. "IAF to Station MiG-29s in Tajikistan," *The Times of India,* April 20, 2006.

9

Iran, Turkey and the Reshaping of West Asia in the Post-9/11 Scenario: Implications for India

Atul Aneja

Background

The invasion of Iraq by the United States, following the attacks in New York and Washington on September 11, 2001, set alarm bells ringing in several countries in West Asia. Key regional powers including Iran, Saudi Arabia and Syria interpreted the U.S. invasion of Iraq as the first major step in a process that Washington had embarked upon of enforcing "regime change" in the region. The acute insecurity that the American invasion caused gradually resulted in a rearguard response from the regional players, initiated by Syria and Iran. Iran had been in Washington's cross-hairs since Ayatollah Khomeini's legions toppled through an Islamic revolution in 1979, the regime of Mohammad Reza Pahlavi, the Shah of Iran, a key U.S. ally in a region rich in oil and gas. Iran, even ahead of the Anglo-American invasion of Iraq, was being subjected to intense pressure. American forces had landed along its eastern borders, to dislodge the Taliban regime in Afghanistan. Much to Iran's discomfiture, the presence of American forces in Afghanistan has inordinately prolonged. According to the current timetable, the U.S. Government would only handover security to the Afghanistan government in 2014.

The U.S. invasion of Iraq was also interpreted in large parts of West Asia as a reinforcement of Washington's alliance with Israel. This generated apprehensions that Israel would play a hyperactive role in the perceived evangelical regime-change agenda that the Bush administration and its neoconservative allies were apparently pursuing. The fears generated by the Iraq invasion ran deep as the Bush administration appeared to be following a Messianic agenda, dictated internally in the U.S. by the neoconservatives and their

Christian-Zionist allies, of knocking out the status quo, and, establishing in its place a firm Israel-friendly political order in West Asia.

Iran and Syria were the first to respond to the post-Iraq challenge posed by the Bush administration. Consequently, they energised a process of security cooperation, which had commenced long before the Americans had arrived in Iraq. Syria's former President, Hafez Al Assad had worked closely with the Iranians to establish in the eighties, the Lebanese Hizbollah, following the Israeli invasion of Lebanon in 1982. After their disenchantment with the Fatah led by Yasser Arafat, the Iranians had begun to cultivate its rival Hamas. This process of engaging Hamas and the Islamic Jihad concluded in the mid-nineties. Syria again has played a major role in building Hamas and Islamic Jihad by hosting the two groups in exile in Damascus, thereby providing them with safe havens outside their Gaza stronghold. In the aftermath of the invasion of Iraq, the Iranians went into top gear to arm Hizbollah. Sharing a common border with Lebanon and for a long time dominating the country's political landscape, Syria has played a critical role in transiting Iranian weaponry to Hizbollah. However, the Syria-Iran alliance was severely tested after the 2005 assassination of former Lebanese Prime Minister, Rafik Hariri. The killing for which Syria was summarily presumed guilty by the West and Israel caused the exit of Syrian forces from Lebanon, resulting in a perceptible drop in Syrian influence there. However, the Hizbollah's strong showing against Israel in the 2006 Lebanon war and its political consolidation that followed has once again brought Syria and Iran right back on to the centre-stage in Lebanon.

The 2006 war between Israel and Hezbollah in Southern Lebanon and Berut, which former US Secretary of State, Condoleezza Rice had initially characterised as the manifestation of "birth pangs of a new Middle East," appeared to have put-off the Bush administration's drive for regime change in the region. [1] Conversely it expanded the political space for Iran and Syria to exploit. Ironically, it was Israel's winter war with the Iran- Syria backed Hamas in 2008-09, which allowed the regional players to play a more active role in this region. Specifically, the Gaza war provided Turkey, which was looking to implant itself in West Asia, after being spurned by the Europeans in its European Union membership campaign, to acquire a prominent niche in the region's politics. Turkey further consolidated itself as a regional player in the summer of 2010 after Israeli commandos killed eight of its citizens who were on-board the Mavi Marmara humanitarian aid ship that was bound for Gaza. Turkey played a leading role in orchestrating a global outcry against the Israeli action. In doing so it appeared to champion the Palestinian cause, a sure shot route to catch the public imagination in the region at the mass level.

Since 2009, a regional and semi-autonomous diplomatic process has been taking root, where apart from Syria and Iran, Turkey and Saudi Arabia have emerged as the lead players. As it evolves and takes shape, the purpose of this intense diplomatic engagement among the prominent countries of the region now appears to be the achievement of the following core objectives: a) Imparting region-wide stability. b) Supporting regime stability especially to Iran, Saudi Arabia and Syria. c) Avoidance of conflict between Iran and Israel/US combine, with Turkey playing a leading role. d) Enhancing economic/energy interaction with Turkey as the centre piece and Syria and Iran as partners.

However, regional diplomacy among the four top players has not been formally structured. It has evolved as a response to the acute sense of crisis that the stakeholders have perceived following the hostile U.S. disposition towards the region in the aftermath of 9/11.At the moment, diplomatic interaction among the stakeholders is need based, ad hoc and has shifting nodal points, defined by the specific issues of concern that keep cropping up at a rapid pace for consideration and action. From its current reactive phase, the four-cornered diplomacy can enter into a pro-active domain, in case the current round of interaction can help prevent a war in Iran, stabilise Saudi Arabia, which is facing an Al Qaeda threat especially from Yemeni soil, and allows Turkey's consolidation in West Asia.

Iran-Syria Alliance in Transition

In recent years, the Syria-Iran relationship has been shaped by their shared perception of two common threats. Both countries fear the United States and Israel as the hostile nations intent on destabilising them. This perception has been reinforced after the U.S. invaded Iraq, a country which shares common borders with Syria and Iran. For Iran, the threat from the U.S. has magnified as the American military forces are already present in strength in neighbouring Afghanistan.

Hostility between Syria and the U.S. rose exponentially soon after the Americans entered Iraq in March 2003. Syrian President Bashar Al Assad was blunt in expressing his hope that the U.S. military plan should fail in Iraq. Former Syrian foreign minister, Farouq al-Shara, went even further when he told the Syrian parliament that "Syria has a national interest in the expulsion of the invaders from Iraq." Syria also looked the other way when anti-US fighters infiltrated into Iraq from its soil. [2]

As the relations between the two countries nosedived, President Bush in early May sent to Damascus his then Secretary of State Colin Powell to read out the riot act to the Syrian government. He demanded that Syria close offices of Palestinian militant groups and turn Hizbollah inert in Lebanon. Later in December, the U.S. Congress passed the *Syria Accountability and Lebanese Sovereignty Restoration Act.* It called for a halt to "Syrian support for terrorism, end its occupation of Lebanon, and stop its development of weapons of mass destruction." The U.N. Security Council also passed Resolution 1559, which called for the Syrian withdrawal from Lebanon and disarming of Hizbollah. [3]

Efforts to marginalise Syria's role in Lebanon accelerated sharply with the assassination of former Lebanese Prime Minister, Rafik Hariri in February 2005. Syria was immediately accused of masterminding Hariri's killing. So intense was the pressure mounted by the United States, Israel, Syria's foes in the Arab world, as well as internally by non-Shia groups in Lebanon, that Syria had no option but to withdraw from Lebanon. Pushed to the back foot in 2005, Syria and Iran worked feverishly to plan together a rearguard action to regain some of the lost ground. Both countries strengthened Israel's arch foes, the Palestinian Hamas and the Lebanese Hizbollah. Iran was in good position to assist Hamas, as it had developed close ties with the group, as well as its Islamic Jihad ally during the nineties. According to Egyptian estimates, Iran has been providing Hamas around US$ 25 million every month to maintain its strength. [4]

The two countries worked hard to beef up the strength of Hizbollah, and in doing so, they fortified their buffer along Israel's northern border. Iran and Syria, were well acquainted with Hizbollah, having worked together to raise this group soon after Israel's invasion of Lebanon in 1982. In a 2008 interview with the daily Sharg, Ali Mohashimi, a former Iran's ambassador to Syria from 1982 to 1985, revealed that Ayatollah Khomeini agreed to the formation of an Iran backed Shia militia in the aftermath of the Israeli invasion. Backed by Iran's Islamic Revolutionary Guards Corps (IRGC) a Herculean effort was mounted to unite Shia groups, either through the method of co-option, and if necessary by taking recourse to the use of force. [5]

Detailing the Iran-Syria role in the evolution of Hizbollah, the London based pan-Arab daily, *Ash-Sharq al-Awsat* noted that Mohammad Hassan Akhtari, Iran's ambassador to Syria from 1986 to 1997, and again from 2005 through 2007 was "the operational father" of Hizbollah, as well as the "engineer of the special relationship" between Syria and Iran. He was also described as the "coordinator of Iran's relations with Palestinian organisations in Damascus". The daily pointed out that "the Iranian embassy in Damascus became the most important Iranian embassy in the world. It represented something akin to a 'regional centre' for Iran's diplomatic activities that extended from Damascus to Beirut and the Palestinian territories and became privy to files on several matters, chief of which was Iran's relations with Syria, Hezbollah, [and] the Palestinian organizations." [6] In their bid to unify the Lebanese Shia militants, which were chiefly divided into Amal and Hizbollah, Akhtari and the then Syrian intelligence chief in Lebanon, Ghazi Kanaan, played a key role. By 1988, Hizbollah was the dominant force in southern Lebanon, bordering Israel, and in Beirut. During the nineties, till the Israeli withdrawal from southern Lebanon in 2000, Hizbollah masterminded more than three dozen suicide attacks against Israeli forces in Lebanon.

As the Hizbollah consolidated, the Syrians not only sheltered the group under their patronage, but they also played in a key facilitating role in arming them. In recent years, the group's operational artillery reach has grown. Experts and analysts generally put the Hizbollah rocket force somewhere between 10,000 and 12,000 missiles. Hizbollah's Iran supplied stocks of around 7,000 to 8,000, 107mm and 122mm Katyusha rockets are at the heart of its arsenal, noted Patrick Devenny, Henry M. Jackson National Security Fellow at the Centre for Security Policy in Washington. [7]

The Iran-Syria project of fortifying Hizbollah as the protector of their interests in Lebanon achieved major success in July-August 2006. Despite relentless aerial bombardment and the invasion of its forces in southern Lebanon, Hizbollah successfully blunted the

Israeli assault. Three years later the Hamas, backed by Syria and Iran, managed to survive the attack on Gaza by Israeli, which used deadly weaponry including phosphorus bombs during its campaign.

Emergence of Turkey

Ironically the events of 2006 and 2009 have also exposed the limits of the Syria-Iran security cooperation. After the unconvincing demonstration of its military might in these two conflicts, Israel has stepped up its diplomatic campaign against Iran. In its assessment, the Israeli intelligence agency, Mossad, is of the view "there is no reason to believe Iran will do anything but use negotiations to stall for time so that by 2010-2011, Iran will have the technological capability to build a nuclear weapon-essentially reducing the question of weaponising to a political decision". [8]

With tensions between Iran and Israel rising, and the threat of a destructive war still on the horizon, Syria is being forced to make a choice. It appears that in case of a conflict between Iran and Israel, Syria would do its best not to get directly embroiled. Since the 2006 war, the emergence of Turkey as an influential player in West Asia has empowered Syria with additional diplomatic and economic options, which it did not have in the immediate aftermath of the U.S. invasion of Iraq.

Turkey has caught the imagination not only of the people in West Asia but also the world following the Mavi Marmara incident. On May 31, 2010 the gun-toting commandos in a pre-dawn raid slithered from helicopters on the deck of the Turkish humanitarian aid ship. The bloodbath which left eight Turkish humanitarian activists dead, and several injured set the world alight. Within hours of the incident, the United Nations Security Council convened in New York. What happened thereafter was truly extraordinary. In a presidential statement, the UNSC condemned the Israeli raid. It also instructed Tel Aviv to free immediately 480 pro-Palestinian activists who were detained following the incident and release the ships. It called upon Israel to lift the three-year-old blockade imposed on Gaza—a narrow stamp-sized coastal strip on the Mediterranean, one of the most densely populated regions in the world. [9]

Turkey's support for the Mavi Marmara mission was not a coincidence. Rather, it was a deliberate exercise to expand its moral influence in the region. Well aware of the deep influence the Palestinian issue exercises over West Asia's collective consciousness, Turkey began to raise its voice against the sufferings of the Gaza residents. The Turks went to extraordinary lengths to slam Israel and empathise with the Gazans, victims of heavy phosphorous bombing, during Israel's 2008-09 winter offensive against Hamas. Turkish Prime Minister Recep Tayyip Erdogan's well-publicised Davos walkout after he had clashed with Israeli President Simon Peres had an electrifying effect among the people in the region. The Gaza war had also brought Turkey closer to three other influential countries—Iran, Syria and Qatar, which stood up for the people of Gaza during the war. Turkey's imaginative moves to ingratiate itself with people and some of the governments in the region have paid off so far. Iran welcomed Turkey as a partner to resolve its nuclear conflict with the West. Turkey's ties with its neighbour, Syria, have also improved exponentially.

Turkey-Iran Ties

Turkey's relations with Iran have improved markedly after the government led by Mr. Erdogan assumed office in Ankara in 2002. There were several factors that have led to this improvement. But most significantly, it is Turkey's decision to embark on a high intensity engagement with West Asia that has caused the turnaround. Turkey's decision to consciously cultivate West Asia was partly on account of Europe's foot dragging on allowing Turkey to enter the European Union. In reaching out to its West Asian neighbourhood, the Turkish foreign ministry, now headed by foreign minister Ahmet Davutoglu, worked out a doctrine that would enable Ankara to deepen its regional influence. In accordance with the new doctrine, Turkey decided to follow a pro-active rather than a "crisis-oriented" approach, armed with a foreign policy which focused on "peace diplomacy". Having "zero problems with neighbouring States," Tehran included, is another basic tenet of Turkey's new foreign policy orientation. Consequently, Turkey is looking at striking a balance between security and democracy, signalling its unwillingness to interfere in the internal affairs of its neighbours, especially on ideological grounds. The new doctrine encourages adoption of a "multi-dimensional foreign policy," meaning that Ankara will no longer be unifocal in pursuing its pro-EU political aspirations. [10]

Based on the foundation of zero conflict with its neighbours, Turkey decided to work closely with Iran. Ankara's ties with Iran revolve around two major considerations. Turkey has decided to respond positively to Iran's requirement to break out of its isolation. In recent years, the controversy surrounding Iran's nuclear programme has been the cause of Tehran's growing isolation. Iran has already been subjected to four rounds of economic sanctions. The nuclear issue and the perception that Iran might be on course to developing nuclear weapon technology now threatens to draw Iran into a war with Israel and the United States. Consequently, Turkey has been working to address the Iranian nuclear issue, and thereby addressing the root cause of Iran's isolation. Turkey and Brazil in May 2010 nearly achieved a breakthrough in engendering a thaw in ties between Iran and the US-led Western camp. After a marathon 18 hour dialogue with Iran, the three countries hammered out the Tehran declaration. The document focused on Iran exporting the bulk of its stocks of low enriched uranium to Turkey. In turn it would get atomic fuel to run a medical reactor, engaged in producing nuclear medicine to treat cancer. The West spurned the deal, which would have greatly improved confidence in Iran's stated intent of using enriched uranium for peaceful purposes. Nevertheless, Turkey in late January 2011 is hosting another key international conference which would deliberate on the Iranian nuclear issue.

On its part, Turkey is looking at Iran to improve its energy security situation. Turkey hopes to reduce its dependence on Russian oil and natural gas, by including Iranian oil and gas to fulfil its growing energy requirements. The Tabriz-Erzurum pipeline which has already been completed has a capacity of transporting 14 billion cubic meters of gas annually. Tehran and Ankara have also signed an agreement which not only allows export of Iranian gas to Turkey as a consumer, but also opens the possibility of its export to third destinations. Iran has also allowed Turkey to explore and extract gas from its huge South Pars gas field. [11]

Turkey-Syria Relations

Turkey's ties with Syria have improved rapidly, symbolised by the signing of a visa free regime for the citizens of the two countries in October 2009. Some the major past irritants have already been removed. Turkey no longer apprehends Syria's support for Kurdish rebels operating on its soil. This has happened after Syria expelled Abdullah Ocalan, the leader of the Kurdistan Workers Party (PKK) in 1998. Cross-border trade between the two countries is already booming. Between 2007 and 2008, trade between the countries doubled. It doubled again in 2009, to an estimated US$ 4 billion, according to the Aleppo Chamber of Commerce. [12] Thc two countries are now looking at developing an energy corridor by connecting an Arab pipeline with a Turkish pipeline that would ferry natural gas. [13]

Given the economic lifeline that Turkey has opened, Syria's critical dependence on Iran, has now been considerably reduced. In the light of the opening of the Turkish option and Syria's developing relationship with Saudi Arabia, Iran may find it difficult to coax Syria to become its trench-mate in a confrontation with Israel. However, short of shedding blood, it would be in Syria's interest to continue working together with Iran on two issues; to beef up the strength of Hizbollah as well as of Hamas, in order to deter Israel to indulge in military adventurism, especially along its shared border with South Lebanon. Consequently, despite its broadening policy options, Syria is unlikely to shut down its supply lines used for transiting Iranian weaponry bound for Hizbollah or Hamas.

After 9/11, Saudi Arabia too Wants a Place in the Regional Sun

The assassination of Rafik Hariri was a big blow to Saudi interests in Lebanon. Hariri had been long recognised as the guardian not only of Saudi political interests, but also of its investments in Lebanon. In a country divided along religious and sectarian lines, Hariri was also seen as the point man to permeate Riyadh's influence in Lebanon's wealthy Sunni community.

The Hariri-Saudi connection took root in the aftermath of the mid-seventies oil boom. In accordance with the surging oil prices, Saudi Arabia's wealth increased exponentially. In relatively quick time, Saudi Arabia became an important political and business centre in the region. Hariri benefited greatly from this after Saudi Arabia's King Khaled sought the services of his business partner to construct a new hotel in Taif. [14] The Saudis set a short duration time line for the construction of this hotel. Hariri rose to the occasion, mobilised capital through Banque Méditerranée in Paris. For construction, he tapped the then declining construction firm Oger. Aware of the high stakes involved, Hariri delivered the hotel ahead of schedule, thereby coming in the good books of Saudis. This was a development which caused his career to zoom, and became the basis of his solid relationship with Riyadh. Hariri was to eventually takeover Oger, turn it into Oger International, which became the firm to execute all the major projects undertaken by the Saudis.

It was therefore not surprising that it took the Saudis considerable time to absorb the shock of Hariri's death. Rafik Hariri's son, Saad Hariri, who led the anti-Syrian alliance after his father's assassination emerged as the natural successor to safeguard Saudi interests. However, by 2008, it became clear to Riyadh that Saad Hariri's main challenger, the pro-Syrian Hizbollah, could not be steamrolled. The turning point came in 2008 when Lebanon's pro-US government backed by Saudi Arabia tried to control Hizbollah's military communication network, as well as the airport through which military supplies for the Shia group were funnelled. Hizbollah retaliated by wiping out pro-government street gangs, whom the Saudi's apparently funded. [15] Since then the Saudis decided not to topple Hizbollah, and, consequently, protect their investments in Lebanon. A top level dialogue to stabilise Lebanon has subsequently commenced involving Saudi Arabia's King Abdullah bin Abdulaziz and Syrian President Bashar Al Assad. Saad Hariri, who became Prime Minister in 2009, has now visited Syria as well as Iran. With its lines open to Ankara, Tehran and Riyadh, Syria has acquired a position of great prominence, capable of emerging as the region's power broker. It is now well poised to actively mediate, especially between Iran and Saudi Arabia—an initiative that can go a long way to stabilise West Asia. Consequently, an autonomous but uncoordinated process of regional diplomacy that has already commenced has a chance of acquiring a more formal appearance.

India and the Regionalisation of West Asia's Geopolitical Space

The growing regionalisation of West Asia's political space chiefly by Iran, Turkey, Syria and Saudi Arabia has major implications for India. Without a deep engagement with these countries, India's capacity to enhance its influence in West Asia is bound to be limited. Iran would be the key to safeguarding India's interests not only in Afghanistan, but also in oil rich Iraq and beyond. Given, lack of physical access in Afghanistan, there appears to be sufficient realisation in New Delhi that without accessibility to the route heading from the Iranian port of Chabahar towards Herat, India's physical accessibility to Afghanistan would be severely restricted. However, there does appear to be insufficient appreciation in the Indian foreign and security establishment about Iran's strategic importance in advancing Indian influence in energy rich Iraq, where

Iran is the chief power broker. Given the centrality of Iran for pushing Indian influence in an arca strctching from the Hindukush mountain ranges in Afghanistan to the Lebanon's Mediterranean coast, New Delhi may have no choice but to invest more political capital to firmly anchor its relationship with Tehran. This existing shortcoming of not having sufficient strategic cement to bind Indo-Iran ties can be overcome if India establishes a deep and well established energy partnership with Iran.

Despite the obvious objections that would come from Washington, India can establish an enduring and weighty relationship with Iran, by signing the Iran-Pakistan-India gas pipeline. Alternatively, it can consider having gas pumped to India along a deep sea pipeline, avoiding the trouble torn energy corridor that passes through Pakistan's Baluchistan province. A new proposal promoted by a consortium called "SAGE" or South Asia Gas Enterprise, envisions drawing gas from Qatar, Iraq and Iran, and funnelling it to Oman. From Oman gas can be carried to western India through an undersea pipeline that can be laid to depths of up to 3,500 meters. [16]

Regarding Saudi Arabia, the political road blocks to an enhanced relationship with Riyadh have been removed following the visit to India in 2006 by Saudi monarch King Abdullah bin Abdul-Aziz and the reciprocal visit to Riyadh in 2010 by Indian Prime Minister Manmohan Singh. Energy including establishment of petrochemical plants have been identified. The legal basis for security cooperation which would allow both countries to extradite suspect criminals is in place. The two sides are now exploring enhanced military cooperation including training that could help the Saudis to better tackle extremists operating in the mountainous border areas of Saudi Arabia and Yemen. A deeper and sustained engagement with Turkey and Syria would now be warranted, notwithstanding India's close security ties with Israel.

Conclusion

Since the U.S. invasion of Iraq in 2003, Iran, Syria, Turkey and Saudi Arabia have played their part to prevent further conflict and turmoil in West Asia. A cycle of diplomatic communication whether direct or indirect, has been established within this quartet, in the backdrop of the belligerent US-led "war on terror." Each of these countries have their unique strengths and advantages which are now being gradually leveraged to help distance forces of conflict from the region.

Turkey's willingness and ambition to emerge as a benign but credible regional heavyweight has become a major factor influencing West Asia since 2009. Turkey's cooperative but independent foreign policy, self-consciously aimed at integrating the region on a common economic and cultural platform, wherever possible, is helping to impart a new dynamic of regional consciousness among some of the key countries in the region. Turkey's pragmatism, non-ideological posture and reluctance to interfere in the internal affairs of its neighbouring countries is generating trust and further animating the spirit of regional cooperation along fresh lines. Turkey has already developed a special relationship with neighbouring Syria, marked by the signing of visa free regime, booming border trade and ambitions to develop a cross-border energy corridor. It is also playing a lead role among regional countries to defuse the crisis surrounding Iran's nuclear programme; a move that in the long run may help in averting a war between Iran and a US-backed Israel. Because of its new economic and diplomatic initiatives, Turkey has strongly interjected and become a third major political player with Syria and Iran to strongly influence the region. In doing so, it is playing a significant role to lay the groundwork for the emergence of genuine regional autonomy in West Asia in the aftermath of the U.S. invasion of Iraq.

After suffering a blow to its regional profile following the assassination in 2005 of former Prime Minister Rafik Hariri, Saudi Arabia is clawing back in Lebanon. Ironically, it is Syria, with whom Riyadh has had a patchy relationship in past, which has emerged as its de facto ally in this exercise. Given Syria's close ties with Turkey and Iran, Damascus is now well positioned to mediate and bridge deep seated differences experienced between post-revolutionary Tehran and Riyadh.

Iran continues to remain the focus of attention in West Asia. Already subjected to four rounds of international sanctions, the threat of war is likely to loom over Iran, as long as a breakthrough over the Iranian nuclear issue remains unachieved. Syria continues to remain Iran's chief ally, and the two together provide critical support to the Palestinian Hamas and the Lebanese Hizbollah—two organisations positioned on the frontlines facing Israel. Notwithstanding their close ties, the Iran-Syria equation is undergoing a modification. With Turkey emerging as its major ally and on account of its improving relations with Saudi Arabia, Syria's critical dependence on Iran has been considerably reduced. It is now unlikely that Iran would anymore be in a position to exhort Syria to join it in a possible war against Israel, should the need arise. But despite its expanding options, Syria is likely to keep open its transit lines to enable weapons supplied by Iran to reach Hizbollah and Hamas. This would be in Syria's interest for Hizbollah's growing military clout is likely to enhance its capacity to deter Israel from pursuing military adventurism, either in Lebanon or against its arch-foe Iran.

With the war against Iran, which is likely to lead to regional turmoil still a distinct possibility, Turkey is engaged in a diplomatic exercise to prevent conflict that would embroil Tel Aviv and Tehran. Turkey, on account of its role in nuclear diplomacy surrounding Iran, and Syria, which remains an ally of Iran backed anti-Israel groups have together some leverage to moderate Tehran's behaviour. With their lines of communication open to Riyadh, the two, Turkey and especially Syria, can also help generate a détente between Iran and Saudi Arabia. In case some progress is achieved on the Iranian nuclear track, based on the Tehran declaration of May 2010, it is likely that the unstructured but growing diplomatic integration among the region's stakeholders may get formalised into a semi-autonomous process of regional engagement in the future.

Despite 9/11 and the Iraq war that followed, the countries of the region have so far managed to ward off the threat of regime change. The stage is now set for the loosening of Western hegemonic influence and the emergence of greater autonomous space for regional forces and influences to work, in order to shape West Asia's destiny in the future. For India, the recognition of an autonomous geopolitical space that is emerging in West Asia is vital for enabling it to safeguard its interests, related especially to energy security in the future. India may need to take imaginative steps to anchor a strategic relationship with Iran. The signing of the Iran-Pakistan-India gas pipeline or its deep sea alterative which avoids the turbulence in Pakistan can provide the foundation for elevating Indo-Iran ties to the next level. India's relationship with Saudi Arabia is moving along a positive trajectory. However, much more political capital may need to be invested to shore India's ties with Turkey and Syria, which would allow New Delhi to emerge as an independent and credible player in the region.

End Notes

1. Tony Karon, "Condi in Diplomatic Disneyland," Time, July 26, 2006. Available at http://www.time.com/time/world/article/0,8599,121932500.htm.
2. Robert G. Rabil, "Has Hezbollah's Rise Come at Syria's Expense?", The Middle East Quarterly, Fall 2007. Available at http://www.meforum.org/1755/has-hezbollahs-rise-come-at-syrias-expense.
3. Ibid.
4. Wikileaks Cable, Admiral Mullens Meeting with Egis Chief Soliman, April 30, 2009, Available at http://www.guardian.co.uk/world/us-embassy-cables-documents/204990).
5. See, Michael Rubin, "The Enduring Iran-Syria-Hezbollah Axis, AEI Middle Eastern Outlook, December 2009, available at http://www.meforum.org/2531/iran-syria-hezbollah-axis.
6. Ibid.
7. Patrick Devenny, "Hezbollah's Strategic Threat to Israel," *Middle East Quarterly* Winter 2006. Available at http://www.meforum.org/806/hezbollahs-strategic-threat-to-israel.
8. Wikileaks, "US embassy cables: Iran bent on nuclear bomb, Israel warns," 18/11/2009. Available at http://www.guardian.co.uk/world/us-embassy-cables-documents/235361.
9. See Atul Aneja, "The tide turns against Israel," *The Hindu*, June 11, 2010. Available at http://www.thehindu.com/opinion/lead/article452262.ece.
10. See Mehmet Efe Biresselioglu, "Changing Dynamics in the Turkey-Iran Relationship," Balkananalysis.com, November 4, 2010. Available at http://www.balkanalysis.com/turkey/2010/11/04/changing-dynamics-in-the-turkey-iran-relationship/.
11. Ibid.
12. See Robert F. Worth, Relations with Turkey Kindle Hopes in Syria, NY Times, December 14, 2009. Available at http://www.nytimes.com/2009/12/15/world/middleeast/15syria.html.
13. See Sebnem Arsu, "Turkey and Syria Signal Improved Relations, NY Times, October 13, 2009. Available at

http://www.nytimes.com/2009/10/14/world/europe/14turkey.htm l.

14. See Rafic Hariri, Wikipedia, the Free Encyclopaedia, available at http://en.wikipedia.org/wiki/Rafic_Hariri.
15. Andrew Lee Butters, "Saudi Arabia and Syria Try to Douse Lebanon's Next Fire," Time, Jul. 31, 2010. Available at http://www.time.com/time/world/article/0,8599,2007875,00.htm l.
16. Peter Lee, "The Natural Gas Game," Counterpunch, Feb 19-21, 2010. Available at http://www.counterpunch.org/lee02192010.html.

10

China Factor in Indo-Iranian Relations

Srikanth Kondapalli

Introduction

Although China had become the second largest economy in the world, it tends to identify on the political issues with that of the other developing countries, including India and Iran. While the Chinese leadership sees a changing world order in which several power centres today— unlike the bipolarity in the Cold War period between the then two superpowers- vying for enhancing their comprehensive national power. In the backdrop of the United States involvement in the Iraq, Afghanistan and North Korean issues, several Chinese view decline in the US power in the 21st century and this offers scope for working together or opportunities to emerge as a major power in the medium term. In this context, equations with other powers–regional and global-become crucial for China.

Other factors as well highlight the importance of India and Iran for China. Historically, cultural and religious exchanges marked the evolution of these three countries. Prakrit (from India) and Saka (from Iran-an extinct language) are still spoken among some ethnic minorities in Xinjiang in China. Chinese leaders, in their interactions with Iran and India, highlight the beneficial historical contacts with these countries. With Iran, such relations with China are traced to the Han dynasty's interactions with Persia in the 2nd Century B.C. [1] Chinese traveller and historian Zhang Qian's account mentioned about the contacts between the two countries, although these appear to be sporadic in nature. Chinese emperors provided refuge to the Persian kings in times of trouble. Historical evidence related to the findings of coins in several parts of China indicated to the establishment of trade contacts between the two. This is facilitated by the four silk routes, specifically the southern route which connected western areas of China with Sassanid Iran. Tang dynasty period is said to have further consolidated relations between the two empires with mutual influences in poetry, magic, religious and cultural aspects. [2] Likewise, historical contacts between China and India had also been fruitful to both in terms of the spread of Buddhism, visits by Buddhist pilgrims such as Faxian (337?-422?), Xuanzang (627-45) and Yijing (635-713), trade through the silk route and the like. [3]

Even though major countries in Asia, viz., China, India and Iran had suggested to a glorious past and frequently referred to by their elites as civilisational entities- these three countries depleted considerably in the 19th and early 20th centuries due to the on-set of colonialism. To some extent, 20th century proved to be a period of nation building and rejuvenation in these countries with several possibilities for their growth in stature in the 21st century. These three countries had been interacting in a mutually beneficial relationship at the bilateral and multilateral levels for considerable number of decades. While United States and Europe still are major factors in India-Iran interactions, China is emerging as a factor in the bilateral equations between Tehran and New Delhi, albeit marginal and implicit currently.

Apart from the civilisational glue, China's considerations vis-à-vis Iran and India also include the energy factor. China in 2010 is expected to import 200 million tonnes of oil – a majority of which originating from the West Asian region and the Persian Gulf. Iran and India are major factors in this consideration–Iran as a supplier and India due to its geographical local in the Indian Ocean region, besides the Chinese interest in the proposed Iran-Pakistan-India oil pipeline.

Another issue that had tested both China as well as India is the recent controversy related to the Iranian nuclear issue, specifically after Iran announced an active weapon programme, despite being a member of the Nuclear Non-Proliferation regime. While China had an active role in the Iranian nuclear build up in the 1990s, it had changed its position in the last few years due to the US pressure. India, likewise, had been taking steps perceived by Iran as close to that of the US position, as exhibited in the International Atomic Energy Agency (IAEA) deliberations.

This article traces those issues which could possibly indicate to the China factor in the bilateral relations between India and Iran. Specifically, issues such as global and regional order, revival of civilisational dialogue, trade, energy and nuclear issues, as well as multilateral grouping such as Shanghai Cooperation Organisation become relevant here. At the outset, it needs to be mentioned here that sharp differences exist between the three–such as on the US role, future of Afghanistan, counter-terrorism, Shia-Sunni factor, hot spot issues like Kashmir and Xinjiang, etc. Yet at a general and strategic level, the three have several issues of commonality with which they are currently focused upon.

The Trilateral Context

All the three countries–China, India and Iran–as with the others have gone through a historical phase of consolidation, decline and currently in the nation-building process for the last few decades. A major factor then that influences these three countries is while harking back to the perceived glorious past of traditional empires in India, Sassanid Persia and imperial China, all of them are focused on protecting their perceived sovereignty and territorial integrity and on enhancing their respective comprehensive national strengths. Nobel Laureate Rabindranath Tagore's visits to China in 1928 and to Iran in the 1930s were mainly to invoke Asian unity. [4] In 1947, during the Asian Relations Conference at Delhi, the mood of several Asian political constituents emphasised on working together in the nation-building process. Subsequently, there were other efforts - notably the Bandung conference in 1955 and the Afro-Asian unity movement which tried to bring together the newly formed post-colonial independent countries. Yet, this period did not witness any major sustainable architecture that could effectively address the issues faced by these countries, and partly were influenced by the rivalry of the Cold War period between the then two superpowers. While the local context and issues are different for each of these three states under discussion, viz., the Arab-Palestinian-Israel or India-Pakistan or China-Taiwan conflicts, it needs to be pointed out that Iran, India and China have been able to sustain individually over a long period of time – in contrast to a number of other states at similar levels of socio-economic and political development that are now either in the process of failing or failed states.

In the last two decades, with the disintegration of the Soviet Union and September 11, 2001 incident the world and the region ushered into new challenges apart from the agenda of protection of territorial integrity and national sovereignty. These three countries have now also to address non-traditional security challenges in addition to the previous agenda of tackling traditional security issues.

Specific challenges to these three countries are not uniform though and hence their national responses, including foreign policy postures, are varied in nature.

Specifically, reflecting on the historical trajectory of the three Asian countries, viz., Iran, India and China, it can be pointed out that broadly these three–by being relatively large in the international system in terms of territory, population, economy, natural resources, geographical location and the ability to influence the power structure at the regional and global levels–have been able to retain a high level of nationhood, maintain relatively higher socio-economic development and are emerging as significant poles in the international system.

Another unique aspect of all these three countries is the independent actors in the international system, given their foreign policy objectives of not aligning with any major power nor have any military alliances. This factor can work for the benefit of any one of the three countries, specifically in their equations with the US, the sole super power in the world today. While the ruling elites in many of these countries face significant challenges of political legitimacy, internal turmoil caused by ethnic or regional disparities or other causes, periods of relative peace and development have made them as powers to reckon with. Over a period of time, these three countries were able to usher in relative political stability internally and also carve niche areas of strength and rejuvenation– such as in the energy fields for Iran, manufacturing sector for China and service and IT sectors for India.

Relative stability and prosperity of these three states are also reflected in new ideas emanating from these countries. Iran, India and China have been toying with several new initiatives at the regional and global levels. India and China have been carefully evaluating the Iranian suggestion on the dialogue among civilisations as one of the ways of political interaction. All the three have expressed concerns on the US debates on "clash of civilisation" phenomenon for its impact internally in these ethnically/religiously diverse societies. The Iranian debates in this regard for dialogue and close coordination among Iran, India and China should be noted in particular. All the three suggest that the United Nations Charter should be respected and advocate multi-polarity and multilateralism as forms of interaction and are part of the Shanghai Cooperation Organisation–with India and Iran as observers. India and China have significant stakes in the Iranian energy and economic fields–with the multilateral grouping Gulf Cooperation Council as one such arena of cooperation. Free Trade Area proposals, market integration, energy pipeline construction or other joint infrastructure projects are being explored by these three countries to expand complementarities for mutual benefit.

However, significant differences between these three countries exist on the type of political systems to be followed, form of governance, religious beliefs and the like. At times the international and regional power dynamics as well impinged on the interactions between these three countries, specifically the United States factor. Some of these are reflected in at-times heated debates and latent animosities on a number of issues. These differences are related to the nuclear factor, ethnic issues in China and India, equations in Afghanistan and the like which shall be discussed in brief below.

The China Factor

For both Iran and India, the significance of the China factor in their bilateral as well as at the regional and global levels is obvious. By being one of the permanent members of the United Nations Security Council, China's voice on a number of issues affecting regional and international security in general and directly on both Iran and India is important, if not decisive. On a number of issues affecting Iran and India, China did influence, to an extent, the outcome at the UNSC. For Iran, broadly, these are related to Israel-Palestinian issues and regional security themes such as West Asian peace proposals, Iran-Iraq war and on the recent Iranian nuclear programme. [5] For India, the issue of prisoners of war during the India-Pakistan war of 1971 and the subsequent Bangladesh membership as an independent country at the UN or on the nuclear and Kashmir issues between India and Pakistan, there is certainly the China hangover at the UNSC.

Secondly, if one of the main considerations of Iran, India and China in the last several decades are based on minimalist foreign policy goals of protecting sovereignty, territorial integrity and maintaining freedom of judgement and action as independent actors in the international system, then the responses of each of these states vis-à-vis each other in these spheres is also important. From China's minimalist foreign policy objectives, Iran, as with any other Islamic country, could be a source of succour vis-à-vis Xinjiang Uighur region, where pan-Turkic population has exhibited not only restiveness but also pan-regional networks. [6] Hence, in order to stabilise the far-flung western areas and consolidate China's hold over the region, it is essential to rope in the concerned countries, including Iran. It is not surprising, then, following from this perspective, most of the Iranian leader's visits to China had Xinjiang as a part of the itinerary. [7]

However, this issue could also be a source of tension between Tehran and Beijing. The continuing unrest in Xinjiang by the Uighurs elicited positive interest from Tehran recently. On July 5, 2009, Xinjiang region had witnessed one of the large scale violence in the region's history. Although from the early 1990s, trouble was brewing for Beijing in its hold over these western areas, the 2009 incident rattled the Chinese leaders, as reflected in the sudden departure of President Hu Jintao from the G-8 extended meeting in Italy. On that day, a toll of nearly 200 people was reported–mostly Han victims at the hands of the suspected restive Uighurs. Subsequently, with the law enforcement agencies, thousands of Uighurs were arrested, incarcerated or even executed. In this backdrop, while China's partners sided with Beijing–notably Russia, Central Asian States, Pakistan and others-Tehran was critical of Beijing's handling of this incident and sided with Turkey and Organisation of Islamic Unity's position that the interests of the Muslims in Xinjiang should be protected.

As for India, the recent controversy from 2008 about the Chinese revival of its policy vis-à-vis Kashmir in the form of issuing of stapled visas to Kashmir residents in India, investments in the infrastructure projects in Pakistan Occupied Kashmir and Northern Areas (renamed as Gilgit and Baltistan) and invitation to the Hurriyet leaders – all these have tested the India-China relations in the recent period. On the part of Iran, fresh trouble seems to be brewing between New Delhi and Tehran on the continuing protests and violence in the Kashmir valley. For Tehran recently had voiced concerns at the OIC meeting on the Kashmir issue.

However, on the Mumbai terror attacks of November 26, 2009, the responses of Beijing and Tehran were different. Although China had announced that it opposes all forms of terrorism, it stopped short of being critical of Pakistan's based outfits' role in cross border terrorism incidents in India. Iran's response on this issue was different. Its foreign minister Manuchehr Mottaki said on December

31, 2008 that "Certain extra-regional powers are carrying out activities that cause instability in South Asia. They have organized plans that lead to extremism...". [8] The focus of the Iranian critique obviously was the US here.

Thirdly, as China and India are rising fast and influencing the geopolitical environment at the regional and global levels, relations between Iran, India and China have been acquiring new features. At least three issues can be outlined here, viz. energy imports from Iran by both India and China, responses of Beijing and New Delhi on the renewed Iranian nuclear programme, and regional stability issues such as post-International Security Assistance Force (ISAF) withdrawal from Afghanistan operations in 2011/2014 framework. The outcome on these three issues could be divisive or also has the possibilities of bringing together the three. Hence, these are significant issues that need some elaboration. As a predominant power as well, the China factor in these three issues would be carefully monitored by the other two as with other countries in the near future. An indication of the China factor is reflected in the Chinese systematic interaction at the bilateral and multilateral, institutional and long-term contacts with both Iran and India and also seen in the appointment of a Middle East Envoy, formulation of comprehensive policies towards West and South Asian regions and the like. [9]

Energy Security Issues

Both China and India have become largest energy importers as a result of their economic development in the last two decades. Since 1993, China became the net importer of energy resources. Today, it had become the largest energy importer in the world, surpassing US and Japan in quick succession. As conflicts became rampant in the West Asian region and sustainable supplies of energy became a main problematic, in addition to their affordability (as oil prices are shooting up), China and India are also concerned with the political stability in the region.

China is dependent on the West Asian oil resources for nearly 60 percent currently and this figure is expected to rise to about 70 percent in the near future. [10] While Saudi Arabia constitutes an overwhelming proportion of the Chinese oil imports, Iran too is emerging as a major oil exporting countries. [11] China's energy dependence on Iran is currently about 13.6 percent, but expected to rise to about 17 percent in near future – a figure which is almost the percentage of Indian energy imports from Iran. [12] By 2010, China emerged as the second largest export destination for Iranian energy products, while Iran emerged as the second largest supplier of oil for India. [13]

In order to secure oil and gas resources from Iran, China has unveiled an ambitious policy of prospecting, drilling and exporting energy resources from Iran. While China has amassed US$ 2.4 trillion in foreign exchange reserves by June 2010, it has made major commitments of investing a portion of this reserve mainly in the energy field across the globe and in Iran in particular–as against the US$ 5 billion promised by India in Iran in June 2009. In March 2004, for instance, one of the four major oil companies of China-Zhuhai Zhengrong–signed a MoU with Iran to import 110 million tonnes of LNG for over 25 years. [14] Subsequently, Iranian vice-oil minister Hadi Nejadhosainaian visited Beijing to negotiate a deal with China Petroleum & Chemical Corp (Sinopec) - the second largest Chinese oil firm-on the nearly US$ 100 billion deal to supply China with at least 5 million tonnes of LNG a year. Sinopec succeeded in its drilling efforts in Iran in December 2003 at Kashan oilfield. In October 2004, both countries signed a MoU on energy exploration. According to this, Sinopec is to develop the Yadavaran oilfield in south-western Iran in lieu of purchase of 10 million tonnes of liquefied natural gas a year for the next 25 years. [15]

Further, China is believed to have concluded an energy agreement with Iran in February 2006. [16] In December 2006, China National Offshore Oil Corp (CNOOC) and National Iranian Oil Company signed a MoU to jointly explore North Pars gas field in Iran. This field has an estimated 80 trillion cubic feet of natural gas and requires about US$ 16 billion (including US$ 11 billion to develop downstream segment). The project is to be completed in about eight years and the offer to supply gas to the Chinese will be for 25 years. [17] In January 2009 the National Iranian Oil Company signed an agreement worth US$ 1.7 billion to develop Iranian North Azadegan oil field that has estimated reserves of six billion barrels of oil. [18] Later, in March, a consortium of three Chinese energy companies signed an agreement with National Iranian Oil Company to produce LNG from South Pars field. This deal is worth US$ 3.3 billion. [19] In April 2009, Iranian Vice-president, Parviz Davoudi visited China to attend the BoAo Forum for Asia meeting. He underlined the Iran-China cooperation in the energy field. [20]

China is also involved in other related projects in Iran. In January 2006, in a contract worth US$ 33 million, a Chinese company COSL signed an agreement with Iran's North Excavation Company for maintenance, repair, and management of semi-floating Iran-Alborz platform in the Caspian sea for a three year period. [21] Further to consolidate its linkages with Iran, China intends to build a 386-kilometer pipeline from Iran connecting to Kazakhstan from where already a pipeline is in operation by 2006. [22]

As mentioned above, India's dependence on energy resources from Iran is also increasing in proportion in terms of imports as well as investments in the energy sector in Iran. Iran also needs India as the latter accounts for nearly 40 percent of imports of refinery oil for the domestic consumption in Iran. In addition, India is also involved in several infrastructure development projects across Iran, including the Chabahar port and Zarang-Delaram road that could link India with the Central Asian region, without going through the troubled Pakistani territory. In this context, significant differences between India and China exist regarding the entry points and these are based on their respective national interests. While China is for opening up the Gwadhar port in the Makran coast of Pakistan, India is for depending on Bandar e-Abbas. Another project, though stalled for the time being, is the proposed Iran-Pakistan-India pipeline project on which china had recently expressed its interest. If the laying down of nearly US$ 7 billion worth Iran-Pakistan-Indian oil pipeline succeeds, China would like to extend this farther into Yunnan province as well–with or without India participating. [23]

The trilateral relations are also exhibited in burgeoning, if in overall terms meagre, economic and trade relations. [24] By 2010, Indian and Chinese trade with Iran is almost equivalent to about US$ 30 billion each–expanding from a meagre figure a decade ago.

Iranian Nuclear Issue

After the Iranian declaration in 2005 that it had started the process of uranium enrichment, developments in 2006 were swift. Specifically, the Chinese position vis-à-vis the Iranian nuclear issue underwent a gradual change. [25] China's (and Russian) position on the Iranian nuclear issue differed with that of the western countries. The European Union (EU)-3 (Germany, Britain and France) and the US threatened to refer the issue to the United Nations Security

Council with possible imposition of sanctions. Both China and Russia initially indicated that they are opposed to sanctions and that they could scuttle the EU-3 and US moves by vetoing the proposals for stalling Iranian nuclear programme. In September 2004, for instance, Chinese ambassador to the 35-member IAEA Board of Governors issued an unprecedented statement that it would use its veto power in the UNSC if the Iranian nuclear issue is forwarded. The Chinese envoy also said that his country supports the Non - Aligned Movement position on the Iranian issue. [26]

By June 2006, however, China was in broad consensus with the US and EU-3 that sanctions could be imposed on Iran if it proceeds with its nuclear programme. However, the sanctions, according to the decisions of the Vienna meeting of the permanent five plus Germany, have to abide by the UN Charter. [27] The following events, although details of actual negotiations are unavailable, indicate to the changes in the Chinese positions on the issue. Initially, Chinese position was that the Iranian nuclear issue should be solved through negotiations and that any resort to sanctions on Iran would be detrimental to peace and stability in the region.

To recount events in 2006, in January, the Chinese ambassador to the UN Wang Guangya called on Iran to cooperate with the EU-3 in negotiating a solution to the nuclear issue and that if it does not, then Tehran "could face difficulties." [28] Ali Larijani, secretary of Iran's Supreme National Security Council visited Beijing, after his trip to Moscow, on January 26, 2006 to meet high-level Chinese officials to enhance "mutual cooperation". [29] At the end of January, and before the February 2-3, 2006 IAEA emergency meeting, the Chinese foreign ministry spokesman, in the backdrop of Ali Larijani's visit to Beijing, supported the plan to have Iran's uranium enriched in Russia. [30] While meeting German foreign minister Steinmeier, Li Zhaoxing suggested in February 2006 that Iran should suspend all uranium enrichment, while at the same time calling the IAEA meeting of March 6 to observe restraint on Iran. [31] Vice foreign minister Lu Guozeng visited Teheran in February 2006 and conducted "in-depth and candid" discussions with the Iranian president and other leaders. He said, "China is willing to work with Iran to further enhance bilateral exchanges and cooperation in such fields as politics, economy, trade and culture". [32] Lu reportedly said that Iran "could take positive action and demonstrate flexibility so as to create conditions for the solution of the Iranian nuclear issue through diplomatic negotiations". [33] In April 2006, at a meeting of defence ministers of SCO, Chinese defence minister Cao Gangchuan said that Iran is entitled to harness nuclear energy for peaceful purposes, although he said that diplomatic talks should be given a chance to solve the issue. [34]

However, during the visit of Chinese president Hu Jintao to Washington in April 2006, a "consensus" was arrived at between China and the US on the Iranian issue. [35] Coinciding with the Iranian announcement in April 2006 that it had reached the stage of uranium enrichment to the level needed to make reactor fuel, China dispatched assistant vice foreign minister Cui Tiankai to discuss with Ali Larijani and nuclear negotiator Javad Vaidi. [36] On the US proposal in early June 2006 that Iran should stop uranium enrichment before negotiations could take place, China argued that no conditions should be imposed on Iran and that "arbitrary sanctions" should not be imposed on Iran. Later, China suggested, during the visit of German chancellor to Beijing on June 11, 2006, that China is keen on participating in talks.

By August 2006, China dispatched assistant foreign minister Cui Tiankai to Iran on a "working visit". Cui conveyed the message that "China hopes that Iran will seize the opportunity to respond to the package put forward by the EU side in a positive way". [37] In January 2007, meeting the Iranian special envoy, president Hu noted that "The UN Security Council unanimously adopted Resolution 1737, which reflects the shared concerns of the international community over the Iranian nuclear issue, and we hope Iran will make a serious response to the resolution". [38] In March 2007, during the visit of deputy foreign minister Abbas Araghchiry, Li Zhaoxing suggested that while China advocated peaceful negotiations to resolve the nuclear issue, the Iranian side should "positively address " the concerns of the international community on this issue. [39]

Subsequently, a six-nation initiative on resolving the Iranian nuclear issue was formed in September 2007 at New York to include China, Russia, the EU-3 (UK, France and Germany) and the United States. After Iran agreed to resolve the nuclear issue within four weeks at the January 13, 2008 IAEA meeting, the six nations met at Berlin on January 22, 2008 reached a consensus on major points to be adopted by the 3rd UN Security Council resolution. While China underplayed the role of sanctions as a part of this consensus, pressure is mounting on Iran. The Chinese foreign minister Yang Jiechi, this time, urged "creative" diplomatic work to overcome the deadlock. [40] In April 2008, China hosted six party talks to revive negotiations on the Iranian nuclear issue. However, no concrete outcome was forthcoming. [41] China's assistant foreign minister Liu Jieyi participated at the E3+3 meeting on Iranian nuclear issue at Wiesbaden, Germany in February 2009. [42] Liu reportedly said at the meeting: "The six countries should seize the present opportunity, enhance diplomatic efforts and manage the issue with flexibility and creativity in a bid to seek comprehensive, long-term and proper methods to solve the issue". [43] In June 2010, the United Nations passed the resolution 1929 that imposed sanctions on Tehran for a fourth round, this time as well with full consent from Beijing and Moscow. [44]

While India has no direct linkage to the Iranian nuclear issue in terms of cooperating with the latter in its nuclear capability (as was the case with Russia and China), this issue had torn the Indian establishment from its previous positions. For India, the Iranian nuclear issue is a complicated subject, as Tehran had been a member of the NPT regime but, in violation of its pledges to the NPT and IAEA, wishes to enrich uranium for weapon programme. Hence, at the 2005 IAEA meeting, India voted against Iran on the nuclear issue, although US "coercion" is said to be one of the main considerations during this voting patterns. [45]

Afghanistan Issue

Another issue on which the China factor is likely to be impacted in the near future is on Afghanistan. While currently, Iran, India and China are relatively aloof from the situation in Afghanistan, given the multi-national International Security Assistance Force (ISAF) presence for stabilizing Afghanistan and restoring law and order in the hands of the national government in Kabul, in the light of recent escalation in violence and the resurgence of the Taliban, the role of these regional states may increase as these countries would be affected by any post-withdrawal scenarios in Kabul. Iran currently has three million refugees from Afghanistan and shares porous borders.

In the light of the post 911 situation a number of Afghans, including the retreating Taliban may have escaped to the border regions of Iran. However, the Taliban was suspected to be involved in a series of attacks on Iranian interests, including the 1998 Mazar-e-Sharif assassination of score of Iranian diplomats. In addition, both have different views and interests. While the Shia majority Iran has some influence among Hazaras, the Sunni Pashtun elements predominate among the Taliban.

While Iran and India supported the Northern Alliance, China and Pakistan have supported the Taliban. For India as well, the resurgence of the Taliban has critical security challenges as was reflected in the IC814 hijacking and release of militants by India. India's assistance in several infrastructure projects, including the building of Chabahar port and Zarang-Delaram road, could provide access for India and Iran to the Afghan interior as well as to Central Asia, although China and Pakistan would like to explore alternate routes.

In this backdrop, the China factor in the India-Iran relations could become crucial, although all the three agree that stability, reconciliation and reconstruction in Afghanistan is vital to the security of the peripheral regions of these states. It is interesting to note an Iranian view in this context. The Iranian president Mahmud Ahmadinezad argued that "by keeping its forces in Afghanistan, the US has inflicted a heavy financial burden on its economy" suggesting that Washington seeks "to bring down the economies of India and China by causing instability...Their ulterior motive is to weaken India and China." [46]

Conclusions

The above analyses indicates that China as a major power in the world today had been influencing the bilateral relations between Iran and India, while the latter two are also responding in several ways. China's relations with Iran and India today are improving and are more composite in comparison to the earlier period. Bilateral political, diplomatic, military and economic visits and relations improved considerably. In the last decade, such relations became more focused in nature as well. At the multilateral level, new ideas are being publicised and adapted. Over a period of time, these three countries have built considerable stakes in each other.

Nevertheless, despite being largely mutually beneficial, such ties have also exhibited tensions–specifically for Tehran. [47] As was pointed out earlier, while economic and trade relations improvement with Beijing and New Delhi benefited Tehran from international isolation, the other two issues, nuclear and Afghanistan have a different outcome. On the Iranian nuclear issue, clearly, despite intensifying energy and economic linkages between these three countries, the role of Beijing and New Delhi underwent significant revisions–as with the revisions in Tehran. The June 2010 UN Resolution of 1929, had called for sanctions on the military and financial sectors of Iran. China had consented to this resolution, despite having wide financial and military cooperation with Tehran. [48] To what extent will China be actually ready to implement these resolutions or even use force against Tehran is unclear. Nor is it clear that China will be able to guarantee Iranian security in lieu of Tehran giving up its nuclear option. [49] None of these scenarios were made explicit by Beijing.

However, it can be safely predicted that China may not lose its stakes in Tehran in the near future, specifically diplomatic, economic, commercial and military ties which proved to be useful. For instance, in August 2009, vice premier Li Keqiang (expected to replace Wen Jiabao as Premier in 2012 Party Congress) assured Iranian Oil Minister Massoud Mirkazemi that these interests and cooperation with Iran would continue. [50] However, how China could wriggle out of the UN sanctions in Iran and protect its commercial or strategic interests in Iran are not clear. It is likely that Beijing could club up with others, such as Moscow, New Delhi, or other capitals which would be equally affected by the above sanctions. Or some of these affected states could seek Presidential exemption from the US. [51] There is also the lingering suspicion in New Delhi as well that the Chinese forays in Iran could upset the West Asian apple cart, specifically as the US faces set-backs and prepares to withdraw. [52]

On the energy security issues, tensions may also be brewing, although these now appear to be bleak. For instance, Iran had declared in 2008 that if it is attacked by the US based on the nuclear issue, then Tehran is likely to retaliate by controlling Strait of Hormuz. Indeed, in early 2008 a US-Iran naval incident took place in the Hormuz. This situation complicates China's relations with Iran as China is dependent on these Straits and it had helped build Gwadar naval port. Currently, one-third of China's oil imports flow through the Hormuz Strait. [53]

On Afghanistan, it is likely that the regional states say on the post-ISAF withdrawal situation may increase the role of these three countries. On this issue, despite peripheral inclinations, Beijing is likely to follow Pakistan to the detriment of both Tehran and New Delhi's interests and security. Yet, there could be other possibilities as well, although the bottom line for Beijing appears that any post ISAF withdrawal scenarios in Kabul should be conducive as it had invested in the extraction of raw materials and infrastructure projects, besides training the Mujahedeen against the Soviet Union during the 1980s.

The above prospects and limitations lead us to argue that while China had not yet become an explicit and decisive factor in the India-Iran relations–in the same mould as that of the US factor (or even Europe), China's rise in the 21st Century has significant possibilities in this direction, albeit implicit in nature.

End Notes

1. See Ye Feng, "*Zhonghua renmin gonghe guo yu Yilang guanxi*" [People's Republic of China and Iran relations] in Tang Jiaxuan Ed. *Zhongguo Waijiao Cidian* [Dictionary of China's Diplomacy] (Beijing: World Knowledge Publications, 2000), p. 680.
2. see John W. Garver, China & Iran: Ancient Partners in a Post-Imperialist World (Seattle: University of Washington Press, 2006).
3. See A. Rahman Ed India's Interaction with China, Central Asia and West Asia (Oxford University Press, New Delhi, 2002). Tan Chung argued that a "Himalayo-centric perspective" can be applied to the India-China bordering areas. Utilising recent archaeological findings at Yuanmou in Yunnan province, Tan argued that the trans-Himalayan region could be considered to be "an important cradle of human civilisation" and that both Indian and Chinese civilisations are "twins emerging from this cradle."(p127). He linked archaeological finds of Wushan County (Sichuan Province), Yuanmou (Yunnan Province), Lantian Man (Shaanxi Province), Peking Man with Hoshangabad (Madhya Pradesh) fossils to arrive at such a picture. See Tan Chung in A. Rahman Ed. *Ibid* Chapter 4.
4. Tagore gave a clarion call for all Asian countries to unite in spiritual terms. Tagore stated: "In Asia we must seek our strength in union, in an unwavering faith in righteousness, and never in the egotistic spirit of separateness and self-assertion.

...In Asia we must unite, not through some mechanical method of organisation, but through a spirit of true sympathy. The organised power of the machine is ready to smite and devour us, from which we must be rescued by the living power of spirit which grows into strength, not through mere addition, but through organic assimilation. That we should borrow science from the West is right. We have a great thing to accept from the people of West, their treasure of intellect, which is immense and whose superiority we must acknowledge. But it would be degradation on our part, and an insult to our ancestors. If we forgot our own moral wealth of wisdom, which is of far greater value than a system that produces endless materials and a physical power that is always on the warpath." See Tagore, "China and India" in Tan Chung Ed. *In The Footsteps Of Xuanzang: Tan Yun-Shan and India* (New Delhi: IGNCA, 1999) accessed at <http://www.ignca.nic.in.

5. See for the overall Chinese objectives vis-à-vis the West Asian region, Lee Deng-ker, *Lengzhanhou Zhonggong dui Zhongdong diqu de waijiao zhengci* [Foreign Policy of Communist China towards Middle East during the post Cold War] (Taipei: Zhengzhong shuju, 1995).
6. Wang Meng, "*20 shiji Zhongguo can yu Zhongdong shiwu de yisilan yinsi*" [The Islamic factor in China's participation in Middle East in the 20th Century] *Ningxia Shehui Kexue* [Ningxia Social Sciences] March 2007 vol. 2 issue 141 pp. 87-94.
7. See Garver, chapter 5. See also Willam van Kemenade, "Iran's relations with China and the West" at <http://www.clingendael.nl/publications/2009/20091100_cdsp_paper_kemenade_iran.pdf .
8. "Iran says ready to broker India-Pakistan talks" Iranian news channel Press TV website on 31 December 2008 at BBC.
9. On West Asia see Srikanth Kondapalli, "China's Relations with West Asia" in Srikanth Kondapalli and Emi Mifune Eds. China and its Neighbours (New Delhi: Pentagon Press, 2010) pp. 243-82.
10. This is based on Srikanth Kondapalli, "Sino-Iranian Relations: Cobbling a United Front" in Anwar Alam ed. Iran and Post-9/11 World Order: Reflections on Iranian Nuclear Programme (Delhi: New Century Publications, 2009) pp.75-100.
11. See Manochehr Dorraj and Carrie L. Currier, "Lubricated with

Oil: Iran-China Relation in a Changing World" at http://www.mepc.org/journal/middle-east-policy-archives/lubricated-oil-iran-china-relations-changing-world and Charles E. Ziegler, "The Energy Factor in China's Foreign Policy" Journal of Chinese Political Science Vol. 11, No. 1 (Spring 2006).

12. See "Iran's petrochem exports to China to rise to US$ 1b" May 11, 2008 http://www.iranmania.com/News/ArticleView/Default.asp?NewsCode=59736&NewsKind=Current percent20Affairs> accessed on May 18, 2008.
13. See "India-Iran-China energy" Oxford Analytica at <http://www.menasaforum.ae/research_reports/files/Oxford_Analytica_IRAN_CHINA_INDIA_Energy_ties_deepen_despite_sanctions_tmp77E.pdf.>
14. Liu Weiling and Xie Ye, "Sino-Iranian LNG deal in pipeline" China Daily April 12, 2004 at http://www.chinadaily.com.cn/english/doc/2004-04/12/content_322445.htm.
15. See Peter S Goodman, "China Rushes Toward Oil Pact With Iran" Washington Post February 18, 2006 at http://www.washingtonpost.com/wp-dyn/content/article/2006/02/17/AR2006021702146.html accessed on May 15, 2006 and "'US$ 100b Iran-China energy deal ready to be inked'" April 30, 2006 at http://www.iranmania.com > accessed on June 13, 2006.
16. See Peter S Goodman, "China Rushes Toward Oil Pact With Iran" Washington Post February 18, 2006 at http://www.washingtonpost.com/wp-dyn/content/article/2006/02/17/AR2006021702146.html accessed on May 15, 2006.
17. Details of this MoU at Wang Yu, "CNOOC to develop Iranian gas field" China Daily December 22, 2006 at http://www.chinadaily.com.cn/bizchina/2006-12/22/content_765293.htm.
18. "Iran, China sign 1.7bn-dollar deal for developing oil field" Mehr (Tehran) January 14, 2009 at BBC and "China, Iran Oilfield Cooperation To Help Stabilize Market, Spokeswoman" Xinhua, January 15, 2009 at BBC.
19. See "Iran, China sign €2.6bn gas deal" March 14, 2009 at

http://www.presstv.ir/detail.aspx?id=88560 > accessed on April 20, 2009.

20. See "Iran to promote energy and financial cooperation with China" Xinhua April 18, 2009 at http://news.xinhuanet.com/english/2009-04/18/content_11211926.htm > accessed on April 20, 2009 "Iran open to China energy investments" April 19, 2009 at <http://www.presstv.ir/detail.aspx?id=91899&sectionid=351020 103 > accessed on April 20, 2009.
21. "Iran, China sign excavation agreement" January 19, 2006 at http://www.iranmania.com> accessed on June 13, 2006.
22. See Kaveh L Afrasiabi, "China's energy insecurity and Iran's crisis" Asia Times February 10, 2006 reprinted at http://indiamonitor.com/news/readNews.jsp?ni=10484> accessed on May 22, 2006 and "Iran to push ahead with trans-Afghan corridor" January 6, 2005 at http://www.iranmania.com> accessed on June 13, 2006.
23. Raman Iyer, "China likely to replace India in Iran-Pak gas pipeline project" February 6, 2010 at http://www.topnews.in/law/china-likely-replace-india-iranpak-gas-pipeline-project-26861.
24. Garver chapter 9.
25. See Xiong Xiaoqing, Yang Xingli and Liu Jinzhao, "*Neigudezhi zheng dui Zhong-Yi guanxi zouxiang de yingxiang*" [The impact of Ahmedinejad's government on China-Iran relations] *Chongqing Gongxueyuan xuebao* [Journal of Chongqing Institute of Technology], March 2006.
26. "China supports NAM position on Iran nuke" September 16, 2004 at http://www.iranmania.com> accessed on June 13, 2006.
27. See Frank Ching, "US-China Conflict on Iran Nukes" The Korean Times June 9, 2006 at www.hankkoki.com> accessed on June 20, 2006.
28. "China cautions against new complications" January 15, 2006 at http://www.iranmania.com> accessed on June 13, 2006.
29. "Iranian nuclear negotiator arrives in China" January 26, 2006 at http://www.iranmania.com> accessed on June 13, 2006.
30. See "China backs plan to have Iran's uranium enriched in Russia" China Daily January 26, 2006 at http://www.chinadaily.com.cn/english/doc/2006-

01/26/content_515834.htm > See also Jephraim P Gundzik, "The ties that bind China, Russia and Iran" Asia Times June 4, 2005 at <http://www.atimes.com/atimes/China/GF04Ad07.html.

31. Li cited by Reuters at "Iran nuclear crisis can be resolved: China" China Daily February 23, 2006 at http://www.chinadaily.com.cn/english/doc/2006-02/23/content_523222.htm.
32. "Iran, China pledge to enhance cooperation" Xinhua February 25, 2006 at <http://news.xinhuanet.com/english/2006-02/26/content_4229046.htm > accessed on May 15, 2006 and "China joins Russia in Iran diplomacy" February 24, 2006 at http://www.iranmania.com> accessed on June 13, 2006.
33. Lu cited by the Chinese foreign ministry spokesman at "China willing to play 'constructive role' in Iran"> March 1, 2006 at http://www.iranmania.com> accessed on June 13, 2006.
34. "China: Iran entitled to access nuclear energy for peaceful use" IRNA April 26, 2006 at http://www.irna.ir/en/news/view/menu-236/0604264715150138.htm > accessed on May 12, 2006 and "China hopes Iran nuclear issue solved with diplomatic means, defence minister" Xinhua April 27, 2006.
35. "Chinese FM discusses Iran nuke crisis with Rice" May 28, 2006 at <http://www.iranmania.com> accessed on June 13, 2006
36. "Chinese official hold nuclear talks with Iran" April 17, 2006 at http://www.iranmania.com> accessed on June 13, 2006.
37. "Assistant Foreign Minister Cui Tiankai Pays Working Visit to Iran" August 16, 2006 at http://www.fmprc.gov.cn/eng/wjb/zzjg/xybfs/gjlb/2818/2820/t268721.htm.
38. "Hu Jintao Meets with Special Envoy of Iranian Supreme Leader and President Larijani" January 5, 2007 at http://www.fmprc.gov.cn/eng/wjb/zzjg/xybfs/gjlb/2818/2820/t287792.htm.
39. "Foreign Minister Li Zhaoxing Meets with Iran's Deputy Foreign Minister Araghchiry" March 1, 2007 at http://www.fmprc.gov.cn/eng/wjb/zzjg/xybfs/gjlb/2818/2820/t301143.htm.
40. "Six-nation talks add pressure on Iran, keep diplomacy going" Xinhua January 24, 2008 cited at http://english.people.com.cn/90001/90777/90853/6344403.html

>. See also "Foreign Minister Yang Jiechi Attends the Six-Nation Foreign Minister's Meeting on the Iranian Nuclear Issue" January 23, 2008 at http://www.fmprc.gov.cn/eng/wjb/zzjg/xybfs/gjlb/2818/2820/t402614.htm.

41. See Chris Buckley, "Iran nuclear talks in China fall short of agreement" Reuters April 16, 2008 at http://www.reuters.com/article/topNews/idUSPEK25932320080416 > accessed on April 27, 2008.
42. "Chinese Assistant FM To Attend Meetings on Iran Nuke Issue, UN Reform" Xinhua, February 3, 2009.
43. "China Hopes US Mideast Policy Will Aid Peace Progress" Xinhua February 5, 2009 BBC.
44. For a comprehensive view of the subject, see Ariel Farrar-Wellman and Robert Frasco, "China-Iran foreign relations" July 13, 2010 at <http://www.irantracker.org/foreign-relations/china-iran-foreign-relations > See also Jian Junbo, "Iran vote shows China's Western drift" Asia Times June 25, 2010 at http://www.atimes.com/atimes/China/LF25Ad02.html.
45. See Anwar Alam (ed.) Iran and Post-9/11 World Order: Reflections on Iranian Nuclear Programme (Delhi: New Century Publications, 2009).
46. "Iran says ready to broker India-Pakistan talks" Iranian news channel Press TV website on 31 December 2008 at BBC.
47. See Mohsen Shariatinia, "Iran-China Relations: An Iranian View" Iran Review October 3, 2010 at http://www.payvand.com/news/10/oct/1019.html.
48. Peter Lee, "China plays lap-dog in sanctions ploy" Asia Times May 25, 2010 at http://www.atimes.com/atimes/China/LE25Ad02.html.
49. For this scenario, see Robert Haddick, "This Week at War: Could China Disarm Iran?" Foreign Policy April 16, 2010 at http://www.foreignpolicy.com/articles/2010/04/16/this_week_at_war_could_china_disarm_iran.
50. See John Park, "Iran Primer: Iran and China" at http://www.pbs.org/wgbh/pages/frontline/tehranbureau/2010/10/iran-primer-iran-and-china.html.
51. See for such a prospect, NV Subramaniam, "China drives India Iran ties" August 9, 2010 at < http://the-diplomat.com/indian-decade/2010/08/09/china-drives-indian-iran-policy.

52. See "India, China denounce unilateral sanctions on Iran" Tehran Times July 7, 2010 at http://www.tehrantimes.com/index_View.asp?code=222677.
53. Yitzhak Schichor, "Blocking the Hormuz Strait: China's Energy Dilemma" China Brief vol. 8 Issue. 18 September 22, 2008 at http://www.jamestown.org.

11

Indo-Iranian Ties: Is there an Israel Factor?

Sujata Ashwarya Cheema

India's strong relations with both Iran and Israel, regional adversaries constantly at loggerheads with each other, confound West Asia watchers. India and Iran have collaborative engagements over a wide range of issues. There are significant trade ties, particularly those related to crude oil imports into India and diesel exports to Iran. They have not so overt strategic ties, which includes cooperation on a shared threat of terrorism emanating from Pakistan and Afghanistan. Iran is also India's gateway to the Central Asia region and Afghanistan, theatres where India seeks to deepen its economic activities and, more importantly, consolidate a presence by projecting greater power. Iran is, thus, a complex relationship, combining important policy drivers such energy security and strategic considerations. India and Israel have developed profound defence and intelligence ties, which began soon after the establishment of diplomatic ties.

Israel has become India's largest foreign military supplier and civilian trade has jumped significantly in the past few years. There is vigorous co-operation in areas of agriculture and science and technology. India has associated Israel publicly with its sophisticated space programme by launching Israeli satellites on its rockets. Their bond, to begin with, was boosted by the fact that both countries had hostile relations with Muslim neighbours, although the Indian side was reticent to articulate this aspect in public. [1] The above substantive thrust in India's relations with Iran and Israel is largely as old as the demise of the Cold War. With the fall of Communism and its eventual removal, the vision of a bipolar contest between the first and the second world became redundant.

The related notion of a non-aligned Third World was also emptied of all meaning. The states, unshackled from the rigidity of ideological divisions, moved on to maximize their gains by forming varied and amorphous coalitions. In the context, India's foreign policy witnessed an inevitable reorientation: ideology-based engagements gave way to interest-based relations. In West Asia, India became more clear-eyed and aggressive in pursuing its interests. Consequently, countries that had received insufficient attention during the years of the Cold War–Iran, Israel and Saudi Arabia–acquired centrality in India's new West Asia policy. India has sought to balance its ties with the two regional actors by indicating its intent to pursue bilateral relations consistent with its interests and requirements, irrespective of the conflicts they have with each other. This 'strategic autonomy' in its dealing with countries locked in outstanding disputes has been the hallmark of India foreign policy behaviour since independence and also accounts for its sophisticated and complex set of bilateral and multilateral relations. [2] India relations with Iran and Israel are tenuously balanced, largely independent and non-parallel, although contentious issues have intermittently upset the much sought-after equilibrium.

While Iran has been generally indifferent towards India's proximity to Israel, the latter has expressed concerns over many issues in New Delhi-Tehran relations. A look at India's extensive ties with both Iran and Israel in the following sections, would explain why New Delhi constantly seeks to balance the two relationships, even as it aspires to fashion bilateral relationships that do not impact any third country.

Contours of Indo-Iranian Relations

During the Cold War years, ties between India and Iran were constrained by contradictory alliances and leanings. While Iran aligned itself with the West, a newly-independent India adopted the policy of non-alignment i.e. a relationship of equidistance from the superpowers. Iran's preference for Pakistan as an ally and its support for the latter during the Indo-Pakistan wars strained Indo-Iran relations. Iran's support for insurgency in Kashmir and its efforts to 'export' the Islamic Revolution caused the weakening of the bilateral ties even further. Although economic cooperation between them continued throughout this period, it was generally low-keyed and confined primarily to trade in petroleum products. However, the end of the Cold War presented both India and Iran with new challenges and opportunities. A perceptible change in relations followed as both countries tried to articulate their foreign policies in light of altered global environment. There emerged a parallelism of political and economic interests and a shared perception of emerging geo-strategic realities between the two countries. Since then, the ties have advanced from a modest engagement to become more broad-based, registering significant upturns in many areas, including military and intelligence.

Indo-Iranian ties in the energy sector are the most significant, wherein, Iran's interest in exporting its abundant hydrocarbon resources, dovetails perfectly with India's energy-deficient status and growing demand. With high rates of economic growth and over 17 percent of the world's population, India has become a significant consumer of energy resources. Already India imports more than two-third of its hydrocarbon requirements and this dependency is growing rapidly. [3] In this scenario, India's policymakers are well aware of the need to diversify sources of energy supply. This is where Iran comes into play: the Persian Gulf nation accounts for roughly 10 percent of the world's total proven petroleum reserves. [4] Iran in 2007 accounted for 17 percent of India's crude oil imports making it the second-largest supplier of oil after Saudi Arabia at 23 percent. [5] In addition to diversifying its sources of supply, an aspect of India's international energy strategy has also been to acquire stakes in energy production facilities in Iran, in order to ship back liquefied natural gas (LNG). India's investment in Iran's energy sector stands around US$ 100 million. [6] Natural gas is set to become the major component of India's import from Iran, especially as domestic demand rises and India begins to face higher prices in the international market.

Iran, given its unique geo-strategic location, has also emerged as a gateway for India's trade with Central Asia and the land-locked Afghan territory. The availability of the region's market to Indian goods was lost with the disintegration of the Soviet Union. Through the Iranian territory, the India-Central Asia trade has not only revived but has also expanded with the discovery of oil and natural gas deposits in the region. The Central Asian reserve has become crucial to India's Delhi's efforts to locate the widest possible set of alternatives to meet its growing energy requirements. [7] With an accelerating economy, India aspires to emerge as a power that is recognised beyond the perimeters of South Asia. This is reflected in New Delhi's developmental efforts in Afghanistan and in carving of trade routes to Central Asia for a 'presence' in this proximate neighbourhood. If China's great power ambition and its extensive relations with Pakistan are factored in, Iran, is strategically placed to leverage India's power projection and expand its presence in these prized geopolitical areas. [8]

Iran has also become integral to India's growing trade with northern Europe and Afghanistan. A major commercial venture between India and Iran, the North-South Transportation Corridor Agreement, signed in September 2000, would permit facile transport of goods from ports in India to the European ports via Iran. From the Iranian ports across the Arabian Sea, internal rail links would ferry the cargo to the Russian sector of the Caspian Sea and then it would be shipped onward to northern Europe through the Volga River. In pursuance of this ambitious trade route, India is expanding the Iranian port of Chahbahar, which would also open up an alternate route into Afghanistan. India would, thus, be able to sidestep Pakistan's dominance of mainland trade routes to the Afghan territory. New Delhi's expansion of trade here is part of a trilateral agreement signed by India, Iran and Afghanistan in January 2003. [9] This agreement and the North-South Corridor initiative have become key milestones in the promotion of India's trade with Iran, Central Asian countries, Afghanistan, and northern Europe. However, the optimal potential of the North-South corridor is yet to be realized as a project of this magnitude requires large investments and years of sustained effort to make it efficient in the long run.

A shared threat from Sunni radicalism emanating from Pakistan and Afghanistan has emerged as one of the most significant area of cooperation between India and Iran. Currently, both countries share similar concerns about the role of Pakistan in fostering anti-India and anti-Shia terror outfits, including the al-Qaeda, on its soil, and providing support and safe haven to Taliban on its western and southern frontiers. The Pakistani military considers them as counterweights to India's presence in Afghanistan and as a means to deepen its own strategic depth in the war-torn country.

Taliban and its affiliates, at the behest of their masters in Pakistan, have been carrying out attacks on Indian targets in Afghanistan in order to compel India to wrap up its developmental activities there. In a similar vein, Pakistan also dislikes Iran's easy access to Afghanistan and Tehran's deep cultural ties with the Afghan people. Iran is also feeling the heat from increasing Sunni militancy within its territory, especially in Zahedan–a predominantly

Sunni city along Iran's frontier with Pakistan–which has been attributed to Pakistan-based Jundallah (with possible links to Taliban or al-Qaida or elements within the Pakistani government). [10]

Therefore, both India and Iran, have expressed strong reservations on the United States' policy of resolving the Afghan conundrum by negotiating with the so-called 'good' Taliban, with Pakistan as the mediator. The strategy of President Barack Obama's administration has been to ensure that it can divide the Afghan Taliban–that seek to regain power lost in the wake of American attack after 9/11–from the Al Qaeda-led extremists, the 'bad' Taliban, who have a global agenda. Such a strategy places Islamabad back deep into Afghan politics, which is a matter of great trepidation for New Delhi. [11] Pakistan lost its influence in Afghanistan to India after the fall of the Taliban regime and is eager to reverse the situation as much as possible. Any push to reintegrate the Taliban into the government would redouble Islamabad's leverage in Kabul to New Delhi's detriment. What India wants is a relatively benign and non-extremist Afghanistan as a way of limiting Pakistan's influence in the region. Iran is an important ally on the issue whose help is crucial to ensure that India is not left to bear the brunt of a resurgent Pakistan-backed radical Islamist in Afghanistan in the event of a withdrawal of NATO forces from the region. [12]

One of the key instruments of the New Delhi Declaration, a joint Indo-Iranian statement of 2003, is the 'Road Map for Strategic Cooperation', which envisages a robust defence cooperation between the two countries, including training and exchange of visits. [13] Although, defence ties between India and Iran have been clouded in secrecy, a number of reports from secondary sources seem to suggest that India would cooperate with Iran on upgrading the latter's Russian-supplied weapon's system, supply conventional military equipment and spare parts, provide expertise in development of military hardware, and train Iranian armed forces. [14] Several reports indicate that Iran has 'allowed India to have access to its military bases in the event of war with Pakistan.'

If true, this could fundamentally alter regional relations in India's favour. [15] Several analysts also speak of close security ties between New Delhi and Tehran, inferring from the presence of an unusually large number of Indian consulates at strategic locations on the Iranian territory. The Indian consulate in Zahedan indicates a possible intelligence presence. India's consulate in Iranian port city of Bandar Abbas, founded in 2002, amidst protests from Pakistan, permits New Delhi to monitor movement of ships in the Persian Gulf and the straits of Hormuz. Observers in Pakistan note that the Indian engineers working to upgrade the Iranian port of Chabahar can easily monitor their country's activities at the Gwador port, currently being developed as a naval base, with assistance from China. [16] However, cooperation in this area appears to indicate a reinforcement of 'strong Indo-Iranian political relations rather than a broader defence alliance.' [17]

Indo-Israeli Normalisation

In pursuance of a non-ideological approach to foreign policy in the post-Cold War period, India normalised relations with Israel in January 1992. With the establishment of diplomatic ties, bilateral relations witnessed rapid expansion, particular in fields of trade and economic cooperation, defence, science and technology, and culture. From being described as the 'most controversial aspect' [18] of India's foreign policy and subject to criticism from some quarters, Indo-Israeli bilateral relationship has now come to enjoy widespread acceptance and support. There has also been a fundamental understanding of long-term convergence of security interests in the Indo-Israeli ties. A counterterrorism dialogue started in 2000, as both countries foresaw a serious danger from Islamic terrorism. Though this dialogue, the security officials of India and Israel keep track of extremist activities in West Asia, including operations near crucial sea lanes. Training of personnel has been an important aspect of defence relationship. Jane's Terrorism and Security Monitor reported in August 2001 that Israel was 'heavily involved' in training Indian counterinsurgency forces in Kashmir. [19]

India-Israel defence cooperation has broadened over the years to include supply of military equipment, intelligence sharing, and joint defence-related research. Since the defence sales began in 2000, with the lifting of a self-imposed restriction by Israel on military exports to India, the emphasis has been on high-end technology. One of the early sales, in 2004, was the Phalcon airborne early warning radar, a system Israel had rescinded from selling to China after vigorous US objections. The United States' green signal to Israel for the sale of Phalcon to the Indian Air Force, was indicative of a new chapter in US-India relationship, heralded with establishment of formal ties between New Delhi and Tel Aviv. The first of the three arrived in

2009 and would be mounted on Russian-built aircraft. Israel has replaced Russia as the leading defence and military supplier to India. Israel crossed the US$ 1 billion mark in defence contracts in both 2007 and 2008 in comparison to Russia, which has been supplying India with US$ 875 million of defence equipment per year. [20]

In recent years, India has obtained a host of sophisticated military equipments from Israel, which includes surface-to-air missiles, sophisticated censors, upgrades for MiG and Jaguar aircrafts, fast attack boats and aircrafts, reconnaissance and observation system, battlefield surveillance radars, and specialised equipments for counter-insurgency purposes. During the Kargil War in 1999, Israel provided India with military hardware including, artillery and rifle ammunitions, laser-guided bombs and unmanned aerial vehicle. India has also negotiated a deal to buy the advanced Arrow anti-missile systems from Israel, built to intercept and destroy ballistic missiles on a national level. Because of the close ties between Israeli and the US defence industries, many of the items Israel sells includes components that are subject to the US licensing requirements. As the Indo-US ties have improved, so has the US readiness to permit Israeli sales to India.

Scientific and technical collaboration is another growing area of vigorous collaboration between India and Israel. Some of this cooperation has been in the field of missile defence system. There is an agreement between the two countries on joint development and production of a long-range version of the Barak surface-to-air missile. Indo-Israeli agreement for cooperation in space research technology was concluded in 2002. India main contribution is satellite launch services, whereas Israel's construction is more sophisticated and both hope to benefit from each other's expertise. In January 2008, an Indian space launch vehicle put into space Israel's most sophisticated spy satellite ever launched, the Polaris or TecSAR.

The commercial launch of Polaris by ISRO (Indian Space Research Organization), in addition, underscored the growing military and intelligence connections between Israel and India. In April 2009, India launched another Israeli-made spy satellite (RISAT-2) in a bid to keep a round-the-clock surveillance on its international borders, necessitated by the glaring loopholes in the defence apparatus, exposed in the wake of the Mumbai attacks of November 2008. The satellite will help India track movements of militants on its borders with Pakistan and within its own territory. [21]

India-Israel commercial ties, too, have expanded rapidly. Bilateral trade crossed US$ 4 billion at the end of 2008, primarily in the high-technology sector, rising from just US$ 200 million in 1992-93, when India established full diplomatic relations with Israel. [22] Information technology and related services were recognised as crucial areas right in the beginning and cooperation agreements were signed between industry associations in both countries.

Contrary to India's initial apprehensions, the West Asian countries have been rather indifferent to Indo-Israeli normalisation. India's Israel policy in the post-1947 period was guided by primarily two factors: the sentiments of Indian Muslims and deference to Arab sensitivities. Earlier, India, as an incipient state under the Indian National Congress, had opposed the Zionist goal of establishing an ethnic-religious state based on Jewish exclusivism in Palestine. The imperatives of leading a unified national movement (in terms of the Hindu-Muslim unity) led the Indian National Congress to adopt a pro-Arab policy in the Arab-Israeli conflict. The Indian nationalists argued that the consent of the Arab inhabitants was essential for the creation of a Jewish national home in Palestine. As a member of the United Nations' Special Committee on Palestine (UNSCOP), India proposed a minority plan which called for the establishment of a federal Palestine with internal autonomy for the extant Jewish population. When the UN General Assembly voted for the majority plan for partition of Palestine, India joined the Arab and Islamic countries in opposing it. It not only established a crucial link between Indian policy towards its Muslims and the trans-Muslim issues in the Arab world, but also caused Indian leaders to view their Israel policy through the prism of the Arab-Israeli conflict. [23] When India established full diplomatic relations with Israel in the 1990s, important countries of the region such as Saudi Arabia and Iran, far from taking an exception to it, responded to India's new Israel policy by actively engaging with it. [24]

The 'Israel Factor' in Indo-Iranian relations

While Iran has been indifferent about India's relations with its regional adversary, Israel has frequently expressed its misgivings over India-Iran ties. Given India's attempt to institute bilateral relations independent of one another, Israel does not figure significantly in Indo-Iranian relations. Iran, regardless of its anti-Israel rhetoric, has not allowed the 'Israeli factor' to come in the way of its relations with India. Bearing in mind that Iran was the only West Asian country to have expressed displeasure at India's move to normalise relations with Israel in 1992, New Delhi and Tehran have come a long way in developing an understanding of each other strategic necessities. While, Pakistan and Egypt continue to make occasional noises about Indo-Israeli ties, Iran has assiduously avoided making references to Israel in its dealings with India.

However, in recent years, Iran's belligerent rhetoric against Israel has put India in a bind. Ahmedinejad's repeated calls for destruction of Israel and denials of the historicity of the Holocaust have made Israel very apprehensive. In the context of Iran's intransigence on the nuclear issue, Israeli threat to attack Iran's nuclear facilities has introduced a new factor into the equation: the question of regional stability in the near future. As a country that seeks close ties with both Iran and Israel for critical needs and requirements, India is clearly uneasy over the dangers posed by escalating tensions in its proximate neighbourhood. While Ahmedinejad may be driven by domestic and regional compulsions to take an increasingly radical stand on Israel, which may have very little to do with destroying the Jewish state or using military force against it, India is clearly wary of such utterances. [25] A stronger and occasional criticism of Israel could be acceptable to New Delhi but to call for the destruction of a sovereign country would be crossing explicit red lines.

In the backdrop of its own adversarial relations with Iran and growing Indo-Iranian ties, Israel, from time to time has expressed fear over the prospect its military equipment or technology reaching Tehran via New Delhi. The former Prime Minister of Israel, Ariel Sharon, sought explicit guarantees from India on this issue during his visit to the country in September 2003. Assuring that there was no possibility of 'leakage' of Israeli technology, India spelt out clearly that the deepening strategic ties with the Israel would not dilute New Delhi's relations with Tehran. [26] Israel raised this question once again at a meeting of the Indo-Israeli joint working group on counterterrorism in November 2004.

Some point out that 'both India and Israel have considerable expertise in providing maintenance and upgrades for legacy Russian weapons platforms. As such there is an explicit symmetry between the kinds of defence-related services that Israel has furnished to India and the kinds of services India seeks to provide to Iran and other Central Asian states. Israel has helped India with avionics upgrades with its MiGs, and in turn, India hopes to provide similar services to countries throughout the region.' Therefore, it is argued that 'Israel has good cause for unease, and India is not insensitive to this discomfiture.' [27]

Conversely, others draw attention to the fact that 'in 1980s, the Middle East being the prime customer for Chinese weapons did not inhibit Israel from actively exporting military hardware to China. Until the Phalcon deal was throttled by the US in 2000, Israel pursued its military ties with China without worrying about the boomerang effect.' Hence, 'Indo-Israeli military ties should not be any different from Sino-Israeli regarding "illegal" transfer of Israeli technology. Moreover, despite its long political and economic ties, India, unlike China has never supplied arms to the Middle East.' [28] Notwithstanding, India's impressive track record in containing illegal transfer of technology received from a third country, Israeli concerns as India's the largest arms supplier will remain a part of New Delhi's strategic evaluation in any future military engagement with Iran.

On the other hand, India-Israel strategic relations have occasionally unruffled feathers in Tehran. The launch of the Israeli Polaris satellite in January 2008 stirred a political controversy following media reports which suggested that satellite was meant to help Israel monitor developments in its neighbourhood. While the *Jerusalem Post* wrote that the 'launch will dramatically increase Israel's intelligence gathering capabilities regarding the Islamic Republic's nuclear program since the satellite can submit images in all weather conditions, a capability that Israel's existing satellites lacked,' the *News Middle East* reported Israeli officials confirming that 'TecSAR is of particular interest to their country because it can be used to keep tab on Iran's nuclear program.' [29] Iran voiced its displeasure over the launch, when it stressed that India should have considered the 'political dimensions' of the deal. [30] Although, Iran reacted with extreme restraint, such events have the potential to drag India into crossfire between Tehran and Tel Aviv and derail its vital interests in the region.

In the context of the projected and possibly prolonged instability in Pakistan and Afghanistan, both New Delhi and Tehran share a common strategic objective of regional stability in south-west Asia, which makes them a long-term strategic partner. Containing extremism and militancy of Taliban in Afghanistan and Pakistan remains integral to that goal. Therefore, an Indo-Israeli joint approach towards terrorism clearly has its limits, when Iran is factored into the equation. During his deliberations in New Delhi, former Israeli Prime Minister Ariel Sharon called Iran the "epicentre of terrorism"–a depiction that carried little resonance on the Indian side. Israel's perception of Iran is rooted in the latter's long-standing support for the virulently anti-Israeli Hezbollah in Lebanon and Hamas in the Palestinian territories. These Islamist groups are products of Israeli occupation and operate in a localised context. No such fears exist in India pertaining to their motives or of their backers. [31]

Iran's antipathy towards extremism and militancy of the Taliban and their ideological brethren in Pakistan makes the Islamic Republic, in effect, a political ally of India in West Asia. Moreover, in presenting shared political and strategic interests in dealing with Islamic fundamentalism and terrorism, India has been careful not to appear as aligning with anti-Islam forces, which given its substantial Muslim population, could also create domestic infelicities. Israel perception of Iranian nuclear programme also creates an uncomfortable situation for India. Israel's position is underscored by security concerns and question of survival in a hostile regional environment. [32] With Iran openly calling for its elimination, Israel clearly sees a nuclear-armed Iran as an existential threat. Israeli leaders have been unequivocal in their opposition to Tehran's nuclear programme and have threatened to carry out military strikes to destroy it. [33] Israel would like India to acknowledge the threat posed by a nuclear-armed Iran. However, India believes that Iran is pursuing a nuclear weapons programme motivated essentially by its own security concerns.

Hence, New Delhi's suggestion that Iran's nuclear ambition should be addressed within the context of a regional security framework beginning, significantly, with an accommodation with the Arab countries of the region. [34] By advocating an anti-sanction stance on Iran notwithstanding its consistent votes against Tehran at the IAEA, India has set aside the Israeli (and Western) argument that ratcheting up sanctions and keeping the threat of force on the cards can force Iran to abandon its nuclear programme.

On the contrary, New Delhi contends that the sanctions inevitably hurt the Iranian population and the threat of military action would only reinforce Iran's desire for some kind of a deterrent capability. India's position has been to hold Iran accountable to its obligations under the NPT, IAEA and UNSC guidelines and insist that Iran address questions related to its nuclear programme to the satisfaction of the international community. This, India believes, will not only allay Israel's fears but also contribute to its own security in the region. [35]

Conclusion

While Iran is pivotal to India's security strategy, access to Central Asia and Afghanistan, energy security, and power projection beyond the South Asian region, Israel, on the other hand, is critical to the strengthening of India's defence infrastructure and counter-terrorism measures. In effect, both provide vital inputs to India's global power aspirations. Even as India is sceptical of endorsing Israeli position on Iran, whether it is on transfer of technology, terrorism or the Iranian nuclear programme, there are explicit red lines that New Delhi, conceivably, recognizes. For example, any cooperation with Iran on the nuclear issue would damage Indo-Israeli relations. Conversely, support for the Israeli position on military strikes on Iran would not only spell trouble for India vis-à-vis the Islamic Republic but also with other Muslim countries. It is pertinent here to recall Pakistan's rhetoric of an 'Indo-Israeli axis' against the Islamic world and its potential for distorting perceptions about India's foreign policy. So, while India would have liked to conduct its relations with Iran as a strictly bilateral issue, this has not been wholly possible. However, by placing national interest at the core of its strategic calculus, India is constantly trying to keep a balance between the two regional adversaries in an essentially non-aligned fashion.

Endnotes

1. Teresita C. Schaffer, *India and the United States in the 21st century: reinventing partnership* (Washington: Centre for Strategic & International Studies, 2009), pp. 155-56.
2. For an exposition of the independent/autonomous strain in Indian foreign policy and its impact on India's future international relations, see Sumit Ganguly, "India's Alliances

2020," in *South Asia in 2020: Future Strategic Balances and Alliances*, ed. Michael Chambers (Carlisle, Penn.: Strategic Studies Institute, 2002), pp. 363-79; Schaffer, 2009, pp. 154-17; Schaffer quoted in Sheryl G. Stolberg and Jim Yardley, "Countering China, Obama Backs India for U.N. Council," November 8, 2010, http://www.nytimes.com/2010/11/09/world/asia/09prexy.html?_r=1.

3. "Integrated Energy Policy," *Report of the Expert Committee,* New Delhi: Planning Commission, 2006, http://planningcommission.gov.in/reports/genrep/rep_intengy.pdf, p. 9.
4. "Country Analysis Brief: Iran," *Energy Information Administration Official Energy Statistics from the US Government*, January 2010, http://www.eia.doe.gov/emeu/cabs/Iran/Full.html.
5. *World Trade Atlas*, quoted in, "Country Analysis Brief: India," *Energy Information Administration (EIA) Official Energy Statistics from the US Government,* March 2009, http://www.eia.doe.gov/emeu/cabs/India/Full.html.
6. "ONGC to use Iran LNG facility for Farsi gas," December 8, 2009, http://www.business-standard.com/india/news/ongc-to-use-iran-lng-facility-for-farsi-gas/80224/on.
7. With Central Asian energy reserves being estimated at 2.7 percent of total world oil reserves and 7 percent of total natural gas reserves, the region has a huge potential as a future energy source for India. See Nivedita Das Kundu, "Hamid Ansari's Visit to Turkmenistan and Kazakhstan," April 24, 2008, http://www.idsa.in/idsastrategiccomments/HamidAnsarisVisitto TurkmenistanandKazakhstan_NDKundu_240408; Harsh V. Pant, "India and Iran: An 'Axis' in the Making," *Asian Survey*, Vol. 44, No. 3 (May-June, 2004), p. 377; Stephen Blank, "India's Rising Profile in Central Asia," *Comparative Strategy*, Vol. 22, 2003, pp. 139-157; Teresita C. Schaffer and Vibhuti Haté, "India's 'Look West' Policy: Why Central Asia Matters", *South Asia Monitor*, No. 110, September 5, 2007, http://csis.org/files/media/csis/pubs/sam110.pdf; John Calabrese, "Indo-Iranian Relations in Transition," *Journal of South Asia and Middle Eastern Studies*, Vol. 25, No. 5 (Summer 2002), pp.

75-76.

8. C. Christine Fair, "Indo-Iranian Ties: Thicker than Oil," *Middle East Review of International Affairs*, Vol. 11, No. 1 (March 2007), p. 46; Fair, "India and Iran: New Delhi's Balancing Act," *Washington Quarterly*, Vol. 30, No. 3 (Summer 2007), pp. 145, 148; Meena Singh Roy, "India's Interest in Central Asia," *Strategic Analysis*, Vol. 24, No. 12 (March 2001); Stephen Blank, "Central Asia's Deepening East Asian Relations," *Analyst's Biweekly Briefing*, November 8, 2000, http://www.cacianalyst.org/?q=node/257/print; Satu Limaye, "The Weakest Link, but Not Goodbye," *Comparative Connection*, Vol. 4, No. 4 (Winter 2003), http://csis.org/files/media/csis/pubs/0204qindia_easia.pdf; Sushil J. Aaron, "Straddling Faultlines: India's Foreign Policy Toward the Greater Middle East," *CSH Occasional Papers*, No. 7 (2003), p. 30.
9. An exposition on the North-South Transport Corridor can be found in Fair, "Indo-Iranian Ties: Thicker than Oil"; Donald L. Berlin, "India-Iran Relations: A Deepening Entente," *Asia Pacific Centre for Security Studies*, October 2004, http://www.apcss.org/Publications/SAS/AsiaBilateralRelations/India-IranRelationsBerlin.pdf; Pant, "India and Iran: An "Axis" in the Making?" p. 377; Regine A. Spector, 'The North South Transport Corridor', *Central Asia-Caucasus Institute Analyst*, July 3, 2002, http://www.cacianalyst.org/?q=node/165/print; and Schaffer & Haté, "India's 'Look West' Policy: Why Central Asia Matters"; Sudha Ramachandran, "India, Iran, Russia map out trade routes," *Asia Times Online*, June 29, 2002, http://www.atimes.com/ind-pak/DF29Df02.html.
10. Michael Slackman, "Iran Blames US and Britain in attack," October 19, 2009, http://www.nytimes.com/2009/10/20/world/middleeast/20iran.html; Arthur Bright, "Sunni Rebels Claim Deadly Terror Attack in Iran; Car Bombing by Jundullah Insurgents Kills at Least 11 of Iran's Elite Guards," *Christian Science Monitor*, February 14, 2007.
11. "Afghanistan, the United States, Pakistan, India, Russia, and Iran," *STRATFOR*, November 9, 2010.
12. Iran is no friend of al Qaeda and a bitter enemy of the Taliban. Intelligence sharing and diplomatic coordination with Tehran

helped the United States rout the Taliban (whatever its history with the United States) and later install Hamid Karzai's government in Kabul in the months following 9/11. Even as far back as the early 1990s, the consolidation of Taliban in Afghanistan emerged as a major source of anxiety for both India and Iran. Both India and Iran were worried of Taliban's harsh treatment of Afghan Shia population; Iran was particularly concerned over the hostility from a militant Islamic group which considers Shiism as apostasy. India was chary of Taliban's jihadist ideology and its potential for fomenting trouble in Kashmir and other parts of the country. As opposed to Pakistan that quickly recognised the Taliban regime, India and Iran – faced with serious challenges from the extremism of the Taliban – instead backed Afghanistan's anti-Taliban Northern Alliance. When, the Northern Alliance routed the Taliban with the help of the United States in November 2001, post 9/11, India and Iran welcomed its demise and made Afghanistan's reconstruction and development a common critical goal. Since then, India and Iran have been collaborating to prevent the comeback of the Taliban in the teeth of opposition from the Pakistani military and intelligence agencies. See Ali Ansari, *Confronting Iran: The Failure of American Foreign Policy and the Next Great Crisis in the Middle East* (New York: Basic Books, 2006); Harsh V. Pant, "India in Afghanistan: The 'Soft Power' Question", October 15, 2009, http://www.isn.ethz.ch/isn/layout/set/print/content/view/full/73?id=108562&lng=en; M.K. Bhadrakumar, "Pakistan warns India to back off," October 10, 2009, http://www.atimes.com/atimes/South_Asia/KJ10Df01.html; Stephen M. Waltz, "Delusion Point", *Foreign Policy*, November 8, 2010, http://www.foreignpolicy.com/articles/2010/11/08/delusion_points?page=0,7; Sachin Parashar, "Afghanistan to top India-Iran talks," *Times of India*, March 7, 2010; Ahmed Rashid, "The End Game," *Outlook*, March 12, 2010, http://outlookindia.com/article.aspx?264681; Robert D. Kaplan, "Obama Takes Asia by Sea," *New York Times*, November 11, 2010, http://www.nytimes.com/2010/11/12/opinion/12kaplan.html?pagewanted=1&hp.

13. C. Christine Fair, "Indo-Iranian Relations: Prospects for Bilateral Cooperation after 9/11," in Robert M. Hathaway (ed.), "The 'strategic partnership' between India and Iran," *Asia Program Special Report, No.120* (Washington: Woodrow Wilson Centre, 2004), p. 10; Pant, "India and Iran: An "Axis" in the Making?" p. 371; "The New Delhi Declaration," January 23, 2003, http://meaindia.nic.in//declarestatement/2003/01/25jd1.htm.
14. More specifically, Indian aeronautical engineers will help Iran maintain and provide mid-life upgrade for its MiG fighter aircraft. Iran has also sought India's help to refit and maintain tanks, infantry fighting vehicles, and artillery guns. India is also planning to sell Konkurs anti-tank guided weapons and spare parts. In the past, India has helped Iran adapt four Russian-built Kilo-class submarines for warm water conditions in the Persian Gulf. Iran is also seeking combat training for missile boat crews and hopes to purchase simulators for ships and submarines from India. Rizwan Zeb, "The Emerging Indo-Iranian Strategic Alliance and Pakistan", *Central Asia Caucasus Institute Analyst*, February 12, 2003, http://www.cacianalyst.org/?q=node/902; Ehsan Ahrari, "As India and Iran snuggle, Pakistan feels the chill," February 11, 2003, *Asia Times*, http://www.atimes.com/atimes/South_Asia/EB11Df01.html; John Calabrese, "Indo-Iranian Relations in Transition," *Journal of South Asia and Middle Eastern Studies*, Vol. 25, No. 3 (Summer 2002), pp. 75-76.
15. As cited in Berlin, "India-Iran Relations: A Deepening Entente," p. 1; Ahrari, "As India and Iran snuggle".
16. Berlin, "India-Iran Relations: A Deepening Entente".
17. Ronak D. Desai & Xenia Dormandy, "India-Iran Relations: Key Security Implications", March 26, 2008, http://belfercenter.ksg.harvard.edu.
18. P.R. Kumaraswamy, "Ties with Israel: Sooner the Better", *Times of India*, August 27, 1991.
19. Sudha Ramachandran, "India and Israel united in defence," *Asia Times Online*, June 26, 2002, http://www.atimes.com/ind-pak/DF26Df02.html.
20. "Israel Becomes India's Top Defence Supplier with Phalcon Deal," *India Defence*, February 15, 2009, http://www.india-defence.com/reports-4221.

21. "India launches spy satellite to boost security," April 20, 2009, http://in.reuters.com/article/idINIndia-39134120090420.
22. "India Israel Bilateral Relations," August 2010, http://www.mea.gov.in/meaxpsite/foreignrelation/israel.pdf.
23. For a definitive book on India's policy towards the Zionist Movement and Israel, see, P.R. Kumaraswamy, *India's Israel Policy* (New York: Columbia University Press, 2003). Also see, Subhash Kapila, "India–Israel Relations: The Imperatives for Enhanced Strategic Cooperation," *South Asia Analysis Group Paper*, http://www.southasiaanalysis.org/papers2/paper131.html; Farah Naaz, "Indo-Israel Relations: An Evolutionary Perspective," *Strategic Analysis*, May 1999, Vol. XXIII, No.2, pp. 241-254.
24. India's relations with Saudi Arabia and Iran have seen an upward trend throughout the 1990s and beyond. Cooperation with both the countries has expanded in diverse fields. Indo-Saudi bilateral issues include trade and commerce, economics, investment opportunities, education, security, labour, issuance of visas and Indian community welfare among others. Saudi Arabia remains India's largest source of oil followed by Iran. See A.K. Pasha, "Indo-Saudi relations: past and emerging challenges", and Javed Ahmad Khan, "New trends in Indo-Saudi economic relations" in Gulshan Dietl et al, *Contemporary Saudi Arabia and the Emerging Indo-Saudi Relations* (Shipra Publications, New Delhi, 2007).
25. The reluctance of Prime Minister Manmohan Singh to participate in the Shanghai Summit Meeting in June 2006, after lobbying hard to get into the grouping, was associated with the Iranian presence there. India was keen not to be seen making a common cause with Iran at a Summit which was taking on an anti-US (and anti-Israeli) hue. See Sudha Ramchandran, "India gives Shanghai the cold shoulder," *Asia Times*, June 17, 2006, http://www.atimes.com/atimes/South_Asia/HF17Df01.html.
26. "India-Israel: Sharon's visit: Vow to jointly fight terrorism," *India News Online*, September 15, 2003, http://news.indiamart.com/news-analysis/india-israel-sharon--773.html.
27. C. Christine Fair, "Indo-Iranian Ties: Thicker than Oil," pp. 52-53.
28. P.R. Kumaraswamy, "Indo-Iranian Ties: The Israeli

Dimension," in Robert M. Hathaway (ed.), "The 'strategic partnership' between India and Iran," *Asia Programme Special Report*, No. 120 (Washington: Woodrow Wilson Centre, 2004), p. 29.

29. Both sources quoted in Ninan Koshi, "India and Israel eye Iran," *Foreign Policy in Focus*, February 13, 2008, http://www.fpif.org/fpiftxt/4959.
30. "India-Israel space ties irk Iran," *Rediff.com*, February 13, 2008, http://www.rediff.com///news/2008/feb/05iran.htm.
31. Kumaraswamy, "Indo-Iranian Ties: The Israeli Dimension," p. 29.
32. For an comprehensive analysis on implications of nuclear weapons on Israel's, see Ephraim Kam, "Israel and a Nuclear Iran," *Institute for National Security Studies Memorandum*, No. 94, July 2008,
33. See, "Israeli Military Calculations towards Iran: A Looming Showdown," *IISS Strategic Comments*, Vol. 12, Issue 9, November 2006.
34. See Raja Karthikeya, "India's Iran Calculus," *Foreign Policy*, September 24, 2010,
35. India's position on Iran's nuclear programme hasn't been without Iranian charges of hypocrisy, given the exceptional status accorded by the NSG's (Nuclear Supplier's Group) waiver to India, an non-signatory to the Nuclear Non-proliferation Treaty (NPT),and its stand that the treaty promotes institutionalized segregation between nuclear 'haves' and 'have-nots' and, therefore, discriminatory. To the Iranian attempts to draw a parallel between their nuclear programme and that of India's, New Delhi draws attention on its impeccable non-proliferation record, indicating the A.Q Khan network's role in Iranian programme and its troubles with the IAEA and NPT. See C. Christine Fair, "India and Iran, New Delhi's Balancing Act," *The Washington Quarterly*, Vol. 30, No. 3 (Summer 2007), pp. 146-47; P.R. Kumaraswamy, "India's Persian Problems," *Strategic Insights* (California: Centre for Contemporary Conflict, Naval Postgraduate School), July 2008, http://www.nps.edu/Academics/centers/ccc/publications/OnlineJournal/2008/Jul/kumaraswamyJul08.pdf.

12

Growing Afghan Maze: An Opportunity for Indo-Iranian Re-Engagement

Vishal Chandra

I would today reiterate the need for structured, systematic and regular consultations with Iran on the situation in Afghanistan……We need to move beyond mere articulation of positions as the Afghan conundrum deepens and could have a deleterious impact on our two countries and the region in case the forces of extremism and obscurantism are made arbiters of the fate of the Afghan people [1]

Ms. Nirupama Rao, Indian Foreign Secretary, July 5, 2010

The Indian and the Iranian priorities as far as the Afghan war is concerned are different if not exactly divergent. Despite the supposed convergence of interest on the Taliban issue and commitment to Afghan reconstruction, the two countries have so far not been able to appreciate the exigency as well as prospects of full scale cooperation on the Afghan issue. While India wants the West and its forces to remain engaged in the Af-Pak region, Iran has been consistent in its stance that the Western forces, especially the US, should withdraw lock, stock and barrel from both Iraq and Afghanistan.

Similarly, while India has been primarily concerned over the prospects of resurgent Taliban making a comeback in Afghanistan, for Iran a bigger priority has been to check the expanded presence of the US in the region. Taliban resurgence is apparently a secondary issue. Iran has time and again been accused of supporting sections of the Taliban to ensure that the Western forces remain bogged down in Afghanistan. Iran's policy towards Afghanistan is thus largely determined by its adversarial relations with the US.

The two countries perhaps have different notions of regional security and threat perceptions, and are also at variance on key sources of trouble in Afghanistan. While India and Afghanistan regard the role and policies of the Pakistani establishment as the key destabilising factor, for Iran there can be no stability in Afghanistan unless the Americans withdraw from the region. Ironically, countries opposed to the Western presence in Afghanistan have no view on ways and means of effectively dealing with post-withdrawal challenges from the Pak-Afghan frontiers. They also pathetically fail to factor in the impact of Pakistani establishment's policy of nurturing, sponsoring, and using a range of local and foreign sunni militant Islamist and terrorist organisations on regional stability and security. Be it the Lashkar-e Toiba or the Jundullah; the Taliban or the al Qaeda; the Uighur or the Uzbek militants; all have safe havens and training infrastructures inside Pakistan. Similarly, be it the Mumbai attacks of November 2008 or the Chabahar bombing of December 2010; be it the suicide bombings in Afghanistan or in Pakistan, the centre of gravity of this violent phenomenon remains in Pakistan.

This paper looks at the prospects of Indo-Iranian re-engagement on the Afghan issue, despite the two countries having divergent regional priorities and threat perceptions, as the US remains engaged in the region as well as in the post-withdrawal scenario. The paper at the very outset recognises the most elementary gap at two levels: Firstly, in the discourse on Indo-Iranian relations and, secondly, in the Iranian discourse on Afghanistan. As regards the first elementary gap, it may be stated that while there is a good amount of understanding about the importance of Iran for India, one simply does not know how relevant or significant India is for Iran. Where does India figure or does India at all figure in the Iranian perception of regional security? Similarly, in the Afghan context, it is difficult to gauge the perceptions and views of the various elements of the Iranian establishment regarding India's presence and role in Afghanistan since 2001. It is not known if there are divergent views within the Iranian establishment on the nature of Indian involvement in Afghanistan. To what extent Iran is amenable to the Indian role, presence and policy towards Afghanistan, and extent to which it shares or differs with the Pakistani perception on the same, is quite open to speculation.

It may be said that the Iranian foreign policy is overwhelmingly oriented to its immediate East as well as the distant West. A competitive civilisational/Islamic/cultural identity perception in the West Asian or the Middle Eastern context, on one hand, and an ideationally conflicting/adversarial politics with the Western world, on the other hand, have largely shaped the Iranian world view, its insecurities, and thereby its foreign policy assertions. Perhaps, Iran needs to balance it with a more nuanced 'look-east' policy. It is not clear to what extent the Iranian policy-makers look at the turmoil to its immediate east in terms of 'Af-Pak'; what is the Iranian position over Pakistani establishment's direct support for the Afghan Taliban and presence of al Qaeda in its tribal agencies; and also its perception of the alliance between Pakistan and the United States.

The paper posits that the Indo-Iranian cooperation on the Afghan issue shall depend on four factors–position on the US presence and its policy towards the region; the Kabul-led efforts for reconciliation with the Taliban and allies; perceptions about Pakistan's role in the Afghan war; and how the Afghan and regional politics shape up in the post-withdrawal scenario. The paper argues that the Indo-Iranian cooperation can at best be tactical and not strategic or ideological on the Afghan issue in the coming years. Though both India and Iran along with Afghanistan are wary of the growing influence of Wahabi-Salafi form of Islamism in the region, any possibility of 'strategic' or 'ideological' cooperation between India and Iran to counter such regressive forces are remote. It is ironical that while Iran was opposed to the Taliban regime, it had never really recognised the Pakistani establishment as the key sponsor of militant extremism inside Afghanistan and by way of its support to the Taliban regime along with Saudi Arabia to parts of Central Asia and regions beyond.

It may be noted that Iran for very obvious geo-historical factors has always exercised a strong influence over parts of Afghanistan. However, there has been a perception that the US has made significant inroads among the supposedly pro-Iranian Afghan factions, especially the Hazaras and the Tajiks, since the overthrow of the Taliban regime in November-December 2001. The Iranian imprint on the Afghan polity since historical times, and its ability to work its way through Afghanistan's complex socio-political networks, is nevertheless unmistakable. However, as the role and relevance of the West is likely to decreases in years to come, Iran is likely to be more assertive and bold in its Afghan ventures. Iran is far better positioned to play an important role in any regional effort for Afghan stabilisation. Unlike Pakistan, it has settled borders with Afghanistan and has strong state institutions. In prospective, if the Pakistan-Saudi Arabia dimension unfolds in a big way in the run up to the post-West Afghanistan, the prospects of Iran and India working together in a more visible and concrete way along with like-minded regional countries will be stronger. However, the Russian response and the Chinese stance too will be an influencing factor in the post-withdrawal scenario.

This is not to suggest that India and Iran have not worked together on the Afghan issue earlier. The two countries along with Russia and the Central Asian countries had played a key role in supporting the Afghan coalition against the Pakistan-backed Taliban between 1996 and 2001. Thereafter, the agreement between Iran-Afghanistan-India in 2003 on improving Afghan connectivity by developing a link road connecting Afghanistan's national highway with the Iranian Chabahar Port was indicative of the trilateral cooperation that had evolved in the early years of the post-Taliban phase. It is also notable that much of the Indian goods bound for Afghanistan to this day is shipped and transported via the Iranian port of Bandar Abbas. As per the tripartite agreement, India has already completed and handed over to the Afghan Government the Zaranj-Delaram road linking the Afghan Garland Highway with the Iranian border.

As Barack H. Obama took over the US Administration and enunciated in March 2009 a new Af-Pak strategy which later in December laid out a time frame for starting the withdrawal of its forces from Afghanistan, both India and Iran again seem to be cautiously reaching out to each other keeping in view the post-withdrawal scenario. Some initiatives have recently been taken at both informal and official levels to revive regular consultations between New Delhi, Kabul and Tehran.

In August 2010, the Iranian Deputy Foreign Minister Mohammad Ali Fathollahi was on a three-day state visit to India to discuss the Afghan situation and explore prospects of trilateral dialogue among India, Iran and Afghanistan. This was preceded by Indo-Iranian Joint Commission meeting in New Delhi on July 9, 2010 where the two countries agreed to expedite the development of Chabahar Port. Earlier in February 2010, Indian Foreign Secretary Nirupama Rao had paid a two-day visit to Tehran. This all the more acquires significance as the US is likely to begin withdrawal of its troops in July 2011 and as Kabul with backing from the West rushes for reconciliation with the Taliban and other armed opposition groups.

The paper is broadly divided into four sections – (i) the elusive regional approach (ii) the US/Western policy in the region (iii) politics of reconciliation with the Taliban and its likely implications, and (iv) prospects of Indo-Iranian cooperation on Afghanistan.

Elusive Regional Approach

The US intervention in Afghanistan and Iraq in a way had initially worked to the advantage of Iran by ousting the Taliban to its east and the Saddam Hussein regime to its west respectively. India too felt vindicated when the US-led Western coalition overthrew the Taliban regime end of 2001. In fact, India and the US for the first time had their interests converging, while that of the US and Pakistan diverging, on a regional issue.

As the US sounded a premature victory in Afghanistan and moved into Iraq in 2003, the nascent regional cooperation that had evolved immediately after 9/11 petered away. Until early 2002, the American intelligence was said to be working closely with the intelligence organisations of all the regional countries, including Iranian and China. Later, the preponderance of the US factor began to weigh on the regional politics as the US invaded Iraq in early 2003 and declared Iran as part of the 'axis of evil'. This in turn impacted on prospects of regional cooperation on the Afghan issue. The responses of the regional countries on the Afghan issue were thereafter determined by their respective perceptions of the US role and intent in the region and the nature of their bilateral relationship with the US. If India was seen as getting too close to the US during the presidency of George W. Bush, Iran was accused of stoking tension in Iraq and supporting sections of Taliban in Afghanistan.

Subsequently, India and Iran came to have mutually diverse relationship with the US which in turn impacted on their respective approaches towards the Afghan issue. The Indian position on the Iranian nuclear stand-off further complicated the relationship between India and Iran. Driven by their respective notions of national interest, the two countries subsequently failed in coordinating their policies on the challenges emerging from the Afghanistan-Pakistan region. It would be useful to briefly look at the regional initiatives on Afghan issue, both in the Western discourse and at the regional level, prior to examining the US and Taliban factor.

When the NATO-led forces moved into southern Afghanistan in mid-2006, they soon realised their limitations against a well-organised Taliban guerrilla force. The NATO forces were evidently not prepared for a full-scale counter-insurgency/terrorism operation. They were clueless about the strength of the Taliban and suffered from differing rules of engagement and national caveats. The idea of seeking a negotiated political settlement with the Taliban, and exploring regional approaches to stabilising Afghanistan, rapidly emerged in the European discourse on Afghanistan thereafter.

In November 2006, former French President Jacques Chirac had first proposed the formation of a contact group on Afghanistan in consultation with Kabul which would also include Afghanistan's neighbouring countries. The NATO Secretary General Jaap de Scheffer and the European Union (EU) foreign policy chief Javier Solana had backed the proposal. [2]

Thereafter, one finds even some of the influential American think tanks clearly recommending for a regional approach to dealing with the worsening Afghan situation. *The Atlantic Council of the Unites States* (ACUS) in one of its report on Afghanistan released in January 2008 suggested that the US should explore prospects for a regional approach and regional solutions to the Afghan crisis as one of its four strategic recommendations:

"Bringing in interested parties and neighbours could be done through a meeting or conference that could include the Shanghai Cooperation Organization (of which Russia and China are key members); India; Iran; and of course Pakistan." [3]

Again, in January 2008, the *Afghanistan Study Group*, in its report argued that there is a need to "initiate a regional process to engage Afghanistan's neighbours and potential regional partners in future sustainable development of Afghanistan," which "can begin with relatively minor confidence building measures and the establishment of a regional forum for discussion of common challenges." The report envisages "a multilateral accord involving Afghanistan, all its neighbours, relevant major powers, and the UN." The report further suggested that "such an accord would recognize Afghanistan as a permanently neutral state, provide international recognition for Afghanistan's borders, pledge non-interference in internal Afghan affairs, ban the clandestine supply of arms to nongovernmental actors, and establish a comprehensive regime to promote the flow of trade through Afghanistan." [4]

A year later in March 2009, the new US President Barack H. Obama in his new Af-Pak strategy put forth the idea of a Contact

Group on Afghanistan and Pakistan. The new strategy stated, "…..together with the UN, we will forge a new Contact Group for Afghanistan and Pakistan that brings together all who should have a stake in the security of the region – our NATO allies and other partners, but also the Central Asian states, the Gulf nations and Iran; Russia, India and China." [5] However, in the revised US strategy for Af-Pak region presented by the Obama Administration in December 2009 there was no reference at all to the Contact Group for Afghanistan and Pakistan. Instead, the US decided to broaden its engagement with Pakistan with the objective of seeking latter's cooperation in controlling sources of violence inside Afghanistan.

The annual tripartite talks involving the US, Afghanistan and Pakistan too has been part of the American effort to improve the coordination among the three. Having announced surge in troops, initially 21,000 in March 2009 and thereafter 30,000 in December 2009, the next logical step for the US Administration should have been to reach out to all regional countries rather than over relying on the Pakistani establishment in view of the July 2011 time frame for beginning withdrawal of its forces from Afghanistan.

For most of the regional countries, especially Iran, Russia and China, Afghanistan has been a predominantly Western (to be more specific a US) affair. Added to it has been a weak and fragmented regional effort that began with the Shanghai Cooperation Organisation's (the SCO) special conference on Afghanistan in Moscow the day Obama Administration declared its new policy for the Afghanistan-Pakistan (Af-Pak) region on March 27, 2009. The American presence in the conference was notable. There have also been efforts by Turkey and Iran as part of the trilateral arrangement to improve understanding between Kabul and Islamabad.

However, none of the above efforts have helped improve the situation in the region so far. One is tempted to argue that lack of coordination & cooperation among the regional countries has only widened the scope for extra-regional powers to remain engaged in their common neighbourhood. Ironically, even if the West, especially the US, withdraws from Afghanistan, the region is not prepared, and is neither expected to be, for the post-withdrawal scenario. Unfortunately, a comprehensive regional effort, even if the US withdraws from the region, is not a possibility given the mutually diverse interests of the neighbouring countries.

Assuming that the American presence and the rising influence of the Pakistan-backed Taliban and allies are a determining factor as far as Indo-Iranian cooperation on the Afghan issue is concerned, it is important to dwell on the future prospects of both the US mission in Afghanistan and the Taliban as a factor in regional politics.

US Withdrawal from the Region: Debatable Issue

If one goes by the general perception, then the US and the NATO is on the verge of withdrawing from the Af-Pak region. The rising casualty levels among the Western troops, downturn in the global economy, and growing domestic compulsions are commonly suggested and cited as reasons for West looking for a quick exit from the Af-Pak region.

There is no doubt that the continuing military and political stalemate in Afghanistan has made Afghan mission appear un-winnable and unsustainable for much of the Western world. The Taliban and allies have over the years expanded the geographical spread of their guerrilla operations and have raised the casualty levels among the Western troops to a record level. All these years, the weaknesses inherent in the Bonn and post-Bonn process, wavering American commitment, and chronic divisions within the Western coalition, has provided the Pakistani establishment with ample opportunities to re-assert its influence by reinventing the Taliban into a force to reckon with. Nevertheless, it would be premature to conclude that the West is departing from the region. Both the US and NATO are not likely to completely withdraw their forces or disengage from the region. Even the withdrawal of troops is likely to be a long-drawn affair.

The biggest challenge before the Obama Administration has been to control the violence and bring the Afghan situation to a manageable level. The Obama Administration had announced an additional deployment of 21,000 American troops in March 2009 followed by another 30,000 in December 2009. The deployment of 30,000 American troops has just got over, taking the total strength of the International Security Assistance Force (ISAF) to well above 100,000 troops in Afghanistan.

The counter-insurgency/terrorism tactic of the ISAF, though slow in adapting to the unconventional nature of Afghan warfare, has certainly evolved over the years. One commonly gets to hear more about the shortcomings, constraints, limitations, caveats and failures of the ISAF, rather than their achievements. Right since 2007, the policy of the ISAF has been pretty consistent in terms of taking on the mid and low-level Taliban commanders active inside Afghanistan. In the last one year or so, the US Special Forces have achieved a certain success in reining in the elements of the Haqqani network as well. The US-led Afghan mission today is far more well-resourced, focused and innovative since the early years of the Bush Administration. However, at the same time, troops from some of the NATO member-states who have been involved in combat operations are on the verge of withdrawing from Afghanistan. The Netherlands has already pulled out its troops from the Urozgan Province and the Canadians and Germans are intent on starting withdrawal in 2011. The pace of withdrawal will also depend on the European threat perceptions and the US diplomacy in times to come.

As regards the July 2011 deadline for beginning the withdrawal of American troops, it is more likely to be symbolic and minimal at the operational level. In recent months, it has been clearly stated by the senior officials of the Obama Administration that withdrawal of troops will depend on the ground situation which is unlikely to improve within a year. Thus, any substantive reduction in American troop levels is not likely to take place before 3-4 years. There is no doubt that most of the Western countries, including the US, want to pull out their troops at the earliest possible, but withdrawal of troops should not be construed as complete withdrawal of Western presence from the region. The West has not invested and lost billions of dollars or taken in casualties among its troops in thousands in the AfPak region for nothing. In times to come, the US and the NATO are likely to retain their presence in the Afghanistan-Pakistan region with minimal number of troops deployed in support of the Afghan army and the government in times of exigency. However, much will depend on: (i) the success and failure of the current military operations underway in the Taliban strongholds in southern Afghanistan and (ii) the success and failure of the Kabul-led efforts to reintegrate elements of the armed opposition groups, and (iii) extent to which Pakistan and the US are able to reconcile with each other's interests.

Kabul-led Peace and Reconciliation Process

The idea of integrating, co-opting, engaging, accommodating and incorporating the Taliban and other anti-government Afghan armed groups into the post-2001 political process is not new.

However, it gained momentum as the violence began to spiral in 2006-07. It has been part of the largely European (specifically British) discourse on a negotiated political settlement of the Afghan problem with 'good' or 'moderate Taliban'. With the Obama Administration laying down a time frame for beginning the withdrawal of American troops, and acquiescing to the idea of negotiating with the 'non-ideologically' committed 'reconcilable' Taliban elements, there has been a surge in efforts to reach out to the Taliban at multiple levels. The January 2010 London Conference on Afghanistan, where President Karzai presented his plan for peace and reconciliation, to the National Consultative Peace Jirga in Kabul in June, to Kabul Conference in July 2010, are reflective of Kabul's intensified effort to forge a national and international consensus for its plan to open formal negotiations with the Taliban.

The issue of reconciliation with the Taliban leadership based inside Pakistan is tricky and hazardous. The growing Pakistani thrust for a central role in any power-sharing agreement between Kabul and the Taliban leadership especially in view of a post-withdrawal scenario is a matter of serious concern. The intent of the Pakistani establishment has throughout been questionable. Key issue here is to what extent the Pakistani establishment is willing to co-exist with a strong, stable Afghanistan. Interestingly, differences between Islamabad and the Afghan Taliban and even within the Quetta Shura on Kabul's offer for talks cannot be ruled out. However, Pakistan is likely to scotch Kabul's effort for reconciliation with the Taliban until it has made a grand bargain with the West which is likely to be at the expense of the interests of other regional countries.

Any reconciliation with the Taliban in its current form and at a time when it thinks that it has an upper hand is bound to prove counter-productive. Where is the incentive for the Taliban leadership to deal with Kabul in view of Americans and Europeans scripting an exit strategy from the region? It will only strengthen the resolve and conviction of the hardcore elements within the Taliban movement, and work to the advantage of pro-Taliban section of the Pakistani polity. It is important to note that Kabul too does not have the institutional capacity to withstand the impact of sharing/ceding power to the Taliban as part of the negotiated deal. It is the strong trans-border dimension of the Taliban movement and activism which is more likely to add instability to the already fragile situation than bringing social and political stability to the war-torn country.

Kabul will have to take into account the likely implications of reconciliation with the hardcore elements of the Taliban leadership for the country's constitution, foreign policy, judiciary, and various state structures. Integrating Taliban guerrilla fighters into the upcoming national army may impact on its orientation and internal cohesion. It is also not clear whether the Taliban leadership is willing to work with the minority ethnic groups from north and parts of central and western Afghanistan. So far there has not been any indication in this regard from the top Taliban leadership. Most of the regional countries, especially Iran, India, Russia, Uzbekistan, Tajikistan and Kyrgyzstan remain sceptical of the 'peace' initiatives aimed at the top Taliban leadership based in Pakistan.

The perceptions and views of the non-Taliban Pashtuns; the minority ethnic factions; and the regional countries, are significant to any reconciliation process. In the given situation, it is worth stating that Kabul and the international community should work towards a well-resourced and a comprehensive integration strategy aimed at weaning away and suitably rehabilitating the low-level Taliban fighters and relatively independent mid-level Taliban commanders, rather than hankering for reconciliation with the top leadership at this point of time.

Prospects of Indo-Iranian Re-engagement on Afghan Issue

Despite divergent views on the American role in the region and the value of Pakistan in any regional strategy, India and Iran have enough common ground for cooperation on the Afghan issue. India can play an important role in getting Iran onboard as far as Western efforts for Afghan stabilisation are concerned since the American forces are likely to maintain their presence in the region next 3-4 years or may be more. In fact, Iran may have to be prepared for a long-term Western presence in the region. Iran, on the other hand, occupies a significant place in India's quest for access to Afghanistan and the Central Asian region. Since India is being kept out of the regional initiatives whether by Turkey or Russia, Iran will be critical to India's continuing contribution to the ongoing state-building process in Afghanistan. Bilateral and trilateral mechanisms are thus critical to sustenance of India's presence in Afghanistan in the long-term.

For countries opposed to the Western presence in Afghanistan, it is important to understand that in the absence of an effective regional strategy and a minimal consensus on the issue of tackling the menace of militant religious extremism emanating from Pakistan, extra-regional powers will continue to find space for expanding their role in the region. A regional approach will also be indispensable to facilitating an Afghan solution for the Afghan crisis. Unfortunately, as brought out earlier in the paper, there is hardly any regional strategy in the making. The regional efforts have so far been fragmented and largely a touch-and-go affair. The region is simply not prepared for the post-withdrawal scenario.

Interestingly, though friction between the US and its supposed allies in the region has been growing, opposition to the large presence of Western forces at the same time appears to be mellowing in some of the regional capitals. It is difficult to say at the moment as to what direction the US-Pakistan relations will take in years to come. As of now, the US strategy for Afghanistan and Pakistan appears to be going nowhere. If the situation continues to exacerbate then given the strong element of inter-dependence in the US-Pakistan relationship, the prospect of a new political arrangement to manage the Afghan situation at the expense of the security concerns of Iran, India and Russia cannot be ruled out.

The Afghan war has gone beyond Mullah Omars and Osama bin Ladens. It is the legacy of their ideas that the region will have to confront for decades to come, irrespective of the Western presence in the region. There can be no military solution to the war of ideas in the long run. India and Iran, two countries with strong state institutions and rich civilisational heritage, can collectively play an important role in strengthening the Afghan state-building process. At a larger level, the two countries can explore prospects of initiating a new regional discourse on stabilising Afghanistan. Meanwhile, India and Iran can potentially contribute to strengthening the Afghan infrastructure and economy, and certainly the Afghan security institutions. The two countries can jointly work on many large and small development projects in parts of Afghanistan; the Indian and Iranian researchers can jointly work with Afghan think tanks and academic institutions. In this regard, the SAARC/South Asian University coming up in Delhi offers a ray of hope.

On the issue of Taliban resurgence, India and Iran appear to be somewhat on the same page. However, the two countries need to work together on a long-term strategy to deal with Afghan crisis that is not likely to abate for decades to come. Going back to the counter strategy of the 1990s cannot be the way forward. Last thirty years of Afghan war has shown how proxy-politics has brought destruction to Afghanistan and reinforced regressive tendencies in the wider south-central Asia region and beyond. The objective of the Indo-Iranian cooperation on the Afghan issue should be to strengthen the capacity of the Afghan state in terms of reviving its infrastructure, its economy, its trade; and also improving Afghanistan's connectivity with the regional economies. The idea should be to assist Kabul extend its reach to the provincial, district, and village levels. At the political level, the two countries can use their enhanced leverages in years to come to bring various Afghan factions together, including Taliban elements willing to work with Kabul, as part of national reconciliation in Afghanistan. In this context, it is important for both India and Iran to factor in the whole range of Afghan view.

However, the Indo-Iranian cooperation on Afghanistan is likely to remain constrained by divergent view points on the relevance of Western role in the region. Withdrawal of Western forces at this stage is not going to help improve the Afghan situation either. It is not going to provide regional countries, other than Pakistan, with any great options in Afghanistan. sA post-West scenario is no assurance for any strategic partnership between India and Iran on regional issues of common concern given the two countries' differing perception of Pakistan's role. It would be an irony of history if the two failed to "move beyond mere articulation of positions" in view of both immediate and long-term ideational challenges emanating from what can be here referred to as the *Indo-Iranian neighbourhood.* Until then, both countries will have to wade through the complex maze of Afghan and sub-continental politics, enmeshed with the interests of extra-regional powers and actors, to pursue their common stakes in Afghanistan and regions beyond.

End Notes

1. Ms. Nirupama Roy made these observations in her keynote address during the IDSA-IPIS Bilateral Conference at IDSA, New Delhi. See "Speech at IDSA-IPIS Strategic Dialogue on India and Iran: An Enduring Relationship", IDSA, New Delhi, July 5, 2010, at http://www.idsa.in/KeynoteAddressIndiaandIrananenduringrelationship_nirupamaroy.
2. Jacques Chirac, "Europe Must Shoulder its Share of the NATO

Burden", *The Guardian*, November 28, 2006, at http://www.guardian.co.uk/commentisfree/2006/nov/28/comment.nato.

3. "Saving Afghanistan: An Appeal and Plan for Urgent Action", *The Atlantic Council of the United States*, International Security Program, Issue Brief, January 2008, p. 5.
4. General James L. Jones (retd.) & Ambassador Thomas R. Pickering, "Revitalizing Our Efforts Rethinking Our Strategies", *Afghanistan Study Group Report*, Centre for the Study of Presidency, January 30, 2008, p. 38.
5. See "President Obama's Remarks on New Strategy for Afghanistan and Pakistan", *The New York Times*, March 27, 2009, at http://www.nytimes.com/2009/03/27/us/politics/27obama-text.html?_r=1&pagewanted=all.

13

India's Energy Security and Caspian Sea Region

Elaheh Koolaee and Masoud Imani Kalesar

Introduction

Indeed, according to power criteria of Richard Muir (physical, demographic, economic, organizational, military, and power from external relationship) India falls in the category of powerful states (Dwivedi 2004: 15). The world's second biggest populated country and the seventh largest in terms of size, India with its military, man power and a growing technology, industry and especially economy, is indeed amongst the world's influential countries. As a nuclear power and thanks to its rapid economic growth in recent years, India, for many scholars, is going to join the club of the big powers. To do so, sustaining economic growth would be of the prime importance and the prime necessity to keep that trend on would be having secure access to energy supplies.

Meanwhile Indian economy has proved doing well during last five years. India scored the second fastest growing economy of the world in the 2003-04. The UN ranked India as the world's 10th largest economy, the 4th largest in Purchasing Power Parity (PPP) and in Asia the 3rd after Japan and China (UN, July 2005).

But India's position in the world ranking of hydrocarbon resources is not as promising as is its coal and hydropower production. In fact, except hydropower consumption which stands lower than its production, India consumes other energies more than it produces. India stands in 25th and 23rd places in terms of proven natural gas and oil reserves (CIA 2007). India's coal consumption catches the production level approximately. According to Energy Information Administration (EIA, March 2009) though coal with 53 percent and hydropower with 630.6 billion kilowatt hour's consumption are standing as the two main sources of Indian energy, the obvious fact is that these supplementary sources to hydrocarbon sources of energy alone cannot sustain the 7.9 percent annual Indian economic growth (The New York Times 2009). India imports about three-fourths of its crude oil and its gas consumption is also ten times higher than its production.

Indian Energy Consumption and Production

India's total energy consumption is 15.4 quadrillion Btus, as follow: coal (53 percent), oil (33 percent), natural gas (8 percent), hydroelectricity (5 percent) and nuclear (1 percent). It is predicted that India's demand for oil and gas will increase within coming two decades. Tata Energy Research Institute has estimated that in 2010 "India's import dependence in crude oil" would "touch 80 percent and in natural gas 77 percent. Supplies are expected largely from the Persian Gulf...Central Asia, Southeast Asia" (Baru 2005: 218).

According to CIA's 2007 estimation, India's oil production was 880,500 bbl/day and its consumption was (2.722 million bbl/day). Currently India is dependent on imports for 68 percent of its oil consumption. Ranking India as the seventh largest net importer of oil in the world in 2006, the "EIA expects India to become the fourth largest net importer of oil in the world by 2025, behind the United States, China, and Japan." India imports about three-fourths of its crude oil from the Middle Eastern partners, Saudi Arabia (23 percent) and Iran (17 percent). India's gas consumption (41.7 billion cu m) also is ten times higher than its production (31.7 billion cu m) (CIA and EIA 2007).

Many research institutes and scholars have predicted that India's demand for oil and gas will increase within coming two decades. Thus, Indian decisions makers are well-aware that nuclear reactors cannot pump Compressed Natural Gas (CNG) into green coloured auto-Rickshaws and public buses, running in New Delhi alone in millions. In India where more than one billion people's transportation fuel is fossil, nuclear reactors won't offer much. Neither they can run 7.9 percent annual growth of Indian economy's gears, nor can direct more than 72 percent of the population in 550,000 villages to their farms. Fossil fuel is not substituted by nuclear or any other energy sources yet.

Indian Energy Import Options

If feasible, practical and economically managed states prefer oil or gas pipelines as secure means of energy transportation to interruptible transportation by rail or sea tankers. In this regard India has shown great interest on pipeline and importing natural gas by focusing on the last two of the following major options of importing oil and gas from:

1. Southeast Asia: Bangladeshi or Myanmar's natural gas through either territory of Bangladesh or deep-sea pipeline through the Bay of Bengal that would bypass Bangladesh,
2. Latin America and Africa,
3. Middle East/Persian Gulf oil and gas reserves: either by tankers or from Iran via IPI gas pipeline through Pakistani territory,
4. Caspian Sea Region:

- Turkmen natural gas through TAPI gas pipeline via Afghanistan and Pakistan;
- Azeri-Kazakh oil via BTC, Turkey and via Red Sea by tankers;
- Caspian Sea region's oil and gas, on-land via Iran and Pakistan territory; or
- Caspian Sea region's oil and gas, via Iran's Persian Gulf ports and by tankers.

India could import gas in three ways; via tankers over sea in liquefied Natural Gas (LNG) form, through under sea pipeline, or overland pipeline which comes four times cheaper. India has opted for the last option. The two top choices to bring gas to home via pipeline are either from Daulatabad of Turkmenistan or from South Pars field of Iran. Transit fees and handling costs would make other choices expensive.

Caspian Sea Region's Oil and Natural Gas Reserves

If India decides to finalize a major deal with any of Caspian republics, the prime question could be naturally the sufficiency of CSR's oil and particularly natural gas reserves. According to an early optimistic estimate, proven or recoverable 200 billion barrels of oil were believed to lie under the Caspian Sea, though most geologists accepted the figure of 40 to 60 billion barrels as the ultimate reserve base of the Caspian region. Early differences and inaccurate geological assessment were due to geological and technical difficulties, insufficient scientific survey and exaggerations by some beneficiary institutes and states (Sharma 2007: 99). To some analysts early "commercially meaningless" figures and exaggeration were "derived for political purposes and for the U.S entry into the Trans-Caucasus and Central Asia" (Chenoy 2007: 114). However, there is for sure a concord on adequate oil and gas reserve and hydrocarbon potential of the CSR.

Among Caspian littoral states and in terms of oil reserves, Azerbaijan with proven 7 bbl of oil and Kazakhstan with proven 9-40 bbl oil are the richest. Though Iran (0.1 bbl) and Russia's (0.3 bbl) oil deposits are said to be negligible, one cannot comment on their Caspian Sea deposits with confidence as their parts of the sea have not been fully studied and explored. Till recent gas discovery in Azerbaijan's Shah Deniz field, Turkmenistan with proven 2.0 and possible 4.49 Tcm gas reserves was considered a leading country, a status which it still preserves. Uzbekistan's oil deposit is not considerable but as a gas-rich state its importance lies in its gas export potential and its geographical position on the way of energy export either toward China or South East Asia.

While multinational oil companies have initiated numerous large-scale projects in Kazakhstan and Azerbaijan, Turkmenistan has achieved only smaller-scale deals. Oil and gas development in the Russian sector have been similarly less important and in Iranian part of the Sea almost inexistent. Yet, despite the high cost of energy exploitation and transportation, legal and environmental problems, and uncertainties of the surrounding governments, oil and gas companies are competing in the CSR to sign contracts, especially in Kazakhstan and Azerbaijan (Crandall 2006: 54). Several complicated issues have prevented maximum hydrocarbon exploitation of the CSR. Difficulties and realities of technical, ethnical, economic, logistical, legal regime of the Caspian Sea, geopolitical, and social issues have led to the exploitation of only few of the major oil fields and have forced some other key contracts and pipeline projects to remain on the paper. Several obstacles should be tackled first in order to maximize the energy extract of the CSR and its export to the world markets (Jaffe 2000: 150-151).

Thus, CSR is not comparable with Persian Gulf but with the North Sea. To some percent 2 and to some others percent 3 to percent 4 of the world hydrocarbon reserves lies in the Caspian Sea. So there is enough oil and gas.

Indian Geopolitical Interests in the CSR

Massive energy need for fast growing economy puts heavy weight on Indian energy security. To sustain high economic growth rate, India will need to increase its hydrocarbon energy import. One of the nearest potential region from which India can import energy is the CSR. To do so India needs to pursue a persuasive long-term energy relation with the CSR which New Delhi has not yet followed. Beside trade, and investment factors there could be three major motivations behind the Indian CSR interests:

1. Energy Security.
2. Regional stability (the question of extremism).
3. Relation with the U.S and balance of power between its two immediate neighbours:

- Powerful rival, China and
- 'Traditional foe', Pakistan.

Meanwhile two main factors which are challenging Indian energy security and energy imports from the CSR are A) transportation limits B) and absence of a defined CSR doctrine (Peyrouse, 31 October 2009).

Despite increasing interest and besides the lack of a strong and clear-cut doctrine toward the CSR as a whole, what handicaps India's CSR politics are the limitations of transportation of either goods or energy? Though India enjoys geographical proximity but unlike China, shares no border with any Caspian republics. This limits Indian access to CSR energy and hampers its import-export from/to the region.

Compared with China and Pakistan, with the exception of Afghanistan toward which India periodically and according to the geopolitical changes has defined a clear political approach, Indian diplomacy and especially its energy politics toward energy-rich CSR has not been a continuous, competitive, evident, and a persuasive one. Apparently instability in Afghanistan and New Delhi's concerns and rivalry with Pakistan over Afghanistan's politics has engaged and diverted the Indian diplomacy which otherwise would have been diverted on the CSR as well.

India, Regional Stability and States

One of the important issues for India is the religious extremism and terrorism which India has been suffering from. India shares the same view than as China and other big global and regional powers on the security of the CSR, especially Afghanistan. A calm, democratic and secular CSR is in accord with Indian interest. New Delhi's worries on Islamic extremist elements of Pakistan and especially Afghanistan have shaped its security concerns vis-à-vis the region. In fact, elimination of such elements has been a cooperation factor between India and other powers since Taliban time, as New Delhi had joined Iran, Russia, the U.S and China to financially and militarily arm and support the anti-Taliban Northern Alliance of Ahmad Shah Masoud versus the Taliban of Mullah Mohammad Omar and Al-Qaeda of Osama Ben Laden.

To secure the region for energy transit and to contribute to the worldwide peace and security, regional states, the U.S and allies must target long-term socio-ideological changes and economic improvement of the war-torn or self-ruled areas. India as an Asian power should contribute its own share to the stability and peace of the region.

Though the physical core of the ongoing game is situated in the CSR but the major energy and geopolitical plans are planted by external players and non-Caspian regional states. Oil and gas rich republics care is want to sell their reserves and convert it into hard currency. Land-locked republics are not the crucial part of the decision making of the projects. Rather it is the politics of the surrounding regional and extra-regional actors which are affecting the issue of the energy security the most. However, this is not to say that the republics are passive players and have no impact on the outcome of the deals and the game. In fact, the rivalries between big powers (USA-Russia, India-Pakistan and India-China) have increased Caspian republics' bargaining power, autonomy and manoeuvrability.

Afghanistan as a landlocked state and poor in hydrocarbon reserves (in world ranking; number 64 in proven natural gas and 97 in proven oil reserves) has less natural sources of power. Afghanistan's last two centuries geo-strategic importance and at the same time its miseries have been derived from bordering regional geo-strategic powers; China (76 km.), Iran (936 km.), Pakistan (2,430 km.), and CSR countries of Turkmenistan, Uzbekistan and Tajikistan. It is more likely that as it has been for at least last two hundred years Afghanistan will remain a 'bargaining tool' and 'buffer interests' of the big powers, namely Russia, China, the US and even India and Pakistan. Therefore, Afghanistan's role in the New Great Game is mostly and solely due to its unique geographical location in both Rimland and Heartland not because of its extremists elements only. On the other hand, stability of Afghanistan is in the interest of all the states involved in the energy sector of the CSR (Shkolnikov 2002: 7,8).

The energy dimension of its geography, as well as the American military presence in the Middle East and its campaign in Afghanistan are directly linked to strategic petroleum reserve which "will greatly affect China's oil strategy in the Middle East and Central Asian countries" (Li 2002) and (Cole 2003: 53). Though since Taliban time projects are crumbling on the paper, the U.S opposition to transit of any pipeline through Iran, makes insecure and instable Afghanistan a potential though controversial energy transit route. Following September 1996 Taliban takeover of Kabul and consolidation of its Islamist administration in Afghanistan, an energy transit plan was actively persuaded and discussed by the American company Unocal in 1997-08. The pipeline plan was so serious at a time that Taliban representatives went to Texas and Washington in December 1997 for negotiations (Li 2002) and (Cole 2003: 53). However, Unocal, though very keen and interested in building a pipeline route from Turkmenistan to India via Afghanistan and Pakistan, had to for political reasons withdraw from the consortium in 1998.

Landlocked Turkmenistan holds huger reserves of gas than oil and is projected to become a second Kuwait. Its foremost natural geostrategic power is derived from one element only that is natural gas. According to CIA, Turkmenistan stands as the 12th largest gas reservoir but to BBC and some experts, Turkmenistan rank is the 5th largest natural gas reservoir of the world (Gjedrem 2003). Being number 12th and 49th in world's proven natural gas and oil ranking, Turkmenistan's rich hydrocarbon deposits is compensating for its weak military, economic, demographical and organizational natural sources of power as well as for its weak 'power from external relationship'.

Despite its low population (5 million) and huge natural gas reserves, Turkmenistan economic profile is not promising as its US$ 1,340 GNI per capita reveals. About 85 percent of Turkmenistan's hard currency comes currently from natural gas export and the majority of its gas is exported via Gazprom owned pipeline and through Russian territory (Mesamed 1999: 211). However, in order to have an alternative pipeline and to be in a bargaining position with Moscow, Ashgabat is looking toward Iran as a potential option among its several export choices. Turkmenistan and Iran are swapping gas for more than a decade. Turkmenistan feeds northern populated areas of Iran with Turkmen gas via a pipeline and in return, Iran releases the same amount of received gas via its Persian

Gulf gas exporting facilities (KeyhanHavai, 15 August 1998:23).

The 9th largest country of the world Kazakhstan, rich in hydrocarbon deposits has the best potential of all Caspian republics. Equipped with two factors of natural sources of power (size and resources), with 15.4 million people, reasonable post-independence economic growth record and US$ 2,930 GNI per capita, Kazakhstan shows a more steady development. To understand Kazakh politics, one needs to look at its relationship with two big powers of Russia and China. Located next to two great powers and sharing long border with them (Russia 6,846 km. and China 1,533 km.) is in itself a major task for any state which requires good neighbourly relations and a cautious foreign policy. Economic trade of Kazakhstan with Russia and China is a clear-cut indication of Kazakh relationship with these two powers. In 2006 Russia and China were the number one import and export partners of Kazakhstan (Koolaee and Tisheyar, 2010).

While China stood in top among Kazkhstan's export partners with 15.2 percent, Russia stood as the most important import partner of Kazakhstan with 34.6 percent. Thus for years to come, as Kazakhstan's location, ethnic, demography and economy reveal, Astana will remain under direct and continuous influence of Russia in first place and upcoming growing influence of China in second place. With full construction of the third phase scheduled to begin in 2011 and full operation of Sino-Kazakh oil pipeline, Kazakhstan's present dependency on Russian oil exporting pipelines will be reduced, as Chinese growing economy and its need for energy will consume huge bulk of the Kazakh oil.

Sino-Pakistan and the US Factors

With Iranian 1979 revolution and Soviet invasion of Afghanistan and formation of Taliban, regional geopolitics underwent considerable changes. Following the Iranian Islamic revolution the US-Iran alliance collapsed and the US turned to Pakistan in order to deal with Soviet intervention of Afghanistan. The US-Pakistan alliance weakened following the withdrawal of the Soviet Union from Afghanistan. By early 1990s Soviets were out of Afghanistan but pro-Pakistan Taliban was in place. However, the US and Pakistan re-allied following the Parvez Mosharraf presidency and 11th September 2001 Al-Qaida attack of the World Trade Centre.

With the emergence of Taliban and takeover of pro-Iranian

strongholds of northern alliance-Mazare Sharif and Bamiyan-and the killing of eight Iranian diplomats, Tehran-Islamabad relations soured severely. While Iran was viewing Sunni Taliban as a main threat to its own Shiite faith and Shiites of Afghanistan and also to the security of its eastern border, Pakistan was treating Taliban as a means of having a footprint in Afghanistan. One of the reasons behind Pakistan's involvement in the politics of Afghanistan and support of Taliban was the issue of energy. The Telegraph reported once that "oil industry insiders say the dream of securing a pipeline across Afghanistan is the main reason why Pakistan, a close political ally of America's, has been so supportive of the Taliban and why America has quietly acquiesced in its conquest of Afghanistan"(Monbiot, October 23, 2001).

The more Iran got involved in the Afghan conflict, the more it "turned into direct conflict with Pakistan." (Hussain, 2002: 533). India's common interests with Russia, Iran and China on containing extremism and Taliban were not matching with Pakistan's Central Asian interests. Thus, India, Iran and Russia and to an extend China came closer. Following the September 11 and the US-led attack of Afghanistan, the entire scenario changed once more as Russia, India and Iran supported the coalition forces' military operations. Therefore, being left alone Pakistan had no option but to join the U.S in its war against terror and Taliban and in return for the USA's financial support. Unlike the early 1990s competition with Turkey and Iran for influencing the CSR, Islamabad's later competitive policies have been more evidently shaped by New Delhi's moves. Through economic, expertise, and diplomacy means, both Pakistan and India have attempted to gain more influence in the region. While Islamabad has tied with both Washington and Beijing, India has opted for the US. Nonetheless, Sino-Indian hidden and implicit rivalry and power balancing act in Asia has bestowed Pakistan with China's strategic cooperation and significant military assistance.

On the other hand, since Soviet withdrawal from Afghanistan and its collapse in 1991, India's CSR energy, security and strategic interests and especially Afghanistan politics are shaped by its traditional rival China in first place and by its traditional foe, Pakistan in the second place. However, compare with China's steady, active and long-term initiations, plans, and participations in CSR's politics, energy and pipeline, India's involvement has not been considerable. And, when it comes for having a footprint in CSR, despite 'having the second largest Muslim population in the world', centuries-old ties with the largely Muslim populated CSR and geographic proximity, New Delhi lags behind Beijing. Paradoxically, India shares more commonalities with the region than China. While China is pursuing a long-term measures vis-à-vis the CSR and through SCO (Koolaee and Moradi, 2011, 226-228) for instance, it seems that Indian administration in spite of India's growing economy and energy needs has not yet prescribed a long-term CSR doctrine for its foreign policy. Instead of a broader approach which could contain the entire CSR, India has opted for bilateral relations with Caspian republics.

Despite several wars, the three nuclear states of China, Pakistan and India have common grounds for cooperation and have so far maintained a balance of power in the region. Organizations such as SCO in which both India and Pakistan have observer status could provide a cooperation ground. It has brought the three states together, though with different interests. However, beside the small-scale cooperation initiatives in the realms of commerce, counter-narcotics and environment protection, security and terrorism are what Islamabad, Beijing and New Delhi are worried about, therefore persuading almost unified politics in that regard (Hill, May 2001: 4). The three most populated countries of the world, India, Pakistan and China's fast growing economies and swelling energy demands make them potential markets for the CSR's oil and gas (Weitz, Summer 2006: 155,163).

The U.S. influencing and strategizing of its 'energy stakes' in the CSR is affecting all main traditional regional players as well as India. In fact, the US "is keen to create regional security architecture, marginalizing if not fully ending the influence of traditional actors Russia and Iran and new stakeholders like China." In this game, "India is being roped in with promises of help in becoming a recognized great power in return for acquiescing in the role of creating an Asian balance vis-à-vis an emerging powerful China. Washington is also trying to exploit the undercurrent of suspicion in the Sino-Russian relations" (Kaushik 2007:83). Moreover, as Ajay Patnaik puts: "US control over the oil and energy resources of Central Asia will make it neither cheap nor accessible to others. If the US succeeds in controlling most of the energy resources, it will use this as an instrument of its external policy. That would make emerging powers like India most vulnerable" (Bedi 2002). Indeed, the US uses energy issue as a tool of its foreign policy. When it comes for IPI for instance, the US uses its leverage openly to discourage India. Condoleezza Rice said once: "if India is buying Iranian gas my country will get upset" (BBC Persian, February 4, 2006). The USA sanctions namely D'Amato Act threatens European companies with heavy fine, and the Iran-Libya Sanctions Act (ILSA) forbids companies investing more than US$ 20 million in Iran.

The coming Indo-China competition for leadership in Asia, Indo-Pakistan hostility and instability in Afghanistan and competition for secure energy will leave a negative impact on large-scale involvement of South Asian states in the CSR's politics and energy. Nonetheless, "If Chinese expansion coincides with declining Russian influence, India will have no choice but to expand its political, economic and military capabilities in Central Asia" (Sachdeva 2006: 34).

Indian Energy Deals with the CSR

India has signed several Memorandum of Understandings and agreements with Afghanistan, Turkmenistan, Iran and Kazakhstan on transportation, pipelines and energy. However, its involvement in the Caspian energy is not promising and matching with that of the China. For instance, India's trade with Central Asia is approximately US$ 200 million which is a negligible portion of India's overall international trade. (Schaffer and Haté 2007). Indian-owned Oil and Natural Gas Company (ONGC) has invested US$ 3.5 billion in overseas exploration since 2000, while Chinese-owned China National Petroleum Corporation (CNPC) has made overseas investments of an estimated US$ 40 billion (Bajpaee 2005).

In the December 2004 summit with Russia, India had announced a US$ 3 billion investment in the Sakhalin-3 oil field and the joint Russian-Kazakh Kurmangazy oil field in the Caspian. It has also formally bid for participation in the Kazakhstan's Tengiz and Kashagan oil fields and the Kurmangazy and Darkhan exploration blocs. Besides, it had also shown interest in exploration of nine other blocs in and around the Caspian Sea. India's Gail Ltd., a gas infrastructure firm, had offered its services as a project consortium partner in Sino- Kazakh pipeline. Along other Indian public-sector companies, Gail was also eager to invest in gas processing and petrochemical plants in the Kazakh towns of Atyrau and Akhtau and to improve oil recovery in older fields. Both sides had agreed to establish a joint working group to examine and develop various projects for cooperation. As far as Kazakh energy is concerned and as of today, both India and Kazakhstan are unclear how they are going to transport Kazakh oil or gas to India (Blank 2005).

So far and in practice, the only Indian energy purchase from a Caspian state is from Iran and that from Iran's Southern energy fields. In 2005, India signed a US$ 40 billion deal with Iran to import 7.5 million tons of liquefied natural gas annually over a 25-year period. It also obtained stakes in the development of Iran's largest onshore oilfield, Yadavaran, as well the Jufeir oilfield. The Yadavaran oilfield is a Sino-Indian-Iranian collaboration with India holding a 20 percent stake, China 50 percent and 30 percent with Iran. In exchange for Iranian gas, India is investing in Iran's ports and energy infrastructure (Bajpaee 2005).

Transportation Limits: Iran, India's CSR Energy Corridor

When it comes for Indian energy security or CSR's energy transportation, the importance of Iran becomes undeniable. Iran not only sits at Hurmoz chock point in the Persian Gulf but also has direct access to both land masses of the east and west energy rich CSR. Geographically, Iran is the best route for Indian export to and energy import from CSR, as none of the other three options of land-routes through its historical rival and foe - China and Pakistan - nor instable Afghanistan suit India. Neither the difficult Leh-Kashgar pass, nor the impracticable route through Afghanistan-Pakistan can serve as an Iranian route can. If the St. Petersburg agreement's potentials have been exploited India could access to both sides of the Caspian Sea through Iran's Persian Gulf port of Chahbahar and its rail and road networks. The Sarakhs-Tajan Rail Link which officially opened on 13th May 1996 connects the Iranian southern ports and railway network to the eastern Caspian region through Turkmenistan. Iran's highways and roads via several points could connect India to the western Caspian region, to Armenia and Azerbaijan (Koolaee, 2005, 21-23).

In 2005, Iran completed the US$ 43 million, 125-km long road from the Dougharoun region to Herat, and announced that it will build a 176-km long railroad from Iran to Herat/Afghanistan. In addition to the Sarakhs-Tajan rail link, Iran completed the 1000 km long Bafq-Mashhad railroad in 2004, which makes the rail journey from Central Asia to the Persian Gulf two days shorter. An improved railroad infrastructure will attract cargos from Russia, China, India, the CSR and Central Asia to reach ports in the Persian Gulf via Iran (Kucera, April 13, 2006).

With Iranian route unexploited, currently and practically Indian access to the CSR is viable by air only. India has signed the St. Petersburg agreement in 2000 with Russia and Iran on establishing a North-South transportation corridor but in reality this corridor's potential has not been exploited. Though India contributes to the developing of Iran's Persian Gulf Chahbahar into a commercial port to access Afghanistan, CSR and Central Asia, but as of today the capability of this port and its connectivity to the Iran's rail network is not up to the level. Nonetheless, a road from Afghanistan to Chabahar has already been completed with Indian help (Sud 2008). The fate of 1997 trilateral agreement between India, Turkmenistan, and Iran on the transit of goods is that of St. Petersburg agreement. India has not exploited the Iran's transit potential and both agreements remain on the papers.

Iran's geo-strategic location and energy factors are not ignored rather are not utilizes by New Delhi. What India needs is more insertion of its crucial regional interest vis-à-vis China and Pakistan. In this regard, Iran can be a useful friend. If India is ever going to enlarge its CSR politics and energy interests, it would then be inevitable for India not to maintain a close relation with Iran. And, what Iran needs is Indian support and backing in the international organizations such as IAEA and the UN. Iran could push forward and facilitate Indian geo-strategic, economic and energy interests and access to the CSR. In return India could facilitate Iranian uneasy international diplomacy. The Iranian value in Indian geopolitical calculation is more at a regional context than at a global level. Indian interests with big powers like the U.S have forced India to take cautious measures and politics vis-à-vis Iran, as Indian congress-led government under direct pressure from White House voted three times against Iran in International Atomic Energy Agency (IAEA).

In sum, if ever India is going to challenge Chinese and Pakistani ambitions and competitions on accessing to CSR's oil and gas reserves, it has no best option than Iran. China has tied with Pakistan and maintains a close relation with Iran. India can do the same. If China has managed to stand the US, EU, and critiques of the international organizations on its cooperation with Iran, then why not India? India can balance its relationship with Iran for its energy needs and meanwhile tie with the U.S and the West for its national interests.

Despite expanding economies and growing energy demands of both China and India, one can observe that India in its CSR gains is lagging behind China. For instance, while Sino-Kazakh oil pipeline is almost to be completed, the Indian gas pipelines call it TAPI or IPI remain on the paper, in case of IPI since 1989. An oil or gas pipeline like IPI can not only foster Indo-Iranian relationship but can also open further the energy transit routes from the CSR to the Indian subcontinent.

Enmity ends not with enmity but with friendship. India is capable of taking initiations to resolve the hostilities with Pakistan. Energy needs of the both nation is an opportunity that could put an end to more than half century hostility. IPI has provided an opportunity for cooperation which should not be lost.

India's Gas Pipeline Options: IPI and TAPI

As analyzed above, one of the best routes for Caspian energy is a Southward gas or oil pipeline via Iran and toward Southeast Asia. This route - if realized - would be beneficiary for all CSR as well as for demanding and growing markets of Asian giants such as India. Azeri and Uzbek oil and gas could be also diverted into the South and toward India.

Kazak, Uzbek and Turkmen oil and gas can reach India via neighbouring countries and through pipelines. By the now it is apparent that India has made its choice by showing interests on CSR gas but not oil though an oil pipeline is not impracticable but due to gas-rich Turkmenistan and Uzbekistan's proximity, India has preferred to work on a gas pipeline. CSR's gas is reachable to India either via TAPI or IPI. If arranged then Iran can receive Turkmen gas for its consumption and pump the same into the IPI pipeline toward Pakistan and India.

The most controversial gas pipeline in the region, Iran-Pakistan-India (IPI), known also as 'Peace Pipeline' would run for 1100 km from Assaluyeh/giant South Pars gas field of Iran in the Persian Gulf and crossing 1000 km. in Pakistan would continue for 600 km. within India eventually ending in Gujarat. With total length of 2,700 km. and US$ 7 billion being the cost, the IPI project would deliver 150 million cubic meters gas per day which will split between Pakistan (60 million cum) and India (90 million cum). IPI project will enjoy Russian support and giant Gasprom's participation. Two decades have passed since conceptualization of the Peace Pipeline by Dr. Pachauri but the U.S opposition to the project and India's security concerns of the pipeline in Pakistani territory have so far prevented the realization of this gas pipeline.

The competitor to IPI is Turkmenistan-Afghanistan-Pakistan-India (TAPI) gas-pipeline which would run from Dulatabad/Turkmenistan. Crossing Herat and Kandahar of Afghanistan, it would reach Quetta and Multan in Pakistan from where it would touch Indian soil at Fazilka. This 1,680 km. long pipeline would require US$ 3.3-4 billion for its construction. It is planned to deliver 3.2 billion Cubic feet gas to be shared by both Pakistan and India. Being shorter and less costly in comparison with the IPI, enjoying the financial aid of Asian Development Bank and World Bank and the U.S backing, this pipeline is politically easier to implement but has serious security problems.

There are several obstacles on realization of both IPI and TAPI. Security concerns in Afghanistan and Pakistan are main challenges. It's less likely that TAPI can enjoy Russian backing as it would hamper Russian strategic oil and gas export plans to Europe. Secondly, any major gas pipeline directed from the CSR southward to the huge subcontinent market would deprive Russia from transit revenue. Losing Turkmen and Uzbek gas through TAPI will go in direct confrontation with Russian 'energy Ace card', thereby making Russia to oppose the TAPI. The U.S President Barak Obama's message to Iranian people and leaders on the occasion of Iranian New Year in March 2009 to end three decades hostilities may open new chapter in the US-Iran relationship. It may leave its impact on IPI as a symbol of a good-will to start with.

On the other hand, when it comes for IPI, there is another problem; 1000 km of 2,700 km IPI pipeline has to pass through Pakistan and mostly throughout Baluchistan and Sind regions. In fact India's major concern could not be the US objection to the deal in the first place but Pakistan's internal turmoil. Indian fear of Pakistan with which it fought three wars isn't baseless but on the other hand India has not any other and better option than dealing with Pakistan which is neighbouring both Iran and India. It is this best obligatory option which imposes psychological pressure on Indian government otherwise oil companies, international banks and consortiums can guarantee the secure flow of gas thorough insecure region. In case of any gas interruption, Iran has also assured India of compensating and delivering the same by all other means and in the first place.

Unlike Pakistan, Indian recent position on IPI is idle. Neither New Delhi has pulled out nor pursued the deal actively. After decades, IPI has provided a chance for the spread of peace in the region. It's up to the US to let the market forces act natural for prosperity of the region and leave the regional security free to shape itself.

Conclusion

India has sensed the urgency and importance of its energy security if Prime Minister Manmohan Singh said: "energy security is second only in our scheme of things to food security." (Blank 2005). If India could not grab its share of the Caspian oil and gas reserves, it will likely face a logjam in the next 10 to15 years. Insufficiency of oil and gas reserves at home, U.S.A.'s ultimate goal of controlling CSR supplies as a tool against others, Myanmar remaining within the Chinese sphere of influence, India's loss of the bid to China on the Canadian-owned oil company in Kazakhstan, Pakistan's enthusiasm to finalize the IPI and to attract Chinese in the project, are enough alarming.

It seems oriental India is not an exception to thinks of cure after the disease establishes itself. This is opposite of occidental habit of 'prevention before cure'. Despite knowing the escalating energy need which can lead to crisis, India is not taking serious and long-term measures to prevent the crisis. India is showing increasing interest but not increasing action, an action unlike of its Asian rival China which predicting the needs and crisis has deconstructed its oriental habit and showing that 'prevention is better and less costly than cure'.

References

Alam, Shah. (October-December 2004), "Iran-Pakistan Relations: Political and Strategic Dimensions", Strategic Analysis, Vol. 28, No. 4.

Bajpaee, Chietigj (2005), "India, China locked in energy game", Asian Times online, [Online: web], URL: http://www.atimes.com/atimes/Asian_Economy/GC17Dk01.html.

Baru, Sanjaya (2005), 'Some Issues for Indian Policy', quoted in:

Kapil Kak, "India's Strategic and Security Interests in Central Asia", in: V. Nagendra Rao, and Mohammad Monir Alam, Central Asia: Present Challenges and Future Prospects, New Delhi: Knowledge World.

BBC News Persian (February 4, 2006) online at: http://www.bbc.co.uk/persian/business/story/2006/02/060204_ra-iran-india.shtml 04. February 2006.

Bedi, Rahul (2002), Front Line, Volume 19 - Issue 19, Sep. 14 – 27.

Blank, Stephen (2005), "Central Asia's Energy Game Intensifies", Yale Global online, [Online: web], URL: http://yaleglobal.yale.edu/display.article?id=6222.

Blank, Stephen (2005), "India's Quest for Central Asian Energy", Eurasia Daily Monitor, Volume: 2 Issue: 40.

British Petroleum, Statistical Review of World Energy", June 2007.

Chenoy, Anuradha M. (2007), "Oil Politics of Central Asia and Caspian Sea Basin: The US Game Plan", in Anuradha M., and Patnaik, Ajay (eds.) Commonwealth of Independent States: Energy, Security and Development, New Delhi: KW Publishers Pvt. Ltd.

CIA world Fact Book (2007), "India", [Online: web], URL: www.cia.gov/library/publications/the-world-factbook/countrylisting.html.

CIA World Factbook and Energy Information Administration, [Online: web], URL: http://www.eia.doe.gov/emeu/cabs/India/Oil.html.

Cole, Bernard D. (2003), "Oil for the Lamps of China: Beijing's 21st Century Search for Energy", Institute for National Strategic Studies, National Defence University Washington, D.C.

Crandall, Maureen S. (2006), Energy, Economics, and Politics in the Caspian region, Dreams and Hopes, USA: Praeger Security International.

Dwivedi, R.L. (2004), Fundamentals of Political Geography, Allahabad (India): Chaitanya Publishing House.

EIA (March 2009), "India", available at: www.eia.doe.gov/india.

Gjedrem, Svein (2003), "The Hazards of Petroleum Wealth", in Tsalik, Svetlana (ed.), Caspian Oil Windfalls: Who Will Benefit?, New York: Open Society Institute.

Hill, Fiona (May 2001), "The Caucasus and Central Asia", No. 80, Brookings Policy Brief, Washington D.C: The Brookings Institution.

Hussain, Nazir (2002), "Pak-Iran Relations in Post-9/11 Period: Regional and Global Impact", Regional Studies, XX (4), Autumn 2002. Quoted in Alam, Shah (2004), "Iran-Pakistan Relations: Political and Strategic Dimensions", Strategic Analysis, Vol. 28, No. 4, The Institute for Defence Studies and Analyses, October-December 2004.

India Daily (March 21, 2008), Online at: http://www.indiadaily.com/editorial/1636.asp.

Jaffe, Amy (2000), "U.S. policy toward the Caspian region: can the wish list be realized?", SIPRI.

Kaushik, Devendra (2007), "The Caspian Cauldron: New Geopolitical Game", in Chenoy, Anuradha M., and Patnaik, Ajay (eds.), Commonwealth of Independent States: Energy, Security and Development, New Delhi: KW Publishers Pvt. Ltd.

KeyhanHavai, 15 August 1998.

Kohl, Wilfrid L. (2000), "The Development of Caspian Sea Oil: Implication for OPEC", in Caspian Energy Resources; Implication for the Arab Gulf, Abu Dhabi: The Emirates Centre for Strategic Studies and Research.

Koolaee, Elaheh and MandanaTisheyar, "Comparative Study on China and Japan Security Approaches in Central Asia, Human Geography Research, No. 71, Spring 2010, pp. 127-144.

Koolaee, Elaheh and Fatollah Moradi, "Impacts of the Shanghai Organization on Central Asia's Security, Politics, Vol. 40, N0. 4, Winter 2011, pp. 217- 136

Koolaee, Elaheh (2005), The New Great Game in Central Asia, Tehran: IPIS.

Kucera, Joshua, "Iran Expanding Ties with Central Asian States to Counterbalance US Geopolitical Pressure", Eurasia Insight, [Online: web], URL: http://www.eurasianet.org/departments/insight/articles/eav041305b.shtml.

Li, Niu. Quoted in Dashan, Xu., "Oil Reserve System Urgently Needed," China Daily, February 18, 2002, in FBIS-CPP20020218000024.

Mesamed, Vladimir (1999), "Turkmenistan: Oil, Gas, and Caspian Politics", in Croissant, Michaeal P. and Aras, Bulent (eds.), Oil and Geopolitics in the Caspian Sea Region, London: Praeger.

Monbiot, George (2001), "America's Pipe Dream", Guardian, 23 October 2001.

Olcott, Martha Brill., and Udalova, Natalia (2000), "Drug Trafficking on the Great Silk Road: The Security Environment in Central Asia," Carnegie Endowment for International Peace Working Paper, No. 11, March.

Peuch, Jean-Christophe (2001), "Central Asia: Charges Link Russian Military to Drug Trade," RFE/RL, June 8.

Peyrouse, Sebastien.,(interview, 31 October 2009), Research Fellow at Central Asia-Caucasus Institute Silk Road Studies Program, Institute for Security and Development Policy, Stockholm-Nacka, Sweden.

Sachdeva, Gulshan (2006), "India's Attitude towards China's Growing Influence in Central Asia", China and Eurasia Forum Quarterly, Volume 4, No. 3, p. 34.

Schaffer, Teresita C. and Haté, Vibhuti (2007), "India's 'Look West' Policy: Why Central Asia Matters", South Asia Monitor, Centre for Strategic and International Studies (CSIS), Number 110 September 05, 2007, USA.

Sharma, R.R. (2007), "Regional Order and Security: Role of External Powers in Central Asia and Caspian Sea Region". Quoted in Anuradha M., and Patnaik, Ajay (eds.) Commonwealth of Independent States: Energy, Security and Development, New Delhi: KW Publishers Pvt. Ltd.

Shkolnikov, Vladimir (2002), Recommendations for Democratization Assistance of the Caspian Region, Caspian Studies Program Policy Brief, No. 7 May 2002, Harvard Universtiy, John F. Kennedy School of Government Caspian Studies Program.

Sud, Hari (2008) "India looks to Central Asia for Energy", [Online: web],URL: http://www.upiasia.com/Economics/2008/06/17/india_looks_to_central_asia_for_energy/5733/.

UN Bureau of Census (July 2005), "India".

The New York Times (30 November 2009), "India Posts Fastest Economic Growth in 18 Months".

Weitz, Richard (2006), "Averting a New Great Game in Central Asia", The Washington Quarterly, Vol. 29, No. 3.

14

Indo-Iran Cooperation in Energy and Energy Security

Shebonti Ray Dadwal

Though Iran-India relations have strong traditional roots, there has been a tendency to view bilateral relations between the two countries through the energy prism.

Of late, even the state of relations amongst these two countries has often mistakenly been identified by the success or failure of negotiations on the Iran-Pakistan-India (IPI) project, and to a lesser extent, the 2005 LNG deal.

Therefore, since the IPI project and LNG deal are both mired in controversy, it would therefore appear that Tehran and New Delhi's relations have undergone a turn for the worse, ignoring the fact that for decades, Iran and India have shared a robust relationship in the energy sector, albeit through the oil trade, with Iran being the second largest OPEC supplier of crude oil for India, while India has been one of the five countries that has been supplying refined petroleum products to Iran.

Recently, there is also a sense in Iranian circles that New Delhi's recent bonhomie with Washington has had an impact on its ties with Tehran.

This paper attempts to look at the state of Iran-India energy relations, and proposes that despite the fact that relations, including ties in the energy sector, between these two important Asian countries have undergone some problems and have dipped from the high point till of 2003-2005, the scope for strengthening and broadening ties in the energy sector are there.

Iran-India Hydrocarbon Trade

India's fast-paced economic growth at an average of 6-7 percent over the last two decades, and the government's goal of reaching double digit growth rates over the next few decades, is to a large extent dependent on its access to energy supplies to fulfil promises of providing modern forms of energy to burgeoning population. In fact, after food and water, energy has been placed at the top of India's national security priorities. However, given the country's ever-growing hunger for energy even its quite large reserves of coal, natural gas and oil has seen India having to resort to ever-increasing imports of all three hydrocarbon resources. In the case of oil alone, India is currently importing 70 percent of its oil requirement and this is expected to increase to 90 percent by 2025, by which time India's oil demand would be around 325 million tonnes. [1]

Its demand for natural gas for the non-power sector alone too is expected to more than double to 391 million cubic meters a day (mcmd) by 2025 from the current 120 mcmd. [2] Similarly, in the case of coal, despite having the fourth largest reserves of coal in the world, India has recorded a compounded annual growth rate (CAGR) of 17.1 percent of coal imports between 2003 and 2008. [3] Given that India would need to add four times its current generation capacity to its power sector, more coal and gas imports are on the cards to meet this requirement.

On the other hand, Iran's stature as a leading oil and gas producer is well known. While it is the second largest producer of oil among the OPEC countries, its gas reserves are of greater interest for the world energy market. With the second largest reserves of natural gas after Russia, its exports are relatively limited. For instance, while its reserves are around 29.6 trillion cubic metres, its production in 2009 was only 130.3 billion cubic metres. [4] However, due to the sanctions imposed on Iran's energy sector by the US [5], much of its gas sector remains unexploited, and therefore holds huge potential for future production and export. In 2005, British Petroleum (BP) terminated its Iran programme on the grounds that the US sanctions made its investments in that country too risky. BP's action was followed by British Gas and, most recently, by Brazilian Petrobras and Norwegian Statoil Hydro. Others, like France's Total, which was developing South Pars gas field's Phase 11, delayed its for five years causing Tehran to replace Total with CNPC in December 2009. [6] In fact, according to recent study by the Majlis Research Centre, a leading official think tank in Iran, the country needs around US$ 4.5 billion of investments in its energy industry, without which it may suffer grave consequences. [7]

Hence, with many of the Western oil companies now increasingly adopting a hands-off policy towards Iran, Iran is looking east. To a large extent, Russian and Chinese firms have benefited. However, with its huge demand for energy, India is a potentially large market for Iran. And as the natural depletion of hydrocarbons the world over takes place, Iran's position is bound to become even more important in the future as a gas supplier. India should therefore take the opportunity to grab a piece of the lucrative Iranian energy pie.

It was with this in mind that India and Iran launched the Iran-Pakistan-India gas pipeline in the late 1980s. In 2005, the National Iranian Gas Export Co., or Nigec, and Indian companies—GAIL (India) Ltd, Indian Oil Corporation Ltd and Bharat Petroleum Corporation Ltd.—also signed an agreement by which Iran was to deliver five million tonnes of liquefied natural gas (LNG) to India, with an option for an additional 2.5 million tonnes per year. The Oil and Natural Gas Corporation (ONGC) also identified the Yadavaran and Azadegan oil fields and South Pars gas field for investment, while state refiner Indian Oil Corporation (IOC) identified the North Pars gas field and refinery upgrades. Gail also aimed to develop new petrochemical plants and city gas distribution networks.

At the same time, despite being a large oil producer and exporter, Iran has to import around a third of its petroleum products (petrol or gasoline) requirement due to inadequate refining capacity. The total daily consumption of petrol is roughly 65.5 million litres, while its daily domestic petrol production stands at 44.5 million litres, according to a Platts report. India is one of the countries that exports petroleum products to Iran.

Differences between Iran and India

Relations between Iran and India suffered some strains following New Delhi's vote in the IAEA against Tehran's nuclear weapons programme in 2005 in line with its official position that Iran had to fulfil its obligations as a signatory of the Nuclear Non-Proliferation Treaty (NPT). This had a fall-out on bilateral relations, including on the IPI project as well as the 2005 LNG deal. Tehran was of the opinion that New Delhi, which was negotiating with Washington for the India-US civil nuclear deal, had succumbed to US pressure on voting against Iran and was also now stalling on the IPI project, though India cited higher prices being quoted by Iran on the LNG deal as well as concerns about the security of the pipeline route through Pakistan as reasons for the same, as well as differences with Islamabad over transit and transport fees. As of now, Iran and Pakistan have decided to go ahead with the project on a bilateral basis, with the option open to India of coming on board at a later date. Iranian and Pakistani sources state that China too has evinced interest on becoming a party to the project, though no official Chinese statements have been made on the same. India, for its part, continues to stress on its commitment to the project.

On the LNG deal too, Tehran revised the price for LNG several times, on the grounds that the rates agreed in 2005 were not approved by higher levels. The IOC's heads of agreement on North Pars also lapsed in 2007, and the firm started to drag its heels on refinery investments. This was followed by Essar Oil withdrawing from a project to build a new US$ 8 billion refinery in Bandar Abbas after it provoked controversy in the US, threatening a major steel deal in Minnesota. [8]

There were also reports that Tehran had trimmed the stake it had offered to the ONGC-Hinduja consortium in South Pars Phase 12 from 60 percent to 40 percent after deciding to assign 20 percent to Angola's state Sonangol. Iran has also assigned a 10 percent slice of the project to Venezuela's state Petroleos de Venezuela. Indian sources further claim that Iran is offering better fiscal terms to the Chinese, including a 3 percent higher rate of return on investments.

In the meantime, Tehran awarded the Indian projects to Chinese rivals one by one. Sinopec signed a US$ 3 billion contract for the Yadavaran oil development in late 2007. This was followed by China National Petroleum Corporation (CNPC) clinching a US$ 2 billion deal for the onshore North Azadegan field in January 2009 and a 70 percent slice of the US$ 2.5 billion South Azadegan project in September. [9]

However, despite the seeming downturn in energy relations, things are not as bleak as they may appear. For instance, ONGC and its overseas subsidiary OVL, along with the Hinduja Group and Petronet LNG have reportedly agreed to take a 20 percent stake in the US$ 4.35 billion LNG export facility Iran LNG is building at Tombak Port, about 50 km north of Assaluyeh in the Bushehr province, which is scheduled to be completed by 2011. ONGC plans to use the facility to liquefy the gas it will produce from the Farsi fields in the Persian Gulf. OVL is the operator of the Farsi block with 40 percent interest, where it along with IOC (40 percent) and Oil India (20 percent) has submitted a US$ 5.5 billion plan to bring to production the Farzad-B gas find. With this, ONGC's stake in Iran LNG could go up to 40 percent. ONGC is keen to ship some 6-8 million tonnes a year of LNG to be produced from Farsi and SP-12 fields. According to source, Iran has agreed to give India up to 6 million tonnes per annum of LNG for its efforts in SP-12 and Farsi gas field. Moreover, OVL and the Hinduja firm, Ashok Leyland Projects Services (ALPS), also signed agreements to take a 40 percent stake in SP-12, which is expected to produce 3 billion cubic feet per day of gas, two-thirds of which is to be converted into LNG for exports. In the SP-12 field, Petropars—a subsidiary of National Iranian Oil Co.—would hold 40 percent while the remaining 20 percent would be with Sonangol of Angola. At 35 tcf, it contains almost 7percent of reserves in the South Pars gas field. [10]

Moving beyond Energy Trade

However, both India and Iran realise that relations between the two countries need to go beyond oil or gas trading for several reasons. First, Iran, which has been seeking to overcome the problems emanating from the US economic sanctions, needs a partner of international standing who can stand up to US pressure. While so far, China has provided that support, for the sake of its own energy security, Tehran needs to diversify its energy markets. India's energy requirements are expanding much faster than most other countries of the world and, together with China, India is expected to account for 45 percent of the total increase in world energy demand by 2030. Rapid economic development, industrialisation, urbanisation and improved quality of life will continue to underpin India's insatiable appetite for energy long into the foreseeable future as ensuring a reliable, affordable and secure supply of energy is arguably the greatest challenge facing the country.

As has been mentioned earlier, India, despite its substantial energy reserves needs to import increasing amounts of oil, natural gas and even coal to meet its requirements. In the case of gas alone, India's imports, which at present are entirely made up by LNG imports, are projected to increase by around 30 percent between now and 2010, when they will reach about 12 billion cubic meters per annum (bcma). Gas imports are expected to further quadruple between 2020-2030, when they will reach an estimated 61 bcma. [11] Hence, India, with its burgeoning energy requirements, is well placed to provide a substantial alternative energy market for Iran.

Given the way the international energy market is transforming and strong diplomatic ties often take precedence over market forces to safeguard energy supplies in a market that may become increasingly tight with regard to oil supplies, India needs to ensure preferential access to residual crude oil, as well as gas, sources.

Secondly, Iran's domestic energy consumption is increasing rapidly as its population grows, while its oil production has been declining, either due to natural depletion or due to lack of adequate and timely investment for upgrading ageing oil fields. For instance, between 1999 and 2006 the average annual growth has been 4.3 percent mainly because of the low domestic prices for oil products, especially motor fuel. In turn, this has resulted in a reduction of oil available for export as well as rising petrol import subsidy which in 2006 amounted to over US$ 4.8 million. Similarly, in the gas sector, the development of the South Pars field has been slow due to administrative delays and problems in negotiations with international oil companies. This has inhibited supplies, both for reinjection in oil fields for secondary recovery as well as limited domestic supplies. Slow development of gas fields in turn have hampered plans for gas exports both by pipeline and LNG, but more importantly, there is growing opposition to exports on the grounds of domestic needs. [12]

On the other hand, India, which is almost self sufficient in petroleum products, and in fact has plans to become a petroleum refining hub in the not too distant future, is one of five countries that exports petrol (gasoline) to Iran. Recently, there have been reports that India's refined products trade has come under pressure from the US, whereby Reliance Industries Ltd., which was the company that was exporting petrol to Iran, stopped its sales to Iran in an apparent bid to escape sanctions by Washington as well as to prevent jeopardizing its bid to buy a US chemical company, LyondellBasell. However, some Iranian sources claim that Reliance is continuing to sell gasoline to Iran, albeit not directly. [13]

Therefore, it is imperative that both India build energy relations and synergies that go beyond bilateral ties and allow both countries to play a larger regional if not global role, with energy as a facilitator.

Potential for Broadening Energy Relations

Even though the pipeline through Pakistan may seem unviable for India for security reasons, other means for bringing Iranian gas to

Indian shores can be looked at. Recently, there has been some talk about reviving the old Oman-India sub-sea pipeline, that had originally been proposed in the mid-1990s but was shelved due to technical and sourcing problems. The current 2,000 km pipeline envisages a line to be laid from Oman to either Gujarat or Maharashtra, at a cost of US$ 6 billion (₹15,150 crore), with gas being sourced from either Qatar or Iran, or both. The proposal was made by South Asia Gas Enterprise Pvt. Ltd (SAGE), a special project vehicle set up as an equal joint venture between the Siddhomal group, an Indian firm, and UK-based Deep Water Technology Co. The project is expected to take five years to be completed and will have a capacity of 31.1 mmscmd. The expected transportation tariff from the project is US$ 1.8 per mm. However, as of now, this project is at a preliminary stage, and given the fact that it will be a sub-sea line, faces technical and economic challenges. Nevertheless, it has the potential to find a solution to sourcing gas from Iran in the event that the IPI project is shelved. [14]

More importantly, beyond ties in the hydrocarbon sector, Iran and India could look at cooperation in the power sector by way of power trade as against gas trade, though issues like political risks, as well as technical and commercial challenges which power generation companies are likely to face including the high cost of laying undersea transmission lines or of laying overhead transmission lines on difficult terrain, remain. Nevertheless, advances in technology may help to diminish such logistic hurdles for electricity transfers.

Iran already supplies electricity to both Pakistan and Afghanistan as well as Iraq and Turkey. As per a contract signed in 2002, Iran was to supply up to 39 MW to Pakistan though the actual import recorded was 25 MW in December 2005. In June 2006, Pakistan signed a memorandum of understanding (MoU) with Iran for increasing the supply to 1000 MW to meet the forecast increase in demand in the Gwadar area. [15] It would therefore be possible for the grid to be extended so as to supply electricity to West or North India.

As an indication that both countries are looking at the prospect of widening their energy ties, Indian power secretary, H.S. Brahma, said that a proposal to set up a gas-based power plant in Iran, with a capacity of 4,000 MW, was being studied with the option for bringing the electricity to India, either over land or through an undersea transmission cable. According to reports, National Thermal

Power Corporation (NTPC) could construct the power station while Power Grid Corporation of India could set up the accompanying transmission network to wheel the electricity from Iran to India. The proposed station is expected to cost over ₹ 20,000 crore (US$ 5.1 billion). Preliminary discussions on the proposal are already supposed to have taken place. Two alternative routes are being looked at for the transmission–a 1,500 km. land route from Iran via Pakistan to Gujarat, which will cost up to ₹ 200 billion, and a 1,000 km. sub-sea route, avoiding Pakistan. However, as was the case with the IPI sub-sea route, it is considered less economical as the cost would almost double. [16] If successful, this could later form a crucial component of a larger pan-Asian energy grid, thereby creating mutual dependencies and allowing all countries involved to have a stake in one another's political and economic stability, with the goal of facilitating regional integration.

India and Iran are also looking at the prospect of cooperation in the renewable energy sector. Currently, Iran's renewable energy consumption is negligible as with abundant oil and natural gas reserves, Iran has expectedly tended to depend on hydrocarbons to feed its domestic energy requirement as well as a means of earning revenue. However, with climate change issues now gaining ground internationally, like other hydrocarbon producing and exporting nations in the West Asian region, Iran too is looking at developing its renewable energy sector. In fact, during his address at the UN sponsored climate change conference in Copenhagen in December 2009, President Ahmadinejad said that all nations must be able to use clean and renewable energy sources, including nuclear power, in a bid to fight climate change. "All countries must gain access to new technologies to diversify their energy resources and be able to use clean and renewable energy such as wind, solar, sea tide, geothermal and nuclear energies," he said. [17]

Iran is believed to have a potential of 6.5 GW of wind energy as well as solar power potential. In January 2009, the Iranian Renewable Energies Organization (IREO) stated that Iran's first solar power plant had gone into operation in Shiraz. The plant has a capacity of 250KW that can be extended to 500KW by establishing larger solar panels. Iran is also reportedly looking at developing geothermal energy as well. [18]

India, on the other hand, has launched a massive programme to develop its renewable energy sector as a means to enhance its energy security by decreasing its reliance on energy imports. According to ministry sources, the country's renewable energy technology capability has matured enough to not only supplement conventional power, but also to provide viable solutions in the off-grid mode to meet the electricity needs of remote villages in the country. [19] For example, the government has launched the Solar Mission whereby some 20,000 MW of solar energy will be generated by 2020. Moreover, the total installed capacity of wind energy has been increased to 10,464 MW by August 2009. [20]

Under the circumstances, India and Iran could expand their energy cooperation in the area of renewable energy in the future, over and above their current engagement in the hydrocarbons sector.

Conclusion

As the recent global economic crisis shows signs of dissipating, the demand for energy is slated to grow as nations begin to recover from the downturn. Projections by the International Energy Agency and Energy Informational for oil demand–as well as gas and coal have indicated that demand will grow above expectations till 2030. [21]

Iran, like other non-OECD producing countries, will benefit from the expected hike in demand. And India, with its burgeoning demand for fossil fuels, particularly oil, is an attractive market. However, Iran will be pushed hard to increase its production to keep pace with the call on demand. But due to natural depletion of its oil wells as well as ever more stringent US sanctions on its energy sector, will find the going hard to inject the requisite investment and technology to sustain as well as increase production. Similarly, its gas sector–both piped gas as well as LNG has not seen development growing at the pace it would like. Iran would therefore prefer dedicated, secure markets it can depend on for the medium to long term to garner the revenues it requires, both for its energy sector as well as for the economy at large. The deal it has struck with China wherein Chinese companies committed to investing US$ 120 billion in Iran's energy sector. Iran is also one of China's biggest oil suppliers. Recently, Sinopec signed a memorandum of understanding with the National Iranian Oil Refining and Distribution Company to invest an additional US$ 6.5 billion to build oil refineries in Iran, despite the sanctions. [22]

Nevertheless, for the sake of diversification of sources and markets, Iran and India will need each other, especially given that the energy market is becoming increasingly uncertain. While Iran's position as a current and future oil and gas supplying giant is indisputable, India can be a potential transit country for the growing South and Southeast Asian markets, particularly if the SAARC energy ring is established in the future, be it for gas or for electricity. Though it is not in India's interest to have a nuclear weaponised Iran in the region, India needs to engage Iran irrespective of pressure from any other country by adopting a strategy that will allow it to keep politics and its energy requirement as separate as possible. As far as India's energy security is concerned, Iran is an important source country. Therefore, New Delhi should deal with Iran from its own national security perspective without succumbing to pressure from other powers. Chinese NOCs as well as some Russian, Turkish and European companies have recently exploited the exodus of Western energy companies in Iran and invested in Iran's energy sector.

Moreover, by stating that India is still welcome to remain a partner in the IPI project, despite New Delhi's tardiness on the negotiations on the project and its flirtation with competing Turkmen-Afghan-Pakistan-India (TAPI) project, Tehran could be sending out a clear signal to New Delhi that it is ready to put aside India's perceived "hostility" with regard to the nuclear issue and move on. India should cash in on this opportunity.

For too long, the world's major energy-producing regions have been considered the domain of the Anglo-American alliance. With the rise of the Asian developing countries, both India and Iran should adopt policies that is not only in their national interest but is also reflective of their status as rising powers, both at the regional and global level.

End Notes

1. India Hydrocarbon Vision, 2025.
2. Ibid.
3. Coal imports growing at 17 percent annually, Business Line, January 9, 2009.
4. Narsi Ghorban, "Potential Gas Export from Iran to Europe by Pipeline", World Energy Council, Berlin, October 29, 2009, www.worldenergy.org/documents/wec_conference_berlin_oct_29th_2009.ppt.

5. On December 15, 2009, the US House of Representatives approved new sanctions against Iran aimed at halting its disputed nuclear programme. The measure empowers US President Barack Obama to ban foreign firms that supply Iran with petroleum products or even tankers and insurance for fuel transports from doing business in the US. The bill, however, can only become law if approved by the Senate. The measure expands an existing US law that punishes any firm that invests US$ 20million a year in Iran's energy sector. ("US House passes Iran sanctions bill amid nuclear row", BBC News, December 16, 2009).
6. "Iran: Falling Energy Investment Threat", Payvand, December 10, 2009, www.payvand.com/news/09/dec/1102.html.
7. Ibid.
8. "Iran: Essar in the spotlight", Energy Intelligence, November 23, 2007, www.energyintel.com/DocumentDetail.asp?documentid=217327.
9. Ammar Zaidi, "Iran: India's Fading Relationship", Energy Intelligence Group, Inc. October 23, 2009, www.energyintel.com.
10. "ONGC to use Iran LNG facility for Farsi gas", LiveMint, December 8, 2009.
11. Speech by André Mernier, Secretary General, Energy Charter Secretariat, at the fifth Asia Gas Partnership Summit: the Asian Gas Market and Energy Security, New Delhi, 14-15 April, 2008.
12. John Mitchell, Paul Stevens and Elisa Cassinadri, "Resource Depletion, Dependence and Development: Iran", Chatham House Working Paper, December 2008, www.chathamhouse.org.uk/files/13182_1108rddd_iran.pdf
13. Iran Says Buying Petrol From Reliance, Business world, December 1, 2009, www.businessworld.in/bw/2009_12-01_Iran_Says_Buying_Petrol_From _Reliance.html.
14. Utpal Bhaskar, "India to revive West Asia pipeline plan", Mint, April 9, 2009, www.livemint.com/2009/04/08233701/India-to-revive-West-Asia-pipe.html.
15. Vladislav Vucetic and Venkataraman Krishnaswamy, "Development of Electricity Trade in Central Asia – South Asia Region", http://siteresources.worldbank.org/INTSOUTHASIA/556101-

1100091707765/21358230/AfghanistanElectricityTradePaperfor DelhiRECC(11006).pdf.
16. "India plans gas-based power plant in Iran", Business Line, August 25, 2009.
17. "Ahmadinejad blames capitalism for climate change", ILNA, December 18, 2009, www.ilna.ir/fullStory.aspx?ID=96582.
18. Cyrus Safdari, "Iran Power Sector and Energy Affairs", Iran Affairs, November 18, 2009, www.iranaffairs.com/iran_affairs/2009/11/iran-nuclea-energy-gas-power.html.
19. "Ministry of New and Renewable Energy Major Achievements and Initiatives in 2008", Year end Review 2008, India Microfinance, January 3, 2009, http://indiamicrofinance.com/blog/renewable-energy/ministry-of-new-and-renewable-energy-major-achievements-and-initiatives-in-2008.html.
20. "Wind Power Capacity May Exceed India's Estimate by Fivefold", Bloomberg, September 10, 2009, www.bloomberg.com/apps/news?pid=20601091&sid=aN14N7WIDbac.
21. See World Energy Outlook, Executive Summary, 2009, IEA, www.worldenergyoutlook.org/docs/weo2009/WEO2009_es_english.pdf and Annual Energy Outlook 2010, Early Release Overview, December 2009, EIA, www.eia.doe.gov/oiaf/aeo/pdf/overview.pdf.
22. "New Energy Game", Zawya News, December 29, 2009, www.zawya.com/Story.cfm/sidZAWYA20091229051117/New percent20Energy percent20Game percent20.

15

Indo-Iran Economic Relations since 1990s

Javed Ahmad Khan

Introduction

India and Iran, the two developing economies in their respective regions, have been living with deep cultural and civilizational links and also, their long geo-strategic and economic ties have been of much significance till very recently with their heavily economic dependence from technology and raw material transfers to the supply of oil and gas as well as consumer products in each other's markets. In recent years, both countries have also embarked on the structural and economic reforms in order to get the best utilization of their resources and potentials in the global market. But, in this age of economic liberalization how far these two emerging economies are prepared to benefit from each others? Are they still on their traditional path of mutual trust and economic cooperation? Or, has the changing international dynamics forced them to stand apart?

In this background of confusion and dilemma of 'strategic interest' this paper focuses on the emerging opportunities for India and Iran to reinforce their economic ties with pragmatic approach. The paper also seeks to examine the economic trends of their past two decades, especially their complementarities and preferences in the area of trade and commerce. This leads to the point that, despite their several domestic and regional inhibitions in recent past, especially with regard to their national interest, the prospect of Indo-Iran business partnership in the twenty first century can be much bright particularly in view of their 'old shared values' and the common interests.

Moreover, India's heavy dependence on the energy-rich Gulf States for its energy needs also provide an emerging markets for Indian products and investments avenues to India's private sector enterprises in that region. India also needs the Gulf's finance for its expanding economy. But as the UN sanctions on Iran is looming, the questions are also raised as how far Indo-Iran economic relations would be beneficial to each others in the coming years? This would much depend how these two countries are prepared to sense their geo-strategic importance and how the economic rationality would prevail over the national interests in this age of globalization and liberalization.

Early Phase: The Governmental Efforts

After India's independence in 1947 the high-level bilateral exchanges could enter only in the 1960s when Jawaharlal Nehru, the first Indian Prime Minister, visited Iran in 1963. A decade latter, the next Prime Minister of India, Indira Gandhi, paid an official visit in April 1974. However, it was P.V. Narasimha Rao's landmark visit in September 1993, the first Indian PM to visit Iran since the Islamic Revolution in 1979 that was seen as heralding a new bilateral cooperation in the era of economic liberalization. In return, the then Iranian president Rafsanjani also paid a State visit to India from 17-19 April, 1995. This process was culminated in the visit of former Indian Prime Minister, Atal Bihari Vajpayee, to Iran in April 2001 that resulted in signing the 'Tehran Declaration'.

In fact, Vajpayee's visit to Iran in April 2001 was seen an opportunity to boost the bilateral relations in economic field when India announced a credit line of USD 200 million for Iran's infrastructure projects. This was a new initiative towards the trade agreement as well as MoUs (Memorandum of Understandings) on technical cooperation, cooperation in Power, Energy, IT and Customs were signed. The Federation of Indian Chambers of Commerce and Industry, (FICCI) and its counterpart the Iran Chamber of Commerce (CII), Industries and Mines also much deliberated to work towards producing a well-thought out business plan for creating the edifice for sustainable and balanced trade, not just in commodities but a diversified portfolio with depth and breadth.

The new transport corridor - India-Iran Caspian Sea – Russia-was visioned as an important step in improving trade in this region. FICCI organized an interactive business meeting in honour of Mr. Ishaghjehangiri, Minister of Mines and Industry of the Islamic Republic of Iran on November 3, 2003 in New Delhi to build synergies in boosting trade and investment cooperation for the development of SMEs, and attracting foreign investments. It further organized jointly with CII an interactive business meeting in honour of Mr Seyed Mohammad Khatama, the then President of the Islamic Republic of Iran, on January 27, 2003 and then again an interactive business meeting in honour of Mr Mohsen Aminzadeh, Deputy Minister of Foreign Affairs for Asia-Oceania of the Islamic Republic of Iran on July 22, 2003 at New Delhi. [1]

India-Iran economic and commercial links have generally been dominated by purchase of oil by India from Iran. [2] However, in recent years, the setting up of free trade zones in Iran and with the India-Iran-CIS trade corridor taking shape rapidly, the climate for investing in Iran has become very conducive. Drugs, petrochemicals, textiles, garments, information technology and chemicals are some areas where joint ventures are considered to be fruitful for both the partners. [3] In November 2003, Iran has invited Indian Mining Machinery Manufacturers to set up joint ventures in Iran. India is working on a preferential trade agreement (PTA) with Teheran which is to take the shape of a free trade agreement (FTA) subsequently, strengthening bilateral trade and defence cooperation became high on the Iranian president's official agenda. India and Iran, jointly with Russia, have also decided to work on doubling their shipments along the North-South corridor by 2005. Thus, these developments provided a whole new world of opportunity emerging with the new trade corridor being set up between India, Iran and CIS.

Economic Ties

In the beginning of 2000, India-Iran Joint Commission had set up a Joint Business Council. This is how a positive intra-regional business climate emerged with the exchange of a number of high-level business delegations started from the beginning of twenty first century. Among these list of some of the important business houses from both side include; Automotive Components Manufacturers Association (ACMA), Indian Oil Company (IOC), tea industry, Federation of Engineering Industries of India (FEII), Ministries of Shipping, Commerce and External Affairs, Gas Authority of India Ltd. (GAIL), APTECH, Maruti Udyog Ltd., Sail Authority of India Ltd. (SAIL), ONGC, Oil India Ltd. (OIL) and Tatas from the Indian side. From the Iranian side delegations from the Ministry of Cooperatives, Ministry of Foreign Affairs, National Iranian Oil Company (NIOC), Ministry of Post and Telecommunications, Industrial Development and Renovation Organisation (IDRO), Pars

Khodro, Ministry of Industry and Mines, Ministry of Roads and Transport, Iran India Business Council. The signing of the Tehran Declaration led to several long-standing and successful projects and further cemented the relationship between the two countries, opened a phase of mutually beneficial cooperation measures, joint research projects, long-term training and exchange of information and provided a new impetus to the relations.

As of now, the non-oil trade balance is significantly in favour of India as both countries have tried to create a positive business environment in recent years. Iran's abolishing of a ban on import of tea from India has created a new opportunity for the Indian tea exporters to boost their business. India, too, has relaxed its norms on import of merchandise from Iran. This would encourage the Iranian businessmen to intensify their efforts towards narrowing the trade imbalance between the two countries.

The bilateral trade during 2000-2007 between the two shows the increasing trend of commercial relationship between the two countries. Expedition in signing agreements on the preferential trade tariff, double taxation avoidance, protection and promotion of investment and presence of Iranian banks in India are amongst the many measures necessary for further expansion of the economic cooperation between Iran and India.

Both governments see this in the context of economic complementarily because on the one hand Iran, with its huge oil and gas reserves is looking to secure a big share in Asian and East Asian markets, and on the other, India is an energy hungry economy. But simply energy cannot the only factor in shaping Indo-Iranian relations. Both are well diversified developing countries, with their skilled manpower and aspiring to strengthen their industrial and managerial know-how and the scientific and technological advancement.

The recent economic developments in Iran have provided fresh opportunities for cooperation between New Delhi and Tehran. During the last three years, Iran's foreign debts have reduced considerably and, at the same time, the country's revenue and foreign exchange reserves have witnessed a significant upswing. Enactment of the Foreign Investment Promotion Protection Act, 2002, the 4 to 10 years tax exemption, particularly in the Special Free Trade Zones, abolition of non-tariff barriers in foreign trade, reduction of taxes from 65 percent to 25 percent, expedition in privatization, establishment of private banks, unification of the foreign currency rate and drop in inflation rate are amongst the positive economic developments taking place in Iran in the course of the country's economic reforms so far.

India's investment interests are in Mining, Minerals, Metals-Iron/ Steel/Aluminium, Automotive, Railways, Construction, Oil, Gas, Petrochemicals, Telecommunications, Textiles, Computer/ Information Technology, Power Transmission/Generation/ Distribution, etc.

Major Trading Agreements

1. **Iran Pakistan India (IPI) Gas Pipeline:** India is yet to arrive an agreement on price of gas and separate transit fee payable to Pakistan.
2. **LNG:** LNG Agreement has been signed by India and Iran in June 2005 for supplying 5 million tons LNG per annum by Iran to India. Iran has since been insisting for increase of gas price.
3. **Steel and Mining Sector:** Essar Group–which has set up their offices in Iran, is setting up a steel plant in Bandar Abbas for developing 4 million tons steel plant. TATA Steel also proposes to set up a steel plant at Bandar Abbas with 100 percent ownership. The steel plant will have capacity production of 3 million tons steel per annum.
4. **Gems and Jewellery:** A MoU between Gem and Jewellery Export Promotion Council (GJEPC) of India and Asian Gem and Jewellery Trade Promotion Co. (AGJTPC) of Iran was signed on 28.4.2007 at Tehran.
5. **ONGC, Hinduja to negotiate with Iran:** Officials from the India's ONGC Videsh and Hinduja companies have met with Iranian Oil Ministry Officials to discuss their participation in development of Azadegan and SP Phase 12 gas fields.
6. **MOU for Petrochemical:** India's Nagarjuna Fertilizers and Chemicals Limited Company signed a Memorandum of Understanding with National Iranian Petrochemical Company (NIPC) for the construction of a Joint Urea and Ammonia Complex in the Pars Special Economic Energy Zone (second phase of (Assaluyeh). The complex nominal production capacity will be 2,200 tons of urea and 3,860 tons of ammonia per day. The estimated budget for the project is 400 million euro.
7. **The principal five export destinations:** UAE, China, Iraq,

India, Japan were the main importers of Iranian goods during the first quarter of the Iranian current year i.e. March 21-June 21, 2008.

8. **The principal five import sources:** United Arab Emirates, Germany, China, Switzerland and South Korea were the main exporters of goods to Iran during the first quarter of the Iranian current year i.e. March 21-June 21, 2008.

Principal five export commodities

- Methanol.
- Liquid gases (Propane, Butane).
- Fresh or dried Pistachio.
- Other Aromatic Hydrocarbon mixtures.
- Ammonia without water.

Principal five import items

- Gasoline.
- Non-alloyed Iron and Steel ingot.
- Non-alloyed Iron and Steel shares.
- Light oils and products other than gasoline.
- Products of Flat iron or steel.

Top five items of export from India to Iran

- Primary and semi finished iron and steel.
- Machinery and Instruments.
- Manufactures of Metals.
- Drugs, Pharmaceuticals and Fine Chemicals.
- Rubber Manufactured Products except footwear.

Top five items of import from the Iran to India

- Organic Chemicals.
- Metalifers Ores and Metal Scrap.
- Non-Ferrous Metals.
- Sulphur and Unrosted Iron Parts.
- Transport Equipments.

Factors Impacting Trade and Economic Relations

1. Indian exporters are facing some problems in operation of LCs due to uncertainties about economic sanctions against Iran,

especially those which are required to be confirmed by third country's banks.

2. Transportation of goods from India to Iran directly takes time (approx. one/two months).
3. Iran's new laws on import of only Standardized and Quality products requiring inspection certificate from the recognized Domestic and Foreign Inspection Agencies is causing delay in release of consignments.
4. Four rounds of negotiations on Bilateral Investment Promotion and Protection Agreement (BIPA) were held to finalize the agreement for promoting investment between two countries. A Double Taxation Avoidance Agreement (DTAA) between India and Iran was held at Tehran on 11th to 16th of March 2007.

Table 15.1: Iran's Foreign Trade: Exports and Import (million dollars)

Year	Oil and Gas	Non-Oil	Total Exports	Imports F.O.B
2001-02	19,339	4,565	23,904	18,129
2002-03	22,966	5,271	28,237	22,036
2003-04	27,355	6,636	33,991	29,561
2004-05	36,315	7,537	43,852	38,199
2005-06	53,820	10,546	64,366	43,085
2006-07	62,011	14,044	76,055	50,020
2007-08	81,764	15,637	97,401	56,582

Contd...

Year	Trade Balance	Total Trade	Growth Rate
2001-02	5,775	42,033	-3.48
2002-03	6,201	50,273	19.6
2003-04	4,430	63,552	26.41
2004-05	5,653	82,051	29.11
2005-06	21,281	107,451	12.79
2006-07	26,035	126,075	16.10
2007-08	40,819	153,983	13.12

Source: Iran Statistical Year Book, 2009.

One significant aspects of Indo-Iran trade is that, at present,

India is one of the major supplier of diesel to Iran. In fact, Iran need to import between US$ 10 billion to US$ 12 billion worth of gasoline and diesel in the year (1387; March 2008-2009). A number of fuel stations in Iran are low because the government had not invested in construction of fuel stations for the past 30 years. Mohamadreza Nematzadeh, Managing Director of the National Iranian Oil Refining and Distribution Company (NIORDC), added that the number of fuel stations will be doubled by 1388 (March 2009-2010).

Iran also wants to make use of the Indian textile industry's expertise in the machinery used in the textile business, Pharmaceutical, textile, food processing, information technology and infrastructure industries which especially offer a huge potential for Indian companies to form joint ventures in Iran. The total bilateral trade in 2000-2001 was of the order of USD 2.38 billion out of which Indian exports amounted to USD 345 million (including USD 118 million export of gasoline. India's imports amounted to USD 2.04 billion out of which non-oil imports constituted only USD 213 million. Oil imports by India account for 3/4th of the total trade. In 2001-02, the volume of total bilateral trade between the two countries stood at US$ 536.86 million compared with US$ 804.67 million in 1997-98. While India's exports to Iran grew from US$ 171.6 million in 1997-98 to US$ 253.03 million in 2001-02, imports from Iran fell from US$ 633.01 million in 1997-98 to US$ 283.82 million in 2001-02. Table 15.2 shows the total trade in US$ and its growth with India by top 10 commodities during the year 2000 to 2008.

Table 15.2: Trade Balance and Growth Rate
(Figures in US$ Million)

Year	Exports from India	Imports by India	Trade Balance	Total Trade	Growth Rate
2001-2002	253.03	1659.82	-1406.79	1912.85	-14.48
2002-2003	655.4	1645.12	- 989.72	2300.52	20.27
2003-2004	935.86	1937.98	- 1002.12	2873.84	24.92
2004-2005	1266.38	2896.87	- 1630.49	4163.25	44.87
2005-2006	1188.71	4822.65	- 3633.94	6011.36	44.39
2006-2007	1490.75	7842.36	- 6351.61	9333.31	55.26
2007-2008	1937.83	11049.24	-9021.06	12896.72	38.18

Moreover, Indo-Iran trade statistics must be higher than the ones indicated in the table because, many Indian goods reach Iran through the re-export route from Dubai. Indian exports are around 1.77 percent in the total Iranian imports (USD 14.35 billion) ranking 21st among the 105 countries exporting to Iran. India is presently exporting more than 67 products to Iran. Similarly, as the above table shows, among Indian exports and import from Iran, the role of petroleum products is of prime importance, where the total bilateral trade of petroleum products has registered 38 percent growth from 2007 to 2008.

The volume of trade between India and Iran has not fulfilled the potential that the two economies have, due to a number of problems like restrictive import regime followed by Iran, non-tariff barriers, absence of short to long term financing arrangements, inordinate delays of opening of LCs, etc. The business organization in India has been much active not only in promoting trade relations and also in identifying the business dynamics in a liberalized environment, specially keeping in view that Iran is well situated for multilateral trade ties in the surrounding regional markets of Central Asian Republics and hence the trade alliance between India and Iran will serve as a gateway to those countries. This would be realized more effectively because the process of economic reforms in Iran which aims at privatization and deregulation needs to be speeded up and the rules governing the inflow of foreign investment are to be reviewed with the intention of providing more incentives to foreign investors.

Thrust sectors of business synergy between India and Iran as identified by FICCI are Information technology, Biotechnology, Energy, Gas, Power generation, Engineering, Food processing and Textile machinery. India has substantial share of Iranian imports in the following categories: Iron ores and concentrates, oil cakes, tea, yarn, organic and in-organic chemicals like sulphonamides, heterocyclic compounds, unsaturated acyclic monocarboxylic acids; drugs and pharmaceuticals like antibiotics; insecticides.

In this age of new WTO regulations, India could consider to supply to Iran a number of agricultural products including wheat, rice and sugar. Since Iran is also agriculture-based economy like India, there is ample scope to find each their market. For example, Iran needs to import 5 million tonnes of wheat and 1.7 million tonnes of rice for its growing population as the annual wheat consumption in Iran stood at 11 million tonnes and it was forecasted in early 2009 that only 6 million would be produced domestically. On the other hand, India has technology in various fields and a developed industry and agriculture. We can cooperate with Iran in developing its industry and agriculture. For example, India could train Iranians in its agricultural institutions and Iranians could also make use of the vast Indian skilled and semi-skilled labour for expanding their industrial sector. [4]

Role of Foreign Capital

The Iranian economy is in need of an infusion of capital and technology especially from Asia and India. While the bulk of financial resources will be generated domestically - by both the government and the private sector - the role of foreign capital will be of crucial importance. In an liberalized financial market of the region, every day, close to one thousand billion dollars are moved across borders, which gives the order of magnitude of resources in international financial markets. Iran has not benefited from this source of finance.

Thus the private sector initiatives in Indo-Iran ties started in mid 1990s where the India-Iran Joint Business Council Agreement was concluded between FICCI and Iran Chamber of Commerce, Industries and Mines (ICCIM). More than 200 Government-owned industries with million of dollars of assets are expected to be privatized in Iran and this provides an excellent opportunity to Indian investors.

India is now in a position to liberalize investment regime, provide an excellent opportunities for trade and investment and also offer its expertise and capabilities in these areas on a competitive basis. Then what is the scope to attract Iran? Obviously, the logic is that India is no longer a producer of traditional items like textiles and handicrafts alone, but its products and services especially in area of engineering and medical sectors, space, science, information technologies have been accepted by sophisticated markets the world over. In fact, in early 1990s, Indo-Iranian relations had started to firm up and provide assistance in area of defence particularly in view of Iran's ambitious plan to develop its Space related facilities like earth-receiving stations, remote sensing satellites etc., India has offered its technology and capability to Iran in this field.

Has the trade and commerce between the two countries expanded to the extent that was expected? For many Indian private sectors enterprises, another problem is how to start joint ventures as foreign companies in Iran? Joint venture in Iran is a contractual form, and not a corporate body - formed under the laws and regulations of Iran. The major distinction between other forms of cooperation and joint venture lies in the actual independence of the joint venture from the business activities of the parties. In other words, a joint venture is seen in factual terms as an independent entry, although it does not have separate legal personality. In short, a contractual joint venture formed under the Iranian laws and regulations is treated as an independent contractual creation. Accordingly a foreign corporation can invest in a subsidiary company register under Iranian law. This enables the parent company to use all facilities extended to Iranian companies, through its Iranian subsidiary, such as holding a Trading Certificate from the Chamber of Commerce. In principle, a Trading Certificate is granted only to the nationals of a country who afford reciprocal treatments to Iranian corporations. [5]

Energy Relations

With global energy demands at an all-time high and supplies becoming increasingly inaccessible, Iran's oil and gas have already started to lure former US allies such as Pakistan and India away from American influence. Over the next decade, Iran's energy supplies look set to radically reformulate the security and diplomatic relationships of Asia and the West Asia. There are also speculations that, because of US trade embargoes on Iran, it is only the US's rivals, such as China, who are able to fully exploit Iran's natural resources, thus powering a new alliance of countries which will act as a counterweight to US global power. [6]

India-Iran economic and commercial links are presently dominated by purchase of oil by India from Iran. India import large quantities of petroleum crude from Iran both by the public and private sector. Is there any scope for growth in this vital area? The prospects in the de-regulated regimes are much bright. The gas pipeline between Iran and India was seen in the context of the confidence with a transnational and political dimension and a positive impact on economic development. Oil imports by India accounted for 3/4th of the total trade, 9.3 MT crude oil worth USD 1.77 billion and USD 0.5 billion of kerosene in 2000-2001. However, this amount accelerated in 2008.

Iran has got considerable reserves of gas and petroleum, which could be a nodal point for India to go for joint venture and production arrangements. It is also in the process of diversifying its exports by focusing on expansion of non-oil exports, export of gas including LNG and development of indigenous quality manufacturing, capability with a view to gradually reducing imports and increasing exports.

There is a reason to understand why Iran is expanding its oil sector. Throughout the 1990s, Iran's oil production averaged only 3.5 mb/d, a level considerably below the pre-revolution production of approximately 6 mb/d. Loss of experienced petroleum executives, political interference and ejecting foreign companies all contributed to Iran's collapse in oil production. In the 1990s Iran selectively re-opened the petroleum sector again to foreign investors under the so called buyback schemes. By this, Iran initially guaranteed foreign investors a certain return on their investments. However, the intensification of confrontation between the reformers and the conservatives is unlikely to have a positive impact on the investment climate in the petroleum sector. [7] Though the economic reform plan had aimed to lure foreign investment into the energy sectors, the parliamentarians in the country on the other hand diluted the energy reform and it could not be made possible to allow the foreign investor's exploration of the oil and gas sectors. [8]

LNG Issues

Signing of a document in January 2005 on Iran selling 7.5 million tons of LNG a year to India for next 25 years and India's participation in developing Iranian oil fields and extracting some 100,000 barrels of oil per day from them was one of the most significant outcomes of the strategic agreements reached upon by the two countries so far. The perception that the LNG and oil deals between Iran and India can provide a solid base for India's energy security and the country's sustained economic and industrial growth is still not well grounded. There is no doubt that the Iranian side has been repeatedly emphasizing that laying the Iran-Pakistan-India Gas Pipeline would be the best and most desirable step towards enhancing the cooperation between Iran and India in the field of energy. However this also could not continue as India's geo-strategic factors becomes the major stumbling block especially when Pakistan became an intermediary in this project. Moreover, one can hardly disagree that the lower cost of the piped gas, creation of fresh job opportunities and speeding of the economic progress as well as foreign investments in the countries of the region are amongst the main motivations for implementing such a big project.

As an alternative to this, the possibility of importing natural gas from Iran strengthened when both countries warmed up again in January 2002, with the Gas Authority of India Limited (Gail) and the National Iranian Oil Company (NIOC) deciding to commission a fresh feasibility study for laying an onshore gas pipeline between the two countries passing through Pakistan. The 2775 km. on land pipeline, costing US$ 4.1 billion, would connect Asslauyah fields in Iran to the HBJ pipeline of Gail near Delhi and have a throughput of 1.5 billion to 3 billion cubic feet per day. NIOC agreed to induct Gail as the fourth partner in the US$ 2 billion liquefied natural gas (LNG) terminal project in Iran where the Reliance Industries Ltd and BP, world's third largest oil company, each have 25 percent stake in the project, while NIOC has 40 percent. [9]

However, as for the Iranian stand is concerned, while addressing the Business Session jointly organized by FICCI and CII in January 2003, Seyed Mohammad Khatami President of the Islamic Republic of Iran welcomed all kind of investments by the Indian petroleum companies in Iranian gas and oil industry and stressed that IIP gas project must play a very significant role in providing India with inexpensive and perennial flow of energy". [10] Consequently, on May 13, 2003 Iran and India signed two separate agreements for the oil sale and for the gas deal, and reached a major long-term gas agreement in October 2003 under which Iran agreed to supply India with 5 million tonnes of liquefied gas (LNG) annually for 25 years and with 100,000 barrels of oil per day for a trial period of one year.

The agreement reflected the two sides' continued cooperation and, in particular, India's determination to expand its relations with its strategic friend Iran despite its also cozying up to the United States. Other major areas of cooperation covered under the agreements included the Iranian government's offering unspecified "discovered and semi-discovered" gas fields to Indian companies for investment. Moreover, it agreed in principle to award a discovered Iranian oil field to ONGC Videsh Limited (OVL), the overseas arm of India's Oil and Natural Gas Corporation (ONGC). The May 13 agreements also provided for Gail India Limited and the National Petrochemical Company of Iran to explore jointly the feasibility of setting up petrochemical projects in Iran and of exporting their products to India and other countries. [11]

In a move to start the process of sourcing LNG from Iran, the National Iran Oil Company invited Gail India Limited and Indian Oil Corporation (IOC) for jointly negotiating import of 2.5 million tonnes per annum (mtpa) of LNG from Iran. For the first phase, Gail has been nominated as the nodal agency by the petroleum ministry. In case a second LNG terminal comes up, IOC will be the lead operator with other oil companies as its partners. Companies interested in Iranian gas include BG, BP, Reliance Industries of India, TotalFinaElf and Petronas of Malaysia. [12]

Iran, which holds some 15 percent of the world's natural gas reserves, is boosting exports of gas to its neighbours in the hope of picking up sales to Asia and Europe in the future. Iran's natural gas reserves of 26.6 trillion cubic meters are the second largest in the world after Russia's. The country's reserves are located in onshore and offshore structures, with South Pars attracting most of foreign investment into the sector. Geologically related to Qatar's 380 North Field, South Pars has been divided into 25 development phases and is estimated to hold 8-10 percent of world reserves. The Iranian government plans to use South Pars to jumpstart a market in natural gas exports to Europe and Asia that can rival Qatar.

With the intention of National Iranian Oil Company to develop the field in phases to secure the increasing internal demand for natural gas, the country also plans to use it for re-injection in its oil fields and export. In order to get the advantage from this initiatives, the government of India formed a consortium, comprising Gail (India) Limited, Indian Oil Corporation and ONGC Videsh Limited (OVL), to look into Iran's offer of a stake in the South Pars gas field to finalise a game plan that will put in place specific strategies for cooperation with Iran in the oil and gas sector. The 3,700 square km. South Pars gas field, which is an extension of the Qatar north dome gas field, is located 105 km southwest of the Assaluyeh port in the Persian Gulf. It has an estimated 14 trillion standard cubic metres (tscm) of in-pace gas reserves and 18 billion barrels of condensate in multiple strata. Indian oil companies plan to invest US$ 3 billion to develop gas fields in Iran's Farsi block which holds estimated recoverable gas reserves of 12.8 trillion cubic feet Iran is drawing interest. The state-run Oil and Natural Gas Corp and Indian Oil Corp (IOC) each hold a 40 percent participating interest in the Farsi block, while smaller outfit Oil India has the rest. [13]

Gail India, a leading Indian LNG importer has already clinched the agreement but with the state-run NIOC. Iran however refused to lower the price of Liquefied Natural Gas it intends to sell to India, claiming that it was already the most competitive at 2.22 dollars per one million British thermal units (MBTU). It may be noted that the price offered by Iran was lower than Qatar's 2.53 dollars per MBTU sale price to petronet LNG. [14] On the other hand, India's private sector energy giant, Reliance had signed a memorandum of association with British Petroleum and the National Iranian Oil Company (NIOC) to undertake a study to examine the possibility of sourcing gas from Iran's offshore South Pars fields and then piping it to an LNG plant in Assaluyeh in the Persian Gulf. [15]

Impact of UN Sanctions on Indo-Iran Economic Relations

However, amid the optimism of Indo-Iranian economic relations in the 21st century, one major hurdle is the shadow of UN economic sanctions on Iran. As far as Iran is concerned, it is not a new experiment for this Islamic republic, as United States imposed the numerous economic sanctions after the hostage crisis of 1979-1981. This could not stop Iran from attracting the global energy market because Iran quickly found new costumers and substituted its customer base. During the 1990s, US concerns about Iran's nuclear program lead to an additional round of sanctions which further weakened its economic strength.

After the US President Barack Obama signed a bill in May 2010, imposing harsh sanctions on Iran that includes cutting off Iran's access to refined petroleum imports, and bans US banks from doing business with foreign banks that provide services to the Revolutionary Guards, India and Iran in July 2010, stepped up increasing bilateral cooperation in the economic sector, which can be considered as a challenge to the unilateral sanctions imposed by Washington to Teheran. India claims that Iran is an important partner as well as an important source for hydrocarbon resources and that it is keen to further strengthen existing ties. Iran is also one of India's largest suppliers of crude oil, and India in turn is also a major supplier of refined petroleum products for Iran. However, the recent studies have also shown that Sanctions are expected to cut only 25 to 50 percent of Iran's petroleum imports. This could be compensated by reducing domestic consumption, as well as increasing domestic refining capacity. [16]

However, the impact of UN sanction can be expected particularly on India's energy sector which is dominant part of Indo-Iranian economic relations. For example, a joint-venture between India's state-owned Oil and Natural Gas Corporation and the Hinduja Group has obtained a 40 percent stake in Phase 12 of Iran's South Pars gas field. The agreement for the project, which is, in total, valued at US$ 7.5 billion, was announced in December 2009. Iran had previously assigned 60 percent of the project to the Indian pair, however reduced the share due to concerns over slow progress and US pressure on India. [17] Moreover, this impact is seen on the prospects of Indian oil companies in Iran because Iran Sanctions Act (ISA) provides for sanctions against persons, including foreign firms, who invest more than US$ 20 million in Iran's energy sector in any 12-month period. A consortium of state-owned oil companies—OVL, IOC, OIL—are developing the Farsi block in Iran. It had submitted a US$ 5 billion master development plan in September 2009 to produce gas from the field. Though India has voted against Iran at the IAEA, it has continued to have energy links with Iran and has conveyed its opposition on imposing sanctions against Iran. [18]

The Obama administration has threatened to slap sanctions against 41 oil firms that include ONGC and Indian Oil Corporation for having energy ties with Iran. [19] With regard to Indian companies' stakes in Iran's energy sector, officials from the India have been of the view that the sanctions would not have an impact on their investments as they have not violated the US law. The Indian consortium comprising OVL-IOC-OIL, which have US Sanctions on Iran have been awarded exploration rights in the Farsi block and the South Pars Phase-12 development, have not invested more than US$ 20 million in any one year, and the barrier will be broken only when Iran awards them the contract to develop the field or if the Indians made investment in the South Pars fields. However, in June 2009, India's Reliance Industries Ltc halted gasoline exports to Iran to avoid possible restriction on sales in the United States, which has increased pressure on companies selling gasoline to Iran. [20] For example, Reliance's decision to terminate exports to Iran came after several US lawmakers urged the Export-Import Bank to suspend the extension of US$ 900 million worth of financial guarantees to RIL to help it to expand its Jamnagar refinery on the grounds that it was assisting Iran's economy with the gas sales.

In order to limit the impact of recent UN sanctions against Iran on Indian economy, India's Ministry of External Affairs proposed "creative mechanisms" in order to protect Indian firms from affects of the UN sanctions. In this context a consortium with companies from Russia, China, and or Kuwait was proposed by the Ministry so that it become difficult to single out single countries or firms, as this new corporate entities would have no financial ties to the US or EU and also enable India to secure its energy interest with Iran. This clearly showed India's keen interest despite the growing international isolation of Iran over its nuclear weapons programme. [21]

In a major push, the Indian government laid out the red carpet for Iranian minister of Economic Affairs and Finance, Seyed Shamseddin Hosseini, who came India with a 30-member delegation to re-energizing business relations and to attend the 16th session of the joint commission on July 8-9. 2010. Huseini invited Indian firms to invest in infrastructure, oil, gas, petrochemicals, mining, automobiles, transport, machinery, chemicals, pharmaceuticals, textiles and agriculture in Iran. He also promised to facilitate access for Indian firms to trade with landlocked Central Asia—Armenia, Azerbaijan and Georgia—besides Russia.

India is not only interested in seeking investment pacts with Iran but also targets to double its trade volume. Iran-India bilateral trade has increased in recent years, totalling US$ 14 billion in 2010—a US$ 1.4 billion increase over the previous year's numbers. [22] The country has sought to buy oil and gas from Iran to help feed its energy needs, generated by the country's rapid development. However, India remained noncommittal on finalization of IPI Gas Pipeline due to a combination of factors, including price disputes with Pakistan, anti-Iranian pressure from the United States, security concerns, and the possibility of less expensive domestic alternatives particularly by the China. [23]

Conclusion

Both Iran and India are moving ahead to the de-regulation of their economies and both are visualizing economic relations beyond the traditional merchandise exports and imports to the emerging opportunities for private investment in each other's potential markets. There is a realization in India that despite the civilizational affinities, the commercial relationship between the two countries, compared to Saudi Arabia and UAE, are still below the required potential and the government and the private sector has to work together in this regard. Though Indo-Iran relations have grown significantly across various sectors, but India's greatest interest lies in secure and economically attractive import of hydrocarbons from Iran. However, can India's current strategy towards Iran help in strengthening India's energy relations with Iran? On the other hand, the economic dilemma of Iran is that even with its second largest natural gas reserves, the Islamic Republic's potential for playing a vital role in supplying gas to India and even to other Asian countries is still in doldrums. Further, it is rightly pointed out that if Iran aspires to have a place on the international economic map as something more than a seller of oil, it has to establish and develop its financial markets (stocks, bonds, foreign exchanges and commodities) and link them to the international capital markets. As a matter of fact, in comparison to the Islamic Republic of Iran, India is in a position to boost of its efficient and transparent capital markets, its high image among the foreign investors and of course, a rather stable and strong economy. Economists in Iran realizes that the role of the financial markets in the country is rather negligible and it does not play a significant part in mobilizing savings, allocating capital, or attracting foreign investments.

End Notes

1. http://www.ficci.com/ficci/media-room/speeches-presentations/2001/apr/apr10-iran- chirayu.htm.
2. http://www.meadev.nic.in/foreign/iran.htm.
3. http://ciionline.org/news/newsMain.asp?news_id=11520033334 1PM.
4. http://www.arabianbusiness.com/521747-iran-needs-to-import-5-mln-tonnes-wheat-minister?ln=en.
5. According to Principle 44 of the 1979 Iranian Constitution the major provision with regard to international trade is contained in principles 44 and 81 of the 1979 Constitution, which prohibits the setting up of foreign concerns and corporations engaged in commercial, industrial, agricultural, mining or services in Iran. On the other hand, Iran had, in the past, compelled foreign concerns to register in Iran, entitling under the new Constitution created difficulties for the Iranian Governmental agencies that had to sign new contracts with foreign companies after the revolution. See, Christian, E. Campbell, *Legal Aspects of Doing Business in the Middle East*, Lulu.com, 2007,pp. 92-96.

6. Roger Howard, *Iran Oil: The New Middle East Challenge to America*, London: I. B. Tauris, 2007, p. 27.
7. Hugo McPherson, W Duncan Wood, Derek M Robinson, *Emerging Threats to Energy Security And Stability*, Springer, 2005, p. 113.
8. *The Khaleej Times* August 24, 2004.
9. *The Business Standard*, (Mumbay) January 18, 2002.
10. http://www.ficci.com/international/international.htm.
11. http://www.atimes.com/atimes/South_Asia/EE22Df01.html.
12. http://www.dailystar.com.lb/article.asp?edition_id=10&categ_id =3&article_id=2852 April 27, 2004.
13. So far the consortium has invested $90 million and if we are allowed to develop the [gas] field, we would be investing around $3 billion," said a senior IOC official. http://archive.gulfnews.com/articles/08/06/14/10221037.html June 14, 2008.
14. The Indian government is asking for a price lower than 2 dollars per MBTU to keep the delivered cost of regasified-LNG to power and fertilizer plants at around 3.50 dollars per MBTU. The delivered price of Qatar gas is 4.80 dollars per MBUT while at 2.22 dollars per MBUT (the Iranian offer), the delivered price would be just over 4 dollars. See, *menareport.com* August 8, 2004.
15. The Iranian South Pars field is the northern extension of Qatar's giant North Field and accounts for 10 percent of the world's and 60 percent of Iran's total gas reserves. Iran's portion of the field contains an estimated 436 trillion cubic feet of gas. See, *The Business Standard*, (Mumbay) October 22, 2003.
16. Shebonti Ray Dadwal and M. Mahtab Alam Rizvi, 'US Sanctions on Iran and their Impact on India, available', at: http://www.idsa.in/system/files/IB_USSanctionsonIran.pdf June 21, 2010, p. 9.
17. 'India May Lose a Gas Project in Iran,' Zeenews, October 4, 2009, http://www.zeenews.com/news568197.html(October 17, 2009) as cited in http://www.irantracker.org/foreign-relations/india-iran-foreign-relations.
18. *The Economic Times* (New Delhi), 15 May 2010.
19. Shebonti Ray Dadwal and M. Mahtab Alam Rizvi, 'US Sanctions on Iran and their Impact on India, available', at: http://www.idsa.in/system/files/IB_USSanctionsonIran.pdf June

21, 2010.

20. 'India's Reliance Halts Petrol Sales To Iran – Report', Reuters, June 4, 2009, as cited in http://www.irantracker.org/foreign-relations/india-iran-foreign-relations.
21. *The Indian Express*, (New Delhi), August 03, 2010.
22. *The Indian Express*, (New Delhi) July 10, 2010.
23. 'China likely to replace India in Iran-Pak gas pipeline project', One India, February 6, 2010 http://news.oneindia.in/2010/02/06/chinalikely-to-replace-india-in-iran-pak-gas-pipelineproje.html;Srivastava, as cited in http://www.irantracker.org/foreign-relations/india-iran-foreign-relations.

16

India's Engagements with Iran: A Geo-Economic Perspective

Faisal Ahmed

I. Evolution of Indo-Iran Relations

Geo-economics is a study of spatial relationships between economic activities, history and politics. The discourses on geo-economics are of larger relevance in the contemporary world order owing to the increasing complexity of international interactions. In the West Asian region, the geo-economic analysis becomes pertinent as there is huge confluence between trade and strategic relations.

Considering the case of India and Iran, it is found that both the states share an evolving trade and commercial relation despite the strategic manoeuvring caused by geopolitical interventions in both South Asia and the Middle East. It is, therefore, imperative to study this geo-economic perspective ranging from civilizational ties to contemporary trade to gain deeper insights which could pave the way for a more constructive and a sustainable bilateral engagement.

The interactions between the two old civilizations including the Indus Valley Civilization in India and the Elamite Civilization in Persia have been quite evident. The Harappan civilization was contemporary with the Proto-Elamite and Elamite civilizations in ancient Iran. Trade links existed between the two civilizations through their ports cities. In Susa (western Iran), the decorated potteries which have been excavated appears to be similar to those of the Kulli culture in the north-west of the Indian subcontinent. Persia was a source of import of silver, copper, turquoise and lapis lazuli from the olden Persia and the Persians used to import Ivory and spices like black pepper from the Harappan Civilization. [1] The grape, introduced from Persia with the almond and walnut, was cultivated in the Hindukush and western Himalayas and also one of the earliest Indian words for a coin, that is, Karsa traces back its origin into Persian. [2]

Among the interactions between the two civilizations were the friendly and diplomatic ties during the Gupta Period as well. Chandragupta Maurya, who founded the Mauryan dynasty, had friendly relations with the successor of the Macedonian conqueror in Persia. Seleucus Nicator, the Grecian ruler of Persia sent Megasthenes as the Persian envoy to the Mauryan court in Pataliputra. Persian nobles were also present in the courts of Mauryan kings, for instance, Tushaspa of Persia was present during the reign of Chandragupta Maurya. The rise of Safavid Dynasty in Iran in the 16th Century and its contemporary Mughal Empire in India helped in strengthening larger engagements and relations between them in terms of politics, diplomacy, culture, literature, trade, and religion. The language of the Mughal court was also Persian and the Mughal patronage of culture constantly attracted Persian scholars to India.

With this brief historical backdrop, the study of bilateral engagement post the Iranian Revolution acquires vital significance. The Iranian Revolution led to the collapse of the Pahlavi Dynasty and Iran officially became an Islamic Republic on April 1, 1979, through a national referendum. It was in December 1979, that the country approved a new constitution, making Ayatollah Khomeini the Supreme Leader of the country. Later, the Iran-Iraq war (1980-88) caused great loss to the Iranian economy and as a result of this war, a significant share of the Iranian government's revenue, which was obtained primarily from sale of oil, was directed to military expenditures rather than on industry, agriculture and infrastructure. [3] Later, President Rafsanjani followed a pragmatic pro-business policy of rebuilding and strengthening the Iranian economy within the ideological framework of the revolution. After 1997, President Mohammad Khatami, a reformist, established good models of governance by engaging civil society and also through his efforts in improving Iran's economic policies and diplomatic relations with the world. Since 2005 Mahmoud Ahmadinejad became President of Iran.

After the Iranian Revolution of 1979, Iran withdrew from the Baghdad Pact, originally the Middle East Treaty Organization. Iran's diplomatic initiatives seem to be based on three fundamental concerns, namely, eliminating external strategic interventions in the region, finding a trusted friend in South Asia, and, preparing itself as a powerful strategic ally for Asian countries. And if the alignment of India-Iran relations is viewed in the strategic context, it is observed that it has not been very fortunate. Moreover, historically, India and

Iran have enjoyed friendly relations. There have been significant trade ties, particularly in crude oil imports into India and diesel exports to Iran. India welcomed Iran's inclusion as an observer state in the SAARC regional organization, though India has also opposed Iran and voted against it in the IAEA in 2005 and also in 2009.

II. Determinants of Geo-economic Relations

The determinants of geo-economic relations between India and Iran in the contemporary global order can be outlined as:

1. The Hydrocarbon Factor: The endowment of natural resources in the Middle East has huge bearing on the global geo-economics through its role in redefining the dynamics of international interactions. Iran, one of OPEC's founding members, holds the world's third-largest proven oil reserves and the world's second-largest natural gas reserves. It is also OPEC's second largest oil producer after Saudi Arabia. It possesses vast amount of oil resources with proven oil reserves (as January 1, 2010) of 137.6 billion barrels and the oil production being 4.2 million barrels per day, of which 3.9 million barrels per day was crude oil (as of year 2008). [4] This huge endowment has also helped Iran in its geo-economic positioning especially with non-Gulf countries in the Asian region.

Oil and natural gas are strategic goods and their abundance has compelled many nations to rethink their foreign policy with Iran. Even the United States and EU have only a fraction of the oil reserves as compared to West Asian countries including Iran. If we see India's oil production and its consumption pattern, it is found that India would continue to meet its energy requirements from the oil-rich states of West Asia, and Iran definitely would a major source. Iran also has a sizeable amount of natural gas reserves though large concentrations of natural gas are also found in Russia and the countries of the former Soviet Union. The underlying principle of oil diplomacy has witnessed a shift from strategizing to improve supply curve to the complete management of oil demand and supply since the oil shocks of the 1970's. Owing to their resource endowments in oil, Iran has been able to magnify its impact on the global geo-economic architecture in several ways including a prominent role in OPEC. [5] Iran has already been elected to chair OPEC in 2011, which is the first time since the Islamic revolution, and that too at a time when Western governments are seeking to target Iran's energy sector over its nuclear programs. [6]

Moreover, Iran is also endowed with natural gas with a Proven Natural Gas Reserves (as of January 1, 2010) of 1,045 trillion cubic feet and the Natural Gas Production (as of 2008) being 4.1 trillion cubic feet. [7] And thus it is a source of India's natural gas requirements. Moreover, the proposed Iran-Pakistan-India (IPI) gas pipeline, deemed to deliver natural gas from Iran to Pakistan and India, has been subject to halt largely because of geo-economic reasons. In the year 2009, India withdrew from the project over pricing and security issues, however, the hope for its restoration still continues.

Also, the transportation link called the North-South corridor project is also playing a defining role in India's cooperation with Iran. [8] The corridor was proposed as part of an agreement among India, Iran and Russia in the year 2000. This would also boost the trade among the member nations.

2. Liberal Trade Policies: Iran introduced economic reforms during its successive regimes. This has led to relaxed rules and regulations on foreign investment and helped in attracting FDI. There is an increase in the foreign trade and investment and also in Iran's engagements with the international economic integration agreements. The Economic policy in the early years of the Iranian Revolution was heavily influenced by socialist thinking. [9] Moreover, a paradigm shift toward market policies took place with the Second Development Plan (1995-1999), and later more specifically with the Third Development Plan (2000-04) which included reforms related to privatization and anti-trust legislation.

Moreover, in their bid to encourage export-oriented industries and technology transfer which is associated with foreign direct investment, the Bank Markazi Iran (BMI) [10] lifted nearly all foreign exchange restrictions to encourage export industries and open the way for foreign investors. But, while having all advantages for attracting FDI like rich natural resources (in oil and gas), infrastructure, large domestic market and strategic position regarding the accessibility to market of other countries in the region, educated youth and low cost workforce, it is not receiving much higher FDI as compare to other developing countries.

3. Diversification of Trade Portfolio: Owing to the scare nature of hydrocarbons, there is a realization in Iran and other oil-exporting countries to diversify their trade portfolio. Many countries have started diversifying from commodities based trade to services based trade and also oil trade to non-oil trade. Though hydrocarbon constitutes a major chunk of India's import from Iran, yet Iran is also increasing its portfolio of non-oil exports to India.

4. Focus on FDI: Iran is already focusing on export-oriented industries and has the potential to receive FDI into various sectors of the economy, though the rate of inbound FDI is slow owing to strategic reasons. It has the potential advantages to attract FDI because of its hydrocarbon endowments, liberal trade policy regime, growth in infrastructural development, and ability to provide larger market access. On the other hand, India also has the huge potential for attracting FDI and remains one of the most preferred destinations. The cumulative amount of FDI flows into India from April 2000 to August 2010 is estimated at US$ 1,75,941 million. [11] This is again an important geo-economic factor that can help India and Iran engage bilaterally.

III. Bilateral Trade

India's trade with Iran has been showing dynamic progress in recent years. Table 16.1 shows that in the WANA region, Iran is India's fourth major export destination and third largest source of India's import as of 2009-10. This suggests Iran is emerging both as a major export market as well as a source of imports.

India's export to Iran was worth US$ 1,853.17 million in 2009-10 (see Table 16.2). Moreover, India's import from Iran was US$ 11,540.85 million in 2009-10 as compared to US$ 12,376.77 million in 2008-09. India's total trade with Iran has been US$ 12870.15 million in 2007-08 and in the three quarters of 2008-09 (i.e. April-December) it has been US$ 12093.85 million.

Cereals (HS Code 10) are India's major export to Iran while Mineral fuels, mineral oils and products of their distillation (27) are our main imports.

IV. Areas with Potential for India-Iran Cooperation

There are several areas besides oil which have a potential for cooperation between India and Iran. Some of these areas include: Petroleum Products, Food Security, Pharmaceuticals, Tourism, OEMs, SME, and investments.

1. Petroleum Products: Hydrocarbon resources endowment including oil and natural gas has helped Iran in evolving and strengthening their bilateral trade ties with India and other countries. India is already heavily dependant on imports to meet its current oil demand, and more so because domestic oil production is forecast to fall to 0.6 million barrels per day by 2030. [12] India's oil consumption was 2.748 mn b/d in 2007 as compared to whole of Middle East's consumption which was 6.203 mn b/d. [13] Even though the IPI Gas Pipeline Project have suffered a blow, India's competitiveness in petroleum products which is increasing, can help both India and Iran mutually invest in oil and gas infrastructure to secure advantages of capital flows, desired infrastructure and cost-advantage.

Table 16.1: India's Trade with WANA (US$ million)

S.N	Country	Export	Import
		2009-10	2009-10
1	Algeria	574.19	995.32
2	Bahrain	250.21	502.86
3	Egypt	1,403.88	1,692.36
4	Iran	1,853.17	11,540.85
5	Iraq	477.13	7,026.93
6	Israel	1,968.59	1,885.06
7	Jordan	245.62	823.43
8	Kuwait	782.45	8,249.49
9	Lebanon	131.33	6.78
10	Libya	221.98	622.64
11	Morocco	250.47	861.51
12	Oman	1,032.93	3,499.89
13	Qatar	536.97	4,648.52
14	KSA	3,907.00	17,097.57
15	Sudan	461.06	475
16	Syria	345.43	144.69
17	Tunisia	213.55	252.83
18	UAE	23,970.40	19,499.10
19	Yemen	727.39	1,575.55
	Total	39,353.76	81,400.40

Source: Export Import Data Bank, Ministry of Commerce and Industry, Government of India.

Table 16.2: India-Iran Bilateral Trade (US$ million)

	2005-06	2006-07	2007-08	2008-09	2009-10
Export	1,188.35	1,449.67	1,949.46	2,534.01	1,853.17
Imports	702.46	7,621.85	10,920.69	12,376.77	11,540.85
Total Trade	1,890.81	9,071.52	12,870.15	14,910.78	13,394.02

Source: Export Import Data Bank, Ministry of Commerce and Industry, Government of India.

2. Food Security: India is one of the world's major food producers. Food production and food security are the major areas in which India can assert its global competitiveness. India produced an estimated 230.78 million tons of food grains in 2007-08, while it was estimated that in 2008-09, the production would be 229.85 million tons as per the third advance estimates. [14] Moreover, India is the world's largest producer of milk, the second largest producer of food grains and fruits and vegetables, and also one of the world's leading producers of meat, poultry and marine products. India's food processing sector is also destined to grow at a huge pace with the government strategy aimed at doubling the size of this sector to ₹ 13,50,000 crore by 2014-15. [15] In this wake, India has the potential to cater to the global requirement of food and thereby an opportunity to enhance its international food trade which at present accounts for less than 1.5 percent of the world's total. On the other hand, Iran's food import is growing drastically and between 2005-06 and 2007-08, it increased by 114 percent from US$ 698.7 million to US$ 1500.1 billion. [16]

3. Pharmaceuticals: The pharmaceutical industry in India has gained strong competitiveness in pharmaceuticals and medicinal research; R&D costs; production technology; drug development; and clinical trials. The Indian pharmaceutical industry ranks 4th in terms of volume and 13th in terms of value globally thereby producing 20-24 percent of the world generic drugs in terms of value. According to Pharmexcil, the pharmaceutical exports from India were US$ 6.68 billion in 2007-08 as compared to US$ 5.73 billion in 2006-07; thus showing a growth rate of 16 percent. [17] IBEF notes that 15 of the 20 largest pharmaceutical companies in the world have their presence in India; and that, during April 2000 to October 2007, drugs and pharmaceuticals have been the tenth largest FDI attracting sectors in

India. On the other hand, the pharmaceutical and bio-medical research is Iran is still evolving and Iran can get the advantage of low-cost medicines and higher accessibility if they enhance cooperation with India in this sector. There were nearly 4,000 kinds of pharmaceutical products available in Iran; 70 percent of which was provided by imports and the remaining 30 percent was produced domestically. [18] Total healthcare spending in Iran is expected to rise from US$ 24.3bn in 2008, to US$ 50.0bn by 2013, reflecting the increasing demand on medical services. [19]

4. Tourism: Indian tourism industry has a remarkable growth trend owing to its culture, heritage, historical importance, beaches and scenic landscapes. According to the United Nations World Tourism Organization (UNWTO), the Indian tourism industry may witness a growth of 200 percent in 2010. The Ministry of Tourism, Government of India has been taking several steps including the 'Incredible India' campaign to boost tourism. On the other hand, Iran's travel and tourism demand is set to grow by 6.6 percent for the next ten-year period (2006-2015) topping the list of Middle East countries, according to World Travel and Tourism Council. [20]

5. Original Equipment Manufacturing (OEMs): The manufacturing industry in India including the OEM sector has grown by three times in 2008-09 as compared to 2005-06. India competitiveness in manufacturing and OEMs is attributed to the following factors: cost of castings and forgings, established production lines, full service supply capability, increasing domestic and international demand. Iran's manufacturing sector comprises 20 percent of the GDP but is heavily dependant on oil revenue as a major source of financing the imports of raw materials and intermediate goods. [21] This implies that both India and Iran can explore the possibilities of mutual investments in the manufacturing sector based on advantages in cost, quality and efficiency.

6. Small and Medium Enterprises (SME): India has a high degree of competitiveness in terms of cost, manpower and export market in SME, and, therefore, a mutual sharing on this front could be beneficial for both. According to an EXIM Bank (India) Research brief, the sectors that contribute to SME exports include readymade garments, engineering goods, chemicals and pharmaceuticals, electronics and computers and processed foods. In terms of export orientation, the areas in the SME sector include sports goods with a 100 percent orientation, readymade garments, leather, marine products and chemicals and pharmaceuticals. SMEs are also on the rise in Iran and constitute a large chunk of market. Mutual cooperation between India and Iran can help boost each others competitiveness in SMEs.

7. Investments: FDI in India is increased from US$ 5.55 billion in 2005 to US$ 7.23 billion at the end of November 2006, which account for 30.3 percent. [22] Mauritius and USA are the biggest investors in India, accounting for 40.8 percent and 13.8 percent respectively of the total FDI in India. India and Iran can enhance mutual investment in the fields of energy infrastructure, real estate, medicines, education, biotechnology, agriculture and services.

8. Services: India and Iran can also strengthen ties in the services sector in major services category like higher education and training; management consulting; telecommunication services; software services; engineering services; and, financial services.

V Recommendations and Conclusion

It is imperative to understand that India's trade engagements with Iran and vice versa is cannot be evolved purely on an economic basis owing to geopolitical consideration. Therefore, based on the geo-economic analysis undertaken in this paper, the following recommendations can be made:

1. People to People interactions can be used a Confidence Building Measure for business houses in the two countries, considering their strong civilization and cultural ties.
2. India and Iran should look forward to engaging more on a bilateral level instead of going for multilateral or inter-regional fora.
3. Mutual investments in oil and gas infrastructure can help to secure advantages of capital flows, desired infrastructure and cost-advantages.
4. A Free Trade Agreement (FTA) between the two countries can help in enhancing trade, but such facilitations require a strong diplomatic relation between the two countries.
5. India and Iran can explore the possibilities of forming a food-based arrangement.
6. For the purpose of investment both India and Iran can develop a Joint Fund like the India-Oman Joint Investment Fund, for enhancing the pace and volume of investment in areas with potential for cooperation.

7. Both entities need to understand that their role in global power balancing is necessary to develop a platform for the sustainable growth of trade diplomacies both in regional agreements as well as internationally.

Therefore, as there will be far greater ideological cohesion at the policymaking level in Tehran in the current regime [23], it can be concluded that larger diplomatic engagements and Confidence Building Measures can help both nations in their pursuits for excellence in geo-economic affairs.

End Notes

1. See A. A. Jorfi, (1994). "Iran and India: Age old Friendship", *India Quarterly*, Vol. 50, No. 4, pp. 65-92.
2. Basham, A. L. (2004). The Wonder That Was India, Picador India.
3. See Karim Chashm Banam (2010). Impact of Financial Liberalization on Economic Growth in Iran: An Empirical Investigation, Middle Eastern Finance and Economics, Issue 7, pp. 6-37.
4. U.S. Energy Information Administration (EIA), Country Analysis Briefs, Iran
5. However, the large number of sanctions imposed by UN has severely affected its oil trade. Major oil importers like India and China are also finding it difficult to import from Iran and in order to maintain trade partnership Iran is offering discounts on crude sales as well. Also see news-article "Iran cuts oil prices as sanctions bite" by Reihaneh Mazaheri, 10 July 2010, Asia Times Online, Available: http://www.atimes.com/atimes/Middle_East/LG10Ak04.html.
6. See article "Iran Elected to Chair OPEC Next Year; Dismisses Western Energy Sanctions as Ineffective" by Patrick Goodenough, 15 October 2010, Available: http://www.cnsnews.com/news/article/iran-elected-chair-opec-next-year-dismis.
7. U.S. Energy Information Administration (EIA), Country Analysis Briefs, Iran.
8. The North-South Transport Corridor comprises of the ship, rail, and road route for moving freight from South Asia to Europe through Central Asia, the Caucasus, and Russia. The corridor is intended to link Mumbai-via Bandar Abbas in Iran-and with St.

Petersburg in Russia and thus the Indian Ocean with the Baltic Sea and Europe. Further, in the year 2003, India, Iran, and Afghanistan signed a memo on the "Development and Construction of the Transit and Transport Infrastructure". This aimed toward improving the route from Chabahar in Iran to the Afghan cities of Zaranj and Delaram; with India making a commitment of US$ 70 million for the construction of a road linking Zaranj and Delaram.

9. See Djavad Salehi-Isfahani (2005). "Iran's Third Development Plan: A reappraisal", Available: http://www.filebox.vt.edu/users/salehi/ReplytoAmuzegar.pdf.
10. Central Bank of Iran.
11. Data based on the statistics of Department of Industrial Policy and Promotion (DIPP), Ministry of Commerce and Industry, Govt. of India.
12. See M. Thirlwell and A. Bubalo, (2006). "India looks West; the GCC Looks East", *GCC-India Research Bulletin*, Issue 2, June 2006, pp. 5-6.
13. BP Statistical Review of World Energy, June 2008.
14. See "Foodgrains Production to Go Up" by G. Parsai, The Hindu Online, 14 May 2009, http://www.thehindu.com/2009/05/14/stories/2009051454661800.htm.
15. See "Indian Food Processors set for Growth" by M. Stones, 11 May 2009; http://www.foodproductiondaily.com/Supply-Chain/Indian-food-processors-set-for-growth
16. Based on data from web link http://www.iran-foodhospitality.com/ (2009).
17. See article on Pharmaceuticals, India Brand Equity Foundation (IBEF), 19 May 2008, http://ibef.org/Archives/ViewArticles.aspx?art_id=17906&cat_id=90.
18. See K. Basmenji (2001). "Pharmaceuticals in Iran: An Overview", Available: http://www.ams.ac.ir/AIM/0472/021.htm.
19. See "Iran Pharmaceuticals and Healthcare Report", Q2-25/03/2009, Business Monitor International, 2009, Available: http://www.payvand.com/news/09/apr/1027.html.
20. Refer to "Iran's Tourism Industry Poised for Robust Growth", WTTC, 05/05/2005, Available:3 http://www.payvand.com/news/05/may/1038.html.

21. See R. Gholami, S. Moshiri, and S.T. Lee, (2004). "ICT and Productivity of Manufacturing Industries in Iran", *The Electronic Journal of Information Systems in Developing Countries*, Vol. 19, No. 4, pp. 1-19.
22. See web link http://www.dailyexcelsior.com/web1/07feb13/busi.htm#4to read "India expecting $2 bln investment from GCC".
23. See M. K. Bhadrakumar, (2009). "Revisiting the Iranian Revolution", *Mainstream*, Vol. 47, No. 28.

17

Preservation of Cultural Heritage between Iran and India

Mandana Barkeshli

Introduction

The relations and exchanges between the great civilizations would contribute not only to the growth of the peoples of the involved civilizations but also to enrichment of lives throughout the globe. The cultural relations between Iranians and the inhabitants of the Indian Sub-continent have produced exceptional results, especially in the realm of art and culture. Looking at the history of Iran and India we can recognize the strong relations of these two cultures from Pre-Aryan civilizations and later Pre-Islamic Persia and Vedic civilization era to Muslim cultures of Mughals and Safawids. According to Pandit Jawaharlal Nehru "India and Iran are the cradle of ancient culture and civilization that continue to have their impact on the world for about 5000 years".

Protection of a culture depends, to a great extent, on the preservation of the material cultural heritage–a branch of knowledge that has received ample attention during the past couple of centuries, especially in the western world. The Eastern world, chiefly those with rich historical civilizations, too has engaged serious efforts to this task. Iran and India enjoy a common civilization background; they share interdependent cultural heritages and face similar problems in preserving them. Their joint efforts could minimize the energy input and maximize the results. It is therefore essential for the two countries–and the few other nations with whom we share a great deal of our rich history–to join hands in preserving something that may well be regarded as "world cultural heritage".

In this paper the author will present the issues of the preservation of cultural heritage in both countries and the joint efforts that has been attempted by individuals, and at the level of government bodies, to fulfil this task from 1979 to the present time.

After 1979 the issues of cultural heritage in Iran entered a new phase. This new phase was because of the formation of the new university programs and establishment of the new organizations in the field. In this phase we can also notice the interest that Iran has shown towards India and its heritage. A number of people made efforts and were pioneers to fulfil these tasks. Here in this paper I try briefly to highlight some of these joint efforts, the reason behind and their impacts towards the elevation of the preservation of cultural heritage. These joint efforts will be discussed based on my involvement in certain projects, as well as my experiences - with help of other individuals to strengthen the already established ties between Iran and India in the field of education and preservation of cultural heritage. These include programs at the level of higher education, recognition of Indian academic institutions by the Iranian bodies, initiation of researches, training course, workshops, as well as a wide spectrum of quality publications in the field.

Cultural Heritage Issues in Iran and India

Cultural Heritage can be categorized to two main important realm; tangible and intangible. The relationship between these two realms is so close that it is impossible to separate them. We know the tangible comes to life because of intangible, and at the same time the tangible carries the intangible within.

The realm related to tangible cultural heritage usually is referred to the body of the heritage. There are many issues that Iran and India share when it comes to the tangible cultural heritage since they have influenced each other along the history in terms of the style, materials and technique of applications. Among them we can give examples such as beautiful Safawid and Mughul manuscripts and miniature paintings, elegant Kashmir shawls and Kerman hand embroidery textile works and other master pieces that many of them are in the safeguard of museums around the world. Curators and conservators may face the same type of deterioration factors and ultimately more or less the same solutions for their preservation techniques. This is where both countries Iran and India with so many similarities in their tangible cultural heritage have learned from each other's valuable experiences.

There are of course number of issues that need to be addressed individually and are different from one to another. Among them buildings and monuments can be noticed. Due to the geographical conditions and materials available we can see that bricks and tiles are mostly used in Iran whereas in India stone is the most popular construction material. Due to material behaviour, naturally, the conservators of the two countries face different problems. In addition to this, factors such as climate and environment have their own serious impact to accelerate or prolong the deterioration process.

On the other hand Iran and India share a great deal in the domain of intangible cultural heritage. This is perhaps because both countries have common historical as well as spiritual and cultural backgrounds in the areas such as literature, poetry, music, dance, etc. It is clear that preservation of cultural heritage needs to be addressed to both body and spirit; in other words we have to look at the issues of tangible and intangible as a whole.

The whole notion of preservation of cultural heritage is indeed a modern one. The very discussion of the need to preserve the tangible and the intangible speaks of a modern crisis of cultural identity. No need to say that in the olden days where the cultural identity was well and alive it was not considered as a "Heritage"; and there was naturally, not much of the need for scholars and practitioners to focus on the issue of preserving them. It is about a century ago that the elite became conscious of a dyeing heritage that needed to be rescued and revived. A handful of pioneers, Ali Asghar Hikmat, Seyed Mohammad Hossein Mashayekh Faridani, Jalali Na'ini, Amir Hasan Abedi, Ziauddin Desai, Nazir Ahmad, Ananda Coomaraswamy to name just a few were involved in introducing such cultural heritage. The number of such scholars and thinkers were indeed small but their contributions in terms of creating awareness were immense. In the course of the last three decades we witnessed the fruition of some of their efforts in the form of educational courses, training programs, and university degrees, academic and other publications, seminars and conferences. In this paper I try to present concise pictures of the movements and activities in the following passage.

Joint Efforts in the Level of Higher Education after 1979

Both countries started to recognize the importance of institutionalizing education in preservation of cultural heritage in university level almost at the same time. From 1960's to the present we have witnessed a growth of awareness and establishments of various programs both at academic institutions (universities, etc.) and professional bodies:

Academic Institutions

To look at the history of education in the field of the preservation of cultural heritage in both countries one can see that Iran during 1979 to 1989 has already established the infra structure in the field of education in comparison to India by offering programs on M.A. and later B.A. level. On the other hand from 1989 to the present Indian government has been more focusing in higher level of education; offering M.A.s and Ph.Ds in History of Art, Conservation and Museology. In Iran the Pardis College of Art in Isfahan was a pioneer of offering M.A and B.A. degrees in Preservation and conservation of cultural heritage and monuments. Later on, Pardis College of Art grew to become a full fledge university in the art related field known as The Art University of Isfahan. A few years later the Iran Cultural Heritage Organization established its own program of higher education in the related field. This is because Cultural Heritage Organization is an umbrella institution responsible for the preservation of the museum collections and historical monuments nationwide. In India, On the other hand the National Museum Institute was the pioneer. They offered M.A.s and Ph.Ds in History of Art, Conservation and Museology. The uniqueness of this institute is that it is part of one of the biggest museums in India. The students would therefore have the opportunity to examine original artifacts and get involved in their restoration under experienced practitioners.

Professional Bodies

No need to say that there were and still are, professional bodies dealing with the issue of conservation and restoration of historical artifacts and monuments. Most of such activities were taking place in museums, archives, libraries and as a part of archaeological sites. The practice of conservation in such places was mostly following traditional methods, but was later on combined scientific and modern methods to enhance the practice.

In Iran there are number of centres that are active and quite advanced as well. Among them Conservation labs of Astan Quds Razavi in Mashhad, Iran Parliament Library in Tehran, Marashi Najafi Library in Qum, is of special significance. However the largest and the best equipped for scientific research in the field of conservation and restoration is Research Centre for Conservation of Cultural Relics (RCCCR). The history of this centre goes back to year 1988 as a small conservation laboratory of Iran archaeological centre. Later in year 1988 this conservation lab turned into research laboratory and in year 1994 became a large and well equipped research centre under the Iranian Cultural Heritage Organization. RCCCR, formerly directed by Dr. Rasool Vatadoust, undertakes national and international level scientific investigations and preventive conservation and restoration projects on histro-cultural materials as well as offering high-level training courses to conservators and conservation scientists. In India there are also numbers of professional bodies that have been active in the field. Among them The National Research Laboratory for Conservation of Cultural Property (NRLC) and The Indian National Trust for Art and Cultural Heritage (INTACH) formerly directed by Dr. O.P. Agrawal can be highlighted.

Recognition of National Museum Institute, New Delhi

Since it is now a prerequisite to hold Ph.D degree to get jobs in academic and high level posts both in Iran as well as in India the demand for studying in Ph.D level increased since 1980s. Only a few institutions throughout the world offered Ph.D in conservation and preservation of cultural heritage. National Museum Institute (NMI) therefore became a target for Indian and Iranian applicants. Interestingly the first Ph.D receivers from this institute were from Iran: Prof. Amir H. Zekrgoo and myself. I was awarded the first M.A. and Ph.D from NMI. I was also the first Iranian woman who ever held Ph.D in conservation and preservation of art works. Before 1979 most of Iranians who were enthusiastic to continue higher education in art and art history were Western educated. After 1979 an Iranian artists Prof. Zekrgoo who had already experienced American education looked at India to explore new inspirations from the East. Right after Ph.D graduation we both went back to Iran joined the Art University as lecturers.

This was the beginning of a fundamental reform in the academic structure in the art arena. The initial step was to get an Indian institute (National Museum Institute of Art History, Conservation and Museology, New Delhi) recognized by the Iran Ministry of Higher Education. This was not an easy task at all, since most of the Iranian academicians in the fields of Fine arts were products of Western universities. Their western biased mind was naturally resisting those with Eastern background. The hard works eventually paid off; doors were opened and the road was paved for the many more Iranian who pursued their post-graduate education in the fields of art history, preservation of cultural heritage and museology in the said institute.

Conferences, Training Programs and Workshops

After the re-opening the universities of Iran in 1983, the academic institutions experienced a reform in art activities, teaching and research projects. Until then most of the outlines and curricula were structured based on European models. The new setup favoured the revival of the traditions based on Islamic perspective, with a kind eye towards its neighbours.

Zekrgoo lived in India from 1986 to 1994. During this period he served as the Director of Art Activities, Cultural Studies and Persian Development Program at the Iran Culture House in New Delhi; he had close relationship with Indian cultural organizations such as IGNCA (Indira Gandhi National Centre for the Arts), ICCR (Indian Council for Cultural Relations), AIFACS (All India Fine Arts and Crafts Society) and the Universities in Delhi and Aligarh. The relations continued and led to further cultural and academic collaborations after his return to Iran in 1994 when he re-joined the Art University, Tehran. With his background on art and philosophy, and exposure to Western and Eastern worldviews, he started giving lectures and seminars on comparative art with special reference to Hindu, Buddhist and Mughul art of India.

Soon after, he offered a course on the 'Art and Culture of Neighbouring Civilizations' with an emphasis on Indian art, philosophy and mythology. In no time the interest in Eastern art and culture grew and, with that, students started writing dissertations on subjects related to Indo-Iranian art and cultural heritage. Lectures on comparative religious themes, especially on Islam, Hinduism and Buddhism comprised another aspect of his contribution to the spread of knowledge with respect to Iran and India. His contribution in the arena of Art is of special significance. He has exhibited his artworks in many countries. Some of his works reflects his fascination for Indian culture. One can detect in his work and effort to establish dialogue among cultures and civilizations through the medium of art.

My contribution, however, was in the field of Preservation of Cultural Heritage. After obtaining my doctorate from the National Museum Institute (NMI) I returned to Iran and continued my academic career with the Art university of Tehran and Isfahan as Assistant Professor and Head of graduate school. During my services I managed to develop few workshops with experts from various Indian conservation institutions. Between 1994 and 1998, Indian authorities in conservation such as Indian Council of Conservation Institute (INTACH) and National Research Laboratory for Conservation of Cultural Property (NRLC) were invited to conduct workshops on paper and textile conservation and deliver lectures on conservation issues and conservation sciences. The above activities prepared grounds for further relation between students, academicians and professional practitioners; and exposure of various traditional as well as modern techniques that each of the two nations had developed.

These were some examples of pioneering academic efforts in the field of Art and Cultural Heritage, which were spearheaded by the Iranians after the Islamic revolution of 1979.

Researches and Publications

From 1979 to the present day many researches initiated and valuable books have been published in Iran and India. Many scholars – in search for common grounds, and in order to pave the way for mutual understanding, have tried to analyze and introduce the art and philosophical point of views of one culture to another. The Indian scholars were particularly active in the areas of Persian language and literature in the subcontinent, and have made invaluable contributions with respect to preservation and introduction of the vast Persian heritage in India–something that Iranians as a nation are extremely grateful. Prof. Dr. Amir Hossein Abedi, late Prof. Nazir Ahmad, Prof. Azhar Dehlavi, late Prof. Z.A. Desai, Prof. S.H. Qasemi, Prof. Yunos Jafari, to name just a few, maybe considered among the pioneers. Dr. Mehdi Khajepiri's works–along with his predecessors and his Indian counterparts–are of special significance. This task was also supported and pursued by Iranian scholars in both Iran and India; the valuable activities of Iranian institutions in Delhi, the Iran Culture House and the Centre for Research on Persian Language and Literature, are remarkable.

Among the scholarly works that has had major impacts on creating awareness of Indian art, mythology and philosophy among the public are the publications of Professor Zekrgoo. Having published nearly a hundred articles and eight books, a significant number of whom were focused on various aspects of Indian culture, he may be regarded as a pioneer of Indian studies in the course of the past two decades. Most of his writings are now regarded as reference sources by students and scholars alike. His pioneering work "اسرار هند اساطیر", on Indian Mythology [1], and his translations and profound commentaries on three books by Ananda Coomaraswamy [2] (one of which was a two time national award winner in Iran in the years 2008 and 2009) elevated the level of scholarship in the domain of Indology to new heights.

In 1997, Zekrgoo established *Honar-Nameh, the Quarterly Journal of Art Research* in the University of Art Tehran, for which he also served as its first editor-in-chief for four years, when he moved to Malaysia. He contributed an article on the *Indian model of promoting traditional art within the academia* in the very first issue; this was a foundation stone for spreading awareness about Eastern arts in general and the Indian art in particular. He tried to present a balanced view of traditionalists and modernists in the journal. The article was then followed by other contributions by him and other writers who shared similar views and interests. Professor Zekrgoo's fascination with Indo-Iranian philosophy, art and culture is also reflected on a number of M.A. and Ph.D dissertations that he has supervised. He joined as the professor of Islamic and Oriental Arts at the International Institute of Islamic Thought and Civilization (ISTAC) since 2001.

My contribution, on the other hand, was more in the field of scientific studies of the Indo-Iranian cultural heritage. My first major publication [3] *The Presence of Saffron in Persian Miniature Paintings and its Preventive Role for the Destructive Effect of Verdigris* was an outcome of part of my Ph.D thesis [4] "Scientific Comparative Study on Materials Used in Persian and Indian Miniature paintings". In this thorough research I have analyzed the materials used in Persian and Indian miniature paintings based on historical treatises from Safawid to Qajar and Mughul period and the scientific analysis from original samples. I continued my research in the same line for nearly last two decades the outcome of which was a number of discoveries based on historical and scientific analysis that could explain the secrets behind the stability of Persian and Indo-Iranian miniature paintings. Among these discoveries that has been published in number of international recognized journals, the role of saffron and henna [5] as an inhibitor and insecticide respectively were highlighted.

Other publication that had a great impact in the preservation and conservation of the manuscripts and documents is "**Conservation and Restoration of Paper Documents**" [6] This was the outcome of a joint effort of reputed Indian scholar, Dr. O.P. Agrawal, the former Director General of Indian Council of Conservation Institute (INTACH) and myself. This book is now a reference in most of the Indian conservation arena. The book was originally published in English in 1997. In 2001 a Hindi version of the book [7] was published due to its demands among the conservation community.

I was invited in Malaysia in 1999 to become the first curator, and to establish the curatorial department, at the Islamic Arts Museum Malaysia. In 2002 as the head curator I was involved in another joint effort project. The Museum hosted an exhibition from the National Museum New Delhi, entitled "Islamic Art of India", also the title of a beautiful catalogue [8] that was published in conjunction with the exhibition. A similar another collaboration was initiated in 2003 and as the head curator I was involved in this joint effort project. The National Museum, New Delhi, hosted an exhibition on Malay Textiles from the Islamic Arts Museum, Malaysia, in National Museum, New Delhi, entitled "Islamic Art of India", also the title of a beautiful catalogue. [9] At present I am teaching subjects related to conservation sciences in International Islamic University Malaysia.

Conclusion

Many important joint efforts have been initiated between Iran and India in last three decades. It is important that it will be continued specially in educational areas such as holding joint workshops and training courses. We need to have more joint researches and try to have more quality publications to elevate the understanding of our cultural links especially among young generations. The awareness about our mutual past and the issues related to preservation of cultural heritage needs to be addressed to the larger target audience and should start from very early stage as primary and secondary level. Then only, we can see that the sense of preservation will come natural around us.

Three decades (1979-2009) may sound a loge time, but it is a blink of an eye in historical scale. We are indeed indebted to those who have created such a great heritage in the ancient past, and grateful to the selfless efforts of the conservators of this great legacy that delivered it to us. It is our historical obligation to do the same for the generations to come. It is the beginning of a long way ahead. We need to stay focused.

End Notes

1. *Secrecy of Indian Myths–Vedic Gods (360 pgs.), Publisher*: Fekr-Rooz Publishing, Tehran, 1998.
2. *Christian and Oriental Philosophy of Art: Translation and Commentary (224 pages), Published by:* The Iran Academy of Art, Tehran, 2007.
3. *The Presence of Saffron in Persian Miniature Paintings and its Preventive Role for the Destructive Effect of Verdigris,* Published in ICOM Committee for Conservation Journal, 12th Triennial Meeting, Lyon, *France,* 1999, Volume II, pp. 489-494, ISBN:1873936923.
4. Scientific Comparative studies on Materials used in Persian and Indian Miniature Paintings », Under Editorial for Publication.
5. *Historical and Scientific Analysis of Iranian Illuminated Manuscripts and Miniature Paintings,* Contributions to the Symposium on the Care and Conservation of Middle Eastern Manuscripts, The University of Melbourne, Australia, 26-28 November 2007, The University of Melbourne, Published by Minuteman Press: Spencer Street, Melbourne, 2008, pp. 74-88, ISBN:978-0-7340404-7-3.
6. Conservation and Restoration of Paper Documents, (Book authored by O.P. Agrawal, O.P. and Mandana Barkeshli), Published by INTACH Indian Council of Conservation Institutes, 1997.
7. Conservation and Restoration of Paper Documents, (Book authored by O.P. Agrawal, O.P. and Mandana Barkeshli), Translated in Hindi, Published by INTACH, Indian Council of Conservation Institutes, 2001.
8. Islamic Art of India, (catalogue, editorial team), Published in Islamic Arts Museum Malaysia), 2002.
9. Cultural Treasures : *Textiles of the Malay World,* (Catalogue, editorial team), Published by Islamic Arts Museum Malaysia, 2003.

References [1]

"A Report of the ASHURA PROCESSION in Lucknow" (Persian), Nameh Farhang, Quarterly Journal on Cultural and. Social Studies, No. 11. 1992.

"An Introduction to Indo-Islamic Architecture" (Persian) Nameh Farhang, Quarterly Journal on Cultural and Social Studies, No. 19, 1996.

"Evolution of Buddhist Figurative Art along the Silk Roads" (Persian), Honar Nameh, Quarterly Journal of Arts Research, University of Art, Tehran, Autumn 1999.

"From Cyrus to Ashoka: A Comparative Study of Ancient Arts and Beliefs of Persia and India" (Persian), Honar Nameh, Quarterly Journal of Arts Research, University of Art, Tehran, Autumn 1998.

"Indo-Islamic Architecture: the Confluence of Contradictions", (Persian) Nameh Farhang, Quarterly Journal on Cultural and Social Research, No. 20, 1996.

"Islamic Scripts in India, Tuqlaq Period, *I*" (Urdu) Rah-e Islam, Monthly Journal of Islamic Culture, New Delhi, 1993.

"Islamic Scripts in India, Tuqlaq Period, *II*" (Urdu) Rah-e Islam, Monthly Journal of Islamic Culture, New Delhi, 1993.

"Islamic Scripts in India, Tuqlaq Period, *III*" (Urdu) Rah-e Islam, Monthly Journal of Islamic Culture, New Delhi, 1994

"Mahatma: The Great Spirit" (Persian), Ayene-e Hind, The Cultural Journal of Indian Embassy, Tehran, 1999.

"Nature, Man and Art: An Irano-Islamic Perspective" (English), In the volume: *PRAKRITI, Man and Nature, An Integral Vision,* Indira Gandhi National Centre for the Arts, New Delhi, 1992.

"Reflections on the Art Theories of Ananda K. Coomaraswamy" (Persian), Art edition, Journal of National Academy of Sciences, Iran, Autumn and Winter 2000.

"The Buddha – Ideal or Idol, A Study on the Evolution of Buddhist Iconography" (Persian), Nameh Farhang, Quarterly Journal of Cultural and Social Studies, No. 22, 1996.

"The Concept of SPIRIT in the Hindu Cosmology" (Persian) Kayhan-e Farhangi, monthly journal of cultural studies, Tehran, 1992.

"The Divine Savior according to Hindu Cosmology", (Persian) Kayhan Farhangi, monthly journal of cultural studies, No. 124, 1996.

"Time and Eternity, Part I" (Persian), translation to Persian of an Essay by Heinrich Zimmer, Nameh Farhang, Quarterly Journal of Social & Cultural Studies, No, 26, 1997.

"Time and Eternity, Part II" (Persian), translation to Persian of an Essay by Heinrich Zimmer, Nameh Farhang, Quarterly Journal of Social & Cultural Studies, No, 29 1997.

"Traces of Persian Art in the Domain of Indian Culture" (Persian) Nameh Farhang, Quarterly Journal on Cultural and. Social Studies, No. 18, 1995.

"Traditional Art Within the Academy: A Survey on Art Education in India" (Persian), Honar Nameh, Quarterly Journal of Arts Research, University of Art, Tehran, Summer 1997.

Zekrgoo, Amir Hossein, "Ananda Coomaraswamy's Perception of 'Form' and Artistic Perfection", Khiyal, the quarterly journal of the Iranian Academy of Arts, No. 18, Summer 2006, pp. 68-75.

Zekrgoo, Amir Hossein, "Buddhist Architecture and its Symbolic Aspects: Part II, 'Chaitya' and 'Vihara'", Khiyal, the quarterly journal of the Iranian Academy of Arts, No. 10, Summer 2004.

Zekrgoo, Amir Hossein, "Buddhist Architecture and its Symbolic Aspects: Part I, 'Stupa'", Khiyal, the quarterly journal of the Iranian Academy of Arts, No. 9, Spring 2004.

Zekrgoo, Amir Hossein, "Christian and Oriental, or True Philosophy of Art" Chapter in a book entitled *New Gathering and Old Wine: Selected Essays on Philosophia Perenis (Jam'e noe va Mey-e Kohbeh: Majmoo'e Maqalat-e Ashab-e Hekmat-e Khaledeh), Published by:* The Institute of Research and development of Human Sciences, Tehran, 2005 (1384), pp. 343-369.

Zekrgoo, Amir Hossein, "Esoteric Buddhism and Islamic Mysticism: An Interdisciplinary Overview of the Sacred Arts and Mystical Literature", in: Esoteric Buddhist Studies: Identity in Diversity (Proceedings of the International Conference on Esoteric Buddhist Studies), March 2008, Koyasan University, pp. 381-398.

Zekrgoo, Amir Hossein, "Ethics and Aesthetics: An Oriental Point of View", Khiyal, the quarterly journal of the Iranian Academy of Arts, No. 23-24, Autumn -Winter 2008, (Late Edition published in January 2010) pp. 4-23.

Zekrgoo, Amir Hossein, *"Islamic Art: Its Contribution to the Hindu Scriptures" (Persian), Saye-e-Tooba: The essays published in conjunction with the 1st painting Biennialof the Islamic World*

Conference, Museum of Contemporary Arts, Tehran, November 2000.

Zekrgoo, Amir Hossein, "Mandala: Manifestation of Supernatural World in Indian Sacred Arts" (Persian), Faslnameh-i- Honar, The Art Quarterly, New series, No. 46, Winter 2001.

Zekrgoo, Amir Hossein, "Manifestation of Mandala in Traditional Iranian Architecture and Music" (Persian), Honar Nameh, Quarterly Journal of Arts Research, University of Art, Tehran, Autumn 2001.

Zekrgoo, Amir Hossein, "Mudrā: The Symbolism of Hand Gestures in Buddhist Iconography", Honar-Nameh, Quarterly Journal of Arts Research, University of Art, Tehran, Summer 2004 , Vol. 7, No. 23, pp. 16-29.

Zekrgoo, Amir Hossein, "Nature in the Oriental Arts: A Study of Coomaraswamy's Perspective", *The Collection of Essays of the Congress: Nature in Oriental Art*, Iranian Academy of Art, Spring 1338 (May 2009), Iranian Academy of Art, Tehran.

Zekrgoo, Amir Hossein, "Religious Art as Reflected in the Ancient Indian Sources and Ananda K. Coomaraswamy's Writings", Khiyal, the quarterly journal of the Iranian Academy of Arts, No. 20, Winter 2007, pp. 4-23.

Zekrgoo, Amir Hossein, "Sufi Sama and the Cosmology of Mandala", Al-Shajarah, Journal of the International Institute of Islamic Thought & Civilization (ISTAC), International Islamic University Malaysia (IIUM), 2008 Volume 13 Number 2, pp. 179-209 (delayed publication).

Zekrgoo, Amir Hossein, "That Beauty is a State": Chapter in a book entitled *New Gathering and Old Wine: Selected Essays on Philosophia Perenis (Jam'e noe va Mey-e Kohbeh: Majmoo'e Maqalat-e Ashab-e Hekmat-e Khaledeh), Published by:* The Institute of Research and development of Human Sciences, Tehran, 2005 (1384), pp. 417-439

Zekrgoo, Amir Hossein, "Time and Myth according the Traditional Indian Cosmology", Ketab-e Mah: The Arts, No: 61- 62, Tehran, September-October 2003.

Zekrgoo, Amir Hossein, "Why Exhibit Works of Art?" Chapter in a book entitled *New Gathering and Old Wine: Selected Essays on Philosophia Perenis (Jam'e noe va Mey-e Kohbeh: Majmoo'e Maqalat-e Ashab-e Hekmat-e Khaledeh), Published by:* The Institute of Research and development of Human Sciences,

Tehran, 2005 (1384), pp. 309-343.
Zekrgoo, Amir Hossein, *Introduction to Indian Art (Translation and Commentary) (Book: 216 pgs), Published jointly by:* Iran Academy of Art and Rowzaneh Publishing, Tehran, 2003.

References [2]

Agrawal, O.P. and Barkeshli. Mandana, Conservation and Restoration of Paper Documents » (book, author), Published by INTACH Indian Council of Conservation Institutes, 1997.

Agrawal. O.P. and Barkeshli. Mandana, Conservation and Restoration of Paper Documents, (Book, author), Translated in Hindi, Published by INTACH, Indian Council of Conservation Institutes, 2001.

Barkeshli. Mandana, Scientific Comparative studies on Materials used in Persian and Indian Miniature Paintings, Under Editorial for Publication.

Barkeshli. Mandana, Cultural Treasures: *Textiles of the Malay World,* (catalogue, editorial team), Published by Islamic Arts Museum Malaysia, 2003.

Barkeshli. Mandana, Islamic Arts Museum Malaysia : *Islam and Islamic Art*, (Book, author), Published by Islamic Arts Museum Malaysia, 200.2

Barkeshli. Mandana, Islamic Art of India, (catalogue, editorial team), Published in Islamic Arts Museum Malaysia), 2002.

Barkeshli. Mandana, Six Centuries of Islamic Art in China, (catalogue, editorial team), Published by Islamic Arts Museum Malaysia, 2001.

Barkeshli. Mandana, Dress for the Body, Body for the Dress : *when Islamic and Western* meet, (catalogue, author of Islamic Arts Museum Malaysia's Forward), Published by Islamic Arts Museum Malaysia, 2000.

Barkeshli. Mandana, Nur Al-Quran: History of Quran; *Islamic calligraphy and illumination; Materials used for decoration of Quran, (*catalogue, author), Published by Islamic Arts Museum Malaysia, 1999.

Barkeshli. Mandana, *Traditional Preventive Measures Used in Persian Manuscripts and Miniature Paintings: Historical and Scientific Analysis of Iranian Illuminated Manuscripts and Miniature Paintings*, Golestan Honar, Quarterly on the History of Architecture, No.16, Summer 2009, ISSN 1735-3890.

Barkeshli. Mandana, Sharing Good Practice, Conservation Issues in Asia: Traditional Preventive Measures Used in Persian Manuscripts and Miniature Paintings, Asian Regional Cooperation Conference, New Delhi, December 24, 2008, INTACH.

Barkeshli. Mandana, *Historical and Scientific Analysis of Iranian Illuminated Manuscripts and Miniature Paintings,* Contributions to the Symposium on the Care and Conservation of Middle Eastern Manuscripts, The University of Melbourne, Australia, 26-28 November 2007, The University of Melbourne, Published by Minuteman Press: Spencer Street, Melbourne, 2008, p. 74-88, ISBN: 978-0-7340404-7-3.

Barkeshli. Mandana, *Historical and Scientific Analysis on Sizing material used in Iranian Manuscripts and Miniature Paintings,* American Institute for Conservation of Historic and Artistic Works (AIC), The Book and Paper Group Annual, Volume Twenty-two 2003, USA, 2003, pp. 9- 16.

Barkeshli. Mandana, *pH Stability of Saffron Used in Verdigris as an Inhibitor in Persian Miniature Paintings*, in Restaurator, International Journals for the Preservation of Library and Archival Material, Volume 23, p.154-164, 2002, issue dedicated to the 13th ICOM Committee for Conservation Meeting, Rio de Janeiro, 22-28 September, 2002, ISSN : 0034-5806.

Barkeshli. Mandana, *The Presence of Saffron in Persian Miniature Paintings and its Preventive Role for the Destructive Effect of Verdigris,* Published in ICOM Committee for Conservation Journal, 12th Triennial Meeting, Lyon, *France,* 1999, Volume II, pp. 489-494, ISBN :1873936923.

Barkeshli, Mansdana and Zekrgoo. Amir. Hossein, Conservation of Living Heritage*: Collection management of Islamic heritage in accordance with the sharia'h of Islam,* International Centre for the Study of the Preservation and Restoration of Cultural Property (ICCROM), Printed by Ugo Quintily S.P.A, Rome, 2005, p.94-101, ISBN: 92-9077-189-5.

Barkeshli. Mandana, Mirror of Heritage (Ayene-ye Miras): *Identification of Sizing material used in Persian Manuscripts and Miniature Paintings Based on Historical and Scientific Analysis*, Quarterly Journal of Book Review, Bibliography and Text Information, New Series, Volume 4, Issues No. 4, (35), Winter, 2007, Special Issues (3): History of Science), Tehran,

Iran, 2005, p. 307-324, ISSN: 1561-9400.

Barkeshli. Mandana, Mirror of Heritage (Ayene-ye Miras): *Discovery of Saffron Trace as an Inhibitor for the Destructive Effect of Verdigris in Persian Miniature Paintings,* Quarterly Journal of Book Review, Bibliography and Text Information, New Series, Volume 3, Issues No.1, (28), Spring, 2005, Special Edition Topic: History of Sciences (2), Tehran, Iran, 2005, p, 183-215, ISSN: 1561-9400.

Barkeshli. Mandana, Spiderwebs and Wallpapers : International applications of the Japanese traditions in paper conservation : *Using traditional Japanese Paper-Making Technique in the Restoration of a Thirteenth Century Iranian Manuscript of the Holy Quran,* Proceedings of the International Seminar on Japanese Paper Conservation (JPC), 14-20 December 1998, *Japan, 1998*, pp. 98-112.

Barkeshli. Mandana, *Islamic textile and costumes*, Stibbert Muséum Journal, Florence, Italy, 2001.

Barkeshli. Mandana, *A scientific microbiological effect of Henna dye in traditional Persian paper dyeing*, ICBCP, Tehran, Iran, 1998: Also published in Honar Nameh, Art University Journal, Tehran, Iran, 1998.

Barkeshli. Mandana, *The presence of saffron traces in green verdigris pigment,* IASC, India, 1997: Also Published in Persian in Honar Nameh, Art University Journal, Tehran, Iran, 1997.

Barkeshli. Mandana, *Preparation of green copper-based pigments According to Persian historical manuscripts*, IASC, India, 1996: Also Published in Persian in Honar Nameh, Art University Journal, Tehran, Iran, 1996.

18

Reflections on Indo-Iranian Relations

Amir H. Zekrgoo

The affection of a day is a link. That of a month is kinship. That of a year is blood-tie. If anyone cuts it off, God will cut him off.

Imam Jafar al-Sadiq [1]

Introductory Remarks

"Relations" between individuals, races or nations are usually spoken of as 'short term' or 'long term', both indicative of "temporality"; that is, to understand and explain events within a time-bound process. Being 'contemporary' in this context would merely mean 'temporal companionship', i.e. occupying or sharing the same geo-physical moment of time on the globe. Temporal companionship may include interaction on different levels based on 'mutual interests' but does not involve deep emotional connections. Strong long-lasting ties, on the other hand, are normally built upon shared ideals, values and worldviews–qualities that are essentially timeless.

Speaking of timeless relations in a time-bound world that is controlled by money, military and media, may sound irrelevant or out of place, but nations like India and Iran, whose identity is moulded by eternal values, need to treat their temporal affairs with timeless ideals, or else the esoteric bounds that have kept them close from time immemorial, will fade into the exoteric superficialities of today.

The backbone of these two ancient civilizations is the inner vision of their sages and seers. Zoroastrian, Buddhist, Hindu or Muslim, these sages and prophets carried with them seeds of blessings that would nourish relationships beyond time and space. This is how great cultures manage to survive the destructive forces of the ages and can themselves become embodiments of an ever-fresh timeless contemporality. Timeless contemporality does not have a date of expiry while governments and political institutions do! It is therefore essential for Indian and Iranian leaders, politicians and academicians to align their internal and foreign policies with shared fundamental values. We need to reform what has been deformed and, as Coomaraswamy rightly states, "must take account of an original 'form'."

"Globalization" is among the concepts that have been deformed. The natural process of globalization started over a millennium ago via the greatest network of highways of all times–the historical Silk Roads, which connected the East and the West. This ancient network of communication is still considered important, not because of the role it once played in the exchange of commodities such as silk and spice, but due to its function in shaping a natural and peaceful environment for the exchange of ideas. It is rightly named by UNESCO "The Roads of Dialogue." Today, Globalization is reduced to a profit oriented agenda by the multinational companies that are supported by the economic super powers that stretch their dominance over the globe. To stay original and loyal to our values does not mean staying away from globalization, for it is neither possible nor desirable. What we need do is engage our efforts to return 'globalization' to its original form–the timeless form derived from inner vision; for, according to Ghazali, "He who lacks the inner vision cannot perceive the inner form, and he cannot derive pleasure from it, love it and incline toward it." [2]

Peace has become the rarest of all commodities: we talk about it more than ever, yet the farther it appears from actualization! In the age of inflation of information, wisdom is marginalized and the very word is regarded as an out-dated concept used ages ago by some old Hindu *rishis* or Muslim sages. It is all about abandoning inner vision and resorting to calculating self-centred greed-oriented temporary solutions. Without an inner peace there cannot be an outer one; the esoteric and the exoteric, the spirit and matter, must necessarily work in harmony to produce desirable results.

It is the age of multilateralism. Having the backbones of rich cultures and old civilizations, India and Iran have serious responsibilities not just towards their own people, but towards the humanity as a whole. Perennial philosophy needs restoration and civilizational renewal is a necessity to put our policies in correct perspective. We must re-educate ourselves about our own forgotten identity and re-evaluate our debts to humanity. Getting engaged in a global economic race of overproduction for the sake of over-consumption is not healthy, nor does it contribute to world peace. After all "the body, for the sake of which we desire wealth, is the ultimate cause of all wars." [3]

Spiritual and Intellectual Fraternity

'Global village' is no longer an idea, it is a reality now. 'Internal affairs' are no longer internal; they have become an integral part of 'foreign affairs'. And with the expansion of media, which has penetrated the most remote corners of the globe and deepest domains of private lives, life is experiencing a transformation from tangible reality to 'virtual territory'. The virtual reality that is created by the media, and is largely controlled by the economic giants, has shaken the very foundations of traditional values and virtues. There are wars everywhere; they are now fought on different grounds, in various fronts and with diverse weapons while the warriors– regardless of victory or defeat–are not sure who the enemy is and why the war must be fought in the first place. The most valuable human asset sacrificed amidst all this is "trust." Peace will not return unless trust is re-established, and trust is a by-product of spiritual and intellectual fraternity. Hence, there is nothing more timely today than the revival of the timeless qualities of brotherhood at a global level.

The first step towards this global goalis the acknowledgement of self, for 'the Kingdom of God lives within you' [4] or, as the famous *hadith* (prophetic tradition) asserts, 'self realization is the realization of the Creator". [5]

The efforts to achieve this fundamental aim must be pursued at personal, cultural as well as racial levels. We need to revive the sense of appreciation of our indigenous art, cultural heritage, and our overall ancient civilization that has contributed so much to the humanity as a whole. Cultural heritage, to most politicians and social reformers, is either a closed book or, at most, an important means to promote tourism for economic prosperity–something that 'qualifies' the country to take a more active part in the dangerous race of 'development'. "The only condition of the renewal of life in India (East), or elsewhere, should be a spiritual, not merely an economic and political awakening, and it is on this ground alone that it will ever be possible to bridge the gulf that has been supposed to divide the East and the West." [6] It is not sufficient to know where we want to be in fifty or hundred years from now; it is equally important to be conscious of where we come from, because the latter defines our identity and is closely connected to our self-esteem. That is why we need to re-educate our public and our leaders alike about the essential position of cultural heritage. A nation without self-esteem is an already defeated party in the global race.

The meaning of *self* in Indo-Iranian context is found in their philosophy. In the Western intellectual tradition the study of philosophy is regarded as an end in itself, and as such it means very little to the ordinary man. But in our tradition, to the contrary, philosophy is an essential ingredient of life: "[it] is not regarded primarily as a mental gymnastic, but rather, and with deep religious conviction, as our salvation (*moksha*) from ignorance (*avidya*) which forever hides from our eyes the vision of reality." [7] We believe that philosophy is the key by which we access the meaning of life and the means of attaining its goal, for 'thoughts become words, words become actions, actions become habits, habits become characters, and characters will eventually become our destiny'.

The modern mentality has distanced us from our 'self', and with it our self-esteem has suffered. The regard that we have for ourselves, as peoples with rich ancient heritage, finds expression mostly, and regretfully, in our nostalgic remembrance of a 'glorious past', without an esteem for what we are 'now' or what will become of us in the 'future'. We often feel that 'we are not good enough', therefore we have doubts whether we deserve a bright future at all! And 'the minute you settle for less than you deserve, you get even less than you settle for'. Self, in Islamic, Hindu or Buddhist philosophy is central, for, as the famous saying goes "in the search for me, I discovered truth. In the search for truth, I discovered love. In the search for love, I discovered God. And in God, I have found everything." As vicegerents of God (*khalifat-Allah*) on earth we – humanity in its totality – do not deserve anything less than everything. As fragmented entities that have been separated from their roots, on the other hand, we cannot be more fragile and hopeless than we already are.

The second stage would therefore be the identification of spiritual allies and the reestablishment of the already existing ties through strengthening them by tangible means; be they academic, economic, social or political. This naturally begins with neighbours. Mahatma Gandhi defined "Swadeshi" [8], or the movement of 'own country' as "that spirit in us which requires us to serve our immediate neighbours before others, and to use things produced in our neighbourhood in preference to those more remote. So doing, we serve humanity to the best of our capacity. We cannot serve humanity by neglecting our neighbours." [9] In another place he described *Swadeshi* as "a call to the consumer to be aware of the violence he is causing by supporting those industries that result in poverty and harm to workers and to humans and other creatures." [10] Gandhi believed that alienation and exploitation often occur when production and consumption are divorced from their social and cultural contexts.

Humanity today is a fragmented entity divided by geographical borders, racial differences, religious denominations, political tendencies and sexual orientations, etc. The fragments are being broken to yet smaller pieces by 'interests'. Military campaigns, economic sanctions and political pressures are used, not to defend legitimate rights but rather the 'interests'–right or wrong–of the mighty. It is mainly these 'interests' that fuel the blazes of hatred and war; and they represent the main obstacles in the path of peace. Reconnection of the cultural, spiritual and intellectual ties could result in restoration of many broken pieces. Reestablishment of 'cultural territories' could provide healthy avenues for intercultural dialogues that would hopefully heal the visions and appreciation of humanity in its beautiful and much wanted diversity. After all 'the flowering of humanity is more important than the victory of any party'.

From Personal to Global

In order to move from personal to universal we have a few social structures–namely 'national', 'regional' and 'international' that, depending on intellectual and spiritual capacity, could serve either as facilitators or obstacles!

Nationalism, as is widely understood today, is a modern phenomenon that originated in Europe in the 18th century. [11] Nationalism, in a sense, is the idealization of a nation: it is an uncritical acceptance and belief in superiority of a group by descent, race or culture that in extreme manifestations lead to fascism. [12] Nationalism, as explained above, is obviously an obstacle. In fact, contrary to the propagated idea that' 'religions are main causes of conflict and bloodshed around the globe', social and political scientists have suggested nationalism is the most significant political and social force in history that have caused the most destructive wars of the globe, i.e. WWI and WWII. [13]

Regionalism, that focuses on the interests of a particular region (I'm referring to region as a domain that includes a few nation-states not the other way around), may have a broader scope, in the sense that one, despite his loyalty towards his own country, shall defend a few others and, at the same time, benefit from their support. Regionalism may be contrasted with nationalism, since national interest, in certain cases, must be compromised for the interests of a greater circle. This interest, however, is–in almost all cases–defined and understood in the economic and political context.

Internationalism, according to an encyclopaedic definition, is 'the doctrine that nations should cooperate because their common interests are more important than their differences'. Nowadays the term 'globalization' is used to express the same concept, that is 'the integration of national economies into the international economy through trade, foreign direct investment, capital flows, migration, and the spread of technology'. Though free trade and capital flow are undoubtedly important aspects of bilateral and global relations, there are "other and perhaps more important freedoms to be considered, which may be called collectively a cultural freedom, bearing in mind that", in countries such as India and Iran, "with millennial and living traditions ... it has never been attempted to live by "bread alone"." [14]

The terms (national, regional and international/global) and their definitions, as explained above, are products of the modern (post-industrial) era, but the concepts have existed long before. In fact the first comprehensive manifestation of the process of globalization, in its most constructive and fruitful appearance, took place along the famous historical network of highways–the Silk Roads. It was through this network of land and maritime routes that mankind experienced for the very first time a multifaceted process of globalization. Through the Silk Route cultures met, ideas travelled, religions spread, and carried with them their languages, scripts and customs. [15]

Maybe it is time for us to revisit and redefine the terms and concepts that are central to our identity as individuals, and to the peace and prosperity of our nations, regions and all of humankind. Ananda Coomaraswamy was both idealistic and realistic in stating that "the chosen people of the future cannot be any nation or race, but an aristocracy of the earth uniting the virility of European

[Western] youth to the serenity of Asiatic [Eastern] age." [16] This could be an establishment of true brotherhood on earth. True fraternity is spiritual in nature; it is based on truth, good intentions and sincere actions, not on selfish interests that aim at one's economic prosperity at any cost. Life must not be looked at as a constant race of gaining more interest; it rather involves selfless acts, providing help, support and guidance to others to preserve a common interest and goal: Salvation.

With the advancement of technology and the widespread access to means of communication, establishment of a 'global aristocracy of the wise and the spiritual' may no longer be a phantom, or an unachievable idealistic thought. This global endeavour, like any other compound project, must start with individuals: the 'wise and the spiritual' must seek their kind within and without the geographical boundaries of their nation-states to form a nucleus of regional think-tanks. These regional circles – that may at the beginning share same language– would then be linked to other circles in other regions through members with bilingual or multilingual skills. This is to connect and relate the people who share the same 'language' but not necessarily the same 'tongue', for there is a "unifying language that sages and mystics refer to it as 'the language of heart', 'the language of presence', 'the language of soul' etc… This language, as Rumi explains in his Mathnavi, is an esoteric one; it unites the people who share the same heart (i.e. the state of spiritual presence), even if they do not speak the same literal language: [17]

همزبانی خویشی و پیوندی است   مرد با نامحرمان چون بندی است
ای بسا هندو و ترک هم زبان   ای بسا دو ترک چون بیگانگان
پس زبان محرمی خود دیگر است   هم دلی از هم زبانی بهتر است

To share a tongue is a sign of kinship and connection
A man among strangers is like a prisoner in chain
Indians and Turks may connect through a shared tongue
While two Turks may be strangers in vain
Therefore the language of hearts is of a different nature
To be one in heart is indeed better than to be one in tongue. [18]

The joining of these circles will eventually lead to the creation a global network of genuine people who want to make things good for both physical and metaphysical use. This network could help reforming the conventional regional and global institutions that have been going through a long phase of de-formation: bodies such as the Non-Aligned-Movement (NAM), Organization of Islamic Countries (OIC), and the United Nations!

Al-Ghazali's Concept of Brotherhood

Al-Ghazali (1058-1111 CE) in the second chapter of his monumental work, *The Revival of the Religious Sciences [19]* provides an account '*On the Duties of Brotherhood' [20]* which I felt would be quite relevant to our discussion. His guidelines to brotherhood could be interpreted both in individual and communal contexts. He introduces eight duties of brotherhood as an aid to spiritual purification and perfection, as well as a source of help in attaining material comfort in life. The eight duties are as follows:

1. **Material Assistance:** [21] Ghazali introduces performing this duty in three degrees of intensity: At the lowest degree you place your brother as the same footing as your servant, attending to his needs from your surplus. At the second degree you place your brother on the same footing as yourself. You are content to have him as partner in your property and to treat him like yourself, to the point of letting him share equally At the third degree, the highest, you prefer your brother to yourself and set his needs before your own.
2. **Personal Aid:** [22] Provide personal aid to your brother for the satisfaction of his needs. The lower degree consists of attending to them without waiting to be asked and when in plenty, though in joy and cheerfulness, showing pleasure and gratitude. The higher degree is doing the same, and with the same attitude, even during times of distress and tight-handedness.
3. **Holding Tongue in Silence:** One should exercise silence regarding secrets his brother has confided in him and on no account disclose them to a third party–not even his closest friends. [23]
4. **Speaking out:** Defending him and his honour in his absence, for 'the rending of honour is harder on the soul than the rending of flesh'. [24] Providing him with wise advices; being like a mirror to him: drawing his attention to his shortcomings, disapproval of what is ugly and approval of what is fine–all in confidentiality and with a compassionate attitude. For, according to al-Ghazali,

"the distinction between rebuke and advice is a matter of secrecy or publicity, just as distinction between courtesy and hypocrisy depends on the purpose motivating your connivance." [25]

5. **Forgiving mistakes and failings:** Everyone makes mistakes and on certain occasions fails to do what is right. Relationships can suffer permanent damages due to hatred caused by the wrong doings of one towards another. Yet longstanding relationships create certain rights and obligations, namely the right to be forgiven for your failings, and the obligation to forgive your brother's mistakes. There must therefore be a distinction between the continuation and the initiation of a relationship, "for mixing with the immoral is to be avoided, and so is separation from dear ones and brethren to be avoided." [26] Prophet Mohammad once said, "The worst of God's creatures are those who spread slander, separating dear ones" and that "Satan likes to cast this kind of thing on your brother, so that you will shun him and break with him. How careful you must be of what is dear to your Enemy!" [27]
6. **Praying:** "Pray for your brother ... that he may have all he might wish for himself, his family and his dependants." [28]
7. **Loyalty and Sincerity:** "Loyalty to a brother includes consideration towards all his fellows, relatives and dependants. To consider these is a greater duty in the heart of a fellow than to consider the brother himself, for his joy for those dependent on him is greater." [29] True loyalty includes sincerity; it can only last if it is for the sake of God, for "a fruit of affection for God's sake is that envy cannot co-exist with it, whether in religion or in worldly affairs." [30] Loyalty, according to al-Ghazali, includes not listening to gossip about one's friend, as well as not befriending his enemies. Here he quotes al-Shafii' I who asserted: "if your friend obeys your enemy, they share in enmity towards you." [31]
8. **Informality for the sakes of comfort and convenience:** Ghazali provides quotations from a few personalities to elaborate on the meaning of informality; among them is Ja'far al-Sadiq who said: "The heaviest of my brothers upon me is the one who discomforts me, and with whom I must observe formality. The lightest on my heart is he with whom I can be on my own." [32] He then encourages a tolerant approach so that one's relation to the others would not lead only to a small circle

of intimates. He commands to seek brotherhood of any intelligent, religious person.

The Ghazalian concept of brotherhood and friendship should not be regarded as merely an "Islamic" perspective, but rather a universal one.

Art and Timelessness

Art is the oldest recorded form of human expression. The history of cave paintings, for example, can be traced as far back as 50,000 years ago. There were other forms of art such as song, music and dance, that due their perishable or non-material nature, we do not have definite dates for their former existence. The existence of music, however, may be traced through musical instruments made of bones that date back to at least 45,000–60,000 years ago. [33] An example of a well developed primitive flute is presented in figure below.

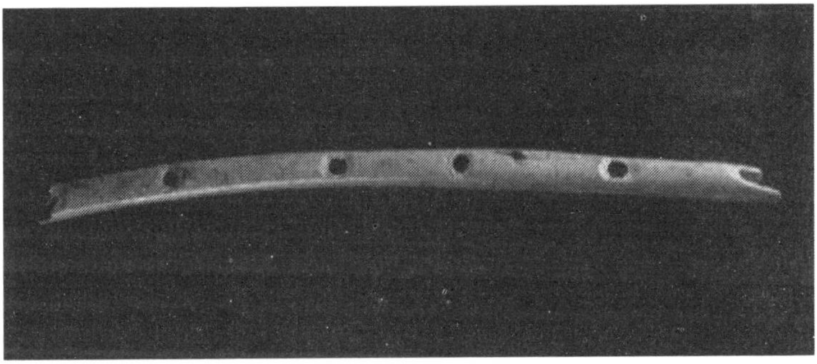

The dates/periods mentioned above indicate the pre-historic era, 'a term used to describe the period before written history'. Evidently, writing occupies such a distinct position in the human mind that we divide our ancient heritage into pre and post writing periods. This is, of course, due to the significant role writing played in recording and transmitting knowledge. During the past few decades, however, this notion has undergone serious modification: as detailed studies of the arts of ancient cultures have revealed art's ability to record and transmit knowledge–sometimes more truthfully and comprehensively than writing. Such discoveries are gradually shifting our perception of prehistory to a wider foundation that allocates a substantial place for art, in its wider meaning. It also makes us rethink about the value of art as a highly sensitive and effective medium of communication.

Art is the embodiment of a race's life experience–matured in time and perfected in form. It's a product of its age, but can leave deep and long-lasting impressions on the body and spirit of an entire culture, long beyond the age in which it was born. Such impressions, if genuine, would continue to grow much like a living being, shaping their environment and influencing people's outlook and tastes. Great civilizations produce great art that lives for ages; they represent cultures in their totality and, at the same time, constitute inseparable ingredients of the culture of its genesis. All the qualities inherent in a culture–such as religious beliefs, social norms and hestatus of men and women, ideals, heroism, ethical values and established relations with other races and cultures–find manifestation in the wide spectrum of arts, i.e. visual arts, performing arts, architecture, music, poetry, etc. That is why arts constitute major components of what is generally known as 'Cultural Heritage'.

Much has been said and written on the historical traces of Iranian art, architecture and poetry in the arena of Indian culture and civilization. The prominent influences, in the realm of art, may be traced back to the Ashokan Lion Capital of Sarnath [34] (Figure on next page) of the first millennium BC, though the Indian Veda and Persian Avesta reveal a much earlier kinship in the domains of religion and mythology. More recent examples are to be found in Mughal miniature painting and architecture, in Urdu poetry, and in numerous other artistic manifestations. On the other hand, the impact of Indian spirituality and art–especially in the arena of music and film–is still evident in the present day Iranian culture. The deep fascination of Iranians for the profundity of Indian culture throughout their long shared history has found its expression especially in the bulk of poems by classical and contemporary poets.

What I would like to propose here is that art should be regarded among the most powerful mediums of communication; it acts and has often acted in the Indo-Iranian cultural context, as solid ground for civilizational dialogue. In fact, no serious discourse on cultural relations between the two civilizations can occur without reference to their arts. Here, we need to have a brief discussion about the nature of cultural heritage.

Art and Identity

Cultural heritage must be preserved because it carries within it accurate references to 'who we were', and helps us establish 'who we are'. Studied well and treated with care, it also contributes to the formation of our 'right and natural future', leading us to 'what should become of us'. In other words 'cultural heritage' forms the backbone of a civilization. A culture with a weak backbone is like a fragile structure that easily collapses, while one with a well-built backbone endures tough circumstance.

Our precious cultural heritage, which we are so rightfully proud of, consists of tangible as well as intangible dimensions. Tangible cultural heritage (TCH) constitutes the material culture, such as painting, sculpture, architecture, objects and artifacts, etc. Their preservation usually means conservation and restoration of the physical. Intangible cultural heritage (ICH), on the other hand, is the spirit that keeps a cultural heritage alive. It comprises, according to the UNESCO's 2003 Convention for the Safeguarding of the Intangible Cultural Heritage, "practices, representations, expressions, knowledge, skills–as well as the instruments, objects, artefacts and cultural spaces associated therewith–that communities, groups and, in some cases, individuals recognize as part of their cultural heritage." [35]

The intangible cultural heritage is manifested, among other means of expression, in the oral tradition, performing arts, traditional craftsmanship and knowledge and practices concerning nature and the universe. We may identify the Intangible Cultural Heritage (ICH) with the qualities stated below:

1. It is transmitted from generation to generation;
2. It is constantly recreated by communities and groups, in response to their environment, their interaction with nature, and their history;
3. It provides communities and groups with a sense of identity and continuity;
4. It promotes respect for cultural diversity and human creativity; etc. [36]

It may be concluded therefore, that:

1. Cultural heritage must be regarded as an organic living entity consisting of body (tangible) and soul (intangible).
2. Preservation of cultural heritage means nurturing this 'living entity' so that it may grow in health.
3. Growth of cultural heritage means continuity of a cultural identity in the people, by the people and around the people. This is to say people are both the creators and true vessels of cultural heritage because the evolution of cultural heritage takes place both in and around people, and never in isolation from society.

The arguments presented above imply that a true preservation of cultural heritage involves creative participation of the people in it, for, how else should we treat a 'living being' that marks not only our past, but our present and future as well?

A Personal Experience of Artistic Expression

My long engagement with India–a living culture with a charismatic and inspiring identity–has been fruitful. The last few years of my stay in India (early 1990s) marked my involvement in a huge art project that provided a unique opportunity for me to leave behind something worth while. The new building of the Iranian Embassy in New Delhi was under construction and I was asked to apply my creative ability and artistic expertise to enrich the project.

My engagement lasted some two years. The first stage was the most confusing; I wanted to develop a visual concept that would reflect the deep ties between the two civilizations. After a couple of months and a few hundred sketches, the idea eventually surfaced: two birds–peacock and Simorgh–where to represent the two civilizations. The peacock has often been associated with India in Persian literature; it symbolizes ultimate beauty and grace. [37] Simorgh, on the other hand, is a famous mythical bird that has been associated exclusively with the Iranian identity. It plays a significant role in the *Shahnameh* of Ferdowsi, symbolizing a connection to heavenly realm and divine protection. [38] The two birds were composed in such a manner that a single line would mark their touching chests–symbolizing the unity of hearts. The forms of each bird was perfected in a few line drawings and then taken to a higher stage of a proper painting with colours to enrich the idea (Figure on next page).

Though the colourful painting was aesthetically pleasing, I felt it didn't quite express what I was trying to accomplish; that is to say, the timeless quality that I pursued, was not quite there! This took me to yet another stage of deliberation; this time to find the 'right medium'–something that would display the firm foundation of an age old relation. After a while of research, 'copper' proved just the right material–a firm surface with an old warm earthy colour that, with the help of high heat and pressure, would take on the forms of delicately engraved lines, embossed curves and graceful volumes. Reintroducing the desired volume to a flat design was not easy; it required experimenting with clay first. Working with clay, I produced a number of three dimensional prototypes before experimenting with copper sheets. The idea was crystallizing bit by bit and step by step.

The next phase was to execute the design on real metal. Two small copper prototypes with slight variations were created–one with a simple shiny polish, and the other with artificial patina to give it an old rustic mood. The plane copper effect was eventually selected for final execution.

The final artwork, which formed the centre piece of the mural, is a colossal embossed sheet approximately 4 meters wide and 8 meters tall. The background contains elements of plant life, such as branches, leaves, blossoms and flowers, and of animal life including snail, fish, birds, eggs and human forms–all intertwined with arabesque designs and, in between, Persian couplets by Shams al-Din Mohammad Hafiz in Nasta'liq style of calligraphy [39]–another shared cultural element of India and Iran. Together they are meant to represent the continuous process of life enriched with art and literature.

To further elaborate the centre piece–both in terms of aesthetic/visual enhancement of the ambiance, and in terms of the message and relevance to historical context–two colossal panels were designed each consisting of 14 individual pieces; these side panels are mirror images of an identical composition, echoing the message in both directions. In designing them, I used elements from the two chief phases of Iranian history–the pre-Islamic and the Islamic period.

The entire mural was designed for, and installed on, three walls of the octagonal entrance hall, with a domed roof elevated some 12 meters above the floor. The design and execution of the dome's interior was also my responsibility. The dome has eight projecting lines issued from the nucleus, echoing the eight sided structure that supports it.

These lines form an eight pointed star, also known as the Mohammadan Star [40], at the centre, harmonized with eight dome-shaped arches at the circumference. Square Kufic script was adopted for decorate of the interior surface of the dome: the Qur'anic expression "Alhamdolillah" (All Praise is to the God Alone) is repeated sixteen times within the eight-pointed star.

Poetic Expression

The art project introduced above was an example of a 'tangible art' and I hope one day it will be regarded as the shared cultural heritage of Iran and India, as I regard them both as 'home'–India was the country of my second birth, and I shall never forget my birth-place(s).

There is yet one more experience I would like to share with our audience. This is (or rather was, before writing this paper, and hopefully publishing it) an 'intangible art'–a poem that I had composed when time came to leave India in, I think, 1993 or 1994. [41] It was a strange feeling: I was going home but the departure was much harder than one would expect! A strong bound was built between my soul and the soul of the land India. It was unusual and overwhelming. All that passion found manifestation in a few Persian couplets quoted bellow:

اسیر هندم و زین رفتن بیجا پشیمانم
هوای هند افکنده شرر بر جسم و بر جانم
روان باید شدن؛ اینست پیشانی نوشت من
ز تقدیر نوشته، من چگونه بر کشم دامن؟
چو سهمم در قدح باشد، من از قسمت نپرهیزم
چو روزی او مقدر میکند، از رزق نگریزم
جماعت را همی گویم: "همین است انچه می جویم"
" ببینیدم رفیقان: سرخوشم، مستم، دعاگویم!"
به چشم خلق من شادی کنم، دستار افشانم
ولی چشم ترم گوید که از رفتن پشیمانم

I translated the couplets to English for this paper. Though the translated version may not totally reflect the essence, I tried to get as close as I could to the original. Both versions are available and the readers may do their own comparison and judge. The translated version is as follows:

To India I'm a slave; it isn't easy to depart
For its sizzling memories still breathe deep in my heart
But I ought to move forward; this is my destined role
How could one ever escape from his ordained goal?!
Everyone's share is fated; I won't refuse mine
Perhaps this episode too, is directed Divine
To all my friends I proclaim: "I always craved for this!
Look how cheerful I am; it must be heavenly bliss!"
In their weak and shallow eyes, merry my face appears
Yet no one stares into my eyes, to see my mournful tears.

While writing my poem Kalim Kashani [42] was present in me. In fact I borrowed the first line (half-couplet = مصراع) of my poem from Kalim–a Persian poet who migrated to India, lived there for 30 years, died there in Kashmir in 1740 and was buried there. And here I was, mourning my departure, inspired by words by an individual who lived some three hundred years ago. It seemed as if my state of mind was, at least for a period–in Hindu terminology–an incarnation of Kalim's deep affection for India. His love for India was so deep that while returning to Iran on the occasion of his father's demise, in the travelling caravan, he composed a poem, lamenting–not his father's death, but his separation from India! Such is the power of art!

When genuine feelings find manifestation in art, they become timeless. Kalim's feeling for India was not a fondness for a land, or the few nice people he met there. His expression reflects a state of deep attachment towards a *'state of being'*–a state of spiritual intimacy – that to him found embodiment in the name 'Hindustan'. The name Hindustan, for us, is a concept much wider than the geo-political boundaries of the present India. That Indian-hood that Kalim, and so many others, fell in love with was the richness of a benevolent old culture that represented esoteric and exoteric aspects of life in totality. So Kalim's touching couplets, and the humble words of mine, shall not be regarded merely as a few individuals' feelings, but rather an artistic manifestation of a race towards that *'state of spiritual intimacy'*. The regard for that *state* did not begin with Kalim, nor did it end in him.

The deep regard of Iranians for India found manifestation in enormous contributions in various areas stretched over two millennia. Such contributions reformed the landscape of Indian soil, culture and thought. The Islamic culture of India, for example, owes a vast part of its magnificent beauty to the richness of the arts that originated from Iran. And again, I shall emphasize that the name Iran–in its cultural and civilizational context–does not refer to the specific geographical boundary that defines it as a sovereign country in the modern geo-political maps. Here we have used the name Iran to identify the Iranian Cultural Continent–a vast domain of many countries that are carriers of Iranian genius in the form of art, architecture, music, literature, etc.–and India has the largest share of this treasure! The value of this heritage is to the extent that an Indian scholar's effort to comprehend the history of his own nation will not be credible without including Iran and the Persian language. An Iranian, on the other hand, is forced to move east, towards India, or rather to 'the Indian Cultural Continent' (to use a more accurate terminology) to understand his identity.

What am I claiming?

Am I considering India as a component of the Iranian Cultural Continent? The answer is definitely affirmative, for history confirms this claim with undisputed evidence. And, how about India; Can she, with all her glorious heritage, claim Iran as a province of her own rich Cultural Continent? Not surprisingly, the response will again be an undisputed Yes!

So where do we stand in the contemporary world? How do we define our identity and base our relations in a world that promotes hostile divisions and profit oriented fragmentations? The answer to this dilemma appears to lie in the realm of 'timeless contemporality'. In order to access that 'state' we need to revive the 'timeless' in our temporal affairs; and this will not happen unless the eyes of self-realization are awakened to view, once again, the essential timeless Self. Art is a miraculous domain that, from time immemorial, has been the vehicle of that eternal quality, and artists are the humble and selfless labourers that move the vehicle around in time and space. Let us value art again. Let art be the medium of dialogue among us–as our history bears testimony to its effective language. Let us prepare grounds for the birth of masterpieces again. The generation of masters and masterpieces is sadly on the verge of extinction and, with that, the ever-fresh melodies of our timeless contemporality is gradually fading away in the noise pollution of 'interest-oriented' temporal companionship.

Our (India-Iran) intimate relation would be a grand blessing for humanity. Our forefathers–sages, intellectuals and artists alike–guarded the sanctity of this relation, and we owe the same to our children and our children's children.

I could not quote here a more accurate, concise and wise statement than the one I began this paper with. I therefore decided to conclude my discussion with a brief elaboration on the same words; words that are simple yet extremely meaningful.

> The affection of a day is a link.
> That of a month is kinship.
> That of a year is blood-tie.
> If anyone cuts it off, God will cut him off.

The above passage uses a metaphoric mode of expression to speak of a universal law:

Affection is introduced as an auspicious and magical ingredient that would transform *days, months* and *years* (quantitative factors of time) to relation-oriented qualitative values, i.e. *links, kinships* and *blood-ties.* And at the end, the entire 'universal law of relation' receives divine endorsement with hazardous consequences for those who break it: Violators shall face a harsh punishment: *God will cut them off*!

People of Iran and India have had blood-ties for at least two millennia; we aren't merely relatives–we are indeed a family! Members of a family, regardless of their 'socio-economic interests' have rights and responsibilities towards each-other. [43] I have sensed the strong presence of that magical ingredient, *affection,* in my soul and in the soul of my Indian brothers–regardless of their race or faith. I feel the responsibility towards safeguarding our priceless bounds, not only on a personal level, but also in intellectual arenas. Our politicians must do the same in their own circles. After all, an affectionate age old relation brings about certain Rights and Duties, precious values that must not be compromised with Interests.

End Notes

1. Narrated by al-Ghazali in *The Revival of the Religions Sciences (Ihya Ulumal-Din).*
2. Al-Ghazali, *Alchemy of Happiness*, translation to English is taken from *Fine Art in the Islamic Civilization*, edited by M. A. Jabbar Beg, The University of Malaya Press 1981, p. 28.
3. Plato, *Phaedo,* 66 c.
4. Plato, *Republic*, 591 e.
5. من عرف نفسه فقد عرف ربه.
6. Dance of Shiva, p. 180.
7. Ibid, p. 23.
8. The Swadeshi movement was part of the Indian Independence Movement. Its aim was to establish economic self-sufficiency through boycotting British products and the revival of domestic-made products and production techniques.
9. Mahatma Gandhi, Young India, 20 August 1919.
10. Mahatma Gandhi, in conversation with Ramachandran, 10/11 October, 1924.
11. The term was coined by Johann Gottfried Hender during the late 1770s.
12. Laqueur, Walter. *Fascism: Past, Present, Future*. Oxford University Press, 1997, p. 90.
13. Joseph Goebbels describes the Nazis as being allied with countries which had "authoritarian nationalist" ideology and conception of the state. See "Goebbels on National-Socialism, Bolshevism and Democracy, *Documents on International Affairs"*, vol. II, 1938, pp. 17-19.
14. Ananda K. Coomaraswamy, "Voice of India", *Washington*, No. 1, 1944, p. 12.
15. Zekrgoo, Amir Hossein, 'Dialogue of Civilizations and Cultural Fusion along the Silk Routes: An Interdisciplinary Study of the Formation of Sino-Arabic Calligraphy', in *Maritime Communication & Islamic Culture* (conference proceedings), Quanzhou Maritime Museum, Fujian, 2008.
16. *The Dance of Shiva*, 2nd edition, Munshiram Manmohrlal Publishers, New Delhi, p. 180.
17. Zekrgoo, Amir Hossein, 'Sufi Sama and the Cosmology of Mandala', in *Al-Shajarah*, Journal of the International Institute of Islamic Thought and Civilization (ISTAC), International Islamic University Malaysia (IIUM), Vol. 13, No. 2, 2008, pp.

179-208.

18. Rumi, *Mathnawi, Book 1*, 1205-1207, The translations to English of the couplets are my own.
19. *The Revival of the Religions Sciences (Ihya Ulumal-Din)* is widely regarded as the greatest work of Muslim spirituality, and has, for centuries, been the most read work after the Qur'an in the Muslim world.
20. By 'brotherhood' he means the 'Communities of Believers'. The English translation of the text is available in Muhtar Hollands's *Al-Ghazali: On the Duties of Brotherhood*, The Overlook Press, Woodstock, NY, 1976.
21. Ibid pp. 21-29.
22. Ibid pp. 30-34.
23. Ibid p. 35.
24. Ibid p. 51.
25. Ibid p. 55.
26. Ibid p. 66.
27. Ibid.
28. Ibid p. 70.
29. Ibid p. 72.
30. Ibid p. 74.
31. Ibid p. 77.
32. *Ibid* p. 80.
33. Stephen Davies, *The Philosophy of Art*, Blackwell publishing, US, UK, Australia, 2006, p. 3.
34. There is convincing evidence that artisans from the Persian Achaemenian dynasty – who are credited with the carvings of the stone lions of Persepolis – had a major role in sculpting the Ashokan Capital, either directly as stone carvers or as advisors for the project. I have elaborated on the subject in my 'From Cyrus to Ashoka: A Comparative Survey of the Ancient Arts and Religious Beliefs of India and Iran', *Honar-Nameh*, Quarterly Journal of Art Research, Volume 1, No. 1, Tehran, 1988.
35. The convention was endorsed in the 32nd session of UNESCO's General Conference meeting in Paris, from 29 September to 17 October 2003.
36. The UNESCO Convention 2003 (ibid).
37. هرکه را طاووس باید، جور هندستان کشد (translation: Whomsoever has the desire of a peacock must face the hardship of travelling to

India). Here 'peacock' symbolizes beauty and perfection, and India was considered a place to travel to for the seeking of knowledge and, hence, the attainment of perfection.

38. **Simorgh (سیمرغ)**, also known as **Angha (عنقا)**, is a fabulous, benevolent, mythical flying creature. The figure can be found in all periods of Iranian art and literature, and is evident also in the iconography of medieval Armenia, Byzantine art, and art of other regions that were within the sphere of Persian cultural influence.
39. The following couplet by Hafiz adorned the lower part of the central mural: شکر شکن شوند همه طوطیان هند زین قند پارسی که به بنگاله می رود.
40. For symbolism of Mohammadan Star see my 'Esoteric Buddhism and Islamic Mysticism: an Interdisciplinary Overview of Sacred Arts and Mystical Literature' in *Esoteric Buddhist Studies: Identity in Diversity, March 2008, Koyasan University, Koyasan, Japan,* pp. 381-399.
41. I am sorry that I cannot recall dates, and also too lazy to search for them in files! May be it is because I'm constantly in a timeless state!!! And the reason I called my poem 'intangible' is that until recently I had it only in my memory, occasionally reciting it to friends. I only wrote it down for the purpose of the conference and this paper.
42. Abu-Taleb Kalim Kashani is among those Persian poets who migrated to India during the reign of Jahangir (1605-27) to seek the favour of the Mughal Emperors. He gained fame both in Iran and India, and this led him into the court of Shah Jahan who made him his poet laureate. Among Kalim's works is *Shah Jahan Nameh,* a poetic account of the history of the Mughals from Tamerlane down to Shah Jahan. Kalim's best work, however, is to be found among his ghazals.
43. I have already elaborated on such rights and duties in introducing Ghazali's view on brotherhood.

19

Iranians and Bollywood Cinema

M.H. Ilias

The current phase of globalization has set in motion an interesting spread of many translocal cultural entities across the world. They are translocal in the sense that they refer to entities which take place within the cultural intricacies and specificities of certain communities, yet are increasingly circulated, identified and consumed by other national communities. 'Indipop' and Bombay cinema (otherwise known popularly as Bollywood) are the two most common forms of cultural expression from India which gained this status with wider global reach.

Wedded to the ideal of mass production, Bollywood, over the years, has created its own popular patterns appealing to outside world. In this way, the films transcend the local, regional or national to reach the universal and it was by endorsing cross-cultural and eclectic narratives, Bollywood cinema acquired its present significance. Bollywood stars and film music are famous throughout much of western Asia, and have influenced mass culture as far away as parts of North Africa. This paper seeks to make an enquiry into how Bollywood cinema as a translocal cultural entity is being perceived by the Iranians within the boundaries of their imagination and aesthetic sensibilities. The enquiry starts from a question why Bollywood is so appealing to a large section of Iranian population.

Thanks to its capacity to engender a cross-cultural circulation of commodities and cultural identifications beyond borders, Bollywood has got an overwhelming presence in Iran. This may not be unique to Iran; there is, of course, a spill-over effect all over West Asia, though the gravity differs. But, unfortunately, this paper does not claim to be a comprehensive study as it is based only on the opinions gathered from Iranians in exile. [1] The recurring ideas in this paper evolved out of a series of conversations with Iranians living in India and the United Arab Emirates (UAE) and broader ethnographic conceptualization is possible only through a detailed field study.

Massive transnational migration of Iranians due to variety of reasons (mainly political and economic) has also engendered a different category of viewership for Bollywood with diverse aesthetic and political sensibilities. Diasporic Iranian viewers are able to easily identify some common and shared cultural currents that keep them connected to Bollywood-dominated now by a genre primarily meant for Non-Resident Indian (NRI). Moreover, they get a chance to watch uncensored prints while lengthy love making sequences, item numbers and kissing scenes always undergo merciless censoring inside the country. In Iran, the commercialization of electronic media has explored new vistas for transnational entertainment products.

With easily available CDs and DVDs, and now satellite television, Bollywood films are making deep inroads to wide audiences. Almost all entertainment channels in Iran have a weekly slot for Bollywood Cinema. Cinema halls exhibit more censored versions of Bollywood films with Farsi subtitles or sometimes with dubbed text. The success of so many Indian films, which were eventually declared as flops in local market, marked a great success in Iran bears testimony to the popularity of Bollywood in the country. Films such as *Dil Se, Lagaan, Devdas, Kuch Kuch Hota Hai, Fashion, My Name Is Khan* and some others were some of the biggest contemporary hits of Bollywood in Iran. The old and middle aged Iranians maintain a fondness for films of 60s and 70s like *Mother India, Mughal e-Azam, Sholay, Sangam* etc., while the preference of youngsters goes to NRI genre.

Asset of 'Political Neutrality'

What Bollywood cinema boasts to catch up the popular imagination in West Asia may be its 'cultural amalgam' that is appealing to an eclectic mix of population without much ideological hassles. Although remains to be an embodiment of the culture of India's English speaking, globalized, upper middle class population, Bollywood is no longer a homogenous entity with a single cultural agenda to promote. It is rather a major locale for the contestation or coexistence of many cultures, tastes, aesthetics and political ideologies. Making possible a plethora of avenues of imagination, people from different cultural milieu get what they expect.

The language of Hindi commercial cinema is a mixture of Hindi, Urdu, Sanskrit and now English. In course of time, especially during and after the 1990s, it has become more anglicized, the language has transformed into 'Hinglish' (a mixture of Hindi and English). This particular language communicates directly with larger Asian audiences in diaspora, irrespective of religious or social differences. It offers similar cultural roots to these communities because of shared cultural past.

Especially the new Bollywood films, which are put under the common rubric of 'NRI cinema', address a multitude of issues cutting across the cultural lines and make inroads into grab a large diasporic population. It is a cinema that appears to be made not essentially for Indians but for a global community and almost entirely calibrated to the globally dominant aesthetics and imagination. Bollywood cinema, thus, began to be looked like a crucial battleground where the conflicts between the 'local' and the 'global', the 'universal' and the 'particular' and the 'traditional and the 'modern' are being fought.

Iranians see Bollywood as their own cinema though the inroads made by Hollywood into Iran have been relatively unlimited. Unlike Hollywood cinema, the liberty that Indian popular cinema takes in story-telling does not go beyond the permissible boundaries of expression. With its episodic nature, its songs, dance sequences and narrative style, Bollywood leads the viewers to a different time and space and transgresses several socio-cultural borders. Bollywood musical revives and energizes a form that became moribund in Iranian cinema a few decades ago. [2] With many tender themes of love and separation, it pushes the margins of imagination further.

For Iranians, Bollywood seldom amounts to cultural hegemony or may be the other way round. The issue of hegemony, normally, does not spring into our mind when we think of spread of Bollywood in Iran. Narrative strategies being used commonly in Bollywood films cannot be regarded as hegemonic 'universal' one, but is actually culture-specific. What is worth-mentioning in this context is the usual reluctance for Bollywood cinema to depend upon loud political issues, while Hollywood always loves to present a meta-narrative of historical or political events (history of wars and high-intensity conflicts for instance). They are being used by Hollywood as pretexts to present their version by linking its own narrative to universal one. Iranians seem to have an uneasiness or ideological hassle in watching these often 'problematized' versions of contemporary history.

The only history known to Bollywood, on the other hand, is family history. The way of interpreting the use of family in Indian cinema is that it is the largest social unit that can exist 'autonomously' without referring to any political issue directly. The film makers in Bollywood concentrate on placing the individual against the background of history of the family and narrate the nation through family. Individuals' or families' destinies blend with the destiny of the country and the two together are pitted against a common enemy. Instead of serving any larger political purpose, these histories are being used as context or background for 'romance' to flourish. Another major worth-mentioning factor is Bollywood's light cultural baggage. For Iranians, these films apparently set up an alternative universe of family values, less violence and clean fun. Likewise, Bollywood Cinema's recent fame in the Islamic world comes from this 'political neutrality'. It is, no doubt, a strategic asset of profound value to attract people of different background and to give Bollywood an added edge over films from other parts of the world.

These do not mean that Bollywood films are politically neutral as they are often being projected. Hindi films are considered to be a fertile land or reflexive of a wide variety of anecdotal insensitiveness especially when it comes to debate over caste, religion and gender. There is a crude caricaturing of Islam and Muslims in some of the films. Nonetheless, for Iranians the otherwise problematic renditions of historical or political events or negative stereotyping of minority or Dalit images seldom matter. Bollywood films have a different narrative strategy and a way of saying something entirely different to their audience in a more subtle manner even they deal with highly sensitive contemporary issues. Even the pre-occupation with political Islam and 'war on terror' on which many of Bollywood films capitalized to garner patriotic appeal becomes a non-issue compared to that of Hollywood.

Despite the crude caricaturing of Indian minorities in many of the films, Bollywood cinema makes a significant headway and wins over the hearts and minds of ordinary Iranians. Iranians have given more importance to the elements like romance, pleasure and freedom than aesthetics and politics. Bollywood cinema, obviously, operates as a realm of pleasure, desire and consumption. The identifying features of Indian popular cinema include the extensive use of music and the dance, and the explicit stylization of acting and mannerisms of male heroes. Politics takes a back seat as the Bollywood tries present itself with an image of being 'politically neutral' to many of the contentious issues in the world politics.

Iranian Cinema: Constrained by Sensibilities

There is, of course, much to be said about contemporary Iranian cinema in the context of a discussion about the popularity of Bollywood among Iranians. It is obvious that Iranian cinema is well recognized as one of the most innovative and exiting in the world, and films by Iranian directors are being screened to increasing acclaim at international festivals. Nevertheless, Iranian cinema in general is still constrained and configured by specifically Islamic sentiments and government sensibilities though there are notable exceptions. The kind of films Iranian directors make is something between documentary and feature films. It is interesting to note that this documentary genre does not serve any artistic function. Instead, they are a result of an effort to overcome governmental measures aimed at controlling and censoring cinema.

A close look at the history of Iranian cinema, for last three decades, would reveal that at different points of time, through its various organizations, the Islamic regime had promoted the creation of a distinctively Islamic cinema. Khomeini regime declared a total disengagement with the drive for modernization and the corresponding takeoff cinema as public entertainment. [3] This move was very much visible in the early 1980s, when the government agencies like the Cinema office of the Ministry of culture used to support and fund only films that serve the state's political interests. Films on political or social subjects relevant to contemporary Iranian society were almost next to nil. At some point of time, documentary films and films released outside Iran were the only tools used by filmmakers to expand the limits of free expression. The themes like love and sex were almost absent from the screen due to the Islamization of cinema though women were present behind the camera, even working as directors. [4] In the absence of women, love and other tender feelings could be channelled through children, so stories based on children dominated the screen during this period.

In the mid 1985 this stringency loosened and has witnessed the emergence of an army of internationally renowned film makers like Abbas Kirostami, Mohsen Makhmalbaf, Jafar Panahi and Majid Majidi. While the end of Iran-Iraq war and Ayatollah Khomeini's death in 1998 brought in some shift to the power structure, Khatami's accession to power ultimately paved the way for introducing a reform package with repercussions in the film field. This phase in contemporary Iranian history brought a breakthrough for Iranian film with the re-surfacing of previously taboo topics with a growing battalion of women filmmakers like Tahmineh Milani. The most significant feature of this phase, according to Ziba Mir-Hosseini is the emergence of younger women voices demanding personal freedom and questioning the whole notion of Islamized cinema. [5] Parallel to it, international acceptance for Iranian art cinema in the 1990s has helped the Iranian diaspora to negotiate and identify with the land and issues that characterize the contemporary Iran.

Another major genre which dominates over others is children-centred cinema. This also refers to a peculiar social condition. When one is not able to express his/her words in the language of adults because of strong censorship regime, he/she transfers them to the children and speaks through their language in a subtle manner. Moreover, the emergence of the new Iranian cinema can be traced to the historical and political particularities that created a distinctive space for critical social issues.

It is true that despite the purification measures the transformation of cinema entailed a major cultural and ideological shift that could not take place abruptly. Iranian cinema has now attained the position of a re-conceived public sphere for social and political discourses. It also provides a framework within which the public issues of the day are discussed.

In this peculiar mix, Iranian art cinema appears to be an important political document, but fails to capture the imagination of ordinary Iranians. People see Iranian art films as the form that has become particularly expressive of liberal middle class sensibilities and aspirations. Mainstream cinema on the other side is inhibited by government sensibilities. There is also a regulation introduced by the government restricting foreign films-especially Hollywood movies-in an effort to purify the public space. Watching Hollywood films, to a certain extent, is tantamount to committing a sin and is being treated as an act of 'westoxication' by the state.

Shared Experience of Modernity

Right from the beginning, Bollywood cinema was being viewed

in Asian-African countries as something counter-hegemonic to Hollywood in the name of a cinema of post-colonial nation-building. While the Hollywood reflected the values of 'imperialism', the nation-building films from the third world were concerned with the issues of de-colonization. They reflected a national spirit of formerly colonized Asian-African countries but used conventional narrative strategies which were inextricably a product of neo-colonialism and posed no serious challenges to the ideological signification of basic Hollywood narratives.

Produced in the context of national cinema, Indian cinema in the 50s and 60s was preoccupied with its concerns pertaining to nation-building. This orientation, at the same time, helped crystallize a new trend in the region; a trend that deeply influenced the cultural politics of Asia and Africa was essentially anti-colonial. Moreover, because of their political content of modernity, these films had captured the imagination of many in the third world countries with similar political condition. [6]

Nation-building films of Nehruvian era and their 'Five Year Plan' heroes spoke a universal language besides contributing towards the consolidation of a national imagination on a mass scale. Most frequently, films were institutionalized within the canons of national cinemas and functioned significantly in narrating nations and producing national identities. Still they usually incorporated a un-hegemonic universalism through the logic of secularism, pluralism multiculturalism and cultural nationalism and through nationalist forms of nostalgic globality. Raj Kapoor, definitely, had a different audience outside and his characters survived in Asian and African countries' public consciousness by possessing this element of universalism. As Nagaraj observes, " Raj Kapoor was an enthusiastic modernist who endorsed the revolt of the young against shifting traditions not just in India but all across Asia; for him the best creative space was in the values created by modernity". [7] Although Dev Anand went to London for shooting *Des Pardes*, this 'European' influence was declared less pernicious.

Iranians could easily find some commonalities as nationalist assertion was very much palpable at the grass-root level after the Moassadiq period (1951-53). [8] Although it was not much expressive on the political front, culture seemed to have surrogated this feeling. So, films like *Mother India* didn't appear to be totally alien to the Iranians. It was, of course, beyond the border but very near and felt as something with which they could relate easily. So was the case with the Five Year Plan Heroes' task of bringing modernity and enlightenment to India's village which was whole-heartedly received by the Iranian who were undergoing similar kind of socio-political engineering schemes came attached to modernization drive under Shah.

The presence of Indian migrants in Iran, which later on got declined due to change in policy of the regime over the dependence on the foreign labour in the event of Islamic Revolution, might be the reason for the wide acceptance for Indian cinema in Iran during 1950s, 60s and 70s. Considerable presence of Muslims in Hindi Cinema might have made a peripheral appeal though Iranians did not approach on it this ground and the total appeal went beyond religious concern. As Iqbal Masud noted, "the resonance of film romances involves the tragic lovers *Laila and Majnu*" [9] Widely known throughout Iran and Central Asia, this story has been the subject of five Hindi films (*Laila-Majnu,* 1931, 1931, 1945, 1953, 1976) and has provided the thematic material for many more. The religious overtones of the Muslim *Laila-Majnu* tale are less explicit than those of its Hindu counterpart, the story of Radha-Krishna, though both link the notions of romantic and divine love. Likewise, Hindi cinema has absorbed many of the themes and storytelling techniques of Persian epics, utilizing them as a structural and thematic basis for countless Hindi films. Costumes in the early 'period' films in Hindi cinema were explicitly Persian reflecting civilizational undertones. Shooting sets, plots and dialogues also bore testimonies to the Persian influence.

Although the films of 70s and 80s were recognizably Indian, tailored to suit the needs of Indians leaving behind the conventions of the 60s, eager to sample new stories, new styles, which spoke to the people directly, these films transcended ethnic identities by crossing over so-called fixed religious and cultural boundaries of different communities in Asia. This phase marked a complete dissociation from all sorts of ideological baggage (primarily of modernity). On one side, the films of this period moved to disorientation between the individual and the nation misleadingly presenting former against the state. The dreams and frustrations of the youth have been the favourite themes of Bollywood cinema of that period. On the other, they became a more effective tool for the state to institutionalize the forms of authority. With popular slogans of progress, development, secularism and national security had resonated in Bombay Cinema.

Amitab Bachan starred *Sholay* which was one of the best known Indian films in Iran furnishes a good example. Sholay exhibits the characteristics of Hollywood genre cinema with much of the inspiration for it coming from the Western genre. At the same time, it worked differently within the same structural paradigm and narrative principles. Amitab Bachan represented the common man fighting to overcome political and financial corruption and abuse of power. The 'angry Youngman' image often possessed by him became both an 'ideological phalanx' and a major vehicle of identification and self expression for youth in Iran.

Diasporic Spectatorship

The cross-cultural and cross-political identification is to continue with the new films also. A genealogical overview of the emergence of diasporic Bollywood cinema would reveal that how these films employ and transform aesthetic and cultural strategies in order to attract an international audience. Indian cinema, despite being a national cinema, has now deterritorialized so that its boundaries are no longer identical to those of the nation-state. Its increasing demands in overseas shows that Hindi cinema has developed as a powerful diaspora media. And the globalization of Bollywood has, now, seriously affected the production and circulation of diasporic films with the result, most recently, of blurring the categories with such films as *Bollywood/Hollywood.*

Diasporic Bombay films are now located in relation to the dominant and 'hegemonic' Hollywood in many places. With efforts to challenge the global domination of Hollywood cinema, Indian cinema is familiar to viewers from West Asia to parts of Asia and Africa. Increasingly, many Iranians cite Indian cinema as appealing because it is seen as an alternative to the Americanness of Hollywood in its Third World or postcolonial sensibilities and structures of feeling.

Hollywood is still a distant cousin, very powerful but demonstrably alien, whose values do not match with the sensibilities of the audience. But Bollywood, though may have turned its gaze towards Hollywood, stays sensibly within the imagination of Iranians. *Lagan* furnishes a serious entry point to this argument. It allows Indians to take pride of an easy, shallow and misleadingly 'all-inclusive' nationalism. No surprise, this film, on account of a strident anti-colonialism, captured popular imagination in Iran. Admirers of *lagan* are struck by its strident anti-colonial posture, though Lagan, for all its anti-colonialism, is not at all far removed from the mediocre stuff that have occupied so substantive place in shaping the culture of the Bollywood cinema.

Briefly put, Boolywood cinema in its new incarnation remains a window to popular India's English-speaking middle class exile communities who are not-yet adjusted to the global aesthetics. [10] It is a cinema that appears terribly flawed by the grammar global film theory and almost entirely disjunctive with the globally dominant aesthetics concept of good cinema. [11] Then what is appealing in these moving images of Bollywood cinema that unites different communities. Broadly, three attributes can be traced in the general structure of post-1990 Hindi films: the filmic language and narration, 'political neutrality' and the centrality of the concept of family. These attributes of Hindi cinema provide a common and united cultural discourse to different communities of Asia.

The 90s was a time when Hindi Cinema was in an intense flowering phase, where the foundation what we call 'NRI' cinema was being laid. Bombay cinema's turning into post-liberalization Bollywood came with massive changes. The shift in orientation of cinema-making more appealing to a diaspora population hungry for nostalgia for the homeland was the major change that took place during this period. Diasporas started registering in the national filmic imaginary; in other words, diasporic lives and experiences became favourite subject of films. To attain a universal appeal, the Indian popular cinema has increasingly tented to become a battleground of eclectic cultures, tastes, aesthetics, and political ideologies with people with different background to identify with.

This phase, broadly speaking, is a phase that works with specific relation to countries like Iran. The development of a diasporic spectatorship creates a new mode of circulation of Bollywood in Iran and Iranians living outside the country. Most commercial Indian films are often characterized as appealing to them because of their content and aesthetic forms that derive from diverse diasporic sources. The focus is on an international involvement and the attempt is to draw attention to the fate of communities determined by an international context.

In addition to this, Bollywood cinema in the new form in its effort to be more appealing to a diaspora audience, contest relationships with nation-states. As a part of it, NRI films present community/family as the significant social unit that can exist 'autonomously' within the narrative without referential links to state and its overarching politics. To reach out to a wider audience across the world, these films try to address the social processes of exile and citizenship and exclusionary practices being faced by various disapora communities. The films discussed here thematically emphasize issues of mobility and location. This includes displacement from homelands as well as exclusion in Western nation states which seem to be appealing to the Iranians who make up a significant portion of Muslim diaspora in the West. With same situation facing in Europe or North America, Iranians in exile can identify easily with Shah Rukh Khan starring film *My Name is Khan.* The theme of this film is poignant story of a diasporic Muslim who often experiences an encounter with the state in the US.

Similarly, the fantasy-rooted construction makes Bollywood a non-mundane field. Keeping a 'different' universe clearly apart from the real one, these films provides the Iranians with a chance to become a part of a collective 'fantasy'. As a medium of pure enjoyment, these fantasies satisfy two types of desire of ordinary Iranians. Firstly, operating from within the realm of pleasure, it offers a site of leisure for a culturally depressed population. Another desire being satisfied by Bollywood cinema is the desire for freedom. This is more significant with regard to an urban generation grown up in the context of modernization under the Shah Regime. There is still a fresh memory of liberal life being nurtured by that generation and Bollywood with its 'freedom and pleasure' strikes a chord for people with 'liberal memory' living under the shadow of conservatism in the post-revolutionary Iran. Nevertheless, Bollywood's popularity does not stop with that lot. With its delicate combination of tradition and modernity, Bollywood becomes appealing to tradition-oriented society also. Similarly, Bollywood brings 'romance' as a compulsory into its narratives as background and most Indian films show the victory of love-even if tragedy prevents mutual love from being finally consummated.

The Bollywood for Iranians becomes a virtually secular space that emanates from a different region and cultural differences, yet addresses them in reality. So Iranian viewers entering a new secular narrative world created and offered by Bollywood Cinema. This, by extending the scope of vision of the Iranians spectators, it takes them to a distant land but with identifiable sights, feelings and people. The three-hour films are often identifiable by their all-encompassing forms that include elements of comedy, melodrama, action, romance, and music that do fit Iranian aesthetic expectations; in particular, the elaborate song and dance numbers, usually six to eight per film, do not pose any difficulties for Iranian viewers.

Another attribute of the contemporary Hindi cinema is its accentuation of the concept of a traditional family. Although, the family has always been at the centre of the filmic narrative, the recent manifestation of family melodrama has placed the global modernity into a specific frame of pan-Asian family tradition. Bollywood, unlike the Hollywood movies, accommodates emotions as well as the rituals related to the family. In Hollywood family dramas are about the families under threat. Indian family dramas are not about families in danger of disintegration, rather, revolving around romantic stories about family bonding or about love with the family serves as a context or background. [12] Most importantly, the happy ending of Bollywood cinema with the re-unification of family gains wide attraction as the gradual erosion of family structure among the Iranian communities in diaspora has become an important social issue. Anyway, Bollywood cinema offers a sense of homecoming to these communities and also provides them a shared space in cultural sphere.

Conclusion

Over the last three decades, age-old civilizational ties between India and Iran seldom overpower the powerful Bollywood images. Raj Kapoor to Shah Rukh Khan add further to the line of actors who energized this relationship with their celluloid charisma. This is a significant phenomenon, especially when other means of cultural interaction between two regions seldom operate. But it is doubtful, whether these two countries have succeeded in translating this cultural affinity and people to people interaction to a mutually beneficial multifaceted relationship.

The basic feature of Hindi commercial cinema is that it visualizes and reflects not the most common image of society in India. The form of film is not, then, the simple representation of Indian society. Inter community relations and attitude towards minorities are some of the complex issues which cannot easily be interpreted. There is the issue, and political stake, of the image of

Muslims, which arises from the way in which the dominant social discourse constructs the identity of the largest minority in India. Another major issue is of the class content. Especially after onset of globalization, the dominant narrative in Bollywood revolves around a typical upper middle class or affluent NRIs. Despite these issues, Bollywood films are being viewed by a highly diverse international audience, many of whom are not acquainted with the culture the films depict and representations they employ.

Iranians find their own images and culture in it. From its part, Bollywood has certain codes and styles that establish its relations with the contemporary socio-political processes in Iran. It is its peculiar mix that has made contemporary Bollywood cinema an important cultural and political document in the region. To sum up, the commercial Hindi cinema in its current form has married to three great obsessions of the Iranian society, namely, pleasure, personal freedom and the quest for love. Negative stereotyping of Indian Muslims and politically insensitive narration of Bollywood cinema becomes a not-so serious issue, when the films operate within the realm of freedom, pleasure and romance.

End Notes

1. The study is based, mainly, on the personal interviews with Iranians living in exile in India and UAE. Opinions gathered here are mainly through direct interactions and online communication. The author wants to acknowledge Iranian friends Reza, Majidi, Mahmoud and Anoush for their contribution to develop the idea of this chapter.
2. The Idea developed from the conversations with Reza and Anoush.
3. Khomeini's regime made a concerted attempt to bring cinema under the domination of state ideology and subject it to a process of Islamization. Films were adhered to a *feqh*-based definition of social reality and constrained by the rules of *halal* and *haram*.
4. Hamid Naficy, "Veiled Vision/Powerful Presences: Women in post-revolutionary Iranian Cinema", in Mahnaz Afkhami and Erika Friedl (eds.), *In the Eye of Storm: Women in Post-revolutionary Iran* (Syracuse, 1997), p. 7.
5. Ziba Mir-Hosseini, Iranian Cinema: Art, Society and the State, *Middle East Report*, No. 219, (summer 2001), pp. 26-29, p. 29
6. The earliest phase, if one could recognize such a phase, tried to

uphold a nationalistic struggle, i.e. the struggle of a nation and its movement towards independence, actually describing the formative years of a young country. Such a depiction within the cultural/social specificities of a nation concentrated on showing the struggle against imperialism.

7. D. R. Nagaraj, "The Comic Collapse of Authority: An Essay on the Fears of the Public Spectator", in Vinay Lal and Ashis Nandy (eds.), *Fingerprinting Popular Culture: The Mythic and the Iconic in Indian Cinema* (New Delhi, 2006).
8. Conversations with Prof. A.K. Ramakrishnan have aided in developing this argument.
9. Iqbal Masud, "The genesis of popular cinema", Cinema in India 1/1: 18-23., 1987.
10. Vinay Lal and Ashish Nandy (ed.), "Introduction", in Vinayalal and Nandy (ed.), *Fingerprinting Popular Culture: The Mythic and the Iconic Indian Cinema,* (New Delhi, 2006)
11. Ibid.
12. M.K. Ragavendra, "Structure and Form in Indian Popular Narrative", in Vinay Lal and Ashis Nandy (eds.), *Fingerprinting Popular Culture: The Mythic and the Iconic in Indian Cinema* (New Delhi, 2006)

Index

Index